OXFOR

THE PASS

AND OTHER LATE PHILOSOPHICAL WRITINGS

RENÉ DESCARTES was born at La Haye near Tours on 31 March 1596. He was educated at the Jesuit Collège de La Flèche in Anjou, and at the University of Poitiers, where he took a Licentiate in Law in 1616. Two years later he entered the army of Prince Maurice of Nassau in the Netherlands, and met a local schoolmaster, Isaac Beeckman, who fostered his interest in mathematics and physics. After further travels in Europe he settled in Paris in 1625, and came into contact with scientists, theologians, and philosophers in the circle of the Minim friar Marin Mersenne. At the end of 1628 Descartes left for the Netherlands, which he made his home until 1648; he devoted himself to carrying forward the mathematical, scientific, and philosophical work he had begun in Paris. When he learned of the condemnation of Galileo for heresy in 1633, he abandoned his plans to publish a treatise on physics, and under pressure from his friends consented to have the *Discourse on the Method* printed, with three accompanying essays on topics in which he had made discoveries. In 1641 his *Meditations on First Philosophy* appeared, setting out the metaphysical underpinnings of his physical theories; these were accompanied by objections written by contemporary philosophers, and Descartes's replies to them. His writings provoked controversy in both France and the Netherlands, where his scientific ideas were banned in one university; his works, however (including the *Principles of Philosophy* of 1644), continued to be published, and to bring him notoriety and renown. In 1648 he accepted an invitation from Queen Christina of Sweden to settle in Stockholm; it was there he died of pneumonia on 11 February 1650.

MICHAEL MORIARTY is Drapers Professor of French at the University of Cambridge. Among his publications are *Early Modern French Thought: The Age of Suspicion* (2003), *Fallen Nature, Fallen Selves: Early Modern French Thought II* (2006), and *Disguised Vices: Theories of Virtue in Early Modern French Thought* (2011). He has edited Descartes's *Meditations on First Philosophy* for Oxford World's Classics.

OXFORD WORLD'S CLASSICS

For over 100 years Oxford World's Classics have brought readers closer to the world's great literature. Now with over 700 titles—from the 4,000-year-old myths of Mesopotamia to the twentieth century's greatest novels—the series makes available lesser-known as well as celebrated writing.

The pocket-sized hardbacks of the early years contained introductions by Virginia Woolf, T. S. Eliot, Graham Greene, and other literary figures which enriched the experience of reading. Today the series is recognized for its fine scholarship and reliability in texts that span world literature, drama and poetry, religion, philosophy, and politics. Each edition includes perceptive commentary and essential background information to meet the changing needs of readers.

OXFORD WORLD'S CLASSICS

RENÉ DESCARTES

The Passions of the Soul
and Other Late Philosophical Writings

Translated with an Introduction and Notes by
MICHAEL MORIARTY

OXFORD
UNIVERSITY PRESS

OXFORD
UNIVERSITY PRESS

Great Clarendon Street, Oxford, OX2 6DP
United Kingdom

Oxford University Press is a department of the University of Oxford.
It furthers the University's objective of excellence in research, scholarship,
and education by publishing worldwide. Oxford is a registered trade mark of
Oxford University Press in the UK and in certain other countries

First published as an Oxford World's Classics paperback 2015

Impression: 2

Published in the United States of America by Oxford University Press
198 Madison Avenue, New York, NY 10016, United States of America

British Library Cataloguing in Publication Data

Data available

Library of Congress Control Number: 2015931305

ISBN 978–0–19–968413–7

Printed in Great Britain by
Clays Ltd, St Ives plc

ACKNOWLEDGEMENTS

For inspiration and support I most warmly thank Terence Cave, Susan James, Ian Maclean, Quentin Skinner, and Rebecca Wilkin. It has been a pleasure, while putting this volume together, to work in the Department of French and Faculty of Modern and Medieval Languages at the University of Cambridge, and especially alongside my early-modernist colleagues. I have benefited especially from Emma Gilby's Cartesian insights, and from her energy in organizing intellectual exchanges, including a conference on Descartes in Cambridge in September 2014. I have also had the advantage of the friendly and stimulating atmosphere of Peterhouse, where my colleagues Tim Crane and Scott Mandelbrote organized a Descartes reading group, and I have had Mari Jones and Claire White as colleagues in French. Many thanks are due also to Judith Luna for commissioning this volume and for all her prompt and effective assistance and generous encouragement. Thanks also to Laurien Berkeley for her vigilant and helpful copy-editing. My greatest debt, as always, is to Morag, James, and John.

Beyond these personal connections, anyone working on Descartes knows how much he or she owes to the generations of scholars in various disciplines and from many countries whose work has illuminated the life, background, and above all the texts of this author. I hope that my own debts are, however imperfectly, acknowledged in the notes.

CONTENTS

ABBREVIATIONS

AT *Œuvres de Descartes*, ed. Charles Adam and Paul Tannery, rev. edn, 11 vols. (Paris, 1996)

Baillet, *Vie* Adrien Baillet, *La Vie de Monsieur Descartes*, 2 vols. (1691); repr., 1 vol. (Paris, 2012). References are to the first edition

Correspondance René Descartes, *Correspondance complète*, ed. Jean-Robert Armogathe, 2 vols., *Œuvres complètes*, viii (Paris, 2013)

Correspondence *The Correspondence between Princess Elisabeth of Bohemia and René Descartes*, ed. and trans. Lisa Shapiro (Chicago, 2007)

CSMK *The Philosophical Writings of Descartes*, trans. John Cottingham, Robert Stoothoff, Dugald Murdoch, and Anthony Kenny, 3 vols. (Cambridge, 1985–91)

Discourse René Descartes, *A Discourse on the Method of Correctly Conducting One's Reason and Seeking Truth in the Sciences* (1637)

Essays Michel de Montaigne, *The Complete Essays*, ed. and trans. M. A. Screech (London, 1991)

Ethics Aristotle, *Nicomachean Ethics*

F French-language version of the *Principles of Philosophy*: *Les Principes de la philosophie* (1647)

L Latin-language version of the *Principles of Philosophy*: *Principia philosophiae* (1644)

Meditations René Descartes, *Meditations on First Philosophy* (1641)

OP René Descartes, *Œuvres philosophiques*, ed. Ferdinand Alquié, 3 vols., Classiques Garnier (Paris, 1963–73)

OWC Oxford World's Classics

Passions *The Passions of the Soul* (1649)

Principles *Principles of Philosophy* (Latin edn 1644; French edn 1647)

ST St Thomas Aquinas, *Summa theologiae*

INTRODUCTION

THIS volume contains a selection of the most important of Descartes's later writings. They were written during his stay in the United Provinces of the Netherlands, where he had lived for most of the time since late 1628. He found it easier to concentrate on his work away from France and the distracting pressures of friends, family, colleagues, and rivals (and, perhaps, away from the eagle eyes of conservative theologians who would object to his critique of the established Aristotelian philosophy). The dominant religion in the United Provinces was Calvinist Protestantism, and Descartes was a Roman Catholic; but in certain regions Catholics could practise their religion without persecution or harassment. However, Descartes's sense of security in the United Provinces must have been severely weakened by a prolonged dispute, running from 1642 to 1648, with the Calvinist theologian Voetius. He had been initially dragged into it by an over-zealous follower, Regius, a lecturer at the University of Utrecht whose indiscreet assertion of Cartesian positions had been censured by Voetius, then rector of the university. But Descartes had involved himself directly by denouncing Voetius in a letter to the French Jesuit Dinet (AT 7. 582–603). The quarrel spread to other Dutch universities, and Descartes found himself condemned for encouraging scepticism and atheism—the very positions he thought he had completely discredited. So much for the peace and quiet for the sake of which he had settled in the United Provinces and which he had there enjoyed for a time. Somewhat reluctantly, he accepted an invitation to Sweden, where Queen Christina was interested in raising the intellectual level of her court. He eventually travelled there in April 1649, and died there, probably of pneumonia, in February 1650.

The works of this late period can be best approached via his two earlier masterpieces, the *Discourse on the Method* of 1637, and the *Meditations on First Philosophy* of 1641. Written in French so as to reach a public outside the scholarly community, the *Discourse* is a narrative of Descartes's intellectual development and achievements, in which he sets out his project of a new approach to philosophy (a term which in the seventeenth century covered not only logic and metaphysics, as it does today, but also what we now call the physical sciences). Existing philosophy (the dominant form of which was the Christianized Aristotelianism of the scholastics) is, he claims, not really knowledge, for it lacks the certainty without which there is no knowledge, and which is currently found only in mathematics. Some way must be found of transporting that certainty from mathematics to other domains: this is the aim of Descartes's method. In Part II of the *Discourse*, he reduces it to four precepts: to accept nothing as true unless he knows it clearly and distinctly to be true; to break down complex problems into simple ones as far as possible; to develop his thinking in an orderly fashion, beginning with the simplest possible objects and moving on to the more complex ones; and to review this process constantly, so as to be sure of having omitted nothing.

The method, first practised in the mathematical domain, further enables Descartes to discover various key items of metaphysical knowledge: his own existence as a thinking substance first and foremost, and the existence of God. He explains how the method would be applied to basic questions of physics, discarding the core concepts of Aristotelian philosophy, and to the understanding of the workings of the human body, which he regards as a kind of machine. There is no need to posit a soul to account for its organic functions; whereas intellectual operations can be ascribed only to an intellectual soul, which, being of a radically different substance from the body, is not condemned to perish along with it. Proofs of the existence of God and the immortality of the soul are thus among the benefits of Descartes's method; but he also envisages its leading to scientific discoveries that will benefit humanity. As we come to know the properties and operations of bodies, we can turn this knowledge to our advantage as a species, transforming nature, so to speak, into an enormous workshop. Despite the differences in their scientific philosophies, Descartes is at one with his English predecessor Francis Bacon in upholding this ambition of controlling nature for the benefit of humanity, and to that extent the *Discourse* can be regarded as one of the founding texts of what is called the Enlightenment, at least in its scientific and technological aspects.

The metaphysical aspect of his thought was developed in the *Meditations*, written in Latin and thus addressed more to scholars. Here he establishes the philosophical underpinnings of his scientific approach far more painstakingly than in the *Discourse*. The text is written from the point of view of a seeker (often conventionally called the Meditator) who resolves to rid himself of all his false ideas and, if possible, replace them with true ones. To this end, he decides to treat any opinion that is in the slightest doubtful as if it were false. Now, he has always been given to understand that all knowledge is based on sense-perception: this Aristotelian view was standard among the scholastics (and was to be reaffirmed by the British empiricists Hobbes, Locke, and Hume). But the senses are often deceptive, and can never vouch for their own reliability. Even mathematical truths are suspect: we can make mistakes in calculation. To power up the sceptical hypothesis to the full, the Meditator imagines that an all-powerful malignant being is systematically deceiving him in all his perceptions (sensory or intellectual). But he cannot think this without becoming aware of his own thinking and hence of his existence. Here, then, is a first item of knowledge that did not, after all, depend on the senses. Reflecting further on his experience of thinking, he becomes aware of himself as essentially a thing, or substance, that thinks—a mind, or soul, in other words—whether or not, as the senses tell him, he has a body. Reflecting on his ideas and what they represent, he comes to focus on the idea of an infinitely perfect being. Infinite perfection is a unique concept, for he has never encountered it in experience, nor can it have been spun out of his own experience of himself, which is that of a finite being, limited and subject to confusion; the concept has therefore been placed in his mind by an outside agency, which can be nothing other than the infinitely perfect being itself—that is, God. Likewise, the Meditator's own finite existence is unintelligible if there is no ultimate cause of it, a being that is self-sufficient because infinite. But, being infinitely perfect, God would not systematically deceive his creature. Therefore, the Meditator concludes, as long as he assents only to what he clearly and distinctly conceives to be true, he can trust his own ideas as sources of knowledge; he will go wrong only if he misuses his power of free choice (vouched for by experience), by assenting to what he does not conceive clearly and distinctly. For instance, he has a clear and distinct idea of body as a kind of substance occupying three dimensions ('extended', to use Descartes's own term). Other properties, such as colour or weight, do not belong to this clear and distinct idea, since they may not belong to the body in itself, but only to our perception of it. Likewise, he has a clear and distinct idea of thinking substance, as essentially immaterial, as not occupying space. But if the ideas are so distinct, they must refer to two fundamentally distinct substances (else God would be deceiving him). The mind, then, exists independently of any body (if, that is, bodies actually exist). However, the Meditator's propensity to believe in an external physical world is so ineradicable that, again, God would be deceiving him if the world were a total illusion. There is, then, a world of bodies. But among all these, the Meditator notes, he has a special relationship with one, his own, the body he experiences as united with his mind. The function of the senses is not to discover the nature of things, but to preserve the union of the body and the mind. There is therefore one sense in which his self is the thinking substance alone, and the body is not the self; there is another in which the self is the mind and the body in union. But this latter aspect is hardly emphasized in the *Meditations*; as a result, to quote Susan James, 'By treating the *Meditations on First Philosophy* as Descartes's philosophical testament, scholars have created a one-sided interpretation of Cartesianism in which the division between soul and body is overemphasized and sometimes misunderstood.'[1] It is largely by engaging with Descartes's later writings that recent scholarship has done much to correct that misunderstanding.[2]

Correspondence with Elisabeth

The union of body and mind is the central theme of the treatise *The Passions of the Soul*, but it figures prominently in the earlier correspondence with Princess Elisabeth of Bohemia, and this for two reasons. First, Elisabeth, a person of remarkable intelligence and unusually well read in a time when women were generally denied the kind of education their brothers received, questions Descartes most searchingly about his dualistic theory qua theory; secondly, she asks him for advice about her own physical and mental health, and her requests and his replies frequently bear on the relationship between the body and the mind.

Elisabeth of Bohemia, born in 1618, was over twenty years younger than Descartes.[3] She was one of the great princesses of Europe. Her

---

[1] Susan James, *Passion and Action* (New York, 1968; Oxford, 1997), 106.

[2] See the Select Bibliography for examples of this scholarship.

[3] Her name is sometimes rendered 'Elizabeth' but she always signs herself 'Elisabeth'. A vivid and detailed account of her life, interspersed with abundant extracts from the correspondence between her and Descartes, is provided in Andrea Nye, *The Princess and the Philosopher* (Lanham, Md, 1999).

maternal grandfather was James VI of Scotland and I of England, under whom the crowns of Scotland and England were united in 1603; the house of Stuart, from which he came, had been kings of Scotland since 1371. Her maternal grandmother was a daughter of Frederick II of Denmark. Her mother, Elizabeth, married Frederick V, Count Palatine of the Rhine, one of the foremost German Protestant princes (he was a Calvinist, whereas most German Protestants were Lutheran). In 1619, the year after Elisabeth's birth, Frederick became king of Bohemia. Elisabeth was therefore the daughter, granddaughter, and great-granddaughter of kings.

But this glory did not last long. Bohemia was technically an elective monarchy, but had for some decades previously been in effect a part of the Holy Roman Empire. The throne had been offered to Frederick by Protestant nobles afraid that the new emperor, Ferdinand II, a zealous Roman Catholic, would abandon the tolerant policy of his predecessors. Ferdinand was hardly going to accept the loss of the kingdom. In November 1620, just over a year after his coronation, Frederick's army was crushed by the Imperial forces, and he fled the kingdom, taking refuge in The Hague. Soon after his hereditary lands in Germany were seized by the Imperialists. In 1629 his eldest son, aged 15, was drowned.

It is not, then, surprising that Elisabeth's letters should mention the misfortunes of her house; but she is probably not thinking just of the catastrophes of her immediate family. The Stuarts were not a lucky dynasty. From James I (reigned 1406–37) on, a succession of Scottish kings had all met premature and (almost all of them) violent deaths, a fate suffered also by Elisabeth's great-grandmother Mary Queen of Scots. During the years of her correspondence with Descartes, Elisabeth would have been only too aware that her uncle Charles I, in conflict with the English Parliament and the Scottish Covenanters, was losing control of his kingdoms; finally defeated, he was to be beheaded in 1649 (Descartes offers his condolences on this event in his letter of 22 February of that year). Her younger brother Rupert (Prince Rupert of the Rhine) had been Charles's most energetic and (for a time) successful general, but was banished from England by the victorious Parliament in 1646. It would be hard for an imaginative person not to be depressed by this family history; and Descartes certainly thought this the chief cause of Elisabeth's melancholy, which he viewed as itself the source of her physical ailments (18 May 1645; letter 12). Perhaps more easily than Descartes, we can see that a good part of her frustration stems from her impatience at the restrictions placed on her by her rank and especially her subordinate position as a woman; and her distressingly frequent (and entirely unfounded) references to her own stupidity can be read not only as the self-directed aggressiveness that seems often to accompany depression but as protests against her lack of opportunity to cultivate her intellectual gifts and interests.

From the start of the correspondence, she addresses him as 'the best doctor for [her] own soul' (16 May 1643; letter 1). No doubt, the exchange of letters itself had a therapeutic value for her, as a relief from her immediate sources of stress (she says as much in the letter of 22 June 1645; letter 15); moreover, Descartes frequently offered psychological remedies for her mental suffering. It seems reasonable to suppose that his reflection on Elisabeth's account of her predicament both encouraged and helped him to develop his thinking about the union of body and soul. In a sense, then, we can see Elisabeth as a collaborator in his later work; not that this process was without friction: the letter of 13 September 1645 (letter 23) shows her unwilling to accept his reassurances and remedies.

Nonetheless, the dominant tone of the correspondence is of strong mutual respect and concern. What other emotions may have been involved we can hardly tell, since the social gulf between them as well as gendered codes of propriety would have militated against explicit expressions of affection. But the letters are fascinating for the light they throw on two remarkable personalities, as well as on the extension of Descartes's philosophy into psychological and ethical areas he had previously ignored.

In 1667 Elisabeth became abbess of a Lutheran nunnery at Herford in Westphalia. She was now at last independent. She used her position to shelter victims of religious persecution, such as the Quaker William Penn. She died in 1680.

Principles of Philosophy

This is the most methodical and sustained exposition of Descartes's total philosophy, though, as he says himself in the prefatory letter, it is not complete: it lacks sections on plants, animals, human beings, medicine, ethics, and mechanics.[4] He hoped that the Society of Jesus, which ran a network of excellent colleges, in one of which, La Flèche, he had himself been educated, would take a favourable attitude to the work, perhaps even to the extent of adopting it as a textbook.[5]

For reasons of space, only Part I, dealing with basic metaphysical issues, is included in this volume. In many ways, it is a straightforward recapitulation of the argument of the *Meditations*, but the change of form from meditation to treatise goes with certain changes of strategy. Thus, in a methodical exposition the so-called ontological proof of God, according to which the concept of a supremely perfect being, God, necessarily entails the existence of such a being, takes pride of place as being the simplest and clearest; whereas in the *Meditations* the existence of God is first demonstrated by the causal proofs advanced in the Third Meditation (my idea of a perfect being must have been produced by a perfect being; my own existence requires that of a supremely perfect first cause), and the ontological argument is postponed until the Fifth Meditation, by which time the Meditator has acquired the habit of forming clear and distinct concepts of things, and of recognizing that metaphysical ideas (like mathematical ideas) have a content independent of one's subjective apprehension of them. The ontological argument there comes across as a supplement to the causal proofs, whereas in the *Principles* the relationship is reversed. The requirements of method also lead Descartes to explain his concept of substance far more fully than in the *Meditations* (and in so doing to expose problems in his philosophical system, as is brought out in the notes).

Other Letters

Five further letters are included, which contain significant discussions of key philosophical themes. The letter to Father Denis Mesland of 2 May 1644 throws light on Descartes's arguments for the existence of God and on his distinctive conception that the eternal truths were created by God, and could thus have been different; together with its successor of 9 February 1645 it offers a far

---

[4] See Stephen Gaukroger, *Descartes' System of Natural Philosophy* (Cambridge, 2002), for an excellent account that integrates what the *Principles* omit.

[5] See to Elisabeth, Dec. 1646 (letter 40); also to Charlet, 9 Feb. 1645, AT 4. 156–8; and to Dinet, 9 Feb. 1645, AT 4. 158–60.

closer examination of the notion of free will than the *Meditations* or
the *Principles* (exegetes differ over whether Descartes has actually
changed his views).[6] The letter to the marquess of Newcastle (23
November 1646) contains one of Descartes's most important treat-
ments of the place of animals in his theory. Pierre Chanut (6 June
1647) receives a fascinating discussion of the religious implications of Descartes's concept of a boundless universe and of the
'unconscious' origin of certain emotional attachments. The letter to
Antoine Arnauld of 29 July 1648 contains an important treatment of
the nature of thought and the problem of the interaction between soul
and body.

The Passions of the Soul

The Passions of the Soul is the last of Descartes's works to be published in his lifetime. It is his fullest account of the interaction
between soul and body, and his most significant contribution to
moral philosophy. Not that he sets himself up as a moral philosopher: he says that his intention is to explain the passions purely as
a natural philosopher (*physicien*), not, as Aristotle had done, from the
point of view of rhetoric or moral philosophy. However, he does not
confine himself to a purely descriptive approach: his theory opens up
a prescriptive dimension. Thus, the first part of the text explains the
nature of passion in general, the second describes the principal passions, and the third the further passions that derive from these; but
each part ends with some definite recommendations concerning the
attitudes or behaviour we should adopt in the light of the foregoing
explanations.

Some sense of the sheer novelty of Descartes's approach can be
gleaned from a comparison with the self-proclaimed first treatise in
French on the passions by the prolific Jean-Pierre Camus (1584–1652),

---

[6] See Étienne Gilson, *La Liberté chez Descartes et la théologie* (Paris, 1913), and
Ferdinand Alquié, *La Découverte métaphysique de l'homme chez Descartes* (1950; 6th edn,
Paris, 2000), ch. 14, who argue that there is a change; and, for the alternative view, Jean
Laporte, 'La Liberté selon Descartes', in Laporte, *Études d'histoire de la philosophie fran-
çaise du XVII*^e *siècle* (Paris, 1951), 37–87, and Anthony Kenny, 'Descartes on the Will', in
John Cottingham (ed.), *Descartes* (Oxford, 1998). For an acute reconsideration, informed
by recent historical scholarship on medieval thought, see Lilli Alanen, *Descartes's Concept
of Mind* (Cambridge, Mass., 2003).

bishop of Belley.[7] Camus's treatment of the subject is ample and informative. One learns what philosophers, theologians, and rhetoricians have said about the passions, generally and severally; they are illustrated by well-chosen extracts from poets such as Virgil and Ovid, alongside quotations from scripture and the Church Fathers. The style is flowing, rich, baroque, metaphorical, embellished with prolonged comparisons and striking juxtapositions. The passions are like the moon—but also like chameleons;[8] Jesus Christ is compared to the emperor Caligula and to Alexander the Great (because, just as they changed their clothes so as to win the favour of their subjects, so he concealed his divinity beneath the garb of humanity).[9] In keeping with early modern precepts, the work pleases as well as instructs. If you were a seventeenth-century scholar required to discourse on the passions you would find more help in Camus than in Descartes. Compared to it Descartes's treatise is distinctly dry. But the lucidity and concision of the work impart to it a certain austere beauty that well complements its rigour and sheer intellectual power.

Though he dismisses all earlier writing on the subject, Descartes's account of the passions shows continuities with that of earlier thinkers. Like Aristotle and Aquinas, for instance, he sees the passions as involving interaction between soul and body. But his theory does involve a radical break with other aspects of their accounts. Essentially, he argues that the soul is nothing other than the mind: it is not the support of the organic functions of life. These can be explained in purely mechanical terms. To show this, Descartes briefly describes the workings of the body in terms of its key organs and processes: digestion; the circulation of the blood via the veins into the heart and thence the lungs, from which it returns to the heart and so to the rest of the body through the arteries; and the movement of the muscles by contraction and extension, in response to the action of the nerves, little filaments originating in the brain and responsible also for sensation. The source of all these processes is a kind of fire kept going in the heart by the blood supplied by the veins. This fire dilates or

---

[7] Camus Jean-Pierre, 'Au lecteur', in Camus, *Traitté des passions de l'ame* (1614), ed. Max Vernet and Élodie Vignon (Paris, 2014), 59. In his erudite and authoritative *French Moralists: The Theory of the Passions, 1585 to 1649* (Oxford, 1964), Anthony Levi observes that Camus's claim to primacy 'is only partly justifiable' (p. 127).

[8] Camus, *Traitté des passions de l'ame*, 74–6.   [9] Ibid. 256.

rarefies the blood, so causing it to flow to different parts of the body. But the most rarefied parts of the blood, what Descartes calls the animal spirits, flow into the brain and out again into the nerves and thence into the muscles, where they produce movement. The animal spirits are described as tiny and fast-moving bodies comparable to the particles of a flame (§§7–10). Their movement is closely related to sensation. Sensory stimuli, external or internal, set off movements in the nerves, which are transmitted to the brain. These can cause movements of the animal spirits, and hence of the muscles. For instance, if someone suddenly moves his or her hand towards our eyes, they will automatically close: the movement of the hand has produced a movement in the brain, sending the animal spirits into the muscles that lower the eyelids (§§12–13). Such motions can be accounted for purely mechanically.

But the same does not apply to thought. What Descartes means by thought can be grasped by the example of sensation, as discussed in the Second Meditation. When I see a white wall, light rays from the wall strike my optic nerve and transmit signals to the brain. But the existence of the wall, and even of my body, nerves and all, can be put in doubt; what remains is my awareness that I *seem to see* a white wall. This awareness, Descartes argues, is therefore distinct from the physical process involved in sensation.[10] The definition of thought in the *Principles* runs along these lines: 'By the term "thought" I mean everything that takes place in us, while we are aware, in so far as there is awareness of it in us' (I. 9). It should be noted that this definition in itself implies the non-identity of physical and mental processes. Suppose, for argument's sake, that all thoughts are necessarily accompanied by brain movements. My feeling of gratitude to a kind friend is therefore accompanied by a brain movement: but though I am conscious of the gratitude, I am not at all conscious of the brain movement as such. In other words, to pick up the terms of the definition, the brain movement takes place within me while I am aware, but there is no awareness of it in me. By Descartes's definition then, the brain movement is not thought. But thought is more than mere passive awareness (perception):[11] the soul is active as well. It is responsible for our acts of will (volitions).

---

[10] Descartes, *Meditations*, II, AT 7. 28–9, OWC 21.

[11] Though the word 'perception' is commonly reserved nowadays for sense-perceptions, Descartes uses it of intellectual acts as well.

Descartes analyses the passions as perceptions in the soul of a bodily process. To that extent they are akin to sense-perceptions of external objects or internal perceptions of bodily states such as hunger and pain. In sense-perception the light of a torch and the clang of a bell arouse different movements in our nerves, which are then transmitted to the brain, so as to produce different sensations in the soul (note that the sensation, as such, occurs only in the soul; what occurs in the brain is a movement). But there is an element of confusion in the perception. We seem to see the light of the torch in the room, to hear the bell ring in the church tower. Likewise with our internal perceptions: we feel a dryness in our throat, a pain in our injured foot. But in each case, what we are in fact aware of is a sensation representing an external object or a bodily state (the pain we feel 'in' our foot is produced by the same mechanism as the pain an amputee feels 'in' the limb that has been removed).[12] Again, as regards the passions, we feel anger or joy 'in' our soul, whereas we are in fact reacting to a physical process produced by a sense-perception (seeing behaviour of which we disapprove or hearing the voice of someone we are fond of).

The passions, then, can be defined as 'perceptions, or sensations, or emotions of the soul that we refer (*rapportons*) particularly to the soul itself, and that are caused, sustained, and fortified by some movement of the spirits' (§27). 'Perceptions' in the general sense of thoughts other than volitions, but not the kind of perception involved in evident knowledge; 'sensations' in that they reach the soul by the same path as sense-perceptions; 'emotions' in that, more than any other kind of thought, they are liable to agitate and disturb the soul (§28).[13] Descartes emphasizes the involvement of the animal spirits in order to distinguish passion as such from acts of will, which we also experience as in the soul, but rightly, because they do originate within it (§29).

The mediating agency between body and soul is identified by

[12] Descartes, in other words, like many other early modern thinkers such as Hobbes and Locke, holds a 'representative' theory of perception: we perceive things not directly but via a representation of them.

[13] *Émotion* in seventeenth-century French denotes a disturbance to the normal order of things. Antoine Furetière defines it as a *mouvement extraordinaire qui agite le corps ou l'esprit* ('an extraordinary movement that agitates the body or soul'; *Dictionnaire universel* (1690), s.v. *esmotion*). The implication of abnormality is taken over from the Greek and Latin terms normally rendered as 'passion': *pathos* ('disease') and *perturbatio* ('disorder').

Descartes as a part of the brain called the pineal gland.[14] Though undoubtedly erroneous, Descartes's ascription of this function to the gland is a brilliant piece of reasoning. He notes that the other parts of the brain are all doubled, as are our sense-organs; so that we need one single part, like the gland, in which the twofold impressions received from our sense-organs can be fused into one (§§30–3).

Descartes is now in a position to reconstruct the whole process of passion. It begins in sensation: to use his example, an animal appears in our field of vision. Light reflected from its body affects our optic nerve, producing two images, one for each eye, on the inner surface of the brain. The surrounding spirits transmit these to the pineal gland, which blends them into a single image. The gland transmits this to the soul, and we see the animal.

But the gland does not simply produce sensations. Some of its movements are naturally designed to induce experiences of passion in the soul—passions that are, so to speak, translations of movements of the animal spirits into the nerves and the muscles.[15] Let us suppose that the animal's appearance is such as to revive prior experiences of danger. The resultant movement of the gland triggers the passion of fear (*crainte*). How we deal with that will depend on our physical or mental constitution and our previous history of dealing with physical threats. In some people, the fear gives place to the passion of boldness (*hardiesse*), and they stand their ground. In others, the spirits reflected from the image formed by the gland will flow partly into the nerves that cause the muscular movements of turning one's back and starting to run, and partly into the nerves that act on the heart so as to cause a flow of spirits to the brain that will keep the first process going. The resultant movement in the gland causes the soul to feel the passion of terror (*peur*).[16] The role of the passions is to 'incite and

[14] See Gert-Jan Lokhorst, 'Descartes and the Pineal Gland', *Stanford Encyclopedia of Philosophy Archive* (Spring 2014), ed. Edward N. Zalta, <http://plato.stanford.edu/archives/spr2014/entries/pineal-gland> (accessed 5 Feb. 2015). This wide-ranging and detailed article offers an excellent account of studies of the pineal gland prior to Descartes's, of the development of his views on the subject, and on the contemporary and subsequent reception of his views. In particular, it points out that his account of the gland was inaccurate in terms of the science of his own time.

[15] Descartes uses the metaphor of translation to explain the relationship (one of causality and not of resemblance) between the objects of our sense-perceptions and the sensations themselves (*The World*, ch. 1, AT 11. 3–6).

[16] Descartes distinguishes *crainte*, an initial affective apprehension of danger, from *peur*, an overwhelming urge to flee.

dispose' the soul to want to perform the action to which the physiological processes are disposing the body: to want to flee, for instance, when the process of flight is set in motion (§§35–40).

But the soul is free: it cannot be compelled to will anything. Moreover, its volitions can move the gland so as to produce the physical process that will enable the body to carry out the will of the soul. However, its freedom as regards the passions is circumscribed. Thus, it cannot directly will the spirits to flow along a different path from the one that is currently producing an unwelcome passion. What it can do is to think thoughts that will arouse a contrary passion, say, boldness: 'it's safer to stand your ground', 'you don't want to feel like a coward because you ran away' (§45).[17] This is easier said than done, because the effect of the bodily process is not only to produce but to reproduce the passion (cf. §36). Where the passion is violent, then, it cannot be immediately replaced by its contrary: we can only refuse to consent to it and restrain, as far as possible, the bodily movements to which it is prompting us. We must wait for the impulse to flee to subside before we can advance to meet the danger head-on (§46).

But how do we avoid being the plaything of contrary passions, oscillating between terror and boldness, say, or desire and shame? We must combat the passions by 'the will's own weapons', that is, 'firm and definite judgements concerning the difference between good and evil, according to which [the will] has resolved to conduct the actions of its life' (§48). (These judgements must, however, be based on the knowledge of truth, else they may be overturned by bitter experience; §49.) Moreover, although there is a natural link between the movements of the gland, the spirits, and the brain that produce certain sense-perceptions and those that produce certain passions, this link can be deliberately uncoupled and other connections made. By this means even the weakest souls can be trained, in theory at least, to master their passions (§50).

Having explained the general mechanism of the passions, Descartes proceeds, in the second part of the text, to explain how the specific passions are generated. He identifies six basic passions, classified in respect of the various ways in which objects of sense-perception

---

[17] Descartes's examples suggest that he is envisaging at least some readers who will have had experience of war, as he himself had had and as most noblemen of the time would have done. See §211 for another example, and §161 for a concession to aristocratic ideology.

can harm or benefit us: wonderment, love, hate, desire, joy, sadness. This taxonomy differs markedly from two influential earlier schemes, those of the Stoics and of Aquinas.[18] Along with each basic passion, he identifies its major derivatives (§§51–69). He then goes through the basic passions again, defining them in more detail and describing the particular physical processes that accompany each one (§§70–111). Next he reviews the external manifestations of these passions: movements of the eyes, facial expression, changes of colour, trembling, lethargy, fainting, laughter, tears, groans, and sighs (§§112–35). (His discussion of facial expressions is generally held to have inspired seventeenth-century art theorists' attempts to codify the expression of the passions in painting.[19]) In the third part, he discusses the derivative passions in detail, along the same lines as the principal ones.

Descartes does not, however, confine himself to merely describing the workings of the passions, and, despite his initial self-distancing from the discourse of moral philosophy, he is led to ask the question moral philosophers have always asked, about our proper relationship to the passions (an essential aspect of Aristotle's conception of virtue).[20] First of all, the passions are functional (so we are not, as the Stoics thought, to attempt to eliminate them);[21] but their functionality is limited. They reinforce and preserve thoughts in the soul that it is good for the soul to retain and that might otherwise be erased; but they may do so for too long, and they may do the same for bad thoughts (§74). Moreover, their functionality is limited to the body, to sustaining the continued existence of the soul–body composite (§137). Even from this point of view, their representation of good and evil is

[18] The Stoics distinguished four basic passions: desire (for a future good), joy (in a present good), fear (of a future evil), distress (at a present evil) (Cicero, *Tusculan Disputations* 4. 6. 11). Aquinas distinguishes two categories of passion: concupiscible, that is, directly related to good or evil objects (love–hate, desire–aversion, delight–sadness); and irascible, where the relationship involves some kind of difficulty (hope–despair, fear–boldness, anger) (*ST* 1–2. 23. 4; cf. 1–2. 23. 1). Descartes jettisons the concupiscible–irascible distinction (§68).

[19] See Jennifer Montagu, *The Expression of the Passions* (New Haven, 1994).

[20] Aristotle, *Ethics* 2. 5. 2–4, 1105^{b}21–1106^{a}6; 2. 6. 10–11, 1106^{b}16–23.

[21] Descartes acknowledges two possible exceptions: faint-heartedness (*lâcheté*) and terror. He admits that faint-heartedness may possibly enable us to avoid unnecessary effort (§§174–6). His follower Malebranche was to argue that terror may have the function of disarming hostility (*De la recherche de la vérité*, V. 3, in *Œuvres*, ed. Geneviève Rodis-Lewis and Germain Malbreil, Bibliothèque de la Pléiade, 2 vols. (Paris, 1979–92), i. 506–7).

potentially misleading and needs correction by experience (§138). But they also need to be evaluated in terms of their effect on the soul. This depends, first and foremost, on whether the perceptions of good or evil that the passions convey correspond to reality: a healthy relationship to the passions thus depends on the knowledge of metaphysical and moral truth. Secondly, love and joy, what we might call the positive passions, are to be preferred to hatred and sadness, since these are irreducibly painful. There is a potential tension between these requirements: Descartes wonders whether joy based on a false opinion might be better for us than sadness based on a grasp of reality (§§139–42).

The effect of the passions cannot be gauged simply in terms of the psychological states they bring about, for they have an impact on our actions through the desires they arouse. A prime goal of moral philosophy is thus to regulate desire by bringing it into line with knowledge: in particular a clear understanding of the distinction between desires whose outcome depends purely on our free will and those whose outcome depends on other factors. (Descartes's inspiration here is the Stoic philosopher Epictetus.[22]) If we concentrate on desires of the first kind, then, provided that we know their object to be good (such as virtue), they cannot be excessive.[23] We also avoid the risk of disappointment and frustration, which is inevitably attached to desires for what is not entirely within our control. We cannot, of course, entirely escape dependence on external events: but when they go against us, we should attribute this not to fortune, for there is no such thing, but to God's providence (§§143–6).

The passions are typically aroused by material objects, inasmuch as they generally derive from sensations. And the good and evil they represent to us is relative, as we have seen, to the body. But we are capable, with the help of the pure intellect or understanding, of conceiving higher goods and evils, and of making judgements accordingly.

---

[22] Epictetus, *Enchiridion*, esp. §§1, 5. The importance of Epictetus is brought out by Charles Taylor in the chapter on Descartes in *Sources of the Self: The Making of the Modern Identity* (Cambridge, 1989).

[23] This is true only if we are sure we know what virtue is. It is not difficult to think of situations in which one person's desire to be virtuous might wreak havoc on other people's lives. Descartes might reply that this only occurs when the concept of virtue in question is unsound; but suppose it is the best the person can come up with? See *Passions*, §49, and Lisa Shapiro, 'Descartes's Ethics', in Janet Broughton and John Carriero (eds.), *A Companion to Descartes* (Malden, Mass., 2008), 455.

And these perceptions and judgements give rise to emotions that are not strictly passions, since they do not result from movements of the animal spirits: there is an intellectual as well as a passional form of love, and the same holds for joy (§§79, 91). Such intellectual emotions may even conflict with the passions, as when the intellectual joy we take in a play coexists with the grief or anger we feel at the events represented. Our good and evil (subjectively speaking, our happiness and unhappiness), Descartes says, depend more on these intellectual emotions than on the passions (§147): this must be because, as in the example of the playgoer, the intellectual judgements determine how we think about the passions we experience, and in that sense transcend them. It is true, however, that, while the soul is joined to the body, a purely intellectual joy in the possession of some immaterial good will normally prompt the imagination to make an impression in the brain that will trigger a movement of the animal spirits resulting in the passion of joy (§91). But this interaction of intellectual emotions and passions, as we shall see, can be ethically beneficial. In any case, inasmuch as the intellectual emotions are generated by our souls, our inner selves rather than our embodied selves, they are potentially more powerful than the passions: so much so that if we have the makings of self-contentment inside ourselves, no disturbance from outside can affect us (§148).

This self-contentment is to be achieved by virtue, and Descartes defines this in a strikingly original way. To live virtuously is to do everything one has judged to be best; and this is a source of satisfaction and tranquillity that no passion can disturb (§148). This conception is developed in connection with the passion Descartes calls *générosité*. What the term refers to is legitimate self-esteem; but it is difficult to find an English equivalent for it. As Descartes more or less admits in §161, he could have used the term 'magnanimity', made famous by Aristotle's *Ethics* (book 4), but he jibbed at the scholastic overtones of the term, particularly because, he says, this virtue is not very widespread in the Schools. This comes across as a rather typical early modern aristocratic gibe at the scholarly community: significantly, Descartes concedes that this justified self-esteem seems to go with noble birth (though anyone can be trained, or train him- or herself, to acquire it). He thus prefers, he says, a term from ordinary usage (§161). His aristocratic and other non-academic readers could have encountered the term he chooses, *générosité*, in the heroic

drama of the day.[24] Given the reference to birth, I have opted to translate *générosité* as 'nobility of soul', though 'greatness of soul' (a literal
translation of Latin *magnanimitas*, Greek *megalopsychia*) would have
done almost as well.

Nobility of soul (legitimate self-esteem) is based partly on a cognitive state (on the knowledge that nothing belongs to us but the
use of our free will, and that nothing but the good or bad use of our free
will is worthy of praise or blame) and partly on a disposition of will,
a determination always to act in accordance with our judgement of
what is best. This is tantamount to virtue (§§152–3). Like Aristotle,
Descartes defines virtue as a habit in the soul, but whereas Aristotle
thinks of the habit as produced by and producing acts, Descartes
thinks of it as produced by and producing thoughts (actions being
considered implicitly in relation to the thoughts that prompt them).
If the thoughts are reinforced by a movement of the spirits, then the
virtues have simultaneously the status of passions. One can therefore acquire the virtue of nobility of soul by exciting the equivalent
passion, and this can be achieved by repeated appropriate meditation on the benefits of the good use of free will (§161). Like Aristotle's
magnanimous man, the *généreux* never thinks of his own advantage
in his dealings with others; but he seems to be keener to benefit them
than his Aristotelian counterpart; and because he values nothing the
acquisition of which does not depend on himself, he is exempt from
any number of passions focused on external objects or involving com-
petitive relationships with other people (§156). Nobility of soul is the
key to the virtues, because it enables us always to act in accordance
with our best ethical judgements; it is thus a general remedy against
all the disorders resulting from passion (§161). By the same token,
it is a means of liberation in that it enables us to realize our free will
in the fullest possible fashion and to attain the full ownership of our
acts (since they have not been dictated by movements in the body, for
which we can be partially responsible at best).

Descartes offers some striking insights into particular passions. He
presents love as an imaginary union of the lover and the object of
love: as he puts it, love incites the soul to imagine itself as united

---

[24] See e.g. Pierre Corneille, *Le Cid*, I. vi. 315; II. vii. 660; III. iii. 844. I have sometimes
translated the adjective *généreux* simply as 'noble', when it is clear from the context that
nobility of soul, rather than rank, is involved, or as 'generous', when, again, there is no
risk of confusion with the nowadays more common sense of 'liberal', 'giving freely'.

with an object represented as beneficial, while hatred seeks to bring about separation (§§79–80).[25] He recognizes a certain disinterestedness in many forms of love (§§81–2). Later seventeenth-century moralists indebted to the Augustinian current (such as Pascal or La Rochefoucauld) will represent human love as pure self-centred concupiscence, seeking sensuous or imaginary gratification, or both, and incapable of any authentic union with or recognition of the other person. The capacity to identify with those we love is highlighted also in Descartes's account of the good sort of anger, which he links to kindness and love, and which is a reaction, on the part of those who are kindly and affectionate, to whatever violates their expectations of how things should be: it is thus akin to indignation, in that it focuses on something bad that affects someone else (§195), but one feels it as if one were oneself affected. Though outwardly conspicuous, it is short-lived, fairly harmless, and amenable to reason (§§201–2); whereas the bad sort, less conspicuous but more dangerous, is fuelled by hatred and sadness, and originates in pride (the bad sibling of *générosité*, since it is self-esteem without a justifiable cause; §157). Alongside the justified and durable self-esteem that is *générosité*, there is a more fleeting self-satisfaction, the joy that comes from performing a particular action one judges good; but if one's judgement is wrong, this self-satisfaction takes the toxic form of pride and arrogance, which Descartes identifies as characteristic of religious bigots, whose supposed zeal for God can lead to the most heinous crimes (§190). This is a striking exception to Descartes's general discretion in referring to contemporary politics.[26]

Descartes's global evaluation of the passions is positive. They are intrinsically good, and only their excess is to be feared. Here, then, he allies himself with the Aristotelian tradition, against the Stoics. But his advice on how to deal with them is reminiscent of the Stoic Seneca's. First of all, Seneca urges the importance of preparation for the various unsettling incidents of life; secondly, he admits that we cannot on occasion resist the shock of passion: we must simply not

[25] This conception of love as union is found in the literature of the period. A striking example is d'Urfé's massively influential romance *L'Astrée* (Honoré d'Urfé, *L'Astrée*, *Première Partie*, ed. Delphine Denis (Paris, 2011); see e.g. I. 3, p. 238; I. 7, p. 438; I. 8, pp. 451, 469). It is ultimately inspired by Plato's *Symposium* 189d–193d.

[26] He condemns religious bigotry also in the letter to Elisabeth of September 1646 (AT 4. 490; letter 36).

give in to it.[27] Descartes has explained how we can prepare ourselves for whatever befalls us, by cultivating the habit of virtue, and in particular nobility of soul; in terms of technique, he advocates learning to '[separate] within oneself the movements of the blood and the spirits from the thoughts to which they are habitually attached'. But he admits that few people are prepared for all situations, and many are naturally susceptible to particular passions, so that they cannot escape being affected by the objects that arouse them. For this his remedy is to cultivate awareness and detachment: when one feels one's blood stirred in this way, one must be alert, and remember that whatever is presented to the imagination tends to deceive the soul and to cause the reasons in favour of the object of one's passion to appear much more convincing than they are, and those against it to appear much less so (§211).

The ending of the treatise is not altogether easy to reconcile with what has gone before. In §147 Descartes states, as we saw, that our well- or ill-being depends primarily on the inner emotions of the soul, produced by itself alone, without reference to the body; these affect us, he says in §148, much more than the passions. Thus, if the soul can achieve contentment from its own resources, it is invulnerable to outside attack; and it achieves this contentment through the pursuit of virtue. Yet in the final article, §212, the specific pleasures of the soul are mentioned, but brushed aside, and the emphasis is on those pleasures that are common to soul and body, and wholly dependent on the passions. The people capable of responding most strongly to the passions are the most capable of experiencing the fullest sweetness of this life. True, the passions can also be a source of misery, but if mastered by wisdom, even those that are painful can be a source of joy (§212). Rightly or wrongly, Descartes is generally thought to have failed to explain how two heterogeneous substances, the soul and the body, can be unified; but the fact of their union is crucial for his ethical thought. The affirmation of joy in the last sentence of what turned out to be his last book suggests that in certain respects his philosophy was crowned with success.

---

[27] Seneca, *Epistles* 76. 34–5; 63. 1.

A NOTE ON THE TEXT, TRANSLATIONS, AND REFERENCES

I HAVE arranged the texts in a broadly chronological sequence to reflect the development of Descartes's philosophical ideas, particularly those concerning the relation of mind and body. I have worked for the most part from the Adam–Tannery edition of Descartes's *Œuvres*.[1] I have supplemented this by the recent edition of the works and letters by Giulia Belgioioso, by the edition of the complete correspondence by Jean-Robert Armogathe, and by Ferdinand Alquié's selected edition of Descartes's *Œuvres philosophiques*. Geneviève Rodis-Lewis's edition of *Les Passions de l'âme* has been immensely useful, and for the letters of 1643 we have the valuable edition by T. Verbeek, E.-J. Bos, and J. M. M. van de Ven. In translating I have been glad to be able to consult the standard English translations of Descartes's works and letters by John Cottingham and others, and that of the correspondence with Elisabeth by Lisa Shapiro.

For the annotation I have drawn largely on the above editions. For biographical and contextual information Baillet's great *Vie de Monsieur Descartes* is still a precious resource, but it needs to be supplemented by modern biographical and historical scholarship: the biographies by Clarke, Gaukroger, and Rodis-Lewis have proved extremely helpful. For such general historical details as these works did not provide I have sometimes turned to Wikipedia.

In translating I have attempted to convey something of the style of the original texts, as well as the content. I have found Furetière's great *Dictionnaire universel* of 1690, the best French dictionary of the century, extremely useful when working on French-language texts (even though it appeared nearly half a century after the texts included here, it can still be relied on as an indication of how Descartes and his contemporaries would have understood the words they used). In the translation of *The Passions of the Soul* I have not substituted modern or more precise medical terms for those used by Descartes. In the correspondence with Elisabeth, I have preserved a good deal of the tone of politeness and even ceremony that enabled the princess and the philosopher to negotiate their dealings. In the dedicatory letter to

[1] Full details of this and other volumes referred to are in the Select Bibliography.

Elisabeth that prefaces the original edition of the *Principles*, Descartes is conforming to the requirements of the genre, which involves extreme formality and hyperbolic compliments. In the ordinary correspondence, he always addresses her as 'Your Highness', as befits her rank.[2]

I do not translate 'Monsieur Descartes' because, had Elizabeth been addressing him in English, that is still what she would have called him. Other Frenchmen are also referred to as 'Monsieur' (or 'M.'), Dutchmen as 'Mijnheer', and the solitary non-titled German as 'Herr'. I have not translated postscripts that give redundant information such as the date of a letter which has already been given in the heading.

Descartes oscillated between French and Latin, depending on the purpose and the audience for which he was writing. He wrote to Elisabeth in French, since she was entirely at home in that language, and, perhaps because *The Passions of the Soul* grew out of that correspondence, and was, he says, originally written for her,[3] he wrote that in French too. But he had earlier written the *Principles of Philosophy* in Latin, as a work intended to be read by a scholarly public, and perhaps to be adopted as a textbook in schools, where Latin was generally the language of teaching. I have translated each text from the original language of its composition. But with the *Principles* a particular problem arises. The French version was produced not by Descartes himself but by the abbé Picot; however, Baillet takes the view that the French versions both of this text and of the earlier *Meditations on First Philosophy* are superior to the originals because in revising them Descartes took the opportunity to clarify his thought.[4] There is a case for holding that the Latin and the French versions of the *Principles* should be treated as different texts.[5] Space precludes a complete translation of both versions here: it is fair to note, moreover, that the

---

[2] Strictly speaking such forms belong to the third person, so that one would say, for instance, 'Your Highness has only to make known her commands to me, and I will do her bidding.' It seemed to me that to follow this rule throughout would result in a certain awkwardness for the modern reader, and therefore, although I keep the form 'Your Highness' whenever Descartes writes 'Votre Altesse', I write, for instance, in the translation of letter 2, 'when I formerly had the honour of speaking to you', rather than 'to her', and 'your clemency' rather than 'her clemency'.

[3] See the Reply to the First Letter preceding *The Passions of the Soul*.

[4] Baillet, *Vie*, ii. 172–3.

[5] This was the view taken by the great Descartes scholar Roger Ariew when I sought his opinion on this point at a conference.

completely new material added in the French version comes mostly in Parts II to IV.[6] However, one cannot simply introduce little bits from the French version into the middle of a translation from the Latin, for one is then translating a hybrid Latin–French text that never existed. Translations of material added in the French version are thus inserted in the Explanatory Notes at the appropriate place. Sometimes, when the changes are great, a whole paragraph is retranslated from the French, and inserted again in the Notes.

French was Elisabeth's first language along with English.[7] She apologizes in the first letter for the awkwardness of her style. This could be read as an index of her proneness to self-criticism and self-doubt, or as a rhetorical modesty topos, a convention whereby the speaker belittles his or her own oratorical ability. True, her style is inelegant and her syntax occasionally incorrect by the standards of the epistolary stylists of the time, such as Descartes's correspondent Jean-Louis Guez de Balzac; Montaigne, however, had lent credence to the notion that a certain roughness of style has an aristocratic charm. Elisabeth's certainly comes across as full of personality in a way Montaigne would surely have appreciated. The translation does not systematically aim to tidy up her sentences, except where comprehension would be otherwise jeopardized. Though the quality of her French is very high, she makes occasional mistakes: thus, she is led astray by English into writing *vous excludez* for 'you exclude' instead of *vous excluez*; elsewhere instead of *vous écrivez* ('you write') she puts *vous escrites* (through a false analogy with the conjugation of *dire*, 'to say'). Her spelling too is shaky: for instance, she spells the word *façon* ('manner') as *fasson*; but it should be pointed out that the spelling of French, even among native speakers, was far more fluid when she wrote than it became later in the seventeenth century. As regards grammar, she sometimes uses the negative particle *ne* by itself, whereas from the late sixteenth century on it became standard, as it is in modern French, to add *pas* or *point* after the verb (thus, she writes *je ne dois négliger* instead of *je ne dois pas négliger*, 'I must not neglect'). She also uses the verb *souloir* ('to be accustomed'), which

---

[6] John Cottingham, 'Translator's Preface', *Principles of Philosophy*, in CSMK i. 178.

[7] Desmond M. Clarke, *Descartes* (Cambridge, 2006), 254. He notes that she also read Latin and Dutch. Andrea Nye states that Elisabeth 'and her brothers and sisters had spoken French between themselves from birth' (*The Princess and the Philosopher* (Lanham, Md, 1999), 11).

was again obsolescent. Her style thus has a certain old-fashioned quality, as measured by mid-seventeenth-century standards.

The standard practice in referring to Descartes's works is to cite the volume and page number in the Adam–Tannery edition (thus, AT 5. 562). For this reason the AT page numbers are mostly reproduced here in the margin (the volume number appears in square brackets, adjacent to the headings to individual letters). The *Principles* and *The Passions of the Soul* are exceptions, however, since the subdivisions of each text are usually so short as to be sufficient signposts to a particular passage. The 'articles' into which *The Passions of the Soul* is divided are referred to as (for example) §52 rather than 'art. 52', though the latter is the form used in the main text. In referring to Descartes's writings outside this volume, I give AT volume and page numbers. For *A Discourse on the Method* and the *Meditations on First Philosophy* I also give the page number in the Oxford World's Classics editions, using the abbreviation OWC. Asterisks in the text indicate an explanatory note at the back of the book.

SELECT BIBLIOGRAPHY

Editions

THE standard edition of Descartes's writings is *Œuvres de Descartes*, ed. Charles Adam and Paul Tannery, 11 vols., rev. edn (Paris, 1996). The correspondence with Princess Elisabeth and the other letters in the present translation are in volumes 3, 4, and 5. The Latin text of the *Principles of Philosophy* is in volume 8, part 1; the French text in volume 9, part 2. *The Passions of the Soul* is in volume 11.

A more recent edition is *Tutte le lettere, 1619–1650; Opere, 1637–1649; Opere Postume, 1650–2009*, 3 vols., ed. Giulia Belgioioso *et al.* (Milan, 2009). This is a parallel-text edition with Latin or French originals and Italian translations and notes. Still more recent is *Correspondance complète*, ed. Jean-Robert Armogathe, 2 vols., *Œuvres complètes*, viii (Paris, 2013).

The standard edition in English is *The Philosophical Writings of Descartes*, trans. John Cottingham, Robert Stoothoff, Dugald Murdoch, and Anthony Kenny, 3 vols. (Cambridge, 1985–91).

There is an excellent selected edition by Ferdinand Alquié: Descartes, *Œuvres philosophiques*, 3 vols., Classiques Garnier (Paris, 1963–73).

Editions of Particular Texts in This Volume

The Correspondence of Descartes 1643, ed. T. Verbeek, E.-J. Bos, and J. M. M. van de Ven (Utrecht, 2004).

The Correspondence between Princess Elisabeth of Bohemia and René Descartes, ed. and trans. Lisa Shapiro (Chicago, 2007).

Correspondence between Descartes and Princess Elisabeth, ed. and trans. Jonathan Bennett, <http://www.earlymoderntexts.com/pdfs/descartes1643.pdf> (accessed 5 Feb. 2015).

Les Passions de l'âme, ed. Geneviève Rodis-Lewis (Paris, 1970).

Other Works by Descartes

A Discourse on the Method of Correctly Conducting One's Reason and Seeking Truth in the Sciences, ed. and trans. Ian Maclean, Oxford World's Classics (Oxford, 2006).

Meditations on First Philosophy: With Selections from the Objections and Replies, ed. and trans. Michael Moriarty, Oxford World's Classics (Oxford, 2008).

What follows is merely a selection from the vast range of Descartes scholarship. In an English-language edition, it seemed natural to give precedence to English-language sources; however, some valuable French-language works are included.

Biographical Studies

Baillet, Adrien, *La Vie de Monsieur Descartes*, 2 vols. (1691); repr., 1 vol. (Paris, 2012). References are to the first edition.

Clarke, Desmond M., *Descartes: A Biography* (Cambridge, 2006).

Gaukroger, Stephen, *Descartes: An Intellectual Biography* (Oxford, 1995).

Nadler, Steven, *The Philosopher, the Priest, and the Painter: A Portrait of Descartes* (Princeton, 2013).

Nye, Andrea, *The Princess and the Philosopher: Letters of Elisabeth of the Palatine to René Descartes* (Lanham, Md, 1999).

Rodis-Lewis, Geneviève, *Descartes: Biographie* (Paris, 1995); trans. Jane Marie Todd as *Descartes: His Life and Thought* (Ithaca, 1998).

General

Daniel Garber and Michael Ayers (eds.), *The Cambridge History of Seventeenth-Century Philosophy*, 2 vols. (Cambridge, 1998).

Collections of Essays

Cottingham, John (ed.), *The Cambridge Companion to Descartes* (Cambridge, 1992).

——(ed.), *Descartes* (Oxford, 1998).

Doney, Willis (ed.), *Descartes: A Collection of Critical Essays* (London, 1970).

Individual Studies

Alanen, Lilli, *Descartes's Concept of Mind* (Cambridge, Mass., 2003).

Alquié, Ferdinand, *La Découverte métaphysique de l'homme chez Descartes* (1950; 6th edn, Paris, 2000).

Baker, Gordon, and Katherine J. Morris, *Descartes' Dualism* (London, 1996).

Brown, Deborah, *Descartes and the Passionate Mind* (Cambridge, 2006).

Clarke, Desmond M., *Descartes's Theory of Mind* (Oxford, 2003).

Cottingham, John, *A Descartes Dictionary* (Oxford, 1993).

——*Philosophy and the Good Life: Reason and the Passions in Greek, Cartesian and Psychoanalytic Ethics* (Cambridge, 1998).

——*Cartesian Reflections* (Cambridge, 2008).

Gaukroger, Stephen, *Descartes' System of Natural Philosophy* (Cambridge, 2002).

Hoffman, Paul, *Essays on Descartes* (Oxford, 2009).

James, Susan, *Passion and Action: The Emotions in Seventeenth-Century Philosophy* (Oxford, 1997).

Kenny, Anthony, *Descartes: A Study of his Philosophy* (New York, 1968).

Marion, Jean-Luc, *Sur le prisme métaphysique de Descartes: constitution et limites de l'onto-théologie dans la pensée cartésienne* (Paris, 1986).

——*Questions cartésiennes: méthode et métaphysique* (Paris, 1991).

Moriarty, Michael, *Early Modern French Thought: The Age of Suspicion* (Oxford, 2003).

Naaman-Zauderer, Noa, *Descartes' Deontological Turn: Reason, Will, and Virtue in the Later Writings* (Cambridge, 2010).

Rodis-Lewis, Geneviève, *L'Anthropologie cartésienne* (Paris, 1990).

Rozemond, Marleen, *Descartes's Dualism* (Cambridge, Mass., 1998).

Shapiro, Lisa, 'Descartes's Ethics', in Janet Broughton and John Carriero (eds.), *A Companion to Descartes* (Malden, Mass., 2008).

Sorell, Tom, *Descartes: A Very Short Introduction* (Oxford, 2000).

——*Descartes Reinvented* (Cambridge, 2005).

Wilkin, Rebecca M., 'Making Friends, Practising Equality: The Correspondence of René Descartes and Princess Elisabeth of Bohemia', in Lewis Seifert and Rebecca M. Wilkin (eds.), *Men and Women Making Friends in Early Modern France* (Farnham, forthcoming).

Wilson, Margaret Dauler, *Descartes* (London, 1978).

A CHRONOLOGY OF RENÉ DESCARTES

1596 (31 March) Born at La Haye in Touraine; his father's official position conferred noble status.

1597 (13 May) Death of Descartes's mother.

1607–15 Education at the Jesuit college of La Flèche.

1610 Galileo Galilei publishes *A Sidereal Message*.

1616 Studies law at University of Poitiers.

1618 Joins the army of Prince Maurice of Nassau in the Netherlands. Meets Isaac Beeckman, a powerful intellectual influence, and starts serious mathematical and scientific work. Outbreak of the Thirty Years War in central Europe and Germany.

1619 Goes to Germany to join the army of the Elector Maximilian, duke of Bavaria.

1620 Francis Bacon publishes *Novum Organum*.

1622 Returns to France.

1623–5 Travels in Italy.

1625–8 Returns to France. Lives in Paris. Has links with the intellectual circle around Marin Mersenne.

1628 (Late in the year) Moves to the United Provinces of the Netherlands, where he will be based, in various places, until 1649.

1629 Works on metaphysics and natural philosophy (science); composes his treatise *The Universe*.

1632 Galileo publishes *Dialogue on the Two Chief World Systems*.

1633 Galileo condemned by the Roman Inquisition: Descartes gives up his plan to publish *The Universe*.

1635 Descartes's daughter Francine born to Hélène Jans, a servant in a house where he had lodged.

1637 Publication of *A Discourse on the Method*, along with three essays: *Dioptrics*, *Geometry*, and *Meteorology*.

1639 Beginnings of dispute with the Calvinist minister Voetius, professor of theology at Utrecht, who accuses Descartes, though not by name, of atheism. Outbreak of the War of the Three Kingdoms in England, Scotland, and Ireland.

1640 Death of Francine.

1641 Publication of *Meditations on First Philosophy* with the first six sets of Objections and Replies. Dispute with Voetius exacerbated.

1642 Second edition of the *Meditations*, including the Seventh Objections and Replies. Beginnings of friendship with Princess Elisabeth of Bohemia, then living at The Hague.

1643 Descartes attacks Voetius in the *Epistola ad Voetium*: this is condemned by the city council of Utrecht. The Prince of Orange intervenes to stop further measures against Descartes. Correspondence with Elisabeth begins.

1644 Publication of the *Principles of Philosophy* (in Latin). (May–Nov.) Descartes visits France, among other things to discuss questions of inheritance with his family.

1646 Last meeting with Elisabeth before she moves to Berlin.

1647 (June–Sept.) Another visit to France. Meetings with Hobbes, Gassendi, and Pascal. Publication of French translations of the *Meditations* and *Principles*.

1648 Descartes returns to Paris in May, but leaves on account of the civil unrest known as the Fronde. The Peace of Westphalia brings the Thirty Years War to an end.

1649 Descartes invited to Sweden at the behest of Queen Christina. He travels there in the late summer. (Nov.) Publication of *The Passions of the Soul*.

1650 Descartes falls ill with pneumonia and dies on 11 February.

CORRESPONDENCE WITH
PRINCESS ELISABETH OF BOHEMIA
1643–1649

[Monsieur Descartes,]

I learned with both much joy and much regret that you intended 660
to visit me a few days ago, and am equally touched by your charity
in being willing to communicate with one so ignorant and unteach-
able as myself, and grieved by the misfortune that deprived me of
so beneficial a conversation. M. Pallotti* has greatly increased this
latter passion by reporting to me the solutions you had given him of
the obscure points in the physics of M. Regius,* which you personally would have better explained to me. The same applies to a question I put to the said professor when he was passing through this 661
town, in response to which he suggested that I consult you in order
to be satisfied on the point. The shame of revealing so disorderly
a style as mine has prevented me up to now from asking this favour of
you in writing.

But today M. Pallotti has given me such assurance of your kindness towards all and sundry, and especially towards me, that I have
banished from my mind all other considerations besides that of taking advantage of it, by asking you how the human soul can act on the
spirits of the body* in order to perform voluntary actions (since it
is purely a thinking substance). For it seems to me that movement
can be produced only by an impulsion applied to the thing moved,
by the manner in which it is impelled by the thing that moves it, or
by the quality and shape of the latter's surface. The first two situations require contact, the third extension. You altogether exclude
the latter from your notion of the soul, and the former seems to me
incompatible with an immaterial thing. For which reason I am asking you for a more detailed definition of the soul than you provide
in your Metaphysics, that is to say, of its substance, as distinct from
its action, thought. For even if we suppose the substance and the
action to be inseparable, like the attributes of God (though this is
hard to prove of an infant in the womb or of an unconscious person),
we can by considering them separately acquire a more perfect idea
of them.

It is because I know you to be the best doctor for my own soul, 662
that I reveal to you so frankly its feeble speculations, and hope that,
in accordance with the Hippocratic oath, you will furnish remedies

for it, without publishing them: I pray you to do so and to tolerate the importunities of

Your affectionate friend at your service,*

ELISABETH

[AT 3]   2. *Descartes to Elisabeth, Egmond aan den Hoef,* 21 May 1643*

663   Madam,

The favour with which Your Highness has honoured me, in conveying your commands* to me in writing, is greater than I would ever have dared hope; and it comforts my inadequacies better than the other favour I had passionately wished for, that of being able to
664   receive them in person, if I had been able to be admitted to the honour of paying you my respects, and offering my most humble services, when I was recently at the Hague. For I would then have had too many marvels to admire at once; and perceiving speech more than human emanating from a body so similar to that ascribed by painters to the angels, I should have been in such ecstasies, as I suppose must befall those who, having just left earth behind, are entering heaven. This would have rendered me less capable of answering Your Highness, who has no doubt already observed this shortcoming in me, when I formerly had the honour of speaking to you; and your clemency decided to spare it this ordeal, by leaving the traces of your thoughts on paper, where, after reading them several times, and familiarizing myself with them, I am indeed less dazzled by them, but all the more full of admiration, observing as I do that not only do they appear ingenious at first sight, but the more they are examined, the more judicious and solid they reveal themselves to be.*

And I may say with truth that the question proposed by Your Highness, seems to me to be the most reasonable I could be asked, in the light of what I have published. For the human soul has two properties, on which all our knowledge of its nature depends, one of which is that it thinks, and the other, that, being united to the body, it can act and be acted on along with it; and of this latter property I have said virtually nothing, and have concentrated only on making the former
665   clearly understood, since my main intention was to prove the distinction that there is between mind and body; and the former point alone conduces to this; the latter would have been an obstacle. But

since Your Highness sees things so clearly that there is no concealing anything from you, I shall here attempt to explain the manner in
which I conceive the union of the soul with the body, and how the
former has the power to move the latter.

First of all, I consider that there are in us certain primary notions,*
which are, so to speak, the originals on the pattern of which we form
all our other knowledge. And these notions are very few; for after the
most general of them (being, number, duration, etc.), which apply
to everything we can conceive, we have only, for the body specifically, the notion of extension, from which those of shape and movement are derived; and for the soul alone, we have only the notion of
thought, which comprises the perceptions of the understanding and
the inclinations of the will; finally, for the soul and the body together,
we have only the notion of their union, from which there derive both
the notion of the soul's power to move the body, and that of the body's
power to act on the soul, by causing its sensations and passions.*

I consider further that the whole of human knowledge consists
purely in properly distinguishing between these notions, and applying each of them only to the things to which they pertain. For then
when we try to explain some difficulty by means of a notion that does 666
not pertain to it, we cannot help going wrong; as we do when we try to
explain one of these notions by another. For, since they are primary,
each of them can be understood only by itself. And, inasmuch as the
use of the senses has rendered the notions of extension, shapes, and
movements far more familiar than the rest, the main cause of our
errors lies in our typically wanting to use these notions to explain
things to which they do not pertain, as when we try to use the imagination to conceive the nature of the soul, or else when we try to conceive the way in which the soul moves the body, on the model of the
movement of one body by another.

This is why, since, in the *Meditations*, which Your Highness was
so good as to read, I attempted to convey an understanding of the
notions that pertain to the soul alone, distinguishing them from those
that pertain only to the body, the first thing I must go on to explain
is how to conceive those notions that pertain to the union of soul
and body, leaving aside those that pertain to the body alone or to the
soul alone. For this purpose what I wrote at the end of my Reply to
the Sixth Objections* may be useful; for we cannot search for these
simple notions anywhere else than in our souls, which has them all

667 in itself in virtue of its nature, but which does not always distinguish them sufficiently from one another, or else does not apply them to the objects to which they ought to be applied.

Thus, I think that we have up to now confused the notion of the force by which the soul acts on the body with that by which one body acts on another; and that we have attributed both, not to the soul, for we did not yet know it, but to the various qualities of bodies, such as heaviness, heat, and so forth, which we imagined to be real, that is, to have an existence distinct from that of the body, and therefore to be substances, although we referred to them as 'qualities'.* And, in order to conceive them, we have sometimes made use of the notions that are in us so that we can know the body, and sometimes of those that are in us so that we can know the soul, depending on whether the property we attributed to them was material or immaterial. For instance, on the supposition that heaviness is a real quality, of which we know only that it has the power to move the body in which it resides towards the centre of the earth, we have no difficulty in conceiving how it moves this body, or how it is attached to it; and we do not suppose that this occurs owing to real contact between one surface and another, because we experience in ourselves that we have a specific notion for conceiving that; and I think that we are using this notion incorrectly

668 when we apply it to heaviness, which is nothing really distinct from the body, as I hope to show in my *Physics*,* but that it has been given us so that we can conceive the manner in which the soul moves the body.*

It would be a proof of insufficient acquaintance with Your Highness's incomparable intelligence, if I used more words to explain myself, and it would be presumptuous of me to dare to suppose that my answer should satisfy you entirely; but I shall try to avoid both these pitfalls, by adding this and no more: if I am capable of writing or saying anything that may give you pleasure, I shall always take it as a great favour to be called on to take up my pen, or to visit The Hague, for this purpose, and there is nothing in the world so dear to me as to be able to obey your commandments. But I cannot find this an occasion to observe, as you instruct me, the Hippocratic oath, since everything you have written to me deserves to be seen and admired by all. I may only say, as to this point, that since I have an infinite regard for the letter I have received from you, I shall treat it as misers do their treasure, which they hide all the more carefully the more they value it; and envying the rest of the world the sight of it, they find their supreme happiness in gazing on it. Thus, I shall be well pleased to be alone in enjoying the benefit of seeing it; and my greatest ambition is to be able to call myself, and to be in truth, &c.*

3. *Elisabeth to Descartes, The Hague, 10/20 June 1643* [AT 3]

Monsieur Descartes, 683
Your kindness appears not only in pointing out and correcting the faults in my reasoning, as I had envisaged, but also in your efforts to make their discovery less painful for me, by consoling me, at the expense of your judgement, with false praise,* which might have been a necessary encouragement to me to strive to remedy them, but for the fact that my upbringing, in a place where the ordinary style of conversation has habituated me to hearing praise from people incapable of sincerity, had led me to assume that I could never go wrong if I believed the opposite of what they said, and thus to accustom myself so much to considering my shortcomings that I now do so with no more emotion than is necessary for me to want to get rid of them.

This makes me admit, without shame, that I have found in myself all the causes of error that you point out in your letter, and that I can- 684 not yet banish them entirely, since the life I am forced to lead does not leave me in control of my time sufficiently to acquire a habit of meditation according to your rules.* Sometimes the interests of my house,* which I must not neglect, sometimes conversations and civilities that I cannot avoid, so crush my weak mind with vexation or boredom, that for a long time afterwards it is incapable of anything else: this will serve, I hope, as an excuse for my stupidity, in failing to understand the idea that we should judge how the soul (unextended and immaterial) moves the body with reference to your earlier idea of heaviness; or why the power (termed a quality) that you falsely ascribed to that property, namely, that of impelling bodies towards the centre of the earth, should more convince us that a body can be moved by something immaterial, than the demonstration of a contrary truth* (which you promise in your *Physics*) should confirm us in the opinion that this is impossible: chiefly, because this idea (which cannot claim the same perfection and objective reality as that of God) may be a fiction produced by ignorance of what really moves bodies towards the centre. And since no material cause presented itself to the senses, we would have attributed this motion to the contrary of matter, immateriality; something that, however, I have never been able to conceive except as a negation of matter, which cannot have any communication with it.*

685   And I admit that it would be easier for me to ascribe matter and extension to the soul, than to credit an immaterial being with the capacity to be move bodies and be affected by them. For if the first of these processes was brought about by the soul's informing the body,* the spirits, which produce the movement, would have to be intelligent, a property you deny to everything corporeal. And although in your *Metaphysical Meditations* you show the possibility of the second process, it is still very difficult to grasp how a soul, as you have described it, having had the faculty and the habit of reasoning correctly, can lose it completely on account of a few vapours,* and how, since it can subsist without the body and has nothing in common with it, it can be so governed by it.

But since you have undertaken to instruct me, I am upholding these opinions only as friends with whom I expect to part company, being confident as I am that you will explain to me both the nature of an immaterial substance and the manner of its actions and passions in the body, no less well than all the other things you have aimed to teach. I beg you also to believe that you cannot do this charity to anyone more sensible of the obligation she has to you than

Your most affectionate friend,

ELISABETH

[AT 3]   4. *Descartes to Elisabeth, Egmond aan den Hoef, 28 June 1643*

690   Madam,

I am greatly obliged to Your Highness, in that, even though you found that I had explained myself poorly in my previous letter, concerning the question you were pleased to put to me, you should yet be so for-
691   bearing as to deign to hear from me again on the same subject, and to give me the opportunity of adverting to the things I had left out. Of these the most important seems to be the following. Having distinguished three kinds of primary ideas or notions, each known in a specific way, and not by comparison with one another, namely, the

notion we have of the soul, that of the body, and that of the union between soul and body, I should have gone on to explain the difference between these three kinds of notions, and between the operations of the soul in virtue of which we have them; and I should have indicated what we can do in order to make each of them familiar and accessible to us. Then, finally, having explained why I made use of the comparison with heaviness, I should have shown that, even if one wishes to conceive the soul as material (which is, strictly speaking, conceiving its union with the body), one can still know, afterwards, that it is separable from it. I think that this covers everything Your Highness is requiring me to discuss.

First, then, I would point to a very great difference between the three kinds of notions, in that the soul is conceived only by the pure intellect; body, that is to say, extension, shape, and movement, can also be known by the intellect, but far more readily by the intellect aided by the imagination;* and finally, the things that pertain to the union of soul and body, are known only obscurely by the pure intel- 691 lect, and even by the intellect aided by the imagination; but they are known very clearly by the senses. As a result, those who never philosophize and who use only their senses, do not doubt that the soul moves the body, and that the body acts on the soul; but they consider body and soul as a single thing, that is to say, conceive their union; for to conceive the union between two things, is to conceive them as a single thing.* And metaphysical thoughts, which exercise the pure understanding, serve to familiarize us with the notion of the soul; and the study of mathematics, which principally exercises the imagination in the consideration of shapes and movements, accustoms us to form quite distinct notions of bodies; and, finally, it is by the experience of life and everyday conversation, and by refraining from meditation and from the study of things that exercise the imagination, that we learn to conceive the union of soul and body.

I am almost afraid that Your Highness may think that I am not speaking seriously here; but to do so would be contrary to the respect I owe you, and that I will never fail to pay you. And I may say, quite truly, that the main rule I have always observed in my studies, and which I think has most helped me to acquire some knowledge, is this: I have never spent more than a very few hours per day on thoughts that occupy the imagination, and very few hours per year in those that occupy the intellect alone, and I have devoted the remainder of 693 my time to giving my senses and mind a rest. Among the exercises of the imagination, I even count serious conversation, and every activity that requires attention. That is why I have retired to the country; for although, in the busiest city in the world, I could have as many hours to myself as I now devote to study, I could not, however, employ them so profitably as I do now, since my mind would be fatigued by the attention required by the hustle and bustle of life. I take the liberty of saying this to Your Highness in order to show you how truly amazed I am that, in the midst of the business and the cares that invariably attend people who are both highly intelligent and highborn, you have managed to find time for the meditations required to get a proper knowledge of the distinction between soul and body.

But I am inclined to think that it is on account of these meditations, and not the thoughts that require less attention, that you have found a certain obscurity in the notion we have of their union; for it seems to me that the human mind is incapable of conceiving quite distinctly, and at one and the same time, both the distinction between mind and body and their union; because that involves considering them both as one single thing and as two, which is contradictory. And this is why (since I supposed that Your Highness still had fresh in your mind the reasons that prove the distinction between soul and body, and since I did not want to request you to discard them, in order to contemplate the notion of union that everyone constantly encounters in their own experience, without philosophizing: namely, that one is a single person, with both a body and a mind,* which are of such a nature that the mind can move the body and experience the accidents that befall the body) I used in my earlier letter the comparison with heaviness and the other qualities we commonly imagine united to some bodies, just as thought is united to ours; and I was not troubled by the fact that the comparison is faulty inasmuch as these qualities are not real, since I believed Your Highness to be already entirely convinced that the soul is a substance distinct from the body.

But since Your Highness observes that it is easier to ascribe matter and extension to the soul, than to ascribe to it, as an immaterial entity, the capacity to move a body and be moved by it, I beg you to feel free to ascribe matter and extension to the soul; for this means nothing else than to conceive it as united to the body. And after having conceived that properly, and experienced it in yourself, it will be easy for you to consider that the matter you ascribed to the mind is not the mind itself, and that the extension of this matter is different in kind from the extension of that mind,* inasmuch as the former is located in a determinate place, from which it excludes all other corporeal extension, which does not apply to the latter. And thus Your Highness 695 cannot fail to return with ease to the knowledge of the distinction between soul and body, even though you have conceived their union.

Finally, just as I believe that it is very necessary to have fully understood the principles of metaphysics once in one's life, because they give us the knowledge of God and our soul, I also believe that it would be very harmful to occupy one's understanding with frequent meditation on them, because it would then be less at liberty to attend to the functions of the imagination and the senses; and that the best course is instead to content oneself with retaining in one's memory and one's belief the conclusions one has once drawn, and then employ the rest of the time one has available for study on thoughts in which the intellect acts in conjunction with the imagination and the senses.

My extreme devotion to the service of Your Highness leads me to hope that my frankness will not be disagreeable to you, and it would have engaged me here in a longer discussion in which I would have attempted to clarify once and for all the difficulties in the question you put to me; but a vexing piece of news has just arrived from Utrecht, where the magistrate is summoning me to make good what I have written about one of their ministers,* although he is a man who has slandered me most undeservedly, and what I wrote about him, in fair self-defence, is only too well known to all and sundry; and for this reason I must finish here, in order to investigate how I may extract myself, as soon as possible, from all this pettifoggery. I am, &c.

5. *Elisabeth to Descartes, The Hague, 1 July 1643* [AT 4]

Monsieur Descartes, 1

I am afraid that you may be as much inconvenienced by my respect for your instructions, and my desire to take advantage of them, as by the ingratitude of those who voluntarily deprive themselves of them, and would wish to deprive the human race of them;* and I would not have sent you a further product of my ignorance, before having liberated 2 you from the results of their persistence, except that Mijnheer van Bergen* induced me to do so earlier, by his obligingness in prolonging his stay in this city, until I could give him a reply to your letter of 28 June, which gives me a clear idea of the three kinds of notions we have, their various objects, and how we are to make use of them.

I find also that the senses show me that the soul moves the body, but do not teach me (any more than do the understanding or the imagination) exactly how it does so. And this is why I think that there are properties in the soul that are unknown to us, and that could perhaps undermine my belief, based on the excellent arguments in your *Metaphysical Meditations*, that the soul is without extension. And this doubt seems to be founded on the rule you lay down in that work* when you speak of the false and the true, and show how all our errors come from forming judgements in the absence of a sufficient perception. Although extension is not necessary to thought, it is not incompatible with it, and could perhaps pertain to some other, no less essential, function of the soul.* At least it demolishes the scholastics' self-contradictory view* that the soul is entire in the body as a whole and in every part of the body. The reason why ordinary people confuse the soul and the body I will not cite as an excuse for myself;* but that does not remove my fundamental doubt, and I shall despair of ever finding certainty in anything at all unless you can give it to me here, since you alone have prevented me from being a sceptic, to

3 which I was inclined by my first reasonings.

Although I owe you this confession in gratitude, I would think it very imprudent, if I did not know that your kindness and nobility of soul are on a par with the rest of your qualities, as I have learned from my own experience as well as from your reputation. You cannot show these in a more obliging fashion than by the enlightenment and advice you share with me, which I prize above the greatest treasures that could be possessed by

Your most affectionate friend and servant,

ELISABETH

6. *Descartes to Elisabeth, Egmond aan den Hoef,*

[AT 4]   *17 November 1643**

38   Madam,

Having heard from M. de Pollot that Your Highness has taken the trouble to investigate the three-circle problem* and that you have found the means of solving it by supposing only one unknown quantity, I thought it my duty to give you the reason why I had supposed several, and the means by which I work them out.

Whenever I am investigating a problem in geometry, I always ensure that the lines I am using to solve it are, as far as possible, either parallel or perpendicular; and the only theorems I consider are, first, that the sides of similar triangles have similar proportions, and, secondly, that in right-angled triangles, the square of the base is equal to the sum of the squares of the other two sides. And I do not scruple to suppose a number of unknown quantities, in order to reduce the question to such terms that its solution depends only on these two theorems; on the contrary, I prefer to suppose more unknowns rather than fewer. For this enables me to see more clearly whatever it is I am doing, and when I work them out I can better find the shortest path to a solution, and spare myself superfluous multiplications. Whereas if one draws other lines, and makes use of other theorems, although one may chance to find a path that is shorter than mine, nonetheless it is almost always the opposite that happens. And one cannot see so well what one is doing, unless one has the demonstration of the theorem one is using at the forefront of one's mind; and in that case, one almost always finds that the theorem is based on the consideration of triangles that are either right-angled or similar, and so one ends up on the same path as mine.

For instance, if we try to solve the three-circle problem with the help of a theorem that shows how to find the area of a triangle from its three sides, we need only suppose a single unknown quantity. For if A, B, and C are the centres of the three given circles, and D the centre of the circle sought, the three sides of the triangle ABC are given, and the three lines AD, BD, CD are composed of the three radii of the given circles, added to the radius of the circle sought; so that if we call this last radius x, we have all the sides of the triangles ABD, ACD, BCD, and can therefore work out the area of each; the sum of these areas is equal to the area of the given triangle ABC. From this

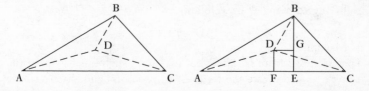

equation one can work out the radius x, which is all that is needed to solve the question. But this road seems to me to lead to so many superfluous multiplications that I would not willingly undertake to work them all out in three months. That is why, instead of the two oblique lines AB and BC, I draw the three perpendiculars BE, DG, and DF, and, putting three unknown quantities, one for DF, another for DG, and the third for the radius of the circle sought, I have all the sides of the three right-angled triangles ADF, BDG, and CDF. These give me three equations because in each one the square of the base is equal to the squares of the other two sides.

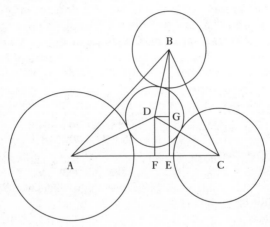

Having thus obtained as many equations as I have supposed unknown quantities, I consider whether, by each equation, I can find one of the unknown quantities in sufficiently simple terms; and if I cannot, I try to solve the problem by combining two or more equations by addition or subtraction; and, finally, if that is not sufficient, I simply examine whether it would be better to change the terms in some way. For if one carries out this examination skilfully, one easily finds the shortest path, and one can attempt a huge number in very little time.

Thus, in the present example, I suppose that the three bases of the right-angled triangles are as follows:

$$AD = a + x,$$

$$BD = b + x,$$

$$CD = c + x,$$

and making AE = d, BE = e, and CE = f, DF or GE = y, DG or
FE = z, I have the following equations for the sides of the same 41
triangles:

$$AF = d - z \quad \& \quad FD = y,$$

$$BG = e - y \quad \& \quad DG = z,$$

$$CF = f + z \quad \& \quad FD = y,$$

Then, making the square of each of these bases equal to the sum of the squares of the other two sides, I have the following three equations:

$$aa + 2ax + xx = dd - 2dz + zz + yy,$$

$$bb + 2bx + xx = ee - 2ey + yy + zz,$$

$$cc + 2cx + xx = ff + 2fz + zz + yy,$$

and I see that by any one of them alone I cannot find any of the unknown quantities, without extracting the square root, which would complicate the problem excessively. Therefore, I turn to the second method, which is to combine two equations together, and I immediately perceive that, since the terms xx, yy, and zz are identical in each, if I subtract one equation from another, as I choose, the terms will cancel one another out, leaving me with no unknown terms besides plain x, y, and z. I see also that if I subtract the second from the first or the third, this leaves me with all three terms x, y, and z; whereas if I subtract the first from the third, I will have only x and z. I therefore choose this second path, which gives me:

$$cc + 2cx - aa - 2ax = ff + 2fz - dd + 2dz,$$

or else

$$z = \frac{cc - aa + dd - ff + 2cx - 2ax}{2d + 2f},$$

or else

$$\frac{1}{2}d - \frac{1}{2}f + \frac{cc - aa + 2cx - 2ax}{2d + 2f}.$$

Then, subtracting the second equation from the first or the third 42
(since the one reduces to the other), and replacing z by the terms I have just found, I have, by the first and the second, the following:

$$aa + 2ax - bb - 2bx = dd - 2dz - ee + 2ey,$$

or else

$$2ey = ee + aa + 2ax - bb - 2bx - dd + dd - df + \frac{ccd - aad + 2cdx - 2adx}{d+f},$$

or else
$$y = \frac{1}{2}e - \frac{bb}{2e} - \frac{bx}{e} - \frac{df}{2e} + \frac{ccd + aaf + 2cdx + 2afx}{2ed + 2ef}.$$

Finally, returning to one of the first three equations, and replacing y or z with the quantities that are equal to them, and replacing yy or zz by the squares of these quantities, we find an equation where x and xx are the only unknowns; so that the problem is planar,* and there is no need to go any further. For what is left does nothing for mental cultivation or recreation and serves only to exercise the patience of some laborious calculator. Indeed, I am afraid of having been tedious here to Your Highness, since I have taken the time to write things you doubtless know better than I do, and which are straightforward, but which are nonetheless the keys to my algebra. I most humbly beg you to believe that I was led to this by the devotion I bear you, and that I am,

> Madam,
> > Your Highness's
> > > Most humble and most obedient servant, DESCARTES

[AT 4]   7. *Elisabeth to Descartes, The Hague, 21 November 1643*

44   Monsieur Descartes,

If my ability to follow your guidance were equal to my desire, you would already be seeing the effects of your charity in my progress in reasoning and algebra, whereas at this stage I can show you only my mistakes. But I am so accustomed to showing you these that, like a hardened sinner, I have lost all shame in doing so. Therefore, my intention was to send you the solution to the problem you gave me, according to the method I was earlier taught, both so that you would have to point out to me what is wrong with that method and because I am not yet so well versed in yours. For I could see that there was something wrong with my solution, since I could not see my way to inferring a theorem from it; but I would never have found out the reason without your last letter, which gave me all

the satisfaction I asked for, and taught me more than I could have 45
learned in six months' working with my teacher. I am most indebted
to you, and would never have forgiven M. de Pallotti if he had followed your instructions.* However, he would not give me your letter
except on condition I sent you my own workings. Do not therefore
take it ill that I am inconveniencing you further, since there are few
things I would not do to obtain these results of your good will, which
is infinitely esteemed by

Your most affectionate friend and servant,

ELISABETH

8. *Descartes to Elisabeth, Egmond aan den Hoef, 29 November 1643* [AT 4]

Madam, 45
The solution Your Highness did me the honour of sending me* is
so sound as to leave nothing to be desired; and not only was I aston- 46
ished when I saw it, but I cannot refrain from adding that I was also
highly delighted and gratified in my vanity to see that the calculation
used by Your Highness is altogether similar to the one put forward in
my *Geometry*. Experience had taught me that most of those who can
readily follow a process of metaphysical reasoning cannot grasp an
algebraical one, and reciprocally that those who can easily understand
algebraical proofs are generally incapable of following the other kind;
and Your Highness's is the only mind that finds all things equally
easy.* It is true that I had so much evidence of this already that I could
not doubt it in the slightest; I was afraid only that the patience necessary at the outset to overcome the difficulties of calculation might
be wanting. For it is a quality that is extremely rare in minds of the
first order and persons of high rank.

Now that this difficulty has been overcome, you will much more
enjoy everything else; and if, as you very often do here, you make
use of a single letter rather than several, the calculation will not be
tedious. This is something one can almost always do, when one is
attempting merely to identify the kind of problem one is dealing with,
that is, to decide whether it can be solved by compass and ruler, or
whether one needs to make use of some other curves of the first or
second category, and what approach one should adopt. I am usually

satisfied to go no further than this, when it comes to individual problems. For it seems to me that the remaining business of seeking out
the construction and the demonstration via the principles of Euclid,
and concealing the algebraic approach, is nothing more than an
entertainment for mediocre geometers, which requires neither great
intelligence nor much knowledge. But when one has a problem one
wants to solve in full, so as to produce a theorem that will serve as
a general rule for the solution of many similar problems, one needs to
keep the same letters one has selected at the beginning right through
to the end; or else, if one alters some to make the calculation easier,
the original ones must be restored later, because normally several of
them will cancel one another out, which is something one cannot see
when one has altered them.

It is useful also to ensure that the quantities designated by the
letters should, as far as possible, have a similar proportion to one
another; this makes for a more elegant and concise theorem, since
what is asserted of one of the quantities can be asserted in the same
way of the others, which prevents one from making mistakes in calculation, since the letters designating quantities with the same proportion to one another should turn out to be similarly distributed; and
when this does not occur, it is a sign one has gone wrong.

Thus, in order to find a theorem which will show the radius of a circle touching three other circles given in advance, we should attach the
three letters *a*, *b*, *c* not to the three lines AD, DC, and DB, but to the

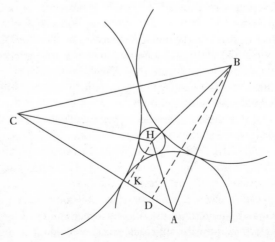

lines AB, AC, and BC, since these latter have the same relation to one another as the corresponding lines AH, BH, and CH, which is not the case with the former. And if one works through the calculation with these six letters, without altering them or adding others, using the method adopted by Your Highness (since it is better for this purpose than the one I had put forward), one should end up with a very regular equation, which will supply a fairly concise theorem. For the three letters *a*, *b*, and *c* are there disposed in the same way as are *d*, *e*, and *f*. 48

But because the calculations involved are tedious, if Your Highness wishes to try this out, you will find it easier if you suppose that the three given circles touch, and use only the four letters *d*, *e*, *f*, and *x* throughout the calculation; for these are in a similar relationship to one another, being, as they are, the radii of the four circles. You will find, first of all:

$$\mathrm{AK} = \frac{dd + df + df - fx}{d+f}, \quad \text{and} \quad \mathrm{AD} = \frac{dd + df + de - fe}{d+f}.$$

Here you can already observe that *x* is in the line AK, as *e* is in the line AD, since it is found using the triangle AHC, as the other is found by the triangle ABC. Then, finally, you will have this equation: 49

ddeeff + ddeexx + ddffxx + eeffxx
= 2deffxx + 2deeffx + 2deefxx + 2ddeffx + 2ddefxx + 2ddeefx.

From this one can derive the following theorem: the four totals produced by multiplying together the squares of three of these radii are twice as great as the six produced by multiplying two of these radii by each other, and by the squares of the other two. This is sufficient to serve as a rule for discovering the radius of the greatest circle that can be described between the three given mutually tangent circles. For if the radii of these three given circles are as follows: *d*/2, *e*/3, *f*/4, *ddeeff* will give me 576, and *ddeexx* will give me 36*xx*, and so forth. From which I will conclude:

$$x = -\frac{156}{47} + \sqrt{\frac{31104}{2209}},$$

if the calculation I have just undertaken is correct.

And Your Highness can see here two very different approaches to one and the same problem, depending on one's intention in dealing

with it. For if I wish to know merely what kind of problem it is, and how one should go about solving it, I take the perpendicular and parallel lines as given, and suppose several other unknown quantities, so as to avoid superfluous multiplication and get a better view of the shortest path; whereas if I wish to solve it altogether, I take the sides of the
50 triangle as given, and suppose only one unknown quantity. But there are a great many problems where one and the same path leads to both destinations, and I have no doubt that Your Highness will see very soon how much progress the human mind can make in this science. I would think myself very fortunate if I could contribute to this in any way, being, as I am, impelled by the particularly zealous desire to be,

     Madam,

        Your Highness's

           Most humble and most obedient servant, DESCARTES.

[AT 5]   *9. Descartes to Elisabeth, Paris, 8 July 1644**

64   Madam,

No misfortune could possibly have affected my journey, since I was so fortunate as to be remembered by Your Highness while I was travelling; the very gratifying letter that shows this to be so is the most
65 precious thing I could receive in this country. It would have made me perfectly happy if it had not informed me that the illness from which Your Highness was suffering before I left The Hague has left you with some residual indisposition of the stomach. The remedies you have chosen, namely, diet and exercise, are in my view the best of all, not counting, however, those of the soul, which certainly has great power over the body, as is shown by the great changes brought about in the body by anger, fear, and other passions. But it is not directly by its will that the soul sends the animal spirits into the parts of the body where they can be beneficial or harmful, only by willing or thinking of something else.* For the construction of our bodies is such that certain movements within them follow naturally on from certain thoughts: as we see, for instance, that shame is followed by blushing, compassion by tears, and joy by laughter. And I know no thought more conducive to the preservation of one's health than a strong conviction and firm belief that the architecture of our bodies is so solid that, once we are in good health, we cannot easily fall ill, unless

we commit some unusual excess or are harmed by the air* or other external causes; and that if we do fall ill, we can easily recover, by the sheer force of nature, especially when we are young. This conviction is beyond doubt much truer and more reasonable than that of some people, who, relying on the word of an astrologer or doctor, delude 66 themselves that they are doomed to die at a certain time, and fall ill for no other reason than that; indeed, it is not uncommon to die as a result, as I have seen in the case of various people.* But I could not help being extremely sad if I thought that Your Highness's indisposition had lasted this long; I prefer to hope that it is altogether over; and yet the desire to be certain of this makes me passionately long to be back in Holland.

I intend to leave here in four or five days, to travel to Poitou and Brittany, which is where I have the business that has brought me to France;* but as soon as I manage to set my affairs somewhat in order, I wish for nothing so much as to return to the places where I was so fortunate as to have the honour to speak on occasion to Your Highness. For although there are many people here whom I honour and respect, I have yet seen nothing here that can detain me. And I am, more than I can say, &c.

10. *Elisabeth to Descartes, The Hague, 1 August 1644*   [AT 4]

Monsieur Descartes,   131

The present Mijnheer van Bergen made to me* on your behalf obliges me to send you my thanks for it, and my conscience accuses me of being unable to do so adequately. Even if I had received nothing more than the benefit you have conferred on our age as a whole, which owes you every reward that former ages have bestowed on the inventors of sciences, since you alone have demonstrated that science exists,* how great must then be my debt, when not only do you enlighten me, you give me a share in your glory through the public demonstration of your friendship and approval. Pedants will say that you are obliged to construct a new morality* to render me worthy of it. But I am taking it as a rule by which to live my life, though I feel myself to be only at the lowest level to which you there give your approval,* that of desiring to inform my understanding and pursuing what it knows to 132 be the good. It is to this intention that I owe my understanding of your works, which are obscure only to those who examine them in the light of Aristotle's principles, or very carelessly; and, indeed, the most reasonable men among the scholars of this country have admitted to me that they have not made a study of them, because they are too old to make a start with a new method, having exhausted body and mind in working with the old one.

But I fear that you may change, and rightly, your opinion of my understanding when I tell you that I do not understand how quicksilver is formed, being, as it is, so quick-moving and so heavy at the same time, thus contradicting your definition of heaviness;* and although body E in the picture on p. 225* presses down on it from above, why should the quicksilver feel the effects of this pressure when it is on the surface, any more than air does when it emerges from a vessel in which it has been compressed?

The second difficulty I have come upon is how the spiral-shaped particles* can make their way through the centre of the earth, without being misshapen or distorted by the fire there, as they were in the beginning when body M* was formed. Only their speed can preserve them from this, and on pp. 133–4* you say that they do not need to move fast in order to continue in a straight line, and, as a result, it is the least agitated particles of the first element that flow in this way through the globules of the second. I am likewise astonished that they should take such a roundabout journey, when they leave the poles of body M, and pass along the surface of the earth, in order to return to

133 the other pole, since they could find a shorter way via body C.*

I am here setting out only my reasons for the doubts to which your book has given rise; those for my admiration are innumerable, as are those for which I am indebted to you, among which I must also count your kindness in keeping me informed of your news and giving me advice for the preservation of my health. Your news gave me much joy on account of the good outcome of your journey, and your continued intention to return, and your advice has brought me much benefit, since I am already feeling the good effects of it in myself. You have not shown Mijnheer Voetius the danger there is in being your enemy as clearly as you have shown me the benefit that flows from your good will; otherwise, he would be as anxious to escape that status, as I am to deserve that of

Your most affectionate and serviceable friend,

ELISABETH

11. *Descartes to Elisabeth, Le Crévis,* August 1644*   [AT 4]

Madam,   136

The favour Your Highness does me in deigning to allow me to testify in public how much I esteem and honour you* is greater and lays more obligations on me than any I could receive from elsewhere. And I do not fear that my having expressed my views on ethics will lead to accusations of attempted innovation;* for what I have written is so true and so clear that I am convinced that any reasonable person will acknowledge it. But I fear that what I have written in the rest of the book must be more doubtful and more obscure, since Your Highness finds difficulties in it.

The one concerning the heaviness of quicksilver is very significant, and I would have tried to elucidate it, except that, since I have not yet sufficiently studied the nature of that metal, I was afraid of putting down something contrary to what I might learn through future investigation. All I can say of it for now is that I am convinced that the particles of air, water, and all other earthly bodies have several pores, through which the very subtle matter may pass; and this follows clearly enough from my account of how they are formed. Now, we have only to suppose that the particles of quicksilver and other   137 metals have fewer such pores in order to explain why these metals are heavier. For, even if, for example, we conceded that the particles of water and those of quicksilver are the same size and shape, and move in similar fashion, we have only to suppose that each particle of water is like a very soft and slack piece of string, whereas the parts of quicksilver, having fewer pores, are like pieces of string that are much more rigid and more compact,* and it will clearly follow that quicksilver must be much heavier than water.

As for the little spiral particles, there is no mystery in their not being destroyed by the fire in the centre of the earth. For this fire is composed purely of very subtle matter, and so can drive them on their way at great speed, but not cause them to crash into other hard bodies, as would have to happen for them to be broken or divided.

Moreover, these spiral particles are not obliged to make too long a detour on their way from one pole to the other and back again. For I suppose that the majority of them are passing through the interior of the earth; so that only those that cannot find a passage by this lower route return through our air. And this is the reason I put forward to explain why magnetic force does not appear so great in the whole mass of the earth as in little magnetic stones.*

138   But I most humbly beg Your Highness to excuse me, if all I have written here is very confused. I do not yet have a copy of the book of which you have deigned to indicate the pages, and I am travelling continuously. But I hope that in two or three months' time, I shall have the honour of paying you my respects at The Hague. I am, &c.

[AT 4]   12. *Descartes to Elisabeth, Egmond-Binnen, 18 May 1645*

200   Madam,

I was extremely surprised to learn from the letters of M. de P.* that Your Highness had been ill for a long time, and I am vexed that my reclusive life prevented me from finding out earlier. It is true that, though I have so much withdrawn from the world that I am completely uninformed about what goes on in it, nonetheless my zeal for the service of Your Highness would not have allowed me to remain so long without news of your health, even if I had had to make a special trip to The Hague to find out about it, were it not for the fact that M. de P. had written to me in great haste about two months ago, promising me to write again by the next post; and because he never fails to inform me how Your Highness is, I supposed, as long as I did not hear from

201   him, that you continued in the same state. But from his most recent letter I learned that Your Highness had been ill for three or four weeks with a slow fever, accompanied by a dry cough, and that, after a respite of five or six days, you had fallen ill again; but that, at the time of writing (his letter took nearly a fortnight to get to me), Your Highness was once again beginning to get better. In all of this, I see the signs of an illness so significant, and yet so certainly amenable to remedies that Your Highness can apply, that I cannot refrain from writing to you with my opinion. For, although I am not a doctor, yet the honour Your Highness did me last summer in asking for my opinion concerning another indisposition from which you were suffering at the time leads me to hope that I am not taking an unwelcome liberty.

    The most common cause of a slow fever is sadness; and the stubbornness with which Fortune persecutes your house* gives you continual sources of grief, so public and so conspicuous, that no great effort of guesswork or close involvement in politics is required for anyone to judge that this is the chief cause of your indisposition. And it is to be feared that you can never be wholly free of it, unless, by the power of your virtue, you achieve contentment in your soul, despite all Fortune's blows. I know that it would be imprudent to try to persuade someone to be joyful when every day Fortune sends them new reasons to be upset, and I am not one of those cruel philosophers* who would have their wise man be immune to feeling. I know also that Your Highness is less concerned with what affects her personally than with what affects the interests of her house and of those dear to her; which I regard as a virtue, and the most attractive of all. But it seems to me that the difference there is between the greatest souls and those that are base and vulgar consists mainly in this, that vulgar souls give way to their passions, and are happy or unhappy only in so far as the things that happen to them are pleasant or unpleasant; whereas those of the other kind can reason so powerfully and convincingly that, although they too have passions, which are often indeed more vehement than those of common souls, their reason nonetheless remains in command, and ensures that even afflictions are of use to them, and contribute to the perfect happiness they enjoy even in this life. For, on the one hand, they consider themselves as immortal and capable of experiencing the highest bliss, and then, on the other hand, considering that they are joined to a mortal and fragile body, subject to many infirmities, and which must inevitably perish in a few years, they certainly do everything in their power to win the favour of Fortune in this life, but nonetheless value it so little, that they consider what results from it almost as we consider the events of a play.* And just as the sad and lamentable events that we see represented on a stage often entertain us as much as the happy ones, even though they draw tears from our eyes, so these greatest souls of whom I speak feel a satisfaction in themselves at everything that befalls them, even the most distressing and unbearable events. Thus, when they feel bodily pain, they steel themselves to bear it patiently, and this making trial of their strength is pleasant to them; thus, when they see their friends in some great affliction, they feel compassion for their trouble, and do all they possibly can to rid them of it, and do not even fear to risk their lives in order to achieve this end, if need be. But, nonetheless, the witness of their conscience that they are doing their duty, and performing a praiseworthy and virtuous action, makes them happier than they are distressed by all the sadness resulting from their compassion.

202

203

And, finally, just as the greatest blessings of fortune never go to their head or make them arrogant, so the greatest misfortunes that can befall them never drive them to despair or depress them so much as to cause the body they are attached to to fall ill.

I would be afraid of falling into ridicule if I wrote in this style to anybody else; but, since I consider Your Highness to possess the noblest and loftiest soul I know, I think that you should also be the happiest, and that you will indeed be such, provided you deign to cast a glance on what is beneath you, and compare the value of the goods that you possess, and that can never be taken from you, with the goods of which Fortune has deprived you and the adversities with which it persecutes you in the person of those close to you;

204 because you will then see how much reason you have to be content with your own goods. It is on account of my extreme zeal on your behalf that I have let myself be so carried away as to address these words to you, which I must humbly beg you to excuse, since they come from one who is, &c.

[AT 4]   13. *Elisabeth to Descartes, The Hague, 24 May 1645*

207   Monsieur Descartes,

I see that the delights of a solitary life have not deprived you of the social virtues. I should have been vexed if your generous kindness towards myself and my friends, which you display in your concern for my health, had induced you to travel as far as here, since M. de Pallotti told me that you judged rest to be essential to the preservation of your own health. And I assure you that the doctors, who saw me every day and examined all the symptoms of my disease, did not

208 discover its cause; nor did they prescribe such efficacious remedies as you have from a distance. Even if they had been knowledgeable enough to suspect the role played by my mind in the disorders of my body, I would not have been frank enough to admit this to them. But I do so to you, Monsieur, with no scruple, since I am confident that an honest account of my shortcomings will not deprive me of my share in your friendship, but will strengthen it all the more, since you will see how necessary it is to me.

I must tell you, then, that my body is imbued to a great extent with the weaknesses of my sex, that it is very quick to feel the effects of the afflictions of my soul, and has not the strength, when my soul recovers, to follow suit, being, as I am, constitutionally subject to obstructions, to which the air where I live makes me more liable. In people who cannot take much exercise, the heart does not need to be oppressed by sadness for long, before the spleen is obstructed, and the rest of the body infected by its vapours. I imagine that the slow fever and the dry cough, which have not yet disappeared altogether, although the warm weather and the walks I am taking are somewhat restoring my strength, are caused by this. For this reason I am accepting the doctors' advice to drink Spa water for the next month (it can be transported here without going bad), since it has been found by experience to be good at clearing obstructions. But I will not take it until I hear your opinion, since you are so good as to want to cure my body along with my soul.

I will go on to confess to you also that, although I do not set my 209 happiness in anything that depends on fortune or the will of man, and I shall not consider myself utterly wretched, even if I were never to see my house restored to its position, and those close to me free from misfortune, yet I cannot consider the harmful incidents that befall them in any other light than that of evil, or think about the vain efforts I make in their service without some kind of anxiety, which, as soon as reason has dispelled it, flares up again under the influence of some new disaster. And I think that if my life were entirely known to you, you would find the fact that a sensitive soul like mine has preserved itself so long, among so many setbacks, in so feeble a body, with no guidance except what its own reasoning can provide, and no consolation except what its own conscience can furnish, stranger than the causes of my present illness.

I have spent the whole of this last winter in business so troublesome that it prevented me from taking advantage of the liberty you have vouchsafed me, to lay before you the difficulties I come across in my studies, and burdened me with other difficulties, of which I needed more insensibility than I possess to rid myself. Only shortly before I fell ill did I find the leisure to read the philosophy of Sir Kenelm Digby,* published by him in English, where I looked to find arguments that would refute your philosophy, since the summary of the chapters indicated two places* where he claimed to have done so; but I was quite astonished, when I got to them, to find that there was a complete misunderstanding behind both his agreement with your views on reflection and his disagreement with you over

210 refraction, since he makes no distinction between the movement of
a bullet and its determination* and fails to consider why a soft and
yielding body slows the one, and why a hard body merely resists
the other. As regards some of what he says about the movement of
the heart, he is more excusable, if he has not read what you wrote on
the subject to the Louvain doctor.* Dr Jonson* has told me that he
will translate those two chapters for you; and I think that you will not
be very curious as to the rest of the book, because it is of the stamp,
and follows the method, of the English clergyman who goes by the
name of Albanus,* although it contains some very fine meditations,
and one could hardly expect more from a man who has spent most of
his life in the pursuit of love or ambition. I myself will never have
stronger feelings of those kinds than my desire to be, all my life long,

Your most affectionate friend and servant,

ELISABETH

Monsieur Descartes,
When I reread what I have told you about myself, I realize that I am
211 forgetting one of your maxims, namely, never to put anything in writing that could be misinterpreted by uncharitable readers. But so great
is my trust both in the diligence of M. de Palotti, that I know that
my letter will be faithfully delivered to you, and in your discretion,
that I know that you will eliminate by burning the chance of its falling
into the wrong hands.

[AT 4]   14. *Descartes to Elisabeth, Egmond-Binnen, May or June 1645*

218   Madam,
I could not read the letter Your Highness has done me the honour of
writing to me without great distress at the thought that such rare and
accomplished virtue is not accompanied by the health or by the prosperity it deserves, and I can readily understand the many vexations
that continually beset you, which are all the more difficult to overcome
because they are often of such a kind that true reason does not command us to challenge them head on and try to drive them away. They are
enemies in the household, with whom one cannot avoid having dealings, and with whom, therefore, one must remain all the time on one's
guard, to forestall the harm they may do. And for this I know only one
remedy, which is to turn aside one's imagination and one's senses from

them as much as possible, and to consider them only with the under-standing, when prudence makes it necessary to do so.

Here I think it is easy to observe the difference between the under-standing and the imagination or the senses; for it is such that I believe that, if a person who had every reason to be happy in all other respects were constantly watching performances of tragedies, with death in every act, and dwelling all the time on stories of sadness and pity, which he knew to be fictitious and invented, so that they only drew tears from his eyes and excited his imagination without affecting his understanding, this would be enough to accustom his heart to being constricted and to sighing; as a result, the circulation of the blood would be so much impeded and slowed, that the coarsest parts of the blood, clustering together, could easily obstruct the spleen, becoming stuck fast in its pores; meanwhile, the decrease in the agitation of the more subtle parts of the blood could have a bad effect on the lungs and cause a cough that, in the long run, would prove very danger-ous. Whereas, on the other hand, if a person with any number of real reasons to be distressed applied himself so thoroughly to turning his imagination aside from them that he never thought of them, except when compelled by practical necessity, and devoted the rest of his time to thinking only about what could bring him contentment and joy, not only would this greatly help him to judge more wisely about matters of concern to him, because he would consider these without passion, I am certain that this alone would be capable of restoring him to health, even if his spleen and lungs were already seriously affected by the bad effects of sadness on the temperament of the blood. Especially if he also made use of medical remedies to thin out the part of the blood that causes obstructions; for which purpose, I judge that Spa water is very suitable, especially if, when Your Highness takes it, you follow the usual recommendation of the doctors, that you should entirely rid the mind of any kind of sad thoughts, and even avoid any kind of serious meditation on intellectual matters, and instead concentrate on doing the same as those people who, when they gaze at the green of a wood, the colours of a flower, the flight of a bird, and such things as require no attention, convince themselves they are thinking of nothing. That is not wasting time, but using it well; for one can in the meantime have the satisfaction of hoping in this way to recover perfect health, which is the foundation of all the other goods one can have in this life.

I know very well that I have said nothing here that Your Highness does not know better than I do, and that in this area it is not the theory that is difficult, but the practice; but the extreme favour you are doing me in letting me know that it is not unpleasing to you to hear my opinions leads me to take the liberty to write down these opinions just as they are, and, moreover, to add here that I can vouch from my own experience how an almost similar illness, in fact an even more dangerous one, was cured by the remedy I have just described. For I was born of a mother who died a few days after 221 my birth,* from a disease of the lung caused by various distresses; and from her I inherited a dry cough and a pale complexion, which remained with me until I was over twenty, as a result of which all the doctors I saw before that age condemned me to an early death. But I think that my lifelong inclination to consider whatever befell me in the most favourable possible light, and to seek my principal satisfaction in what was purely under my control, is the reason why this more or less natural indisposition has over time disappeared entirely.

I am much obliged to Your Highness for deigning to convey to me your opinion of the book of M. le Chevalier d'Igby,* which I shall be unable to read until it is translated into Latin; M. Jonson, who was here yesterday, told me that some people are planning to do this. He also told me that I could address my letters to Your Highness by the ordinary postal messengers, which I would not have dared to do without his saying so, and I would have delayed writing this one because I was waiting for one of my friends to be travelling to The Hague to give it you. I very much regret the absence of M. de Pollot, because through him I could find out about your state of health; but letters addressed to me care of the Alkmaar post office are delivered to 222 me without fail, and just as there is nothing in the world that I desire so passionately as to be able to do Your Highness service, there is nothing, likewise, that can render me happier than to have the honour of receiving your commands. I am, &c.

[AT 4]   15. *Elisabeth to Descartes, The Hague, 22 June 1645*

233   Monsieur Descartes,
Your letters always serve as an antidote for my melancholy, and would do even if they did not instruct me, since they distract my

mind from the unpleasant objects that it faces every day, so that it can contemplate the happiness I possess in the friendship of a person of your merit, to whose advice I can entrust the conduct of my life. If I could also change it in accordance with your most recent precepts, there is no doubt I should be swiftly cured of the diseases of my body and the weaknesses of my mind. But I confess that I find it difficult to withdraw my senses and imagination from things continually represented to them in speech and writing that I cannot ignore without betraying my duty. I can certainly see that if I could remove from the idea of a particular matter everything that makes it distressing to me (and which I think is represented to me purely by the imagination), I would be able to judge no less soundly of it, and would immediately find the same remedies for it as are furnished by the emotion I bring to it. But I have never succeeded in doing 234 so until after passion has played its part. There is something surprising about misfortune, however much it is foreseen, and I cannot get over this surprise until a certain time has passed, during which my body becomes so severely disordered that I need several months to recover, and these hardly ever go by without some new reason to be upset. Not only am I obliged to govern my mind with care in order to provide it with agreeable objects, the slightest period of inactivity causes it to fall back on the reasons it has to feel distressed, and I am afraid that, if I do not keep it active while taking the Spa water, it will become more melancholy. If I could take advantage, as you do, from everything that presents itself to my senses, I would enjoy myself, without exerting it. At this moment I feel the disadvantage of being somewhat rational. For if I were not rational at all, I would find pleasures I could share with those among whom I have to live, so as to be able to benefit from taking this medicine. And if I were as rational as you, I would cure myself as you have done. Moreover, the curse of my sex* deprives me of the contentment I would gain from a trip to Egmond, to learn about the truths you are extracting from your new garden.* Nonetheless, I console myself with the liberty you grant me to ask now and again for news of them, being as I am,

Your most affectionate friend and servant,

ELISABETH

I was delighted to learn that the University of Groningen* has done 235 right by you.

[AT 4]   16. *Descartes to Elisabeth, Egmond-Binnen, June 1645*

236   Madam,

I humbly beg Your Highness to forgive me, if I cannot feel pity for your indisposition, when I have the honour to receive your letters. For I find in them such clear thinking and such solid reasoning that I cannot persuade myelf that a mind capable of conceiving them should be housed in a weak and sickly body. Be that as it may, the knowledge Your Highness displays, both of the disease and of the remedies by which it can be overcome, convinces me that you will also display the necessary skill to use them.

I know well that it is virtually impossible to withstand the initial turmoil that new misfortunes bring about in us, and indeed that it is normally the finest minds that have the most violent passions,* with the most powerful effect on their bodies; but it seems to me that
237 the day after, when sleep has calmed the disturbance to the blood that occurs in such situations, we can set about getting over the shock and restoring calm to our minds. This is done by concentrating on all the benefits we may derive from the thing that the day before we were treating as a great misfortune, and by diverting our minds from the evils we had imagined in it. For there are no events so dreadful nor so utterly evil (as ordinary people regard them) that an intelligent person cannot regard them from a point of view in which they will appear beneficial. And Your Highness can derive this general consolation from the blows of fortune, that they have perhaps contributed a great deal to making you cultivate your mind as much as you have; this is a good you should value more than an empire. Great prosperity often dazzles and intoxicates to such a great extent that it possesses those who have it, more than they possess it; and although this does not occur to minds of the stamp of your own, it nonetheless gives them fewer opportunities to test their mettle than does adversity. And I believe that, just as there is no good in the world, except good sense, that one can call 'good' without reservation, so there is no evil from which one cannot derive some advantage, provided one has good sense.

Up to now, I have tried to persuade Your Highness to take things easy, thinking that excessively serious occupations weaken the body by tiring the mind; but I would nonetheless not want to persuade you not to make the necessary effort to divert your thoughts from the objects that may sadden them; and I have no doubt that intellectual diversions, which others would find very burdensome, may 238 sometimes enable you to relax. I would deem myself extremely fortunate if I could help to make them easier for you; and I have a much greater desire to go to The Hague to learn the virtues of Spa water than to stay here in order to discover the virtues of the plants in my garden, and very much more than to find out what is happening in Groningen or Utrecht,* whether to my advantage or not. I shall therefore follow this letter in four or five days, and will be, every day of my life, etc.

17. *Descartes to Elisabeth, Egmond-Binnen, 21 July 1645*   [AT 4]

Madam 251

The weather has been so continually unsettled, since I had the honour of seeing Your Highness,* and there have been days so unseasonably cold, that I have frequently been worried and fearful that the Spa water would be less healthy and beneficial than it would have been in better weather; and since you did me the honour of indicating that my letters might provide some diversion, while the doctors recommend you not to burden your mind with anything that would tax it, I would be squandering the favour it pleased you to confer on me when you allowed me to write to you, if I failed to profit from it at the first opportunity.

I imagine that most of the letters you receive from elsewhere are sources of anxiety, and that even before you read them you are fearful they will contain some distressing news, since the malignity of for- 252 tune has long accustomed you to such; but as for those that come from here, you can at least be sure that, if they give you no grounds for joy, they will also give you none for sadness, and that you can open them at any time of day without fearing they may interfere with the digestion of the waters you are taking. For since in this remote place I learn nothing of what is going on in the rest of the world, and think of nothing so frequently as of the virtues of Your Highness, which makes me wish to see you as happy and contented as you deserve, I have nothing to write to you about but the means by which philosophy teaches us to acquire the supreme happiness for which common souls look in vain to fortune, and which we cannot have except from ourselves.

One of these means, and among the most useful, it seems to me, is to examine the writings of the ancients on this subject, and to attempt to go beyond them by adding to their precepts; for in this way we can make their precepts fully our own, and prepare ourselves to put them into practice. For this reason, so as to compensate for the shortcomings of my own mind, which can produce nothing from itself that I judge worthy to be read by Your Highness, and so that my letters will not be entirely vacuous and useless, I propose to fill them from now on with considerations derived from the reading of a particular

253 book, namely, Seneca's *On the Happy Life*,* unless you would prefer to select another, or this whole idea displeases you. But if I find that you approve of it, as I hope you will, and especially, furthermore, if you will be pleased to oblige me to the extent of sharing your own observations on the same book, not only will these enlighten me greatly, they will give me the opportunity to make my own more precise, and I shall cultivate these all the more carefully the more I judge you find this exchange of ideas agreeable. For there is nothing in the world I desire so keenly as to demonstrate, in every way in my power, that I am,

> Madam,
> > Your Highness's
> > > most humble and most obedient servant,
> > > > DESCARTES.

[AT 4] 18. *Descartes to Elisabeth, Egmond–Binnen, 4 August 1645*

263 Madam,

When I suggested Seneca's *On the Happy Life*, in the belief Your Highness might enjoy discussing it, I was thinking simply of the author's reputation and the lofty subject matter, without taking into account the way in which he handles it. After further reflection, I find his approach is not sufficiently precise to be worth following. But, to help Your Highness to judge more easily of the matter, I shall here attempt to explain how I think this subject ought to have been treated by a philosopher such as himself, who, deprived of the enlightenment of faith, had no guide but natural reason.

What he says at the beginning is very good, that 'all human beings wish to live happily, but when it comes to discerning what it is that makes a life happy, they are in the dark'. But we need to know what

it means to *vivere beate*; in French I would say *vivre heureusement*,* 264
but *heureusement* can mean 'fortunately', and there is a difference
between happiness and good fortune, which is that good fortune
depends only on things that are external to us, so that those people
to whom some good occurs that they have not obtained by their own
efforts are judged more fortunate than wise, whereas happiness,
it seems to me, consists in a perfect contentment of mind and an
inner satisfaction, which are not typically to be found in those most
favoured by fortune, and that the wise acquire without fortune's help.
Thus, *vivere beate*, to live the happy life, is nothing other than to have
a perfectly contented and satisfied mind.

Considering next what it is *quod beatam vitam efficiat*,* that is, what
are the things that can procure us this supreme contentment, I note
that these are of two kinds:* namely, those that depend on us, such
as virtue and wisdom, and those that do not so depend, such as honour, wealth, and health. For of two equally wise and virtuous men, of
whom one is well-born, healthy, and wanting for nothing, whereas
the other is poor, unhealthy, and disabled, the former can enjoy more
perfect contentment than the latter. And yet, just as a small vessel
can be as full as a large one, although it contains less liquid, so, if
we regard a person's contentment as consisting in the fulfilment of
his or her desires regulated according to reason, I do not doubt that
the poorest and most disadvantaged people (whether their disadvantage comes from fortune or nature) can be entirely content and sat- 265
isfied, no less than the other kind, even though they do not enjoy so
many goods. And this is the only kind of contentment that concerns
us here: because since the other sort is not in our power, it would be
superfluous to seek it.

Now it seems to me that anyone can gain contentment with himself without any need of outside help, provided only that he observes
three requirements, corresponding to the three rules of ethics I laid
down in the *Discourse on the Method*.*

The first is, always to attempt to use one's intelligence to the
best of one's ability, to know what one should do or not do in all
situations.

The second, to have a firm and constant resolution always to act
according to the advice of reason, without being led astray by one's
passions or appetites; and, in my view, it is in the firmness of this resolution that virtue consists, though, as far as I know, no one has ever

explained it in this way; instead, they have divided it, on account of the various objects to which it applies, into several species, to each of which they have given a different name.

The third, to consider that while one behaves in this way, as far as possible according to reason, the goods one does not possess are 266 all equally out of one's power, and in this way to accustom oneself to not desiring them; for nothing can prevent us from being content but desire, and regret or repentance; but if we always do everything that reason dictates to us, we shall never have any occasion for regret, even if the outcome subsequently shows us that we were mistaken, since this was not our fault. And the reason why we do not desire, for example, to have more arms or tongues than we have, whereas we do desire to have more health or wealth, is purely that we imagine that these latter things can be acquired by our behaviour, or else that they are due to our nature, and that this does not apply to the former category. We can rid ourselves of this opinion if we consider that, since we have always followed the advice of our reason, we have failed to do nothing that was in our power, and that diseases and misfortunes are no less natural to man than prosperity and health.

Furthermore, not all kinds of desire are incompatible with perfect happiness, only those accompanied by impatience and sadness. Again, it is not necessary that our reason should never be mistaken: it is enough if our conscience bears witness that we have never lacked resolution and virtue, to carry out all the acts we have judged best,* 267 and in this way virtue alone is sufficient to bring us contentment in this life. But nonetheless, because when it is not enlightened by the understanding, virtue can be false (I mean that willpower and the resolution to do the right thing can induce us to do the wrong thing, in the belief that it is right), the resultant contentment is not solid; and because this kind of virtue* is normally set against pleasures, appetites, and passions, it is very difficult to put it into practice. Whereas the proper use of reason gives us a true knowledge of the good, and prevents virtue from being false; it even reconciles it with legitimate pleasures, and thus renders the practice of it so easy, while, by revealing to us the basic nature of our humanity, it so restricts our desires, that we must admit that the greatest bliss of man consists in this proper use of reason, and consequently that to set ourselves to master this is the most useful way we can spend our time, as it is, beyond doubt, the most agreeable and delightful.

Taking all this into account, it seems to me that what Seneca should have done is to teach us all the principal truths of which the knowledge is required in order to facilitate the practice of virtue, and to regulate our desires and passions, and hence to enjoy natural happiness.* This would have made his book the best and most useful a pagan philosopher could have written. However, this is only my personal opinion, which I submit to the judgement of Your Highness; and if you show me so much favour as to point out where I am going wrong, I shall be most obliged to you, and, by correcting myself, shall   268
reveal myself to be,

> Madam,
>> Your Highness's
>>> most humble and most obedient servant,
>>> DESCARTES

19. *Elisabeth to Descartes, The Hague, 16 August 1645*   [AT 4]

Monsieur Descartes,   268
In my reading of the book you recommended to me,* I have found any number of fine sentences and of maxims well conceived to provide me with the theme of a pleasant meditation, but not to enlighten me as to the subject of the work, since they are put down without any method, and the author does not even follow the method he had pre-   269
scribed for himself. For, instead of showing the shortest route to happiness, he contents himself with showing that his wealth and luxury do not make him incapable of it. I had to tell you this, in case you were to think I am adopting your own opinion out of prejudice or laziness. Furthermore, I am asking you to continue correcting Seneca, not because your way of reasoning is more out of the ordinary, but because it is the most natural I have ever encountered, and seems not to be teaching me anything new,* except that it enables me to draw from my own mind knowledge I had not previously realized was there.

And this is why I cannot yet rid myself of the doubt as to whether we can attain the happiness you speak of without the assistance of things that do not absolutely depend on our will: for there are diseases that entirely deprive us of the power to reason, and hence the power to enjoy rational satisfaction; there are others that diminish our strength, and prevent us from following the maxims formulated by good sense, and that render the most moderate man liable to be swept away by his passions and less capable of coping with the accidents of fortune that require resolution on the spur of the moment. When, during his bouts of kidney stones, Epicurus struggled to assure his friends that he felt no pain,* instead of crying out like an ordinary person, he was leading the life of a philosopher, not that of a ruler, commander, or courtier, and knew that no outside event could befall him that would cause him to forget the part he was playing and to fail to meet the challenge according to the rules of his philosophy.

270 And it is when faced with such challenges that it seems to me that repentance is unavoidable, and the knowledge that error is as natural to human beings as illness is no defence against it. For we also know that we could have avoided any particular mistake.

But I am confident that you will dispel these difficulties, and any number of others I cannot at present call to mind, when you teach me the truths that need to be known in order to facilitate the practice of virtue. Do not therefore abandon, I beg you, your intention of obliging me by your precepts, and please believe that I value them as much as they deserve.

For the past week, the bad frame of mind of a sick brother has prevented me from making this request of you, because it has kept me with him all the time: he will only follow his doctors' instructions to please me, and I must show myself ready to please him by trying to entertain him, since he is convinced that I am capable of this. I hope I am capable of assuring you that, all my life, I will be,

Monsieur Descartes,

Your most affectionate friend and servant,

ELISABETH.

[AT 4] 20. *Descartes to Elisabeth, Egmond–Binnen, 18 August 1645*

271 Madam,

Although I do not yet know if my most recent letter has been delivered to Your Highness, and there is nothing I can write about the subject I had adopted in order to have the honour of conversing with you that you do not, I must suppose, know better than I do, I will nonetheless continue with what I have begun, believing, as I do, that my letters will not be more troublesome to you than the books in your library; for since my letters contain no news you would benefit from knowing immediately, you will have no incentive to read them at times when you are busy, and I shall count the time I take in writing them well spent if you devote to them only the time you feel like wasting.

I have said in my previous letter what I thought Seneca should have dealt with in his book; I will now examine what he does deal 272 with. In his book, I observe in general only these three things: first, he tries to explain what the supreme good is, and he gives various definitions of it; secondly, he argues against the opinion of Epicurus; thirdly, he replies to those who object that philosophers do not live according to the rules they themselves lay down. But in order to show in more detail how he handles these points, I shall briefly discuss the book chapter by chapter.

In the first, he criticizes those who are guided by custom and example rather than reason. *Nunquam de vita iudicatur, semper creditur,** as he puts it. He approves, however, of taking advice from those we think wisest; but he wants us to make use of our own judgement as well, in order to examine their opinions. Here I agree with him most strongly; for although many people are not capable of finding the right path by themselves, there are few, nonetheless, who cannot recognize it well enough, when it is clearly pointed out by someone else; and be that as it may, we have reason to be satisfied with our conscience, and to be confident that our opinions in matters of ethics are the best they could be, when, instead of blindly following the example of other people, we have made a point of seeking guidance from the wisest ones, and used all the powers of our own mind to examine what we ought to do. But, while Seneca takes much trouble 273 here to adorn his style, he is not always sufficiently precise in the expression of his thought; for instance, when he says *Sanabimur, si modo separemur a coetu,** he seems to be teaching that in order to be wise it is sufficient to be eccentric, which is not, however, what he means.

In the second chapter, he does little more than repeat in other words what he has said in the first; all he adds is that what is commonly valued as good is not so.

Then in the third, after many more superfluous words, he finally gives his opinion concerning the supreme good;* namely, that *rerum naturae assentitur,** and that *ad illius legem exemplumque formari*

274   *sapientia est*,* and that *beata vita est conveniens naturae suae*.* All
these explanations seem to me highly obscure: for, when he speaks of
'nature', he cannot, surely, mean our natural inclinations, since these
normally incline us to give way to pleasure, and he is arguing that we
should not do this; but the context suggests that by *rerum naturam*, he
means the order established by God* in all things in this world, and
that, considering this order as infallible and independent of our will,
when he says *rerum naturae assentiri et ad illius legem exemplumque
formari sapientia est*,* he means that it is wisdom to acquiesce in
the order of things, and to do what we think we were born to do; or
rather, to put the matter in Christian terms, that it is wisdom to submit to the will of God, and to follow it in all our actions; and that
beata vita est conveniens naturae suae means that happiness consists
in following the order of the world in this way, and taking everything
that happens to us in the right spirit. This explains almost nothing,
and one cannot sufficiently see how it relates to what he adds immediately after, that this happiness cannot be obtained *nisi sana mens est,
&c.*,* unless he also means that *secundum naturam vivere** is the same
as living according to true reason.*

In the fourth and fifth chapters, he gives various other definitions of
the supreme good, which all have some connection with the meaning of the first definition, but none of them explains it sufficiently;
and by their variety they show that Seneca did not clearly understand
what he meant; for the more clearly one conceives a thing, the more
committed one is to expressing it in one way and one way only. He
seems to me to have come closest in chapter V, when he says *beatus est
qui nec cupit nec timet beneficio rationis*,* and that *beata vita est in recto
certoque iudicio stabilita*.* But as long as he does not share with us the
reasons why we should fear and desire nothing, all of this is very little
help.

In the same chapters, he begins to argue with those who hold that
happiness consists in pleasure, and he continues to do so in those
that follow. For this reason, before I examine these, I shall here give
my own views on this question.

275   I observe, first of all, that there is a difference between happiness,
the supreme good, and the ultimate end or goal at which all our
actions should aim;* for happiness is not the supreme good; but it
presupposes it, for it is the contentment or satisfaction of mind that
comes from possessing the supreme good. But 'the end of our actions'

can refer to both happiness and the supreme good; since the supreme good is surely the aim we should have in view in all our actions, and since the resultant contentment of mind is the attraction that causes us to seek for the supreme good, that too can be legitimately spoken of as our end.

I would next observe that the word 'pleasure' is used by Epicurus with a different meaning from that in which it is used by his adversaries. For they have all restricted the meaning of the word to sensual pleasures; whereas he extended it to cover all the contentments of the mind, as can readily be seen from what Seneca and some others have written about him.

Now, among the pagan philosophers, there were three main opinions concerning the supreme good and the end of our actions, namely, that of Epicurus, who said it was pleasure; that of Zeno,* who held that it was virtue; and that of Aristotle, for whom it comprised every perfection, both of body and of soul. All these three opinions, it seems to me, can be accepted as true, and made compatible, as long as they are favourably interpreted. 276

For Aristotle was considering the supreme good of human nature in general and as a whole, that is, the good that can be possessed by the most perfect human being, and so he was right to see it as comprising all the perfections of which human nature is capable; but this is not relevant to our purpose here.

Zeno, on the other hand, was considering the supreme good a given individual can possess;* this is why he too was perfectly right to say that it consists purely in virtue, because, among all the goods we can possess, this is the only one that depends entirely on our free will. But he represented this virtue as being so severe and so hostile to pleasure, with his theory that all the vices were equal,* that it seems to me that his only followers could have been melancholics, or those whose minds were entirely detached from the body.

Finally, Epicurus was not mistaken, when he considered what happiness consists in, and what the motive is of all our actions, or the end at which they aim, to say that it is pleasure in general, that is, the contentment of the mind; for although the mere knowledge of our duty could induce us to perform good actions, we would not, however, enjoy any happiness as a result, if we did not derive any pleasure from doing so. But because the term 'pleasure' is often applied to false pleasures, which are accompanied or followed by anxiety, grief, and 277 repentance, many have thought that Epicurus was preaching vice; and indeed he was not preaching virtue. But when a contest takes place, with a prize for hitting the target, the prospect of the prize makes people want to take part; but all the same they cannot win the prize, if they cannot see the target; and those who can see the target are not thereby induced to shoot, unless they know there is a prize to be won.* By the same token, virtue, which is the target, does not appear very desirable when it appears by itself; and contentment, the prize, cannot be won, unless you follow virtue.

For this reason, I think I can here conclude that happiness consists only in contentment of mind, that is to say, contentment in general; for though there are contentments that depend on the body, and others that do not, there are none that are not in the mind; and, further, that to enjoy solid contentment, we need to follow virtue, that is, to have a firm and constant will to act always in accordance with our judgement as to what is best, and to use all the powers of our mind to attain a correct judgement.* I shall postpone considering what Seneca has written about all this for another occasion; for my letter is too long as it
278   is, and I have only space enough left to write that I am,

> Madam,
>> Your Highness's
>>> most humble and obedient servant,
>>> DES CARTES*

21. *Elisabeth to Descartes, The Hague, [late] August 1645*   [AT 4]

278   Monsieur Descartes,
I think that you will already have seen, from my letter of 16 August, that I have received yours of the 4th. And I need not add that it has
279   enlightened me more as to the subject it deals with than anything I have ever read or thought about the matter. You know too well what you are doing and what I am capable of, and you have examined other people's efforts too well, to be able to doubt of this, even though, from an excess of generosity, you wish to seem unaware of my extreme obligation to you for giving me so useful and agreeable an occupation as that of reading and thinking about your letters. But for your last letter, I would never have grasped Seneca's views about happiness so well as I believe I do now. I attributed the obscurity of his book, a feature it

shares with most ancient writing, to his way of explaining himself, which is so different from ours, inasmuch as the same things we regard as problematic might among them be considered hypothetical;* and I attributed the lack of connection and order in his writing to the intention to win admirers by capturing the imagination, rather than gaining disciples by informing the judgement; I thought that Seneca uses epigrams, as others use poems and fables, to induce the young to follow his opinion. The way in which he refutes Epicurus' opinion seems to bear out this view. Speaking of Epicurus, he says *quam nos virtuti legem dicimus, eam ille dicit voluptati.** And a little earlier he says, speaking in the person of an Epicurean: *ego enim nego quemquam posse iucunde viuere, nisi simul et honeste viuat.** From which it clearly appears that the Epicureans applied the term 'pleasure' to the joy and satisfaction of the mind, which Seneca himself calls *consequentia summum bonum.** And yet in the whole of the rest of the work he speaks of Epicurean pleasure 280 more as a satirist than as a philosopher, as if it were purely sensual. But I am very grateful to him for this because it is what prompted you to take the trouble to explain their views and reconcile their disputes better than they could have done themselves. In doing so you have removed a powerful objection to the pursuit of the supreme good, which not one of these great minds succeeded in defining, and another powerful objection to the authority of human reason,* since it could not enlighten such distinguished people as to the knowledge of what was most needful and important to them. I hope you will continue, by discussing what Seneca has said or should have said, to teach me how to strengthen the understanding to enable it to judge what is best in all the actions of life; this seems to me to be the only difficulty, since it is impossible not to follow the right path when it is known. Be so frank, then, I beg you, as to tell me if I am taking advantage of your kindness, by making too severe demands on your leisure, for the satisfaction of,

Your most affectionate friend and servant,

ELISABETH.

22. *Descartes to Elisabeth, Egmond–Binnen, 1 September 1645* [AT 4]

Madam, 281

Being uncertain lately whether Your Highness was at The Hague or Rhenen,* I addressed my letter via Leiden, and the letter you did me the honour of writing to me reached me only after the messenger who had brought it to Alkmaar had left. This is why I was unable until now to let you know how proud I am to find that my judgement of the book you have taken the trouble to read is no different from your own, and that my method of reasoning appears to you to be pretty natural. I am certain that if you had had as much leisure as I to think about the subjects discussed in the book, there is nothing I could write about it that you would not have already observed better than I could; but because Your Highness's age, birth, and occupations have made this impossible, perhaps what I write may be of use to you by saving you a little time, and even my mistakes may provide you with opportunities to observe the truth.

For instance, when I spoke of a happiness that depends entirely on our free will, and that all human beings can acquire without any external aid, you rightly observed that there are diseases that deprive us of the power to reason, and likewise of the power to enjoy a rational satisfaction of mind; and this teaches me that what I had said of all human beings in general applies only to those who have the free use of their reason, and who also know the path we need to follow to attain this happiness. For there is no one who does not desire to gain happiness; but many do not know how to do so; and frequently a bodily indisposition deprives us of free will. This happens also when we are asleep; for the greatest philosopher in the world cannot prevent himself from having bad dreams when his temperament disposes him to have them. And yet experience shows that, if we have often had a certain thought while our mind was at liberty, it will still return afterwards, whatever indisposition the body is suffering from; and so I may say that in my own dreams nothing upsetting ever happens, and that there is, no doubt, a great benefit in having long accustomed oneself not to have gloomy thoughts. But we can absolutely answer for ourselves only as long as we are ourselves; and to lose one's life is less bad than to lose the use of reason; for even without the teaching of faith, mere natural philosophy gives our soul reason to hope for a better state after death than it is currently in;* and the most distressing fear it can arouse in the soul is of being attached to a body that deprives it entirely of freedom.

As to other indispositions, that do not completely disturb the senses, but only affect the humours, and cause us to be unusually inclined to sadness, anger, or some other passion, they do certainly give us trouble, but they can be overcome, and can even provide the soul with grounds for a satisfaction that is all the greater, in proportion as the indisposition was hard to conquer. And I believe the same of all external obstacles, such as conspicuously noble birth, the flattery of courtiers, the adversities of fortune, and also its greatest prosperities, which normally are more of an impediment to playing the part of a philosopher than its bad turns. For when everything is as one would like it to be, we forget to think of ourselves, and when afterwards our luck changes for the worse, we find ourselves all the more disagreeably taken by surprise, because we had relied on it so much. Finally, we may say in general that there is nothing that can entirely deprive us of the means to gain happiness, as long as it does not affect our reason; and that the things that appear most upsetting are not always those that do us most harm.

But to gain an exact knowledge of how far different things can contribute to our contentment, we must consider what are the causes that bring it about; and this is also one of the most important pieces of knowledge that can facilitate the practice of virtue; for all the actions of our soul that gain some perfection for us are virtuous, and all our contentment consists purely in our inner awareness of 284 possessing some perfection. Thus, we can never practise any virtue (that is, do what our reason persuades us we should do) without experiencing satisfaction and pleasure as a result. But there are two kinds of pleasure: some belong to the mind alone, and some to the whole person, that is, to the mind in so far as it is united with the body; and this latter kind, which present themselves confusedly to the imagination, often appear much greater than they are, especially before we possess them; which is the source of all the evils and mistakes of this life. For, according to the yardstick of reason, every pleasure should be measured by the greatness of the perfection that produces it, and this is how we measure those whose causes are clearly known to us. But often passion causes us to believe that certain things are better and more desirable than they in fact are; then when we have taken a good deal of trouble to acquire them, and in doing so lost the opportunity to possess other more genuine goods, our enjoyment of them reveals their shortcomings; hence disdain, regret, and repentance. This is why the true function of reason is to examine the real value of all the goods whose acquisition seems to depend in some way on our own behaviour, so that we shall never fail to direct all our

efforts to the attempt to obtain those that are in truth the most desirable; and then if fortune interferes with our plans, and prevents them
from succeeding, we shall at least have the satisfaction of having lost
nothing by our own fault, and we shall be able all the same to enjoy all
the natural happiness whose acquisition was in our power.

Thus, for instance, anger can sometimes arouse in us such violent
desires for revenge that we imagine there will be greater pleasure in
punishing our enemy than in preserving our honour or our life, and
so rashly expose both of these in the attempted revenge. Whereas, if
reason examines what good or perfection is the basis of the pleasure of
revenge, it will find none (barring cases where the point of revenge is
to prevent further offences to us), except that it makes us imagine
that we are superior to the target of our revenge, or that we have got
the better of them. This is often no more than a futile imagination,
which does not deserve to be compared in value to honour or life, or
even to the satisfaction that refraining from vengeance procures, of
seeing oneself master of one's anger.

And much the same occurs in all the other passions: for there
is none that does not represent the good at which it aims more
attractively than it deserves, and that does not make us imagine
pleasures as far greater, before we possess them, than we afterwards
find them to be, when we do possess them. This is why people very
commonly inveigh against pleasure, because the word is only applied
to those pleasures that frequently deceive us by their appearance,
and cause us to neglect other pleasures that are far more solid, but
the expectation of which affects us less, as is normally the case with
the pure pleasures of the mind. I say 'normally' because not all the
pleasures of the mind are praiseworthy, inasmuch as they can be
based on some false opinion, such as the pleasure we take in speaking ill of other people, which has no other foundation than the belief
that the less other people are respected, the more respected one will
be oneself; and they too can deceive us by their appearance, when
they are accompanied by some strong passion, as is clear with the
pleasure produced by ambition.

But the main difference between the pleasures of the body and
those of the mind consists in this: the body is subject to perpetual
change, and indeed its preservation and well-being depend on such
changes, so that all the pleasures that pertain to it are short-lived; for
they result only from the acquisition of something beneficial to the

body, at the moment they are experienced; and as soon as it ceases to be beneficial, they also fade away; whereas the pleasures of the soul can be immortal as the soul itself is, as long as their foundation is so solid that neither the knowledge of the truth nor any false conviction can destroy it.

Moreover, the true use of our reason in the conduct of our life consists purely in dispassionately weighing and considering the value of all perfections, both those of the body and those of the mind, that can be acquired by our behaviour, so that, since we are ordinarily obliged 287 to do without some of them in order to have others, we may always choose the best of those we can have. And since those of the body are least important, we may say, in general, that, without them, it is still possible to be happy. Nevertheless, I am not of the opinion that we should despise them entirely, or even that we should attempt to rid ourselves of the passions; it is enough if we render them subject to reason, and once they have been tamed in this way, the more they have a tendency to excess, the more useful they sometimes are. I myself shall never have any passion more excessive than the one that inclines me to the respect and veneration I owe you, and that makes me,

> Madam
> > Your Highness's
> > > most humble and most obedient servant,
> > > > DESCARTES.

23. *Elisabeth to Descartes, The Hague, 13 September 1645* [AT 4]

Monsieur Descartes, 288

If my conscience could keep itself satisfied by the pretexts for my ignorance you mention, as if they were remedies,* I would be highly obliged to it, and would no longer have to repent my failure to make better use of the time during which I have had the use of reason—a longer time than others of my age have had, all the more because my birth and fortune compelled me much sooner to start making use of my judgement, in order to direct a life that has been fairly difficult and at the same time free both of the prosperity that might have prevented me from thinking of myself* and of subjection to a governess* on whose prudence I would have to rely.

But to my mind it is not such prosperity, or the flattery that goes with it, that is absolutely capable of depriving a well-born soul of its strength of mind and preventing it from accepting changes of fortune like a philosopher. Rather, I am convinced that the multitude of chance events that take people in positions of authority by surprise, without giving them the time to examine the most effective response, often leads them (however virtuous they may be) to carry out actions that they later have reason to repent, which you say is one of the main impediments to happiness. It is true that a habit of valuing goods in proportion to their capacity to contribute to our contentment, of measuring this contentment by the perfections that give rise to pleasures, and of judging these perfections and pleasures dispassionately will protect them from many mistakes. But in order to value goods in this way, we need to know them perfectly; and to know all the goods between which we are compelled to choose when we live the active life, one would need to possess an infinite knowledge. You will say that we can still be satisfied, whenever our conscience bears witness that we have taken all possible precautions. But that never happens, when things do not work out. For we always think back on the things we failed to consider. To measure contentment by the perfection that produces it, we would need to have a clear idea of the value of every perfection, and to know whether those that are useful to ourselves alone should be preferred to those that also make us useful to other people. The latter seem to be over-valued by those whose temperament makes them sacrifice themselves for the sake of other people, and the former by those who live only for themselves. And yet both kinds of people can bolster their inclination by reasons strong enough to maintain it throughout their lives. The same applies to the other perfections of mind and body which our reason approves in virtue of an instinctive sense* that should not be called a passion, since it is innate. Tell me then, please, how far we should follow it (being, as it is, a gift of nature), and how it is to be corrected.

I would also like to see your definition of the passions, in order to know them better; for those who name them 'disorders of the soul'* would persuade me that their power consists purely in bedazzling and subjugating reason, were it not that experience has taught me that there are some that incline us to rational actions. But I am confident that you will give me further enlightenment on this, by explaining how the strength of the passions renders them all the more useful, when they are subject to reason.

I shall receive this favour at Rijswijk, where we shall be living in the house of the prince of Orange,* while this house is cleaned; but you need not change the address on your letters to

Your most affectionate friend and servant,

ELISABETH

---

24. *Descartes to Elisabeth, Egmond-Binnen, 15 September 1645*   [AT 4]

Madam,   290

Your Highness has so accurately discerned all the reasons why Seneca has failed to clearly explain to us his opinion concerning the supreme good, and you have taken the trouble to read his book so   291
carefully, that I would fear to be vexatious if I carried on examining all his chapters one by one in this letter, and so postponed replying to the difficulty it pleased you to put to me, concerning the means by which one may strengthen one's understanding so as to discern the best course of action in all situations. For this reason, without devoting further time to following Seneca, I shall try merely to explain my own opinion of the matter.

It seems to me that, in order to be always well equipped to judge accurately, only two things are required: first, the knowledge of the truth, and secondly, the habit of remembering and acquiescing in this knowledge, whenever circumstances so require. But since God alone has a perfect knowledge of all things, we must be content with knowing those things that are most useful to us.

Among these the first and most important is that there is a God, on whom all things depend, whose perfections are infinite, whose power is immense, and whose decrees are infallible; for this teaches us to take in good part whatever happens to us, as being specifically sent us by God; and because the proper object of love is perfection, when we lift up our minds to consider him as he is, we find ourelves   292
naturally so inclined to love him, that we can even find joy in our afflictions, when we think that our suffering them is the fulfilment of his will.

The second thing to consider is the nature of our soul, in so far as it continues to exist without the body, and is far more noble than the body, and is capable of enjoying an infinity of contentments that cannot be experienced in this life; for this prevents us from fearing death, and so loosens our attachment to the things of this world, that we despise whatever is within the power of fortune.

To this end, it is also very helpful to form a proper judgement of the works of God, and to come to terms with the vast idea of the extent of the universe that I have attempted to convey in book III of the *Principles of Philosophy*;* for if we imagine that beyond the heavens, there is nothing, only imaginary space, and that the heavens themselves were created only for the service of the earth, and the earth only for man, this encourages us to think that this earth is our principal dwelling place, and this life the best we have; and instead of getting to know the perfections that truly exist within ourselves, we falsely attribute imperfections to other creatures, in order to raise ourselves up above them; and, succumbing to presumptuous arrogance, we want to take a share in God's counsels, and in the burden of governing the world, which causes any number of futile anxieties and worries.

293   After we have thus recognized the goodness of God, the immortality of our souls, and the greatness of the universe, there is one further truth the knowledge of which appears to me very profitable; namely, that although each of us is a person separate from other people, and whose interests are thus in some sense distinct from everybody else's, we should nonetheless bear in mind that we cannot exist on our own, and that each of us is, in fact, part of the universe, and more particularly still part of this earth, of the state, of the society, of the family, to which one is attached by residence, by one's oath of allegiance, and by one's birth. And we should always put the interests of the whole of which we are a part above those peculiar to ourselves; yet this should be with measure and discretion, for it would be wrong to expose oneself to a great evil, so as to obtain only a little good for one's kin or country; and if a man is worth more by himself alone than the rest of his fellow citizens put together, he would not be right to try to save the city at the cost of his own life. But if we judged everything in relation to ourselves, we should not fear to do great harm to others, whenever we thought we might derive some slight advantage from doing so, and we should have no true friendship, no loyalty, and in general no virtue. Whereas, if we consider ourselves part of the public, we take pleasure in doing good to everyone, and even do not fear to put our own life at risk for the benefit of others, should the occasion arise; indeed, one would be ready to lose one's

soul, were it possible, in order to save other people's. So that this consideration is the source of all the most heroic actions undertaken by human beings; for as to those who put their lives in danger out of 294 vanity, because they hope to be praised for doing so, or out of stupidity, because they fail to grasp the risk, I think they are more to be pitied than esteemed. But when anyone risks his life because he thinks it is his duty to do so, or suffers some other evil, so that good may come to others as a result, even though he may not be explicitly reflecting that he is doing this because he has a greater duty to the public, of which he is a part, than to himself as a particular individual, he is nonetheless acting in virtue of this consideration, which is confusedly present in his mind. And we are naturally inclined to have it within ourselves, when we know and love God as we should: for then abandoning ourselves entirely to his will, we divest ourselves of our own interests, and have no other passion than that of doing what we think agreeable to him; as a result of which we have a mental satisfaction and contentment incomparably superior to all the fleeting petty joys that depend on the senses.

Besides these truths, which apply to all our actions in general, we need to know several others, which relate more particularly to individual actions. Of these the chief seem to me to be those I pointed out in my last letter: namely, that all the passions represent those goods they impel us to pursue as being far greater than they are in truth; 295 and that the pleasures of the body are never so long-lasting as those of the soul, or so great, when possessed, as they appeared when hoped for. This we must carefully bear in mind, so that, when we feel ourselves stirred by some passion, we may suspend our judgement, until it has calmed down; and so that we do not allow ourselves to be easily deceived by the false appearance of the goods of this world.

There is nothing I can add further, except this: that we should also examine in detail all the customs of the places where we live, so as to know which of them ought to be adopted. And though we cannot have cast-iron demonstrations of everything, we must nevertheless make up our minds, and espouse the opinions that appear to us most probable* concerning all those everyday matters of behaviour, so that, when we have to act, we are never irresolute. For irresolution is the sole cause of regret and repentance.

Moreover, I have said above that, besides the knowledge of the truth, habit is also essential if we are to be always disposed to judge

correctly. For, given that we cannot be continually attentive to the same thing, then, however clear and evident the reasons that have previously convinced us of some truth, our belief in it may be subse-
296 quently dislodged by false appearances, unless, by long and frequent meditation, we have so imprinted it in our minds that it has been transformed into a habit. And in this sense the schoolmen are right to say that the virtues are habits;* for, indeed, when we go wrong it is seldom because we lack the theoretical knowledge of what we ought to do, but only because we lack the practical knowledge, that is, the firm habit of belief as to what we ought to do. And because, while here examining these truths, I am increasingly assimilating them as habits, I am especially obliged to Your Highness, for permitting me to discuss them with you, and there is nothing in which I judge my leisure better employed than in this occupation in which I can bear witness that I am,

> Madam,
> > Your Highness's
> > > most humble and most obedient servant,
> > > > DE CARTES

As I was sealing this letter, I received Your Highness's of the 13th; but I find it so full of matters that deserve consideration that I dare not undertake to reply straight away, and I am confident that Your Highness will prefer me to take a little time to think them over.

[AT 4]   25. *Elisabeth to Descartes, Rijswijk, 30 September 1645*

301   Monsieur Descartes,
        Though your comments on Seneca's views about the Supreme
302 Good would render the reading of his work more profitable to me than I could find it if left to my own devices, I am not sorry to lose them in exchange for such necessary truths as those concerning the means by which one may strengthen one's understanding so as to discern the best course of action in all situations, as long as you also provide an explanation (which my stupidity renders necessary) of the utility of the knowledge you proffer.

        That of the existence of God and his attributes may console us for the misfortunes that result from the ordinary course of nature and the order he has established within it, as when we lose property on account of a storm, or health on account of infection in the air, or friends by death; but not from those visited on us by human beings, whose choice appears to us to be entirely free, since only faith can convince us that God undertakes the governance of human wills, and that he has determined the fortune of every person before the creation of the world.

The immortality of the soul and the knowledge that it is far nobler than the body may lead us to seek for death, as well as despising it, since it cannot be doubted that we would live more happily if we were exempt from the diseases and passions of the body. And I am amazed that those who claimed to be convinced of this truth, and lived without the revealed Law,* preferred a painful life to a beneficial death.

The immense extent of the universe, which you demonstrated in Book III of your *Principles*, serves to detach our affections from the part of it we see; but it also separates particular providence,* which is the cornerstone of theology, from our idea of God. 303

The consideration that we are a part of the whole, and should pursue the benefit of the whole, is indeed the source of all noble actions; but I find many difficulties in the conditions you lay down for these. If we try to measure our efforts for the sake of the public against the good that will result from them, will the efforts not appear greater, inasmuch as the idea of them is more distinct? And what yardstick can we have when it comes to comparing two things of which we have an unequal knowledge, such as our own worth and that of the people we live with? One who is naturally arrogant will always tip the balance in his own favour, and a modest person will value himself at less than his worth.

To benefit from the particular truths you mention, we would need an exact knowledge of all these passions and preconceptions, of which most people are unaware. When we observe the customs and values of the country we are in, we sometimes discover extremely irrational ones, which we have to conform to in order to avoid greater disadvantages.

Since I have been here, I have had most vexing proof of this, because I hoped that a stay in the country would do me good by providing opportunity for study; and yet I find that I have incomparably less free time than I had at The Hague, through having to entertain people who do not know what to do with their time; and although it is very unfair to deprive myself of real benefits in order to provide them 304 with imaginary ones, I am obliged to yield to the irrational laws of civility in order not to make enemies. Since I started this letter, I have been interrupted at least seven times by such troublesome visits. It is your very great kindness that protects my letters from a similar fate in your hands, and that makes you try to render your knowledge more habitual by communicating it to so awkward a pupil as

Your most affectionate friend and servant,

ELISABETH.

[AT 4]   26. *Descartes to Elisabeth, Egmond-Binnen, 6 October 1645*

304   Madam,

I have often put this question to myself: is it better to be cheerful
305 and happy, imagining that the goods we possess are greater and more valuable than they are, and being unaware of or not taking the trouble to think about those we lack, than to be more thoughtful and know-ledgeable, so as to discover the true value of both kinds of goods, if one is sadder as a result? If I thought that joy was the supreme good, I would not doubt that we should make an effort to be joyful, at all costs, and I would approve the brutishness of those who drown their troubles in wine, or dull them with tobacco. But I make a dis-tinction between the supreme good, which consists in the practice of virtue, or, what comes to the same thing, in the possession of all the goods the acquisition of which depends on our free choice, and the satisfaction of mind consequent on this acquisition. This is why, see-ing that it is a greater perfection to know the truth, even if it is to our disadvantage, than not to know it, I admit that it is better to be less cheerful and have more knowledge. Indeed, it is not always when one is most cheerful that one's mind is most satisfied. On the contrary, the greatest joys are often solemn and earnest, and only the middling and fleeting kind are accompanied by laughter. Thus, I do not approve the effort to deceive oneself by feeding on false imaginations; for all the resultant pleasure can affect only the surface of the soul, which
306 at the same time feels an inner bitterness, since it perceives those joys to be false. And even if the soul were so continually distracted by other things as never to perceive this, one would not enjoy the happiness I speak of, because it has to depend on our conduct, and this distraction would be dependent on fortune.

But when we have various considerations at our disposal that are equally true, of which some incline us to be contented, while the others prevent us from being so, it seems to me that prudence requires us to dwell mainly on those that give us satisfaction; and even, since most of the things of this world are such that one can look at them from one point of view in which they appear good, and from another in which their bad side appears, I think that, if there is one area of life in which skill is called for, it is in managing to consider them from the point of view in which they appear best for us, if we can do so without deceiving ourselves.

Thus, when Your Highness observes the causes for your having perhaps had more leisure to cultivate your reason than many other people of the same age, if it pleases you also to consider how much more you have profited from it than those others, I am confident that you will have grounds to feel satisfied. And I cannot see why you should prefer to compare yourself to them from a point of view that gives you grounds for complaint rather than one that could give you satisfaction. For the constitution of our nature is such that our mind needs a great deal of relaxation if it is to be able to make good use of short periods of investigating the truth, and that it would become drowsy, rather than polished, if it were excessively devoted to study; and thus we should not measure the time we have been able to employ in educating ourselves by the number of hours we have had to ourselves, but rather, as it seems to me, by the example of what we see usually occurring in the case of other people, treating this as a sign of the ordinary capacities of the human mind.*

It seems to me also that we have no grounds for repentance, when we have taken what we judged to be the best course of action at the time when we had to make up our minds how to act, even if, subsequently, thinking the matter over again at more leisure, we decide that we made a mistake. But we should, rather, repent, if we have done something against our conscience, even if we subsequently realize that the action turned out better than we intended; for we are responsible only for our thoughts; and it is not in human nature to know everything, or always to judge as well on the spur of the moment as when we have plenty of time for deliberation.

Moreover, although vanity, which gives one a better opinion of oneself than one deserves, is a vice that belongs only to weak and base souls, this does not mean that strong and noble souls should despise

themselves; no, we should do ourselves justice, by recognizing our
308 perfections as well as our shortcomings; and if good manners forbid
us to trumpet them, they do not prevent us from being aware of
them.

Finally, although we do not possess the infinite wisdom that would
give us a perfect knowledge of all the goods among which we may
have to choose in the various situations of life, we should, as it seems
to me, be content with a moderate knowledge of the most necessary
things, like those I listed in my last letter.

In that letter I have already given my opinion concerning the
difficulty raised by Your Highness, namely, whether those who
relate everything to themselves are more right than those who sacrifice themselves for others. For if we thought only of ourselves, we
could only enjoy those goods that are exclusively ours; whereas, if we
consider ourselves as part of some other body, we also have a share in
the goods that are common to it, without thereby being deprived of
any that is ours alone. And the same does not apply to evils; for as
Philosophy teaches us, evil is nothing real, but only a privation;* and
when we are saddened by some evil that is affecting our friends, we
do not for all that have a share in the lack that constitutes this evil;
and whatever sadness or grief we experience in such circumstances,
309 it cannot be as great as the inner satisfaction that always accompanies good actions, especially those that proceed from pure affection
for someone else that one does not relate to oneself—that is, from
the Christian virtue termed charity. Thus, even when one is weeping and deeply grieving, one can be experiencing more pleasure than
when one is laughing and relaxing.

And it is easy to prove that the pleasure of the soul in which happiness consists is not inseparable from physical cheerfulness and
ease; thus, for example, tragedies* please us all the more the more
sadness they arouse in us, and physical exercise, like hunting, ten-
nis, and so forth, is still enjoyable, even when it is very exhausting;
indeed, we often find that the tiredness and discomfort actually
increase the pleasure. And the reason why the soul feels contentment
in these exercises is that they make it aware of the strength, or skill, or
some other perfection of the body to which it is attached; whereas the
contentment it feels in weeping, when it sees some pitiable and tragic
story being enacted on stage, mostly derives from the sense that it is
performing a virtuous action in feeling compassion for the afflicted;

and generally it takes pleasure in feeling itself stirred by passions of whatever kind, as long as it remains mistress of them.

But I must examine these passions in more detail in order to be able to define them. This will be easier for me, writing to you, than if I were writing to someone else; for, since Your Highness has taken the trouble of reading the treatise I formerly drafted on the nature of animals,* you know already how I conceive the formation of different impressions in their brain, some coming from external objects that affect the senses, others from the inner dispositions of the body, or from the traces of previous impressions that have remained in the memory, or from the agitation of the spirits coming from the heart, or also, in human beings, from the action of the soul, which has a certain power to alter the impressions in the brain, just as, reciprocally, these impressions are capable of arousing thoughts in the soul that do not depend on the will. Given all this, we may apply the general term 'passions' to all the thoughts thus aroused in the soul, without the involvement of its will, and hence without any action on its part, due purely and simply by the impressions of the brain (for whatever is not an action is a passion). But the term is normally restricted to those thoughts that are produced by a particular agitation of the spirits.* For the thoughts that come from external objects, or else from the inner dispositions of the body, such as the perception of colours, sounds, smells, hunger, thirst, pain, and so forth, are named sensations, some being external, others internal. Those that depend only on traces left in the memory by previous impressions, and on the ordinary agitation of the spirits, are fantasies, whether they occur in dreams, or else when one is awake and the soul, not focusing of its own accord on any particular object, idly yields to the impressions that happen to occur in the brain. But, when the soul uses its will to apply itself to some thought that is not only intelligible, but imaginable, this thought makes a new impression in the brain, and this is not a passion in the soul, but an action, the specific name of which is 'imagination'. Finally, when the ordinary flow of the spirits is such as, typically, to arouse sad, for example, or cheerful thoughts, this is to be ascribed not to passion but to the nature or temperament of the person in whom they are aroused, which is why we say that one man is gloomy by nature, or that another has a cheerful temperament, and so forth. Thus, we are left with the thoughts that result from some particular agitation of the spirits, the effects of which we experience as being in the soul itself, and these alone are termed 'passions' in the strict sense.

It is true that we hardly ever encounter any that do not depend on several of the causes I have just disentangled; but they are named
312 in respect of the principal cause, or the cause we are mainly considering. This is why many people confuse the sensation of pain with the passion of sadness, and that of titillation* with the passion of joy, which they also call delight or pleasure, and the sensations of thirst or hunger with the desires to eat or drink, which are passions; for the causes that produce pain typically also agitate the spirits, in the manner required to arouse sadness, and those that cause us to feel titillation agitate them in the manner required to arouse joy, and so on.

A further confusion is sometimes encountered between the inclinations or habits that dispose to a given passion, and the passion itself; and yet these are easy to distinguish. For instance, suppose it is announced in some city that the enemy is approaching to lay siege to it; the inhabitants' initial judgement about the evil that may befall them as a result is an action of their soul, not a passion.* And although the judgement itself is common to many people, this does not mean they are all equally disturbed by it emotionally; some will be more affected, some less, according as they are more or less inclined or habituated to fear. And before their soul can feel the impact of the emotional disturbance, in which alone passion consists, it has to make the judgement; or else, without judging, it must at least conceive the danger,* and imprint the image of it in the brain (through another act, which is called 'imagination'); by this means it causes the spirits,
313 which flow from the brain via the nerves into the muscles, to enter the muscles that serve to close the openings of the heart, which slows the circulation of the blood. As a result, the whole body becomes pale, cold, and shaky, and the new spirits, flowing from the heart to the brain, are agitated in such a way that they cannot help forming other images in the brain than those that excite the passion of fear in the soul. All these things follow on from one another so quickly that it seems to be a single process. And in the same way in all the other passions, some particular agitation occurs in the spirits flowing from the heart.

This is what I meant to write to Your Highness a week ago, and my intention was to add a detailed explanation of all the passions;

but having encountered some difficulty in classifying them, I was compelled to let the messenger go without my letter; and having received in the meantime the letter Your Highness did me the honour of writing me, I have a fresh occasion to reply, which obliges me to postpone this examination of the passions for another time, so as to say in this letter that all the proofs that God exists, and that he is the first and immutable cause of all effects that do not depend on man's free choice, prove, it seems to me, in the same way that he is also the cause of those that do. For we cannot demonstrate his existence except by considering him as a supremely perfect being; and he would not be supremely perfect if anything could happen in the world that did not come entirely from him. It is true that only faith teaches us about the grace by which God raises us to supernatural happiness; but philosophy by itself suffices for us to know that the slightest thought cannot enter the mind of a human being, without God's wishing and having wished from all eternity for it to do so. And the schoolmen's distinction between universal and particular causes* has no place here; for the reason why the sun, which is the universal cause of all flowers, is nonetheless not the cause of the difference between tulips and roses, is that their production also depends on various other particular causes not subordinate to the sun; but God is so much the universal cause of everything, that he is also in the same way the total cause of everything; and thus nothing can occur without his will.

It is true also that the knowledge of the immortality of the soul and of the bliss of which it will be capable when released from this life might induce some people who are suffering in this life to put an end to it, if they were convinced that they would afterwards enjoy such bliss; but there are no rational grounds for this conviction;* and only the false philosophy of Hegesias,* whose book was banned by Ptolemy, because several people who had read it had killed themselves, attempts to persuade us that this life is bad; the true philosophy teaches us the very contrary, that, even among the saddest misfortunes and the most oppressive sufferings, we can always find contentment in this life, as long as we know how to make use of reason.

As for the extent of the universe, I cannot see how the consideration of it should lead us to separate particular providence from our idea of God; for God is not at all on the same footing as finite powers, which can be exhausted, and of which we rightly judge, when

314

315

we see them involved in the production of many great effects, that it is improbable that their responsibility extends as far as little ones; whereas the greater we judge God's works to be, the more we become aware of the infinity of his power; and the better we come to know this infinity, the more convinced we are that it extends also to the most particular acts of human beings.

Furthermore, I do not suppose that, when Your Highness refers to this particular providence of God as the cornerstone of theology, 316 you mean that his decrees are in any way altered by actions depending on our free will.* For theology denies the possibility of any such alteration; and when it requires us to pray to God, this is not so that we can inform him of our needs, or attempt to persuade him to change anything in the order established by his providence for all eternity; either of these would be blameworthy; it is only so that we may obtain what he has willed us from all eternity to obtain by our prayers. And I think that all theologians are in agreement over this, even the Arminians,* who seem to be the ones who allow the largest scope to free will.

I admit that it is no easy task exactly to measure how far reason requires us to take an active interest in the public welfare; but at the same time this is not a matter in which great exactitude is necessary: it is enough to follow one's conscience, and in this case we may largely go by our inclinations. For God has so established the order of things, and joined human beings together in so close a society, that, even though each one of us were to act only in his interests, without any charity towards others, he would still ordinarily seek to benefit them in whatever was in his power, provided that he were governed 317 by prudence, especially if he lived in an age where morals had not been corrupted.* And, furthermore, since it is a higher and more glorious thing to do good to other people than to obtain it for oneself, so it is the greatest souls who are most inclined to do good to others, and who set least store by the goods they themselves possess. Only weak and base souls value themselves more highly than they should; they are like those little vessels that three drops of water are enough to fill. I know that Your Highness is not of their number, and that whereas one can only induce these base souls to take trouble for others by showing them that it will benefit themselves to do so, one can only get Your Highness to be mindful of your interests by pointing out that you could not be helpful for very long to those you are fond of, if you neglected yourself, and entreating you to take good care of your health. As does,

> Madam,
>> Your Highness's
>>> most humble and most obedient servant,
>>> DES CARTES

27. *Elisabeth to Descartes, The Hague, 28 October 1645*   [AT 4]

Monsieur Descartes,   321

After you have given such excellent reasons why it is better to know truths that are to our disadvantage than to deceive oneself agreeably, and why only in matters that can admit different and equally true points of view should we adhere to the one that brings us more contentment, I am surprised that you should suggest that I compare myself to people of my own age, in respect of something I know nothing about rather than something I cannot help knowing, even if the former point of view is the more advantageous to me. There is no way in which I can discover whether I have benefited more from cultivating my reason than others have done from their own favourite occupations, and I have not the slightest doubt that, even allowing for the interruptions required by my body, I have had time enough to be able to make further progress than I have done. If we measure the scope of the human mind by the example of the general run of human beings, it would emerge as very limited, since most people use their minds only in relation to the senses. Even among those who apply themselves to study, there are few who use any other faculty than their memory or whose efforts are devoted to seeking the truth. If there is a fault in my reluctance to consider whether I have benefited more than these people, I do not think that it is an excess of humility, which is as harmful as presumptuousness, though less common. We   322 are more inclined to fail to recognize our shortcomings than our perfections. And if we seek to avoid, as inimical to happiness, repentance for things we have done wrong, we could run the risk of losing the desire to correct ourselves, especially when our actions have resulted from some passion, because we naturally love to be stirred by passion and to follow its impulses; only from the painful consequences of doing so do we learn how harmful the passions can be.

And, in my opinion, this is why the sadder a tragedy makes us feel, the more we enjoy it, because we know that this sadness will not be so violent as to lead us to do something irrational, or so long-lasting as to worsen our health.

But this is not enough to justify the doctrine contained in one of your previous letters,* that the more the passions have a tendency to excess, the more useful they are, when they are subjected to reason, because it seems that they cannot be both excessive and subjected. But I suppose that you will be able to satisfy this doubt, if you take the trouble to explain how this particular agitation of the spirits serves to produce all the passions we experience, and how it corrupts our powers of reasoning. I would not dare ask this of you, if I did not know that you never leave a piece of work unfinished, and that, when you undertook to instruct so stupid a person as myself, you were prepared for the trouble you would be put to as a result.

For this reason, I will go on to say that the proofs that God exists, and that he is the immutable cause of all effects that do not depend on the free will of human beings, do not convince me that he is also the cause of those that do depend on human free will. That he could be so follows necessarily from his supreme perfection; that is, he could have created human beings without free will. But since we are aware that we possess it, it seems to me that it runs counter to common sense to think that its operations depend on him in the same way as its existence does.*

If one is thoroughly convinced of the soul's immortality, it is impossible to doubt that it will be happier after separation from the body (which is the source of all the discomforts of life, as the soul is that of the greatest satisfactions); unless one follows the opinion of Sir Kenelm Digby, inculcated in him by his tutor* (whose writings you have seen), who convinced him that purgatory is necessary because the passions which, during our lives, have dominated our reason, still, after the death of the body, leave traces in the soul, which torment it all the more because they find no prospect of satisfaction in so pure a substance. I do not see how this can be reconciled with the soul's immateriality. But I do not in the least doubt that, although life is not bad in itself, it should be abandoned for a condition we shall experience as better.

When I say that particular providence is the cornerstone of theology, I mean the providence by which, from all eternity,* God has decided upon such wondrous devices as his incarnation, for the sake of a part of the created whole, a part so slight when compared to the remainder as, in your physics, you represent the globe as being; and has done so for the sake of his glory, which seems a goal quite unworthy of the creator of this great universe. But I was citing this as an objection from our theologians,* rather than putting it forward as my own; for I have always thought it very unreasonable for finite beings to judge the final cause* of the actions of an infinite being.

You do not believe that we need an exact knowledge of how far reason requires us to take an active interest in the public welfare, on the grounds that, even if everyone were to act purely for their own self-interest, they would also work for other people at the same time, if they were governed by prudence. And this prudence is the whole, of which I am asking you only for a part. For, if we possess it, we cannot fail to deal justly with other people, as well as with ourselves; and it is for lack of it that sometimes a noble soul will lose the opportunity to serve his country, by heedlessly neglecting his own interests for his country's sake, whereas a timid one is ruined, along with his country, because he would not risk his property and position in order to preserve it.

I have always been in a condition that rendered my life quite useless to those I love; but I am seeking to preserve it much more carefully since I had the good fortune to get to know you, because you have shown me the way to live more happily than I was living. I lack only the satisfaction of being able to prove to you how much this obligation is felt by

Your most affectionate friend and servant,
ELISABETH.

28. *Descartes to Elisabeth, Egmond-Binnen, 3 November 1645*   [AT 4]

Madam,

I so rarely encounter sound reasoning, whether in the speech of the people I frequent in this lonely place, or in the books I look into, that I cannot help feeling an extraordinary joy when I encounter it in Your Highness's letters; and I find your arguments so strong that I prefer to admit that they have defeated me rather than to attempt to withstand them. For although the comparison in your favour which Your Highness refuses to make can be easily verified by experience, it is nonetheless so praiseworthy a virtue to judge other people favourably, and one that chimes so well with the nobility of soul that leads you to refuse to measure the powers of the human mind by the example of the general run of human beings,* that I cannot but greatly value both of these qualities.

I would not dare, furthermore, to contradict what Your Highness writes about repentance, seeing that it is a Christian virtue, which helps us to correct ourselves, not only of the wrongful acts we have committed voluntarily, but also of those we have committed in ignorance, when our knowledge of the truth has been impeded by some passion.

And I readily admit that the sadness we feel when watching a tragedy would be unpleasant, if we had reason to fear it might become so extreme as to be harmful. But when I said that there are passions that are all the more useful the more they have a tendency to excess, I meant only those that are wholly good; which I indicated by adding that they must be subject to reason. For there are two kinds of excess:* one alters the nature of the thing from good to evil, and thus prevents it from remaining subject to reason; the other merely increases its quantity and changes it only from good to better. Thus, 332 the excess of boldness shades into temerity only when it goes beyond the bounds of reason; but while it remains with those limits, it can still admit of another form of excess, which consists in being unaccompanied by any irresolution or fear.

I have been thinking these past days about the number and classification of all these passions, in order to examine their nature in more detail; but I have not yet sufficiently digested my opinions on the matter to dare to communicate them to Your Highness, and I will not fail to do so as soon as it becomes possible.

As far as free will is concerned, I admit that when we think only of ourselves, we cannot help thinking it independent; but when we think of the infinite power of God, we cannot but believe that all things depend on him, and therefore that our free will is no exception. For it is self-contradictory to say that God has created human beings of such a nature that the actions of their will do not depend on his will, since this would be tantamount to saying that his power is both finite and infinite: finite, because there is something that does not depend on it; and infinite, because he was able to create this independent entity. But, just as the knowledge of God's existence should not prevent us from being convinced of our free will, inasmuch as we experience it and feel it in ourselves, so the knowledge of our free will should not lead us to doubt the existence of God. For the independence we experience and feel in ourselves, and which suffices to render our actions praiseworthy or blameworthy, is not incompatible with dependence of another sort, in virtue of which all things are subject to God.

As to the state of our soul after this life, I know much less about it than M. d'Igby; for, setting aside what faith teaches us, I confess that, with the aid of natural reason alone, we can make many conjectures in our favour and entertain great hopes, but can gain no certitude. And because this same natural reason also teaches us that we always have more good than evil in this life, and that we should not forfeit the certain for the sake of the uncertain, it seems to me to teach us that, though we should not really fear death, we should never seek it either.

I have no need to reply to the objection to my views on the vastness of the universe that theologians might put forward, since Your Highness has already replied to it for me. I would add only that if this vastness could render the mysteries of our religion less credible, the same would apply to the vastness that astronomers have always attributed to the heavens, for they have viewed them as so great that, in comparison, the earth is only a speck; and yet no one raises this objection against them.

Next, if prudence were the mistress of events, I do not doubt that Your Highness would successfully carry through all her undertakings; but, for that to be so, all human beings would have to be perfectly wise, so that, knowing what they ought to do, we could be certain of what they would do. Or else we would have to know the particular temperament of everyone with whom we have dealings of any kind; and even that would not be enough, because they also have their free will, the movements of which are known only to God. And because we normally judge what other people will do by what we would want to do if we were in their place, it often happens that people with commonplace and mediocre minds, being similar to those they have to deal with, see further into their intentions and succeed more easily in their undertakings than those of the most lofty intelligence, who, dealing only with people far inferior to themselves in knowledge and prudence, judge the business in hand quite differently from them.

This should console Your Highness when fortune runs counter to your plans. I pray God that he may favour them, and I am,

     Madam,

          Your Highness's most humble and obedient servant,

     DES CARTES.

[AT 4]   29. *Elisabeth to Descartes, The Hague, 30 November 1645*

335   Monsieur Descartes,

You may well be surprised that, after hearing from you that my arguments did not seem to you to be totally ridiculous, I have waited so long to benefit from your answers to them. And I am ashamed to tell you the cause for this, because it has overthrown all that your lessons seemed to have established in my mind. I believed that a staunch resolution to seek happiness only in things that depend on my will would render me less sensitive to those occurring from external causes, until the folly of one of my brothers* revealed my weakness to me. For it has troubled the health of my body and the peace of my soul more than all the misfortunes that have befallen me up to now. If you take the trouble to read the gazette,* you cannot fail to know that he has fallen into the hands of a certain group of people who

336 hate our house more than they love their religion, and has let himself be trapped in their snares, to the point of changing his religion and becoming a Roman Catholic, without the slightest outward sign that could persuade the most credulous that he is doing so for the sake of his conscience. I am compelled to see a person that I loved with the greatest affection possible given over to the scorn of the world and (as I believe) the loss of his soul. If your charity were not greater than your sectarian feeling, it would be irrational to write to you in this way, and it would still be so, if I were not entitled to tell you of all my failings, being, as you are, the person in the world most capable of ridding me of them.

I will confess to you likewise that, although I cannot understand why the independence of free will is not less incompatible with our idea of God than its dependence is with its freedom, it is impossible for me to reconcile them, since it is equally impossible for the will to be at one and the same time free and tied to the decrees of providence and for the divine power to be both infinite and limited. I cannot grasp this compatibility between them of which you speak, or how this dependence of the will can be of a different nature from its freedom, unless you take the trouble to explain it to me.

As regards contentment, I admit that present possession is much more solid than expectation for the future, however good the reasons on which this is based. But I find it hard to convince myself that we always have more goods in life than evils, since more is needed 337 to produce the former than the latter; since man can be affected by pain in more parts than by pleasure; since there are an infinite number of errors, for one truth; so many ways of getting lost, as against one only of keeping to the right path; so many people with the intention and the means to do harm, as against the few with both the intention and the power to help. Finally, everything that depends on the will of everyone else and the course of the world as a whole is capable of troubling us; and, according to your own views, there is nothing but what depends completely on our own will that is sufficient to give us real and lasting satisfaction.

As for prudence in relation to human society, I am not expecting to be given an infallible rule; but I should be very pleased to learn what rules you would lay down for a person who, living only for himself, in pursuit of any occupation whatever, would still be exerting himself for other people as well—if I dared ask you for more enlightenment when I have made such bad use of that you have already given to

Your most affectionate friend and servant,

ELISABETH.

30. *Elisabeth to Descartes, The Hague, 27 December 1645* [AT 4]

Monsieur Descartes, 339
The son of the late Professor Schooten* has today delivered to me the letter you wrote to me on his behalf, to forestall my committing myself to supporting his rival. And since I indicated to him that I not only had no intention of harming him, but was obliged to help him as far as I could, since you have enjoined me to love him and be grateful to him, he then requested me to recommend him to the Curators.* There are only two with whom I am acquainted, Mijnheer Wimmenum and Mijnheer van Beveren, and the latter is out of town, so I immediately 340 got in touch with the former, who promises to act in the said Mijnheer

Schooten's favour, even though the plan was to abolish the professorship altogether, as being superfluous.* This seems to be the only difficulty he will have to surmount, since, compared to him, his rival is not highly rated, except by a few narrow-minded men who are afraid young Schooten will inculcate the errors of the Arminian sect in his mathematics lectures. If he had given me the time to ask him to come and visit me again, to let me know the outcome of my recommendations, I should have had the opportunity to inform him of things I think should be helpful to his application; but he was in such a hurry to withdraw, that I was obliged to follow him right to the door,* in order to ask him to whom my recommendation should be addressed. I know that if he had simply considered me as your friend, without thinking of those titles of rank that fluster people who are not accustomed to them, he would have behaved differently, judging, and rightly, that in a matter I knew to be agreeable to you, I would certainly have made no slight efforts. And I beg you to believe that I shall never squander an opportunity to bear witness that I am truly,

Monsieur Descartes,

Your most affectionate friend and servant,

ELISABETH.

341 I am afraid that you did not receive my letter of the 30th of last month, because you make no mention of it. I would be upset if it fell into the hands of one of those critics who condemn any doubt of received opinions as heresy.

[AT 4]   31. *Descartes to Elisabeth, Egmond-Binnen, January 1646*

351   Madam,
I cannot deny that I was surprised to learn that Your Highness had been upset, to the point that your health was affected, by a thing that most people will find good,* and that the rest should excuse for many powerful reasons. For everyone whose religion is the same as mine (that is, no doubt, the majority of the people of Europe) will necessarily approve this step, even if they were to see it as arising from circumstances and apparent motives that were blameworthy; for we believe that God makes use of different means to attract souls to him, and that some have entered a monastery with bad intentions who have afterwards led a most holy life there. As for those who are of another

belief, if they speak ill of it, one is free to set aside their judgement; for, as in all issues where there are different sides, it is impossible to please one side, without displeasing the other. If they were to reflect that they would not belong to the religion they profess, unless they themselves, or their parents or grandparents, had abandoned the Roman religion, they would have no grounds for mockery, or for accusing of disloyalty those who leave their own religion.

From the point of view of worldly prudence, it is true that those who have fortune on their side are right to remain united around her, and to join their forces to prevent her from escaping; but those who belong to a house she has deserted are wise, it seems to me, to agree to follow different paths, so that, if they cannot all find it, at least one of them will. And, in the meantime, because they are each thought to have several sources of support, since they have friends in different parties, this renders them more of a force to be reckoned with than if they were all committed to one. For this reason, I am loath to imagine that those who advised your brother to take this step wished in doing so to inflict harm on your house. But I cannot hope that my reasons will dispel Your Highness's resentment; I hope only that time will have lessened it before this letter reaches you, and I would be afraid of reopening the wound if I expatiated further on the subject.

This is why I shall move on to the difficulty Your Highness raises concerning free will. I shall try to explain how it is both free and dependent by a comparison. Suppose a king has forbidden duelling,* and knows with complete certainty that two noblemen in his kingdom, who live in different cities, are at loggerheads, and that their mutual enmity is such that nothing can prevent them from fighting if they should meet; and suppose he issues an order to the first one to go on such-and-such a day to the town where the other one lives and also orders the other one to go on the same day to the place where the first one is. He knows with complete certainty that they will not fail to meet, and to fight,* thus offending against his ban; but, for all that, he is not compelling them to fight; and, notwithstanding his knowledge, and even his will to determine them to fight in this way, they fight, when they eventually meet, as voluntarily and as freely as they would have done if he had known nothing about it and they had come upon each other for some quite different reason. For this reason, they can be justly punished, since they have transgressed his ban. Now, what a king can do with respect to some free acts by his subjects, God, with his infinite foreknowledge and power, infallibly does with respect to all free human actions. And before he sent us into the world, he knew exactly what all the inclinations of our will would be; in fact, he himself implanted them in us; moreover, he so arranged everything outside us as to bring it about 354 that such-and-such objects should present themselves to our senses at such-and-such times, on which occasions he knew that our free will would determine us to a particular thing; he therefore willed this to happen, but nonetheless he did not will to compel our free will. And just as we can distinguish two different levels of will in the king, one in respect of which he willed the noblemen to fight, since he brought about their meeting, and one in respect of which he did not will it, since he had forbidden duelling, so theologians make a distinction between two wills in God, one absolute and independent, in virtue of which he wills all things to come to pass as they in fact come to pass, and one that is relative, and connected with merit or demerit in human beings, in virtue of which he wills his laws to be obeyed.

I must, furthermore, distinguish two kinds of good, in order to reconcile what I have previously written (that is, that in this life we have always more good than evil) with Your Highness's objection bearing on the many unpleasantnesses of life. When we consider the idea of good as a rule by which to measure our actions, what we mean by 'good' is the total perfection that can be in the thing we call good; and this perfection can be compared to a straight line, which is unique among an infinity of curves (evils, from the point of view of the comparison). In this sense philosophers are in the habit of saying that *bonum est ex integrâ causâ, malum ex quouis defectu.** But when we consider the goods and the evils that can coexist in a single thing, in order to determine how highly we should value it, as I was doing 355 when I spoke of the value we should set on this life, 'good' means whatever there is in the thing that can be of some benefit to us, and 'evil' only that which can harm us in some way; for, as to the other shortcomings that may exist in the thing, we ignore them. So, when someone is offered a position, he considers on the one hand the honour and the profit he can expect from it as goods; and on the other he considers the effort, the danger, the loss of his time involved as evils; and comparing the evils with the goods, he accepts or refuses it, according as he finds the former less or greater than the latter. Now, the reason why I said, in this second sense, that there is always more good than evil in this life is that I think we should set very little store by everything that is external to us, and does not depend on our free will, in comparison to the things that do depend on it, which we can always render good, if we know how to make good use of them; and by their means we can prevent all the evils that come from outside, however great they may be, from penetrating further into our soul than the sadness produced when we see actors performing some dreadful deeds; but I admit that one has to be far advanced in philosophy* to get to that point. And yet I also think that even those who let themselves most often be swept away by their passions always judge, deep down, that there is more good than evil in this life, even if they do not realize this themselves;* for though, when they are undergoing great suffering, they sometimes call on death to help them, it is only, like the man in the fable,* to help them bear the burden, and they do 356 not want to lose their life, for all that; or if there are some people who do want to lose it, and who kill themselves, this is from an error in their understanding, and not the result of a properly reasoned judgement, or of an opinion imprinted in us by nature, like the preference for the goods of this life over its evils.

The reason why I think that those who do nothing except for their own advantage should exert themselves, if they want to do the prudent thing, for other people, and try to please everyone as much as lies in their power, is that we commonly observe that those who are reckoned helpful and ready to please others also receive an abundance of good turns from other people, even from those whom they have never laid under obligation, which they would never receive if they were thought to be of another disposition;* and the trouble they take in pleasing others is less than the advantage they receive from the friendship of those who know them. For the only good turns anyone expects from us are those we can easily do, and we expect no more from other people; but it often happens that something that is no trouble to them is a great help to us, and may even be a matter of life and death. It is true that sometimes our efforts to do good are wasted, and there is, on the contrary, an advantage to be gained in doing harm; but this cannot alter the rule of prudence, which takes account only of what usually happens. As for myself, the maxim I have 357 most observed in the conduct of my life as a whole has been simply to follow the main road, and to believe that the most cunning way to behave is to refuse to have anything to do with cunning. The point of all the common laws of society is to get us to do good, or at least not to do harm, to one another, and these laws, it seems to me, are so well established that whoever follows them sincerely, without any dissimulation or artifice, leads a happier and more untroubled life than those who seek their advantage in other ways.* Such men, to be sure, do sometimes succeed, on account of the ignorance of others and the favour of fortune; but it happens far more often that they fail, and that in seeking to make a position in the world, they come crashing down. With the same frankness and candour I profess to observe in all my actions, I more particularly profess myself to be, &c.

[AT 4]　　　　　32. *Elisabeth to Descartes, The Hague, 25 April 1646*

404　　Monsieur Descartes,

The treaty my brother Philip has signed with the republic of Venice* has given me, ever since your departure,* an occupation much less agreeable than the one with which you left me. The subject in question is outside my knowledge, and I was dragged into it purely by the impatience of the young man who was involved in it. This has prevented me up to now from taking advantage of the permission you gave me to consult you about the obscurities my stupidity has encountered in your *Treatise of the Passions*, though they are very few in number, because one would have to be totally idiotic not to see that the classification, the definition, and the distinction of the passions, and in fact the whole moral part of the treatise, goes far beyond what has ever been written on the subject before.

But since the physical part is not so clear to the ignorant, I cannot see how we can know the various movements of the blood that cause the five basic passions, since they never occur alone. For instance, love is always accompanied by desire and joy, or by desire and sadness, and as it grows stronger, these other passions grow as well, . . .* on the contrary. How can we then observe the differences in pulsation, or digestion, and the other changes in the body that allow us to discover the nature of these movements? Indeed, the specific difference you
405　find in each passion varies with individual temperaments: because of mine, sadness always takes away my appetite,* even when, arising from the death of some friend, it is unmixed with any hatred.

When you speak of the external signs of these passions, you say that wonderment, combined with joy, causes the lungs to inflate in a jerky fashion, producing laughter.* I beg you to add an explanation of how wonderment (which according to your description seems to affect only the brain*) can open the orifices of the heart so promptly as to produce this result.

The passions you observe to be the cause of sighs* do not always seem to be their cause, since habit and a full stomach can also produce them.

But I find less difficulty in understanding all you say of the passions than in practising the remedies you prescribe for their excess. For how can we foresee all the accidents that can occur in life, when they are impossible to count? And how can we help ardently desiring things that necessarily tend to our preservation as human beings (such as health and the means of life) which, nonetheless, do not depend on our will? As to the knowledge of the truth, the desire for it is so justified, that it exists naturally in all human beings;* but only if our knowledge were infinite could we know the true value of the goods and evils that habitually arouse our passions, since there are many more of them than a single person could imagine, and to know them we would have to have a perfect knowledge of everything in the world.

Since you have already told me the most important things, as regards our individual lives, I would be content also to know your maxims concerning civil life, although this makes us dependent on people who are so irrational that up to now I have always found it better to rely on experience than on reason in this context. |406

I have been so often interrupted in writing to you that I am compelled to send you my draft,* and to use the Alkmaar messenger, since I have forgotten the name of the friend you wanted me to address my letters to; this is why I am not sending back your treatise, since I cannot bring myself to risk handing over to a drunkard a document of such great worth, that has given so much satisfaction to

Your most affectionate friend at your service,

ELISABETH.

33. *Descartes to Elisabeth, May 1646*   [AT 4]

Madam, |407
I can confirm from my own experience that I was right to count glory among the passions; because I cannot help being affected by it,

when I see Your Highness's favourable judgement of my little treatise on the subject. And I am in no way surprised at your observing shortcomings in it as well, because I did not doubt that there would be many of them, since this is a subject I had never studied before, and of which I have produced only the initial drawing, without adding the colours and ornaments* that would be required in order to display it to eyes less acute than those of Your Highness.

Nor did I include all the principles of physics which I used to decipher the movements of the blood that accompany each passion, since I cannot expound them in their proper order without explaining the formation of all the parts of the human body; and this is so difficult that I would not yet dare to undertake it, even though I have more or less satisfied myself of the truth of the principles presupposed in this work. The main ones are these: the function of the liver and spleen is to contain a constant reserve supply of blood, less purified than that which is in the veins; the fire in the heart needs to be continually kept going, either by the juices from food, which come directly from the stomach, or, failing that, by the reserve supply of blood, since the other blood, which is in the veins, dilates too easily; there is such a close connection between our soul and our body that the thoughts that accompanied certain movements of the body, at the very beginning of our lives, are still accompanying them, so that, if the same movements are produced in the body again by some external cause, they also produce the same thoughts in the soul, and, by the same token, if we have the same thoughts, they produce the same movements; finally, the machine of our body is so constructed that a single thought of joy, or love, or anything of the kind, is sufficient to send the animal spirits via the nerves into all the muscles required to cause the various movements of the blood that I have said accompany the passions. It is true that I have found it difficult to identify the specific movements that belong to each passion, because the passions never come alone; but, all the same, since their combinations are not always the same, I have tried to observe the changes that took place in the body, when a passion changed company. Thus, for instance, if love and joy were always combined, I would not know to which of them I should ascribe the warmth and expansiveness they cause us to feel around the heart; but since love is sometimes combined with sadness as well, and in that case, we still feel the warmth, but not the expansiveness, I judged that the warmth pertains to love and the expansiveness to joy. And though desire is almost always combined with love, they are not always together to the same extent; for, even when love is strong, there is little desire where there is no hope; and because in that situation we do not have the energy and promptness we would have if desire were greater, it can be judged that these qualities result from desire rather than love. 409

I can well believe that sadness suppresses appetite in many people, but because my own experience has always been that it increases it, I went along with that. And I take it that the reason for this difference is that, for some people, their first cause of sadness, at the beginning of their lives, was that they were not getting enough food; whereas for others, it was that the food they were receiving was doing them harm. And in these latter the movement of the spirits that suppresses appetite has ever since been combined with the passion of sadness. We also see that the movements that accompany the other passions are not entirely alike in all people, which can be explained in the same way.

As for wonderment, though it does originate in the brain, and cannot therefore, unlike joy or sadness, be caused by the temperament of the blood alone,* it can, nonetheless, act on the body, by means of the impression it makes on the brain, as much as any other passion, or even more in some ways, since the surprise it involves causes the swiftest movements of all. And just as we can move our hand or foot almost at the same instant at which we think of doing so, because the idea of the movement, which is formed in the brain, sends the spirits into the muscles that perform this task, so the idea of some pleasant thing that takes the mind by surprise immediately sends the spirits into the nerves that open the orifices of the heart; and the action of wonderment here is simply that, by the effect of surprise, it reinforces the movement that causes joy, and brings it about that, the orifices of the heart being all at once dilated, the blood that enters it via the vena cava and leaves it by the arterial vein suddenly inflates the lungs. 410

The same external signs that customarily accompany the passions can perfectly well be produced by other causes on occasion. Thus, the reddening of the cheeks does not always result from shame; it can also come from the heat of the fire, or from exercise. And the smile known as the *risus sardonicus** is nothing but a convulsion of the facial nerves. And so in this way one may sometimes sigh from sheer habit, or on account of disease, but that does not mean that sighs are not external signs of sadness and desire, when these passions are the cause of them. I had never heard of, or observed, their being caused on occasion by the fullness of the stomach; but when that happens I suppose that it is a movement of which nature makes use to enable the juice from food to flow more quickly through the heart, so that the burden on the stomach is relieved all the sooner. For sighs agitate the lungs, and thus cause the blood they contain to flow more rapidly down through the venous 411   artery into the left side of the heart, thus allowing the new blood, composed of the juices from food, which comes from the stomach to the lungs via the liver and the heart, to be received there easily.

As to the remedies for excesses of the passions, I do indeed admit that they are difficult to put into practice, and indeed that they are insufficient to prevent disorders from occurring in the body; but they are capable of ensuring that the soul is not troubled as a result, and can keep its judgement free. For this purpose I judge that it is not necessary to have an exact knowledge of the truth of each and every thing, or even to have foreseen in detail all the accidents that might befall us, which would no doubt be impossible; but it is enough to have imagined in a general way things that are more upsetting than those that actually occur, and to have prepared oneself to endure them. Moreover, I think that it virtually never occurs that we commit the fault of excess in our desire for the necessities of life; our desires need to be regulated only when their object is bad or superfluous. For with those desires that are directed at the good it seems to me that the greater they are, the better; and even though I wished to gloss over a shortcoming of my own when I listed a certain lethargy* among the excusable passions I nonetheless have far more respect for the energy of those who always enthusiastically set about doing what they think it is in some way their duty to do, even if they do not expect much benefit from doing so.

412   I lead so retired a life, and I have always been so remote from the management of affairs, that I would be as unreasonable as the philosopher who tried to lecture on the duties of a general in the presence of Hannibal,* if I undertook to write down here the maxims one should abide by in civil life. And I have no doubt that the maxim proposed by Your Highness is the best of all, namely, that it is better in this sphere to govern oneself by experience rather than reason, since one rarely has to deal with people who are perfectly rational—as all human beings ought to be, so that we could judge what they will do simply by considering what they ought to do; and often the best plans

are not the most successful. For this reason we are compelled to take risks, and to put ourselves in the power of Fortune, which I wish were as obedient to your desires as I am, &c.

34. *Descartes to Elisabeth, Egmond-Binnen, May 1646* [AT 4]

Madam, 414

It is because the opportunity has come up of giving this letter to M. de Beclin,* who is my very close friend and whom I trust as I do myself, that I take the liberty of confessing here to an egregious blunder I have committed in the *Treatise on the Passions*, where I have flattered my own dilatoriness by listing, among the disorders of the soul that are excusable, a certain lethargy that sometimes prevents us from putting into execution the things our judgement has approved. And my greatest misgivings here come from remembering that Your Highness particularly singled out this passage,* as if you were indicating that you did not disapprove of this behaviour in a matter where I cannot see that it is helpful. I readily admit that it is very reasonable to take time to deliberate before undertaking any business of importance; but when a negotiation is under way, and there is agreement as to the principal issue, I cannot see that there is any advantage in seeking to delay things by haggling over terms. For if, all the same, the negotiations are successful, the slight gains one may have made 415 as a result are less helpful than the annoyance normally caused by such delays is potentially harmful; and if they do not come off, that just shows everyone that one had aims that one has failed to achieve. Besides, for a delay in bringing a business to a conclusion to lead to its eventual failure is far more likely to occur when the advantage to be gained is great than when it is not.* This is why I am convinced that resolution and promptitude are very necessary virtues in the handling of a business already begun. And there are no grounds for fear of the unknown: for often the things we most dreaded, before we experienced them, turn out to be better than those we desired. So the best course of action in all this is to trust to divine providence, and to allow oneself to be guided by it. I am convinced that Your Highness understands what I mean very well, even though I am explaining it very badly, and that you will forgive the great zeal that obliges me to write all this: for I am, as much as I can be, &c.

[AT 4]   35. *Elisabeth to Descartes, The Hague, July 1646*

448   Monsieur Descartes,
         Since your journey* has been fixed for the 3rd/13th of this
         month, I must remind you of the promise you made to leave your
         agreeable solitude so as to give me the happiness of seeing you, before
         my own departure from here takes away the hope of doing so for
         another six or seven months, which is as long as I am allowed to be
         away with the permission of the queen my mother and the prince
         my brother,* and the approval of the friends of our house. But this
         time would seem even longer to me if I were not certain that you
         would continue the kindness of helping me by your letters to bene-
         fit from your reflections; since, without their help, the cold of the
         north and the kind of people I would find myself conversing with
         would extinguish the tiny beams of common sense I was endowed
         with by nature and the benefits of which I recognize thanks to your
         method. I am promised sufficient leisure and calm in Germany to
449   be able to study it, and I am taking no greater treasure there, and
         no greater source of satisfaction, than your writings. I hope you will
         allow me to take the treatise on the *Passions*, even though it was unable
         to calm those aroused by our latest misfortune.* Your presence was
         necessary* for the cure that your maxims and my own reasoning were
         unable to bring about. The preparations for my journey and the con-
         cerns of my brother Philip, along with the obligation to comply with
         the pleasure of my aunt, have prevented me until now from giving
         you the thanks I owe you for the benefits of your visit. I beg you to
         receive them now from
                         Your most affectionate friend at your service,
                                                    ELISABETH.

         I am obliged to send this letter by the messenger, because speed is
         more necessary to me at this time than security.*

[AT 4]   36. *Descartes to Elisabeth, Egmond, September 1646*

486   Madam,
         I have read the book of which Your Highness commanded me to give
         an opinion,* and in it I find many precepts that seem to me very good;
         for instance, in chapters 19 and 20: 'That a prince should always avoid

the hatred and scorn of his subjects, and that the love of his people is better than fortresses.'* But it also contains many others that I cannot approve. And I think that the author's major blunder is that he fails to distinguish sufficiently between princes who have acquired a state by just means* and those who have usurped one by unjust means, and that he has laid down, as applying to all princes, precepts that apply only to the latter category. For just as if one is building a house of which the foundations are so poor that they cannot support thick high walls, one has to make them low and thin, so those who have initially gained power by crimes are generally compelled to go on committing crimes, and could not maintain their position if they tried to be virtuous.

It is with princes of this latter sort in mind that he says in chapter 3: 'That they cannot but be hated by many people; and that it is often to their advantage to do a great deal of wrong rather than a little; because slight injustices are sufficient to inspire the desire for revenge, whereas great ones take away the power to carry it out.' Then in chapter 15 he says: 'That, if they wished to be good men, they would inevitably doom themselves, when there are so many evil people to be found everywhere.' And in chapter 19: 'That one can be hated for good actions just as much as for evil ones.' 487

On these foundations he bases completely tyrannical precepts, as when he recommends 'devastating a whole country, so as to remain master of it; exerting great cruelty, provided one does so swiftly and all at once; making an effort to appear a good man, without really being one; keeping one's word only so long as it is advantageous to do so; practising dissimulation and betrayal; and finally, in order to rule, stripping oneself of all humanity, and becoming the most savage of animals'.*

But there is very little justification in writing a book if one's aim is to lay down such precepts, which, when all is said and done, cannot secure the position of those to whom they are addressed; for as he himself admits, 'they cannot protect themselves against the first man who will be willing to forfeit his own life for the sake of revenge'. On the contrary, to educate a good prince, even one who has newly gained power,* it seems to me that one should present him with the very opposite maxims, and should suppose that the means he has made use of to establish his position are just ones; as, indeed, I think that almost all of them are, when the princes that put them into practice believe them to be such; for justice between sovereigns has different boundaries from justice between private citizens, and it seems in such situations that he who has God's power on his side also has God's justice. But the most just actions become unjust, when they are thought to be so by the agent.*

We must also distinguish between subjects, friends or allies, and 488 enemies. For, as regards this last category, one is virtually permitted to do anything, as long as one thereby derives some advantage for oneself or one's subjects; and in this context I do not disapprove of acting both the lion and the fox,* and combining cunning with strength. Moreover, in the term 'enemies' I include all those who are not friends or allies, since one is entitled to make war on them when one finds it advantageous, and since if they become objects of fear or suspicion, one has reason to distrust them. But there is one form of deception I rule out, which is so directly contrary to society that I do not think it is ever permissible to make use of it, even though our author endorses it in several places, and it is practised all too often; this is to pretend to be friends* with those we intend to destroy, the better to take them by surprise. Friendship is too sacred a thing to be thus perverted; and a person capable of pretending to love someone in order to betray him deserves the complete distrust and hatred of those he afterwards wishes to love sincerely.

As regards allies, a prince should keep his word to them most scrupulously, even when it is disadvantageous to him to do so; for it can never be as disadvantageous as the reputation of always making good his promises is beneficial to him; and he can only gain this reputation in circumstances of this kind, where he stands to lose by keeping his word. But in those where he would be altogether ruined by doing so, the law of nations* releases him from his promise. He must also be extremely wary before giving his promise, so as to be always able to 489 keep his faith. And although it is a good thing to be on friendly terms with most of one's neighbours, I think, nonetheless, that it is best to have no close alliances, except with those less powerful than oneself. For, however much one intends to keep one's promises oneself, one cannot count on others to the same extent; one must expect to be betrayed whenever they find it advantageous to do so; and a more powerful ally may find it so whenever he wishes, whereas a less powerful one will not.

As regards subjects, these are of two kinds, namely, the grandees and the people. By the grandees I mean all those who can form factions against the prince. He must be very certain of their loyalty; or, if he is not, all political thinkers agree that he should make every effort to bring them down, and that, in so far as they are inclined to cause trouble in the state, he should regard them simply as enemies. But, as for his other subjects, he should above all things avoid being regarded by them with hatred and scorn; this, I think, he can always achieve, provided he strictly abides by justice as they understand it (that is, follows the laws to which they are accustomed), and is neither too severe in his punishments nor too indulgent in granting pardons; and he should not rely on his ministers for everything: he should leave them the burden only of the more unpopular condemnations, while demonstrating his own responsibility for everything else. He should preserve his dignity by laying claim to all the honours and signs of respect the people think due to him, but nothing beyond that; and he must expose to the public only his most serious actions, or those that can win everyone's approval, keeping his pleasures to be taken in private, and never at anyone else's expense. Finally, he must be adamant and inflexible, not when it comes to the initial plans he forms in his own mind, for, since he cannot have an eye to everything, he must ask advice and let many people have their say, before reaching a decision; but he must be inflexible as regards the things on which he has publicly resolved, even if they should be harmful to him; for they can hardly be as harmful as a reputation for fickleness and changeability. 490

I therefore disapprove of the maxim in chapter 15: 'That since the world is very corrupt, one is doomed to destruction if one always tries to be a good man; and, in order to maintain his power, a prince must learn to be wicked, when the occasion requires it'; unless perhaps by a 'good man' he means one who is superstitious and simple-minded, who dare not give battle on the Sabbath,* and whose conscience can never be at peace until he changes his people's religion. But if by a 'good man' we mean one who does everything that true reason dictates to him, it is certain that the best thing is always to try to be one.

I do not believe, furthermore, what he says in chapter 19: 'That we can be hated as much for our good actions, as our bad ones,' except in so far as envy is a kind of hatred; but that is not what the author means. And it is unusual for princes to be envied by the mass of their subjects, only by the grandees, or their neighbours, in whom the same

491   virtues as arouse envy also arouse fear; this is why one should never refrain from doing good, in order to avoid this kind of hatred; and there is no hatred that can harm them but that which comes from the people's judgement that they are unjust or arrogant. For we see that even those who have been condemned to death do not usually hate their judges, when they think the sentence is deserved; and people also patiently endure evils they have not deserved when they think that the prince from whom they come is in some way compelled to inflict them, and does so with regret; this is because they judge that it is just for him to put the public benefit before that of individuals. Difficulty only arises when a prince is obliged to satisfy two groups who judge differently of what is just, as when the Roman emperors had to satisfy both the citizens and the soldiers.* In this case, it is rational to offer something to both sides, and one should not undertake to subject people all at once to reason, when they are unaccustomed to hearing it; but one should gradually try, whether by public proclamations, or by the sermons of preachers, or in some other way, to get them to understand what is reasonable. For, when all is said and done, the people will endure whatever one can convince them is just, and resent whatever they imagine to be unjust; and the arrogance of princes, that is, the usurpation of some authority, or right, or honour that they are not thought to be entitled to is odious to the people, only because they consider this as a form of injustice.

492   Next, I also disagree with the author's opinion when he says in his preface,* 'That, just as you have to be standing in the plain to get a better view of the outline of the mountains you wish to draw, so a private citizen is better placed to get a proper knowledge of the duties of a prince.' For the drawing represents only what is seen at a distance; but the principal motives for princes' actions are often such private considerations that no one who is not himself a prince, unless he has shared a prince's secrets for many years, could possibly imagine them.

     This is why I should deserve to be laughed at, if I thought I could teach Your Highness something in this area; and, indeed, that is not my intention. My aim is simply to provide in my letters some kind of entertainment different from those I imagine you will encounter in your journey, which I hope will go perfectly smoothly; as no doubt it will, if Your Highness resolves to act on the maxims that teach us that everyone's happiness depends on himself, and that we should

so withdraw ourselves from the empire of fortune, that, without missing opportunities to seize the advantages it may bring, we do not think ourselves unhappy when it denies them to us; and because in all the situations in the world there are many reasons on both sides, we should dwell particularly on those that tend to make us approve what we see happening. What is most impossible to avoid is diseases of the body, from which I pray God he may preserve you; and I am, as   493
devotedly as possible, &c.

37. *Elisabeth to Descartes, Berlin, 10 October 1646*   [AT 4]

Monsieur Descartes,   519
You are right to think that the entertainment your letters afford me is different from what I encountered on my journey, since it gives me greater and more lasting satisfaction. Although on the journey I received all possible satisfaction from the friendship and affection of my close relations, I consider these as things that could change, whereas the truths your letters contain leave impressions on   520
my mind that will always contribute to my contentment.

I am extremely sorry that I did not bring with me when I travelled overland the book you took the trouble to examine* so as to give me your opinion of it, because I allowed myself to be persuaded that the luggage I was to send by sea to Hamburg would be here before I was; and it has not arrived yet, even though we arrived on the 7th/17th of last month. This is why all I can bring to mind of the author's doctrines is what my very feeble memory retains from a book I have not glanced at for the past six years. But I remember approving some of them at the time, not as being good in themselves, but because they do less harm than those acted on by a number of reckless and ambitious people I know, whose aim is to cause trouble and then leave the rest to fortune; whereas this author's maxims are all aimed at establishing power securely.

It seems to me also that in order to explain how a state should be governed, he sets himself to consider the kind of state that is most difficult to govern,* where the prince is a recent usurper, at least in the people's mind; and in that case, his own opinion of the justice of his cause may serve to bring peace to his conscience, but not to his situation, in which the laws run counter to his authority, the grandees undermine it, and the people curse it. And when the state is in such a condition, extreme acts of violence do less harm than petty ones, because the petty ones too cause resentment and provide grounds for a protracted war; whereas the extreme ones deprive the grandees who might undertake such a war of the courage and means to do so. Again, when the violence is carried out quickly and all at once, its effect is to astonish, rather than anger, and it is also more bearable for the people than the long string of miseries produced by civil war.

It seems to me that he also adds, or rather teaches, by means of the example of the nephew of Pope Alexander,* whom he represents as the perfect politician, that the prince should have these acts of extreme cruelty carried out by a minister whom he can afterwards sacrifice to the hatred of the people;* and although it may appear unjust on the prince's part to put to death one who had obeyed him, I hold that such barbarous and unnatural men, who, for whatever consideration, are prepared to act as executioners for a whole people, deserve no better treatment; and for myself I would prefer to be the poorest peasant in all Holland, than the minister who would obey such orders, or the prince who would be compelled to issue them.

Likewise, when the author speaks of allies, he supposes them to be as bad as they could be, and the situation to be so desperate, that the choice is between the ruin of the whole state and breaking one's word to people who would keep theirs only as long as they stood to gain from doing so.

But, if he is wrong to infer general maxims from what should be done only in exceptional circumstances, he is no more at fault than virtually all the Fathers of the Church* and the ancient philosophers, who do the same; and I think that this is because of their pleasure in uttering paradoxes,* which they can afterwards explain to their pupils. When this man says that to try always to be a good man is to doom oneself, I think that the kind of goodness he means is not obedience to the laws of superstition; he is referring to the general law that we should act towards everyone else as we should wish them to act towards us; a law that princes can virtually never observe towards individuals among their subjects, whom they must destroy whenever the public benefit so requires. And since no one before you has said that virtue consists only in conformity to right reason* (they have simply laid down a number of more specific laws or rules), it is not surprising that they have failed to define it properly.

I believe that the rule you point to in his preface is false, because he never knew a person like you, with an insight into everything to which he turns his attention, and who would therefore be capable, though living a private life far from the bustle of the world, of teaching princes how to govern, as is clear from what you write on the subject.

I have a princely title, but nothing more, and so I direct my efforts only to applying the rule you laid down at the end of your letter, by attempting to make the best of what is around me as far as I can. I do not find this very difficult here, in a house where I have been tenderly loved since I was a child and where everyone makes a concerted effort to show me affection. Although this sometimes distracts me from more useful occupations, I can easily put up with this inconvenience, because of the pleasure one feels at being loved by one's close relations. This is why, Monsieur, I have not had leis- 523 ure up to now to tell you about the outcome of our journey, which did indeed go off without the slightest difficulty, and was as swift as I mentioned above, or of the miraculous spring* of which you spoke to me at The Hague.

I was only a few miles away from it at Schöningen, where we met all the household here, who were just on their way back from it. The elector* offered to take me to see it, but since the rest of the company were in favour of another amusement, I did not dare go against them, and contented myself with seeing and tasting the water from it. There are several springs, all with a different taste, but the water that is used comes mostly from two. The first is clear, salty, and highly purgative; the second is somewhat whitish, has a taste of water mixed with milk, and is supposed to be cooling. There is much talk of them working many miraculous cures; but I have not been able to find out about any from a trustworthy person. They do, indeed, say that the place is full of beggars, who proclaim that they were born deaf, blind, crippled, or hunchbacked, and were cured by the spring. But since these are out for gain, and are dealing with a people rather credulous when it comes to miracles, I do not think that this should convince a rational person. In the whole court of my cousin the elector only his chief equerry has benefited from it. He had a wound under the right eye, the sight of which he had lost on one side, on account of a flap of skin that had grown over it; and when the salty water from the foun- tain was applied to the eye, it got rid of this skin, to the point where he can now make out people with his left eye closed. It is also true that 524 being a man of hearty constitution and bad eating habits, a thorough purge could only do him good, as it has many other people.*

I have examined the cipher you sent me,* and I think it very good, but too prolix when it comes to conveying a whole message; and if one writes only a few words, they could be deciphered by the quantity of the letters. It would be better to construct an alphabetical key to the words, and then mark some distinction between numbers that signify letters and those that signify words.

I have so little leisure to write here that I am compelled to send you this rough draft,* in which you can tell, from the changes of pen, how often I have been interrupted. But I would rather appear before you with all my shortcomings than give you grounds to impute to me a vice so remote from my nature as that of forgetting my friends in their absence, especially one whom I could not cease to care for without also ceasing to be rational, such as you, Monsieur, for whom I will be all my life,

> Your most affectionate friend at your service,
>
> ELISABETH.

[AT 4]   38. *Descartes to Elisabeth, November 1646*

528   Madam,

I received a most signal favour from Your Highness, when you chose to write to me of the success of your journey and your happy arrival in a place where, being highly esteemed and tenderly loved by your close relations, it seems to me that you have as much good as one can reasonably desire in this life. For, knowing the nature of the human condition, it would be to demand too much of fortune to expect of her so many favours that, even with the help of one's imagination, one could not find the slightest reason to be upset. When there are no present objects 529 that distress the senses, and the body is troubled by no indisposition, a mind that follows true reason can readily find contentment. And in order to achieve this, it is not necessary to forget or ignore whatever is remote from us; it is enough if we attempt to avoid all passions associated with those things that may upset us; this is not contrary to charity, because one is often more successful at finding remedies for the evils one examines dispassionately than for those that grieve us. But, just as bodily health and the presence of agreeable objects greatly assist the mind in driving away all those passions with an element of sadness, and welcoming in those with an element of joy, so, by the same token, when the mind is full of joy, this is highly conducive to bodily health, and causes present objects to appear more agreeable.

And, indeed, I dare to believe that inner joy has some secret power to win the favour of fortune. I would not choose to write this to weak-minded people, for fear of encouraging any superstition; but, as far as Your Highness is concerned, my only fear is that you will laugh at me for becoming too credulous. And yet I have a wealth of experiences, not to mention the authority of Socrates, in support of my belief. My experience is that I have often observed that whatever I have done with a cheerful heart, and without any inner reluctance, tends to turn out well for me, to the point where, even in games of chance, which are governed by fortune alone, I have always found her more favour-   530
able when I had quite separate grounds to be joyful than when I had grounds for sadness. And what is commonly called the daemon of Socrates* I think was nothing but this: he was accustomed to follow his inner inclinations, and thought that the outcome of an under-taking would be successful when he had a secret feeling of cheerful-ness, and on the contrary that, when he felt sad, it would turn out badly. True, it would be superstitious to believe in this as much as he is said to have done; for Plato tells us that he would go so far as to stay at home whenever his daemon did not advise him to go out. But faced with the crucial decisions of life, when the element of doubt is so strong that prudence cannot indicate what we should do, then it seems to me that one is perfectly right to follow the guidance of one's inner spirit,* and that it is useful to have a strong conviction that the things we undertake without reluctance, and with the freedom that typically accompanies joy, will not fail to turn out well for us.

And so I dare to encourage Your Highness here, since you find yourself in a place where the objects present bring you only satisfac-tion, to seek contentment also through your own efforts; this, it seems to me, you may easily do by concentrating only on present things, and never thinking of matters of business except when the messenger is due to leave.* And I think it fortunate that Your Highness's books have not been delivered as soon as you expected them; for reading   531
them is less likely to keep you cheerful than to make you gloomy. This is especially true of the book by the instructor of princes,* since it depicts only the difficulties that princes have in maintaining their

position, and the cruelty and treachery he advises them to practise, so that a private person who reads it has less reason to envy the lot of a prince than to pity it.

Your Highness is perfectly correct in perceiving his mistakes and mine; for it is true that it is because he wishes to praise Cesare Borgia that he lays down general maxims to justify particular actions that are hardly excusable; and since then I have read his *Discourses upon Livy*, where I observed nothing amiss. And his main precept, which is either to wipe out your enemies altogether or to win their friendship, without ever following a middle course, is no doubt always the safest; but, when one has no grounds for fear, it is not the noblest.

Your Highness has also penetrated the secret of the miraculous spring, in that there are many poor people who proclaim its benefits, and who are no doubt in the pay of those who hope to make a profit from it. For it is certain that there is no remedy that can deal with every disease; but of the many people who have tried this one, 532   those for whom it has worked speak well of it, and no one hears about the others. Be that as it may, the purgative quality of the water from one of the springs, and the whiteness, along with the sweet taste and cooling quality, of the water from the other, lead me to think that they flow through deposits of antimony or mercury, which are two poisonous substances, mercury especially. For which reason I would advise no one to drink of them. The vitriol and iron of the waters of Spa* are much less dangerous; and because both of these reduce the spleen and cause melancholy to be evacuated, I recommend them.

For Your Highness will permit me, if you please, to finish this letter as I began, and to wish her above all things joy and satisfaction of mind, these being not only the fruit to be expected of all other goods, but often a means as well to increase the graces one has in order to acquire them;* and although I am incapable of contributing in any way to your service, except by my good wishes, I dare nonetheless to assure you that I am, more fully than anyone else in the world, &c.

[AT 4]   **39.** *Elisabeth to Descartes, Berlin, 29 November 1646*

578   Monsieur Descartes,

I am not so accustomed to the favours of fortune as to expect any extraordinary ones; it is enough for me if I am not too frequently visited with mishaps that would give the greatest philosopher in the world good cause for sadness. And since nothing of the kind has befallen me since I arrived here, since present objects are all agreeable to me, and the air of the country is not ill-suited to my temperament, I find myself in a position to be able to put into practice your lessons about cheerfulness, even though I do not expect this to have the same effect on the conduct of my business as you experienced with games of chance, because the luck that favoured you when you were already disposed to joyfulness for other reasons, no doubt came from the fact that in that state you had all the factors that ordinarily lead to one's winning* more at your disposal.

But, if I were fully in control of my life, I would not so easily settle in a precarious state, even in a place where I have found grounds for contentment, as in that from which I come.* And as for the interests of our house, I have long since abandoned them to fate, seeing that all prudence would be exerting itself in vain, unless assisted by other resources at our disposal. A more powerful daemon than that of Socrates would be needed to advance them effectively; for since his own could not enable him to avoid imprisonment and death, he had no great reason to boast of it. I too have observed that in cases where I have followed my own impulses, things have turned out better for me than when I have let myself be guided by the counsels of wiser people than myself. But I do not put this down to any particularly felicitous inner spirit of mine; it is rather that, since I am more attached to my interests than anyone else is, I have also made a closer examination of the courses of action that could harm or benefit me, than the people on whose judgement I relied. If you want me to give some credit as well to the occult qualities of my imagination,* I think you must be wanting me to adapt myself to the disposition of the people of this country, who are even more pedantic and superstitious than those I have known in Holland; this is because the population as a whole is so poor that no one studies or reasons, except in order to stay alive. 579

I have had to take any amount of trouble to keep myself out of the doctors' hands, so as not to suffer from their ignorance; not that I have been ill, but the change of air and diet has given me, not scabies, but a few abscesses on the fingers. From these, these gentlemen judged that there was still harmful matter hidden there, too coarse to be evacuated through the pores, and requiring treatment with purges and bleeding; but since in all other respects I am feeling myself in such good condition that I am getting visibly plumper,* I have resorted to stubbornness where reason could be of no use, and up to now have taken no remedies. I am all the more fearful of taking medicines here, 580 because the ones everyone uses are chemical extracts, the effects of which are both sudden and dangerous.

Those who have investigated the ingredients of the Hornhausen springs think that the saline one contains nothing but ordinary salt; on the other, there is no agreement. They also (this is especially true of the Lutherans*) explain the effects by a miracle, rather than the composition of the water. For my part, I shall take the safer course, according to your advice, and refrain from taking the water.

I also hope never to be in a position to follow the advice of the teacher of princes, since violence and suspicion are things contrary to my nature. Although I condemn tyrants only for planning to usurp a country and then seizing power; for afterwards the means they use to establish themselves, however harsh, always harm the public less than an armed battle for sovereignty.

I am not sufficiently engaged in such studies for them to make me unhappy, for the little time I have over from the letters I have to write and my duties to my near relations is spent in re-reading your works, an hour of which helps me to cultivate my reason more than would a lifetime reading other things. But no one here is rational enough to understand them, though I have promised the old duke of 581 Brunswick, who is at Wolfenbüttel, to have a set sent him to adorn his library.* I do not think they will provide any adornment for his catarrh-ridden brain, already fully stuffed with pedantry. I am letting myself be carried away by the pleasure of talking to you, without reflecting that I am doing the whole human race a wrong by making you waste the time you would otherwise be using for its benefit in reading the idle prattle of

> Your most affectionate friend at your service,
>
> ELISABETH.

40. *Descartes to Elisabeth, Egmond-Binnen, December 1646*

589   Madam,
I have never found such good news in any of the letters I had previously had the honour to receive from Your Highness as I did in your

last of 29 November. For it leads me to judge that you are in better health and more joyful than I have ever seen you before; and I think that, after virtue, which you have never lacked, these are the two principal goods one can have in this life. I cannot regard as serious the little trouble on account of which the doctors were claiming you should employ them; for although it is sometimes a little troublesome, in the country I come from it is so widespread among the young and otherwise healthy that I consider it less as an ailment than as a mark of good health, and a preservative against other diseases. And through experience our doctors have found reliable remedies to cure it, but their advice is to try to get rid of it only in springtime, because the pores are more open then and it is easier to get rid of the cause of the trouble. So Your Highness is entirely right to refuse to undergo treatment for this reason, especially when winter is coming on, which is the most dangerous time; and if the trouble lasts until spring, it 590 will be easily dealt with by means of a few mild purgatives or cooling broths, containing nothing but herbs generally used in the kitchen, and by abstaining from meats that are too salty or spicy. Bleeding might also be very helpful; but because it involves an element of danger, and shortens life if frequently used, I would not advise it, if you are not accustomed to it; for when one has had oneself bled at the same time of year three or four years in a row, one is virtually obliged to do the same every year. Your Highness is also absolutely right to refuse to make use of chemical remedies; even when a doctor has long experience of using them successfully, the slightest change in their preparation, even when intended to improve them, can entirely change their qualities, and turn them from medicines into poisons.

The same, almost, is true of knowledge, in the hands of those who wish to teach what they do not properly know; for, in the attempt to correct or to add to what they have learnt, they transform it into error. It seems to me that Regius' book,* which has finally come out, is precisely a case of this. I would pick out a few points from it, if I thought he had sent it to Your Highness; but it is so far from here to Berlin, that I expect he is waiting to present you with it until you return; and I will postpone giving my views on it until then.

I am not surprised to learn that Your Highness has found no scholars in the country you are in who are not entirely in thrall to 591 the opinions of the Schools;* for I see that in the rest of Europe, and even in Paris, there are so few who are not that, if I had realized this to start with, I would perhaps never have gone into print. Yet I have this consolation, that, though I am certain that there are many people far from unwilling to attack me, no one has so far ventured into the lists;* and, indeed, I am even receiving compliments from Jesuit fathers, who, I have always thought, would have the strongest interest in the publication of a new philosophy,* and who would be the least disposed to forgive me, if they thought they had good grounds for condemning some aspect of it.

Among my many obligations to Your Highness I count your promise to send His Grace the duke of Brunswick, at Wolfenbüttel, a copy of my works; for I am certain that, before you came to that part of the world, I did not have the honour of being known there. It is true that I am not much concerned to be known to many people, for my principal ambition is to be able to bear witness that I am most devotedly, &c.

[AT 4]   *41. Elisabeth to Descartes, Berlin, 21 February 1647*

618   Monsieur Descartes,

I set as high a value on joy and health as you do, although I rate your friendship (not to mention virtue) even more highly, since it is chiefly to that that I owe the first two goods, as well as the satisfaction of mind (which is even more important than joy) that you have taught me how to have. Moreover, I could not but persevere in my resolution not to take any remedy for the one minor ailment that was still affecting me, since it met with your approval. At present, I am so fully cured of the abscesses that I do not think I need take any medicine in the spring to purge the blood, since I have sufficiently got rid of the bad humours, and, as far as I can see, have been spared the fluxions* that otherwise would have been caused by the cold and the stove-heated rooms.

My sister Henrietta has been so ill that we thought we were going to lose her. That is why I have been slow to answer your last letter, since I made a point of being with her all the time. Since she got better, we have had to be with the queen mother of Sweden* all the time: 619   sleigh rides every day, and banquets and balls every night; amusements that are very troublesome to those who have better ones within reach, but that are less troublesome when they are for the sake of and in the company of people whom one has no reason to distrust. This is why I am more willing to take part in them here than I was at The Hague.

Nonetheless, I would prefer to be using my time reading Regius' book and your views on it. If I do not return to The Hague this summer (I cannot be sure that I will: not that I have changed my mind, but it partly depends on what other people want and the course of public affairs), I shall try to have the book sent on one of the ships that make the crossing from Amsterdam to Hamburg, and I hope that you will send me your views by the post. Whenever I read your works, I cannot imagine that you are really sorry to have gone into print, because they will inevitably come, in the end, to be accepted and to benefit the public.

Not long ago I met one man here who has some knowledge of them. He is a medical doctor named Weiss, and a very good scholar as well. He told me that it was Bacon who first caused him to doubt the philosophy of Aristotle, and that your *Method* led him to reject it altogether, and convinced him of the circulation of the blood, which destroys all the old principles of the medicine they study; that is why he admits that he was reluctant to accept your views. I have just lent him your *Principles*, and he has promised to pass on his objections to 620 me; if he comes up with any, and they seem worth it, I will send them to you, so that you may judge of the abilities of the man I find the most reasonable among all the scholars here, since he is capable of appreciating your arguments; but I am convinced that no one is capable of esteeming you more highly than

Your most affectionate friend at your service,

ELISABETH

42. *Descartes to Elisabeth, The Hague, March 1647* [AT 4]

Madam, 624

The contentment Your Highness tells me you are experiencing where you are now prevents me from wishing you back here, although I find it very difficult not to do so, especially at the moment, when I am myself at The Hague. And because I perceive from your letter of 21 February that we should not expect you to be back here before late summer, I intend to travel to France to sort out some personal business, with a view to returning at the approach of winter; and I shall delay my journey by two months, so that I may have the honour beforehand of receiving Your Highness's commands, which will always have more power over me than anything else in the world.

625 Praised be God that you are now in perfect health; but I beseech you to pardon me if I dare to go against your opinion, in the matter of not taking any remedies because the trouble with your hands has gone away; for it is to be feared, with both Your Highness and the princess your sister,* that the humours that were purged in this way* were merely held in check by the winter cold and that in spring they may bring back the same trouble, or expose you to the risk of some other disease, if you do not remedy them by a healthy diet, consisting purely of food and drink that cools the blood and has a naturally purgative effect. For as to drugs, both those of apothecaries and those of empirics,* I value them so little that I would never dare advise anyone to use them.

I do not know what I can have written to Your Highness about Regius' book that made you want to read my comments on it; perhaps I refrained from giving my views for fear of prejudicing you against the book if you happened to have it already; but since I learn that you do not yet have it, I will tell you frankly here that I do not think it is worth Your Highness's taking the trouble to read it. As to physics, it contains nothing but assertions of mine, all in the wrong order, and separated from their proper proofs, so that they come across as paradoxes;* and what he puts at the beginning can be proved only by what he puts at the end. He has put hardly any-
626 thing of his own in it, and very little from my unpublished work;* and yet at the same time he has done me wrong, inasmuch as, though he professed to be my friend and knew perfectly well that I did not want my work on the description of animals to be made public (so much so that I had refused to let him see it, and had excused myself on the grounds that he could not help speaking of it to his pupils if he did see it), he has nonetheless used a good deal of that material; having somehow got hold of a copy of it, unbeknownst to me, he has exactly transcribed the whole section where I discuss the movement of the muscles, and where, for example, I examine two of the muscles that move the eye, of which there are two or three pages he has reproduced, word for word, twice over in his book, he was so fond of them. And yet he did not understand what he was writing: for he has left out the key point, which is that the animal spirits that flow

from the brain into the muscles cannot return by the same channels along which they came. Without this observation, everything he has written is worthless. And because he did not have my illustration, he provided one that clearly displays his ignorance. I hear he currently has another book on medicine in the press,* where I expect he will have copied all the rest of my treatise, to the best of his digestive ability. He would probably have taken a good deal more from it; but I found out that, by the time he got hold of a copy, his book was already nearly printed. But just as he blindly follows what he takes to 627 be my views, on all matters of physics or medicine, even when he does not understand them, he blindly contradicts them on all metaphysical matters—on which I urged him not to write, because they were irrelevant to his subject and because I was convinced that anything he did write about metaphysics was bound to be bad. But my urgings had no effect, except that, since he did not intend to satisfy me on this point, he felt free to disoblige me in other matters.

I shall nonetheless bring her ladyship P. S.* tomorrow a copy of his book, the title of which is *Fundamenta Physices*, along with another little book by my good friend Mijnheer Hogelande,* who has done the exact opposite of Regius, in that Regius has written nothing that he has not taken from me, and that is not, at the same time, directed against me; whereas Hogelande has written nothing that is really mine (for I do not think that he has ever even read my works properly), and yet he says nothing that is not in my favour, inasmuch as he has followed the same principles. I will ask Lady L.* to enclose 628 these two books, which are not particularly large, with the next packet she shall choose to send via Hamburg. I shall also include the French translation of my *Meditations*, if I can get hold of it before I set off, for it is quite a long time since I was told that the printing has been completed. I am, &c.

43. *Elisabeth to Descartes, Berlin, 11 April 1647*   [AT 4]

Monsieur Descartes,   628
I had not once regretted my absence from The Hague until you told me you had been to the city, leaving me feeling deprived of the satisfaction I was accustomed to feeling in your company, when you stayed in the city. It seemed to me that I was more rational every

time I left you, and although the peace I am enjoying here, among
629 people who love and respect me far more than I deserve, surpasses all
the goods I could find anywhere else, it does not come anywhere near
the benefit of your company, which I cannot, however, promise myself
for several months. How many I do not know, because, as far as I can
see, my aunt the electress is in no mood to allow me to go back to The
Hague, and I have no grounds for pressing her to do so, until her son
the elector is back with her, which, to judge by his own requests, will
not be before September; and perhaps his affairs will require him to
come earlier or stay away longer. Thus, I can hope, but not promise,
that I will have the happiness of seeing you again around the time
you expect to be back from France. I hope that your journey there
will be as successful as you wish it to be; and if I had not learned by
experience how firm you are in sticking to your resolutions, I would
be afraid that your friends would oblige you to stay there. I beg you,
though, to give your address to my sister Sophia, so that I may hear
from you from time to time; I will be pleased to have your news, even
if it takes a long time in getting to me.

After Easter, we shall go to Crossen,* which is an estate belonging
to my aunt the electress, on the borders of Silesia,* to stay there for
630 three weeks or a month; there solitude will give me more opportunity to read, and I will use it wholly on the books you have so kindly
sent me, for which please accept my thanks. I was more keen to have
Regius' book because I know it includes material borrowed from
you, rather than for anything he has put in of his own. Besides the
fact that he does everything rather in a hurry, he made use, as he
told me himself, of the assistance of Dr Jonson, who is capable of
confusing his mind even further, having himself rather a confused
mind to start with, and Regius is not patient enough to try to understand what Jonson has read or heard.* But even if I were to excuse
all Regius' other failings I cannot possibly forgive his ingratitude
towards you, and I hold him to be a complete villain, since all his
conversations with you were unable to change his mind.*

Mijnheer Hogelande's book will certainly be worth his efforts, since
he has followed your principles, which I cannot get a single one of
these Berlin scholars to understand, they are so full of scholasticism.
And the one I mentioned in my last letter* has not been to see me
since I lent him your *Principles*, which is an excellent proof that everyone here is very well, since he is one of the family doctors.

When I told you that I would not take any remedies for the abscesses I had last autumn, I meant apothecary's remedies, since cooling and purgative herbs are my regular diet in the spring, when I generally have no appetite for anything else. I intend also to have myself bled in a few days, since I have got into the bad habit of doing so, which I cannot change so late in the day without suffering from headaches. I would be afraid of giving you a headache by this boring news of myself if it were not for your concern for my health; which would also make me extremely vain, if I did not know that its only cause is your extreme kindness towards

631

Your most affectionate friend at your service,

ELISABETH.

44. *Descartes to Elisabeth, Egmond, 10 May 1647*   [AT 5]

Madam,

15

Although I may find reasons when in France for prolonging my stay there, none of them will be so strong as to prevent me from returning here before the winter, provided I still have life and health, since the letter I had the honour of receiving from Your Highness gives me reason to hope that you will return to The Hague towards the end of summer. But I may say that that is the main reason why I prefer living here to anywhere else; since I foresee that the tranquillity, the quest for which led me here in the first place, will be somewhat diminished from now on, because, not having yet received complete redress for the injustices inflicted on me at Utrecht,* I see that these have given rise to more treatment of the same kind, and that there is a gang of theologians, scholastics all, who seem to have joined together in order to bring me down by calumny; so that as long they are plotting in every possible way to damage me to the best of their ability, if I were not on the watch and ready to defend myself, it would be easy for them to subject me to public insult.

16

The proof of all this is that over the last three or four months a certain regent* of the theological college of Leiden, named Revius, has organized disputations* of four different theses directed against me, so as to pervert the meaning of my *Meditations* and persuade people that they contain doctrines both absurd and contrary to God's glory; for instance, that we should doubt whether God exists,

and even that I require the reader for a certain time absolutely to deny that there is a God, and suchlike stuff. But because this man is unintelligent, and even most of his students laugh at his backbiting, my friends in Leiden did not even bother to let me know what he was doing; until Triglandius, their senior professor of theology, brought out another set of theses, including these words:* 'He who regards God as a deceiver, as in the wicked view of Cartesius, is a blasphemer.' From this my friends, even those who are also theologians, judged that the aim of these people, in accusing me of so great a crime
17 as blasphemy, was nothing less than to try, first of all, to get my opinions condemned as extremely pernicious by some synod they could get control of, and then to try also to get the magistrates, who believe in them, to publicly disgrace me; and that to prevent this I had to take action to block their plans. For this reason I wrote a long letter a week ago to the curators of Leiden University to demand redress for the calumnies of these two theologians. I do not yet know what kind of answer I shall get; but, to judge by my knowledge of the attitude of the people of this country, and their reverence, not for integrity and virtue, but for the beard, the voice, and the scowl of a theologian, so that the most powerful people here (as is usual in all democratic states*) are the most brazen and those who can shout the loudest, even when they are least rational, I expect nothing more than a superficial remedy, which will not get rid of the cause of the disease, and only render it more protracted and troublesome. Whereas for my part I think I have no choice but to do my utmost to obtain full redress for these injustices, and also, in doing so, for those from Utrecht; and, supposing I cannot obtain justice (which I foresee will indeed be very difficult), to leave the United Provinces altogether. But because everything happens here very slowly I am certain that it will take more than a year before it gets to that stage.

I would not take the liberty of burdening Your Highness with these
18 trivial matters, if it were not that the favour you do me in choosing to read the books of Mijnheer Hogelande and of Regius because of what they include concerning me makes me suppose that you will not be displeased to learn of my concerns from myself; besides, the obedience and respect I owe you obliges me to give you an account of all my actions.

I praise God that the doctor to whom Your Highness lent my *Principles* has not been to see you for a long time, since this is a sign that no one at the court of the electress is ill, and it feels as if one is in more perfect health when everyone with whom one is living is equally healthy, than when one is surrounded by sick people. The doctor will have all the more time to read the book it pleased Your Highness to lend him, and will be better able to give you his opinion of it at a later date.

While writing this, I have received letters from The Hague and Leiden to the effect that the meeting of the curators has been postponed, so that they have not yet received my letter; and I see that a squabble has been turned into a major issue. I am told that the theologians want to sit in judgement on the case, that is, to put me here under a more severe inquisition than the Spanish one ever was, and to make me pass for an enemy of their religion. In response to this I am being advised to make use of the influence of the French 19 ambassador and the authority of His Highness the prince of Orange,* not to obtain justice, but to intercede on my behalf and block my enemies from going further. However, I do not think I will follow this advice: I shall simply demand justice, and if I cannot obtain it, it seems to me that my best course of action is quietly to prepare to leave the country. But whatever I think or do, and wherever in the world I go, nothing will ever be dearer to me than to obey your commandments, and to bear witness how zealously I am, &c.

45. *Elisabeth to Descartes, Crossen, [late] May 1647* [AT 5]

Monsieur Descartes, 46

Three weeks ago I was sent the foolish corollary of Professor Triglandius,* and was further informed that those who had argued on your behalf were not conquered by reason, but silenced by the uproar that arose in the university; and that Professor Stuart* (a very widely read man, but one of very little judgement) was proposing to refute your *Metaphysical Meditations*. I could well imagine that that would give you the same pain as the calumny of Voetius' pupil,* but not that it would make you decide to leave Holland, as you indicate in your letter of the 10th of this month, because it would be unworthy of you to leave your enemies in possession of the field, and your departure would appear as a kind of banishment, which would do you more harm than the worst these theological gentlemen can do to you, 47 since calumny is not of great importance in a place where the rulers themselves cannot escape it, or punish the authors of it. The people pay this great toll simply for the sake of freedom of speech, and the speech of theologians, which is privileged everywhere,* cannot be restrained in a democratic state. For this reason, it seems to me that you would be right to content yourself with obtaining what your friends in Holland advise you to ask for, although you should not follow their advice in asking for it,* since the resolution you have taken is more worthy of a free man who is sure of his ground. But if you persist in your intention to leave the country, I would also abandon my own intention of returning there, unless called back by the interests of my house, and remain here instead, until the outcome of the Münster negotiations* or some other turn of events brings me back to my own country.

The electress's dower house* is sited in an area that suits my constitution pretty well; it is two degrees nearer the sun than Berlin, and surrounded by the river Oder. The land is extremely fertile. The people here have already recovered better from the civil war than at Berlin, even though the armies were here for longer, and caused more damage by fire. In some villages now there are so many of the flies called *cousins* in French* that many people and animals have been choked by them, or lost their sight and hearing. They arrive in the shape of a cloud and leave in the same way. The local people think
48 they are the result of witchcraft; but I think it is due to the unusually heavy flooding of the Oder, which this year lasted to the end of April, when it was already very hot.

A couple of days ago I received the books of Mijnheer Hogelande and Regius; but dispatches have prevented me* from reading them, except the beginning of the former. I would have great respect for the proofs he gives there of the existence of God,* if you had not accustomed me to seeking for such proofs in the principles of our knowledge.* But the comparisons by which he shows how the soul is united to the body and constrained to adapt itself to the body's form, and share in the good or evil that befalls it, do not quite satisfy me. For the subtle matter he supposes to be enclosed in more solid matter by the heat of the fire or fermentation is nevertheless corporeal, and it can receive pressure or movement from the solid matter only because it has a surface consisting of a quantity of particles; which cannot apply to the soul, which is immaterial.*

My brother Philip, who sent me the two books, tells me that there are two others on the way; and since I have ordered none, I think they must be the French editions of your *Meditations* and *Principles of Philosophy*. I am especially impatient to receive the latter, because you have added some material that is not in the Latin; I think that this must be in book IV, because the three others appear to me to be as clear as they could possibly be.

The doctor whom I have mentioned to you before* has told me   49
that he has some objections concerning minerals, but that he does not dare send them to you before he has had a chance to examine your fundamental principles again. But his practice takes up a great deal of his time. The people here have extraordinary faith in the medical profession; and yet, if both the common people and the nobility were not so dirty, I think they would need doctors less than anyone, because the air here is very pure. And, indeed, my health is better here than it was in Holland. But I would not wish to have lived here all my life, because there is nothing but my books to stop me from becoming completely stupid. I would be completely content here if I could convey to you how highly I value your continued kindness to

Your most affectionate friend at your service,

ELISABETH.

46. *Descartes to Elisabeth, The Hague, 6 June 1647*   [AT 5]

Madam,   59

Passing through the Hague on my way to France, since I cannot have the honour of receiving your commands, and paying my respects to you there, it seems to me that I am obliged to write you these few lines, so as to assure Your Highness that my zeal and devotion will never change, even if I were to change country.* Two days ago, I received a letter from Sweden from the French resident* there, in which he puts a question to me on behalf of the queen,* to whom he made me known by showing her my answer to another letter he had sent me previously. And his description of this queen, and the things he reports her as saying, lead me to esteem her so highly that it seems to me that each of you would be worthy of each other's conversation; and that so few other people are, in the rest of the world, that it would   60
not be difficult for Your Highness to form a close friendship with her;

and besides the contentment of mind it would bring you, this could be desirable from several points of view.* I had previously written to my friend the resident in Sweden, in reply to a letter in which he talked about the queen, that I did not find it hard to believe what he told me of her, since the honour I had of knowing Your Highness had taught me how far those of high birth can excel other people, etc.* But I do not know if this was in the letter he showed her, or in another earlier letter; and because from now on he will probably show her the letters he gets from me, I shall make a point of always including something that will give her a reason for desiring Your Highness's friendship, unless you forbid me to do so.

The theologians who were attempting to damage me have been silenced,* but in a way that panders to them and every effort has been made to avoid offending them, which people now explain by the particular times we are going through; but I am afraid that this time will never come to an end, and that they will be allowed to gain so much power as to be unbearable.

The printing of the French translation of my *Principles* is nearly complete; and because the dedicatory epistle* will be printed last, I am sending Your Highness a copy of it with this letter, so that if there is anything in it that displeases you and that you would like altered, you will be so good as to inform one who will be all his life, &c.

[AT 5]   47. *Descartes to Elisabeth, Egmond-Binnen, 20 November 1647*

89   Madam,

Since I have already taken the liberty of informing Your Highness of the Swedish correspondence* I started not long ago, I think myself obliged to continue, and to tell you that I recently heard from my friend in that country, who told me that when the queen was in Uppsala, where the Swedish university is situated, she wanted to hear a speech by the professor of rhetoric, whom he rates as the most able and rational man in the university, and that the subject she had set him was the supreme good in this life; but having heard the speech, she stated that such people treated the subject only superficially, and that I should be asked for my opinion of it. To this he answered that I was extremely busy working on just this subject; but if Her Majesty wished him to ask for my opinion on her behalf, he did not think I would fail to do my best to satisfy her. Whereupon, she explicitly instructed him to ask for it, and made him promise that he would write to me about it in time for the next post; so that he advises me to give my answer, addressing my letter to the queen, to whom he will present it, and says that he can guarantee it will be well received.

I thought that I could not let slip this opportunity, and, reflecting that when he wrote his letter he could not yet have received the one in which I spoke of the correspondence I had had the honour of having with you on this very subject, I judged that my plan in writing that letter had failed,* and that I would have to try a different approach; and so I wrote a letter to the queen* in which I briefly gave my opinion, and added that I had left out a great deal, because, bearing in mind the number of matters with which the ruler of a great kingdom has to deal, and which Her Majesty attends to personally, I dared not ask her for a longer hearing; but that I was sending M. Chanut a few documents in which I had given my views on the subject in more detail, so that, if it pleased her to see them, he could present her with them.

The writings I am sending to M. Chanut are the letters I had the honour of writing to Your Highness about Seneca's *De vita beata*, up to halfway through the sixth,* where, having described the passions in general, I say that I find difficulty in classifying them. In addition to this, I am also sending him the little *Treatise on the Passions*, which I found quite difficult to have transcribed from the very disorderly draft I had kept of it; and I make it clear to him that I am not requesting him to present these writings to the queen right away, for fear that it might be lacking in respect towards Her Majesty to send her letters I had composed for another person, rather than writing to herself what I might judge to be agreeable to her; but that if he thinks fit to mention the matter to her, saying that it was to him that I sent them, and if after that she desires to see them, I shall be free of this scruple; moreover, I have convinced myself that perhaps she will prefer to see what was written for another person, than if it had been addressed to herself, since she can be all the more certain that I have changed or disguised nothing out of consideration for her.

I did not judge it opportune to say anything further of Your Highness, or even to mention your name, which, however, he must certainly know on account of my earlier letters. But considering that, although he is a very virtuous man, who holds people of merit in high

esteem (so that I do not doubt that he honours Your Highness as much
as he should), he has nonetheless spoken very seldom of you in his
92 letters, although I have mentioned you in all of mine, I supposed that
he had misgivings about mentioning you to the queen, on account of
not knowing whether that would please or displease the people who
sent him.* But if I do in future have occasion to write to her directly, I shall need no intermediary; and my purpose on this occasion
in sending her these writings is to try to get her to devote more attention to this kind of thinking; and if she likes it, as I have been given to
hope, to bring it about that she has an opportunity to discuss it with
Your Highness.* For whom I will be all my life, &c.

[AT 5]   48. *Elisabeth to Descartes, Berlin, 5 December 1647*

96   Monsieur Descartes,
Since a few days ago I received the French translation of your
Metaphysical Meditations, which you had sent me, I cannot but write
to you to thank you, although I cannot express my feelings of gratitude
for your kindness, without requiring of you the further kindness of
excusing the trouble I give you of reading and replying to my letters,
which so often divert your attention from useful meditations onto
subjects that, but for the bias of friendship, cannot be of any importance to you; but I have received so many proofs of your friendship for
me that I presume on it so far as to take the liberty of telling you how
gratified I was to read the above-mentioned translation, since it makes
97 your thoughts all the more mine in that I see them clearly expressed
in a language I am in the habit of using,* although I believe I had
understood them before.
Whenever I read the objections put to you,* I find myself wondering more and more how it can possibly be that people who have
spent so many years in meditation and study can fail to understand
things so simple and clear, that most of them, in debating truth and
falsehood, seem not to know how they are to be distinguished, and
that M. Gassendi,* whose reputation for learning is so high, has
put forward objections less rational than all the rest (except for the
Englishman's).*
This shows you how much the world needs the *Treatise on Learning**
you once intended to write. I know that you are too charitable to reject

an idea so beneficial to the public, and that therefore I have no need to remind you of the promise you once gave

Your most affectionate friend at your service,

ELISABETH

49. *Descartes to Elisabeth, Egmond–Binnen, 31 January 1648*   [AT 5]

Madam,   111

I received Your Highness's letter of 23 December almost immediately after the one before,* and I admit I am in a quandary how to reply to the earlier one, because in it Your Highness expresses the wish that I should write the *Treatise on Learning* of which I once had the honour of speaking to her. And there is nothing I desire more zealously than to obey your commands; but I will give you here the reasons why I decided to abandon the project of this *Treatise*, and if   112 these do not satisfy Your Highness, I will not fail to revive it.

The first is that I could not include all the truths that would need to be included without incurring the ire of the scholastics:* and I am not currently in such a situation as to be able to ignore their hatred altogether. The second is that I have already said some of the things I wanted to include in the treatise in a preface to the French translation of my *Principles*, which I think Your Highness must have already received. The third is that I now have another piece of work in hand which I hope may be more agreeable to Your Highness, namely, a description of the functioning of animals and human beings. For my draft treatment of the subject, produced twelve or thirteen years ago, and which Your Highness has seen, has been through the hands of so many people who have transcribed it badly,* that I decided I would have to tidy it up, in other words revise it altogether. And I have even gone so far (but only in the last week or ten days) as to attempt to explain in it how animals develop from the very beginning of their lives. I mean animals in general, because, as regards human beings in particular, I would not venture to attempt this, for lack of sufficent empirical evidence.

Furthermore, I am thinking of the remainder of this winter as the quietest time I shall perhaps have in the rest of my life; and for this   113 reason prefer employing it on this project than on another that does not require so much attention. The reason why I am afraid I may not have so much leisure after that is that I have to go back to France next summer, and stay there through the following winter; my domestic affairs and several other reasons make this necessary.* I have also been honoured by the offer of a pension from the king of France, for which I never applied; that will not be sufficient to compel me to stay in France, but many things can happen in the course of a year. Yet nothing can happen to prevent me from preferring the happiness of living in the same place as Your Highness, if the opportunity arose, to that of living in my native land, or any other place whatever.

I am not expecting any response for a long time to the letter about the supreme good,* because it was delayed for more than a month at Amsterdam, which was the fault of the person I sent it to* for it to be forwarded; but as soon as I hear anything of it, I will not fail to let Your Highness know. It contained nothing new that deserved to be sent to you. Since then I have received some letters from that coun-
114 try, in which I am informed that my letter is expected; and according to what they tell me of that princess,* she must be unusually inclined to virtue and capable of forming a sound judgement about things. I am informed that she will be presented with the translation of my *Principles*, and assured that she will read the first part of it with pleasure, and would be capable of reading the rest but for the pressure of business on her time.

Along with this letter I send a pamphlet of slight importance,* and do not enclose it in the same packet, because it is not worth the cost of postage; I was compelled to write it by the insults of M. Regius, and it was printed before I expected. The publisher even added a poem and a preface I disapprove of, even though the poem is by Mijnheer Hey[danus];* but he did not put his name to them, and quite rightly. I am, &c.

[AT 5]   50. *Elisabeth to Descartes, Crossen, 30 June 1648*

195   Monsieur Descartes,
A swelling in my right arm, the fault of a surgeon who severed part of a nerve while bleeding me, prevented me from replying sooner to your letter of 7 May,* which reveals to me yet again your extreme nobility of soul, when you say you regret leaving Holland because, while there, you could hope to confer on me the benefits of

your conversation; which is, indeed, the greatest good I had to look forward to there, and the only reason for which I was considering how I might return there—a plan that would have been furthered both by a settlement in England* and by the despair of ever seeing such a thing in Germany.*

In the meantime, there is talk of the journey you proposed some time ago,* and the mother of the person to whom your friend has given your letters has been ordered to bring the matter to a successful conclusion without it being known in her country that she was acting from anything other than her own spontaneous impulse. The good woman is the last person who should have been entrusted with any secret business, since she has never been able to keep a secret. Nonetheless, she is very energetically dealing with the other aspects of her commission, and if it were up to her there is another person* who would be hastening on the same journey; but that person is not intent on making it, but will do as the family decides. They will probably be in favour of the journey, and if they send the necessary money, the person is determined to make the journey, because that will perhaps make it possible for them to be of use in that country to those to whom they have obligations,* and they can return in the company of the good woman mentioned above, who is not minded to stay there either. This is the only thing that has changed since the reasons for not making this journey were communicated to you earlier, and if it does not take place, the most likely reasons will be the death of the woman (who is in rather poor health) or her having to set out on the journey before the other person hears from their family. Three weeks ago, I received a most obliging letter from the country in question, full of kindness and protestations of friendship; but it makes no mention of your letters or of what has been said above; so it was passed on to the good woman only by the word of mouth of a messenger.

I have not yet given you an account of my reading of the French translation of your *Principles of Philosophy*. Although there is something in the preface I need you to explain, I shall say nothing of it here, because that would make this letter too long. But I intend to discuss it with you another time, and promise myself that, when you change your place of residence, you will still retain the same charity for

196

Your most affectionate friend at your service,

ELISABETH

51. *Descartes to Elisabeth, Paris, June or July 1648*

197   Madam,

Although I know well that neither the place nor the situation in
198 which I am at present can give me any opportunity of being serviceable
to Your Highness, I would be failing both in my duty and my zeal if,
having arrived in a new dwelling place, I neglected to renew my pledge
to you of my most humble obedience. The state of things in which I have
found myself here is one that no human prudence could have foreseen. The Parlement, acting together with the other sovereign courts,
is now meeting every day, to discuss certain measures they claim should
be taken with regard to the management of government finances.* At
present they are doing so with the permission of the queen, so in all
probability the business will drag on for a long time: but it is far from
easy to predict the outcome. It is said that their aim is to come up
with sufficient money to carry on the war,* and maintain big armies,
without the people being crushed by taxation as a result. If this is their
approach, I am convinced that this will finally lead to a general peace.
But until that comes about, I would have done better to remain in
a country that is already at peace; and if these storms do not soon clear
away, I mean to make my way back to Egmond in six weeks or a couple of
months, and to stay there until the weather in France improves. And
yet, standing as I am, with one foot in one country and the other in
another, I find my situation a very happy one, inasmuch as it is independent. And I think that the great difference between those most
favoured by fortune and other people is that the former feel the setbacks
199 that befall them more keenly, not that they enjoy more pleasures: for all
the gratifications they can have are familiar to them, and so affect them
less than the misfortunes, which come upon them only when they least
expect it and are altogether unprepared. This must serve as a consolation to those whom fortune has accustomed to its disfavours.* I wish it
were as obedient to all your desires as I shall be all my life, &c.

52. *Elisabeth to Descartes, Crossen, July 1648*

209   Monsieur Descartes,

Wherever in the world you may be, the trouble you take to write to me
with your news will always be a source of satisfaction to me. For I am

convinced that your news must always be good, and that God is too just to send you any misfortune so great that your prudence cannot benefit from it; as with the unexpected disorders in France, which, by compelling you to return to Holland, are preserving your freedom, which otherwise the court would have snatched away from you,* whatever efforts you made to resist it; and the benefit to me is the pleasure of being able to hope for the happiness of seeing you again, in Holland or elsewhere. 210

I think you must have received the letter that mentions the prospect of another journey that was to take place,* if it received the approval of friends, thinking it would benefit them in the current situation; and since then they asked for it to be made, and supplied the necessary funds. Nonetheless, the people who need to take the lead in the business have, day after day, blocked the necessary preparations, their reasons for this being so feeble that they themselves dare not acknowledge them. Meanwhile, so little time is now left for the preparations that the person who was to make the journey cannot be ready in time. And, in the first place, the person is very displeased not to have kept their word; secondly, their friends will think that they lacked the willpower or the courage to sacrifice their health and peace of mind for the good of a house* for which they would be ready to give their very life if it were required. That upsets them, rather, but does not surprise them, for they are well used to putting up with being blamed for what is other people's fault (especially in circumstances where they have chosen not to clear their name) and to seeking their satisfaction only in the witness of their conscience that they have done their duty. And yet that does for a time turn the person's thoughts away from more agreeable 211 subjects; and although you are right to say that the great difference between those most favoured by fortune and other people is that they feel the setbacks that befall them more keenly, not that they enjoy more pleasures, because there are few of them that take pleasure in the right objects;* yet if the pleasure in question were that of doing good to the public and especially to people of merit, a worldly position that offered much scope to it would also produce more pleasures than could be enjoyed by those to whom fortune has denied this advantage; for myself, I would never ask for any greater pleasure than to be able to give you concrete proof of how much I value your kindness towards

Your most affectionate friend at your service,

ELISABETH

[AT 5]   53. *Elisabeth to Descartes, Crossen, 23 August 1648*

225   Monsieur Descartes,
In my last letter, I mentioned someone who, through no fault of
their own, was at risk of losing the good opinion and perhaps the
good will of most of their friends. Now they find themselves released
from this prospect in rather an extraordinary fashion,* because when
they wrote to the other person to tell her how long it would be before
they could join her, the reply came that she (the other person) would
certainly have waited for them, if her daughter had not changed her
mind, thinking that it would make a bad impression if she allowed
people of a different religion to approach her so closely. This behaviour, to my mind, hardly matches up to the praise your friend
bestows on the woman who uses him; at least, that is, if she herself is
alone responsible for it, and the source of it is not her weak-minded
mother, who, the whole time this business has been under consideration, has been accompanied by a sister who is totally dependent for
her keep on the party opposed to the house of the person mentioned
226   above. Your friend could explain what has happened to you, if you
thought it would be appropriate to mention the matter to him. Or
perhaps he will write to you about it of his own accord, since it is said
that his influence over the mind of the person he praises so highly is
absolute. I have nothing further to add, except that I do not think that
this episode should rank among the misfortunes that have befallen
the person concerned. For it spares them a journey the evils of which
(loss of health and peace of mind, plus the unpleasantness they would
have had to suffer from a brutish people) were inevitable, whereas the
benefits that other people might have hoped for from it were anything but certain. And if this behaviour is insulting, the disgrace falls
entirely on those responsible for it, since it is a mark of their fickleness
and instability, and anyone who knows about it also knows that the
person in question has done nothing to prompt such capriciousness.
        As for me, I intend to remain here until I know the outcome of
what is happening in Germany and in England, where things seem
at the moment to be coming to a crisis.* A few days ago something
rather amusing, and yet very disagreeable, happened to us. We, the
electress and her followers, were strolling through an oak wood, when
suddenly a kind of measles-like rash broke out all over our bodies,
except for the face. There was no fever or any other symptom except

an unbearable itching. The superstitious ones thought they had been bewitched; but the peasants told us that there is sometimes a kind of poisonous dew on the trees that drips down and infects passers-by. And it is curious to note that, of all the different remedies everybody thought of for this new disease (baths, bleeding, cupping, leeches, purges), not one worked. I am telling you all this, because I presume   227 that you will find evidence here in favour of some of your doctrines.

> I am most truly, Monsieur Descartes,
> Your most affectionate friend at your service,
>
> ELISABETH.

54. *Descartes to Elisabeth, Egmond-Binnen, October 1648*   [AT 5]

Madam,   232

I have at last had the good fortune to receive the three letters* Your Highness did me the honour of writing to me, and they have not fallen into the wrong hands. But the first one, from 30 June, reached Paris when I had already set out on my return to this country, and so those who received it on my behalf waited to hear that I had arrived before forwarding it to me; hence I received it only today, when I also received the letter of 23 August. The behaviour there described is so insulting I am astonished; and, like Your Highness, I am will-ing to believe that the person to whom it is attributed* is not really responsible for it. Be that as it may, I do not think that one should be distressed at not going on a journey the difficulties of which, as Your Highness very shrewdly observes, were unavoidable, while the benefits were most uncertain. For myself, thanks be to God, I have completed the journey to France I had to make; and I am not sorry to have gone there, but I am even more pleased to be back. I saw no one there whose situation seemed to me enviable, and those who cut the most prominent figure there seem to me to be the most deserving of pity. I could not have gone there at a better time to be convinced that happiness resides in a quiet and retired way of life, and wealth in a very modest income. If Your Highness compares your own situation with that of the queens and the other princesses of Europe, you will find the same difference as there is between those who are finally resting safe   233 in harbour, and those still at sea, tossed about by the storm winds.* And even if one has been driven into the harbour by a shipwreck, as long as one has no lack of the necessities of life, one should be no less satisfied there than if one had arrived there in some other way. The setbacks that befall people engaged in action, and whose happiness depends totally on other people, pierce right to the depths of their heart; whereas the poisonous vapour that came down from the trees under which Your Highness was peaceably walking will have affected, I hope, only the outer surface of the skin; and I think that if this had been washed right away with a little brandy, the trouble would have been altogether removed.

I have not heard for the last five months from the friend* about whom I formerly wrote to Your Highness. And since in his last letter he informed me in great detail about the reasons why the person to whom he had given my letters* had not yet answered them, I judge that he has kept silent only because he is still waiting for an answer, or perhaps because he is rather embarrassed to have no answer to send me, as he had expected he would. That is why I am not taking the initiative and writing to him, in case my letters came across as a reproach; 234 and, while in Paris, I was still kept abreast of his news, thanks to his in-laws,* who heard from him every week. But when they have told him that I am back here, I have no doubt he will write to me here, and tell me what he knows of the business concerning Your Highness,* for he is well aware of my great interest in the matter. But those who have not had the honour of seeing you, and who lack the detailed knowledge of your virtues, will fail to understand that anyone can be, as wholeheartedly as I am, &c.

[AT 5]   **55. *Descartes to Elisabeth, Egmond, 22 February 1649***

281   Madam,
Of the many pieces of bad news* that I have received all at once from various places, the one that most affected me was that of Your Highness's illness. And though I have also heard that you have recovered, there are still traces of sadness remaining in my mind, which cannot be erased so soon. The inclination to write poetry Your Highness experienced during your illness reminds me of Socrates, who Plato says had a similar urge while he was in prison.* And I think that this poetic mood comes from a violent agitation of the animal spirits,* which could altogether unhinge the imagination of someone

whose brain is somewhat unsettled, but does no more than stimulate the strong-minded, so disposing them to write poetry. And I regard this enthusiasm as the mark of a mind stronger and nobler than the common.

If I did not already know yours to be such, I would fear that you would be extraordinarily distressed to learn the bloody denouement of   282 the tragedies of England:* but I am confident that Your Highness, being no stranger to the blows of fortune, and having seen herself not long since in great danger of death, will be less shocked or disturbed to learn of the death of one close to her than if she had never before encountered affliction. And although this violent death seems to have something more horrible about it than an expected death in bed, yet, properly regarded, it is more glorious, more fortunate, and sweeter; so that the aspect of it that particularly distresses ordinary people should be, to Your Highness, a consolation. For there is much glory in dying in a situation such that one is universally pitied, praised, and missed* by all those with any human feeling. And it is certain that, but for this ordeal, the clemency and the other virtues of the late king would never have been so acknowledged and so valued as they are now, and will be in the future, by all those who read his history. I am certain also that, in the last moments of his life, he will have experienced more satisfaction from his conscience than distress from his indignation (the only sad passion that, as it is reported, could be observed in him). And as for the pain, I do not attach great importance to it; for it is so brief that if murderers were able to make use of fever, or one of the other diseases of which nature generally makes use when it takes a person from the world, we would have grounds for thinking them crueller than when they kill their victims with one blow of an axe. But I dare not dwell longer on so gloomy a subject; I will add only   283 that it is better to be entirely rid of a false hope than to be buoyed up by it in vain.

While writing these lines, I have received letters from a certain place* for the first time in seven or eight months; among which there is one from the person to whom I sent the treatise on the passions* a year ago, who writes in her own hand to thank me for it. Since, after all this time, she remembers a man so insignificant as myself, it is most probable that she will not forget to answer Your Highness's letters, though she has waited four months to do so. I am informed that she has instructed one of her scholars to study my *Principles of*

Philosophy, so as to assist her in reading it. However, I do not think that she will be able to find the time to set about it, though she seems to have the intention. She thanks me explicitly for the treatise on the passions, but makes no mention of the letters enclosed along with it,* and I have heard nothing at all from the country in question concerning Your Highness. The only explanation I can guess at is this: since the terms of the German peace treaty* were less advantageous to your house than they might have been, those who have contributed to this outcome are wondering whether you bear them ill will on this account, which inhibits them from offering you marks of friendship.

284

Ever since the peace was concluded I have been distressed not to hear that the elector your brother has accepted it; and I would have taken the liberty before now of letting Your Highness know my views on the subject, if I could have imagined that he was seriously debating the issue. But, since I do not know by what private reasons he may be influenced, it would be rash on my part to pass any judgement. I can only say this, in general: when the point at issue is the restitution of a state that is occupied or disputed by another party that has armed force on its side, then it seems to me that those whose only support lies in equity and the law of nations must never expect to have their claims met in full; and that they have more reason to be grateful to those who ensure that a part, however small, of their territory is restored to them, than to bear ill will towards those who retain possession of the rest. And although they cannot be blamed for pursuing their claims as vigorously as possible, while the parties with armed force at their disposal are deliberating, I think that, when a settlement is reached, prudence obliges them to appear to be satisfied, even when they do not feel so; and to thank not only those who have brought about a partial restitution in their favour, but those who have not deprived them totally, so as to win the friendship of both parties, or at least to avoid their hatred; for this will be very helpful, subsequently, in maintaining their position. Besides, there is always a long road between a promise and its fulfilment; and if the

285 parties with armed force at their disposal come to an agreement by themselves,* they can easily find reasons to divide among themselves what perhaps they were willing to restore to a third party only on grounds of mutual suspicion, and to prevent the new possessor, rich with the spoils of his predecessor, from growing too powerful. The smallest area of the Palatinate is better than the whole empire of the

Tatars or Muscovites, and after two or three years of peace, it will be as pleasant to live in as anywhere on earth. Speaking for myself, as one not committed to living in any particular place, I would be perfectly willing to move to that country from the United Provinces, or even from France, if I were as certain of being left in peace there, even if I had no incentive to go there apart from the beauty of the country; but there is no place in the world, however forbidding and inconvenient, where I would not reckon myself happy to be spending the rest of my days, if Your Highness were there, and I were capable of doing her some service, since I am entirely and unreservedly, &c.

56. *Descartes to Elisabeth, Egmond, 31 March 1649*   [AT 5]

Madam,   330

About a month ago I had the honour of writing to Your Highness, and informing her that I had received some letters from Sweden. I have just received some more, in which I am invited, on the queen's behalf, to travel there this spring, so as to be able to return before the winter. But I have answered in such terms that, although I am not refusing to go there, I think nonetheless that I will not leave here until midsummer or thereabouts. I have requested this postponement for various reasons, and especially so as to be able to have the honour of receiving Your Highness's commands before I set off. I have before now so publicly declared my zeal for and devotion to your service that people would have more reason to think ill of me, if they observed that I was indifferent in matters that concern you, than they will, if they see that I am scrupulously seeking opportunities to perform my duty. Thus, I most humbly entreat Your Highness   331 to do me the great favour of informing me of any way in which you judge I can be of service to yourself or your family, and of believing firmly that you have as much power over me as if I had been your servant all my life.* I entreat you also to let me know what answer you would wish me to give if the letters of Your Highness concerning the supreme good, which I had mentioned last year in my own, were to come to mind* and there should be some curiosity to see them. I am assuming that I will spend the winter there, and return only the following year.* It is most likely that by then there will be peace all over Germany, and if all turns out as I desire, I will come to visit you,

wherever you are, on the return journey, so I may all the more bear
witness that I am, &c.

[AT 5]   57. *Descartes to Elisabeth, Egmond, June 1649*

359   Madam,
Since Your Highness desires to know my decision about the journey
to Sweden,* I will tell you that I still firmly intend to go there, assuming that the queen continues to indicate that she wishes me to; and
360   when M. Chanut, our resident in that country, passed by here a week
ago, on his way to France, he spoke to me of this extraordinary queen
in such glowing terms that the journey now seems to me less long and
tedious than it did before; but I shall not leave until I hear once again
from Sweden, and I shall, if possible, wait until M. Chanut sets off on
his return journey so as to be able to travel with him (since I hope that
he will be sent back there). In any case, I should judge myself to be
very fortunate if, while I am there, I could be of any service to Your
Highness. I will not fail to seek out any opportunity to be so, and shall
not fear to write down openly all my thoughts and deeds concerning
this subject. For since I can have no intention that could be prejudi-
cial to those whom I shall be obliged to respect, and my guiding rule
is that the most just and honourable behaviour is also the safest and
most useful, even if my letters should be read by a third party, I hope
that they cannot be misinterpreted or fall into the hands of people
so unjust as to find fault with my acquitting myself of my duty and
professing myself openly to be, &c.

[AT 5]   58. *Descartes to Elisabeth, Stockholm, 9 October 1649*

429   Madam,
Having arrived in Stockholm four or five days ago, I regard it as
a prime duty to renew the offer to Your Highness of my most humble service, so that you may know that the change of air and place
can change or diminish nothing of my devotion and zeal. I have
had the honour of seeing the queen only twice; but it seems to me
that I already know her sufficiently to dare to say that her merit is no
less and her virtue even greater than reputation proclaims. Alongside

the nobility and majesty that shine forth from all her actions, she displays a gentleness and kindness that compel all who love virtue and who come close to her to be entirely devoted to her service. One of the first things she asked me was whether I had heard from you, and I did not hesitate to say right away what I thought of Your Highness; for having observed her strength of mind, I had no fear of arousing any 430 jealousy by doing so, just as I am confident that I shall arouse none in Your Highness by freely expressing my opinion of the queen. She is very much given to the pursuit of learning:* but since, to the best of my knowledge, she has had no acquaintance with philosophy, I cannot judge whether she will take to it, or whether she will have the time to study it; and therefore I do not know whether I will be capable of satisfying her or benefiting her in any way. Her great enthusiasm for learning is prompting her especially to devote herself to studying the Greek language and to collecting a great number of ancient books; but that, perhaps, will pass. Even if it does not, the virtue I observe in this queen will always oblige me to put the concern to be of service to her above the desire to please her; so that nothing will inhibit me from frankly expressing my opinions; and if these fail to please her (although I do not think they will), then I shall at least have the advantage of having done my duty, and, moreover, a reason to return all the sooner to my solitude, when I am away from which it is difficult to make progress in the search for truth; which is for me the principal good in this life. At Herr Freinsheimius'* prompting, Her Majesty has agreed that I need never go to the palace, except at the hours she thinks fit to set aside* for me to have the honour of speaking to her; thus, I shall not find it troublesome to pay court to her, which suits my temperament very well. But when all is said and done, although I have 431 great veneration for Her Majesty, I do not think that there is anything capable of keeping me in this country longer than the start of next summer; but I cannot absolutely answer for the future. I can only assure you that I shall all my life be, &c.

59. *Elisabeth to Descartes, 4 December 1649* [AT 5]

Monsieur Descartes, 451
Your letter of 29 September/9 October took a roundabout route through Cleves;* but old though it is, it is nonetheless most agreeable,

and a most gratifying proof of the continuation of your kindness for me; it convinces me also that your journey will turn out well, since the reason for it justifies the trouble of making it and since you find even more marvellous qualities in the queen of Sweden than her reputation suggests. But one must admit that you are more capable of recognizing them than the people who up to now have taken it upon themselves to proclaim them. And it seems to me that I know her better, from the little you say of her, than from all I have heard about her from other sources. Do not, however, think, that so favourable a description gives me any cause for jealousy; on the contrary, it gives me reason to value

452 myself a little more than I did before your description conveyed to me the idea of so accomplished a person, who liberates our sex from the slur of weakness and helplessness that pedants have fastened upon it.* I am confident that when she has once tasted your philosophy, she will prefer it to their philology.* But it strikes me as remarkable that the queen finds it possible to apply herself to study as she does, and also to the affairs of her kingdom, two such different occupations, each of which requires a whole person. As to the honour she did me in your presence of calling me to mind, I attribute it entirely to her intention of being obliging to you, by giving you an opportunity to practise a charity to which you have given public expression on many other occasions; this benefit I owe to you, as I shall also owe you, if I gain it, the benefit of having a share of her approval, which I shall have all the better chance of preserving since I shall never have the honour of being known by Her Majesty otherwise than as you represent me. Yet I feel myself guilty of a crime against her interests, in that I am very pleased that your extreme veneration for her will not compel you to remain in Sweden. If you leave the country this coming winter, I hope it will be in the company of Herr Kleist,* which would be the most convenient way of giving the happiness of seeing you again to

Your most affectionate friend at your service,

ELISABETH

My last letter was dated 10/20 November.*

PRINCIPLES OF PHILOSOPHY

PART I

To the Most Serene Princess Elisabeth, first-born daughter of
Frederick, king of Bohemia, count Palatine and elector of the
Holy Roman Empire*

Most Serene Princess,

The greatest benefit I have received from the writings I previously
published is that you deigned to read them through, and that, having
come by their means to be admitted to your acquaintance, I recognized your gifts to be such that I deem it to be for the benefit of the
human race to lay them before future ages as an example. It would ill
beseem me either to flatter, or to make an assertion based on insufficient insight, in this place of all, in which I am about to attempt to
lay the foundations of truth; and I know that the plain and unaffected
judgement of a philosopher will be more pleasing to your noble modesty than the more elaborate praises of men more given to flattery.
For this reason I shall write here only those things I know to be true,
whether by reason or by experience, and in this preface I shall philosophize in the same way as in the rest of the book.

There is a great distinction between true and merely apparent
virtues; and also, among the true ones, between those derived from
an accurate knowledge of things and those conjoined with a certain
ignorance. By 'merely apparent virtues', I mean certain vices that are
not very common, and that are contrary to other more familiar ones:
for because these vices are further away from their opposites than the
virtues that stand in the middle,* they are therefore customarily more
widely celebrated. Thus, because more people are found who fly in
terror from danger than who hurl themselves thoughtlessly into it,
rashness is set against cowardice as if it were a virtue, and commonly
more highly valued than true courage; thus, spendthrifts are often
more highly esteemed than people who are generous;* and thus
no one more easily attains a great reputation for piety than superstitious people or hypocrites.

But among the true virtues, many are derived not purely from the
knowledge of what is right, but even from some error; thus, kindness often arises from naivety, piety from fear, and courage from
desperation. And these differ from one another, as, indeed, they are
known by different names: but the pure and genuine virtues, which
flow purely from the knowledge of what is right, all have one and

the same nature, and are brought together under the single name of wisdom.* For whoever has a firm and effective will always to use his reason rightly, to the best of his ability, and to perform whatever he knows to be best,* is truly wise, as far as his nature permits him to be; and as such he possesses justice, fortitude, temperance, and all the other virtues, but so conjoined together, that none of them is more prominent than any other; and therefore, although these virtues are far more excellent than those which are marked by some tincture of vice, nonetheless, because they are less well known to the multitude, they are not usually celebrated with such praise.

Moreover, two things are required for virtue as thus described, that is to say, perception by the intellect and propensity of the will. Now, no one indeed is incapable of the part that depends on the will, but some people have a far more perspicacious intellect than others. And although it should be sufficient for those who are not naturally very bright, that, despite their ignorance of many things, provided they do at least maintain a firm and constant intention to neglect no means of attaining to a knowledge of what is right, and to put into practice all their judgements of what is right, they can be, within their own limits, wise and as such most pleasing to God; nonetheless, those people are far more admirable in whom we find, along with an utterly firm will to act rightly, a most perspicacious intellect and an absolute commitment to discovering the truth.

That Your Highness's commitment to this is absolute, is crystal-clear from the fact that neither the distractions of the court nor the typical upbringing that generally condemns girls to ignorance have been able to prevent you from exploring all the worthy arts and sciences. Moreover, the supreme and incomparable perspicacity of your intellect appears from the fact that you have delved most deeply into all the innermost parts of those sciences, and acquired an accurate knowledge of them in the briefest possible time. Yet I have a still stronger proof of it, peculiar to myself, that you are the only person I have ever found who has a perfect understanding of all the treatises I have previously published. For to most other people, even those who are highly intelligent and erudite, they seem to be very obscure. For it happens with almost everyone that, if they are versed in metaphysics, they loathe geometry; but if they have made a study of geometry, they cannot grasp my metaphysical writings; I recognize only your intelligence as one to which everything is equally clear, and that is the reason why I call it, as it deserves to be called, incomparable. But when I consider that this varied and perfect knowledge of all things is to be found not in some aged gymnosophist,* who has had many years to devote to contemplation, but in a young princess, who in her beauty and her youth recalls not grey-eyed Minerva* or one of the Muses,* but rather one of the Graces,* I cannot but be lost in utter wonderment.

Finally, not only as regards knowledge, but also as regards the will, I observe that there are none of the qualities required for the most absolute and lofty wisdom that do not shine forth in your behaviour. For it displays a blend of exceptional kindness and gentleness with supreme dignity, challenged by the perpetual injustices of fortune,* but never blighted or broken. These qualities have so won me over that not only do I judge that this philosophical work of mine should be dedicated and consecrated to the wisdom that I revere in you (since philosophy itself is nothing other than the quest for wisdom), but also I would wish to be spoken of no more as a philosopher than as

> Your Serene Highness's
> Most devoted worshipper,
> DES-CARTES

*Letter to the translator of this book, which may here serve as a Preface.**

Sir,

The translation of my *Principles* that you have taken the trouble to produce is so clear and so accomplished that it gives me hope that they will be read more widely in French than in Latin, and that they will be better understood. My only anxiety is that the title may deter a number of people who have not been academically educated* or who have a low opinion of philosophy, on the grounds that the philosophy they have been taught did not satisfy them. This is why I believe that it would be useful to provide a preface setting out the subject of the book, what intention I had in writing it, and what benefits may be derived from it. But although I should be the one to write this preface, since I should know all that better than anyone else, the most I can bring myself to do is to give a brief statement here of the main points I think it should contain and I leave it to up your judgement whether you decide to release this to the public or not.

First of all, I would have wanted to begin with an explanation of what philosophy is, beginning with the most commonplace points: for instance, that the word 'philosophy' means the study of wisdom, and 'wisdom' here does not simply mean prudence in practical life but, rather, a perfect knowledge of everything a human being can know, both as regards the conduct of life, and as regards the preservation of health and the discovery of arts;* and that, in order for this knowledge to be perfect, it must be deduced from primary causes; so that if we are to make the effort to acquire it (which is what philosophy really means), we must start by seeking for those primary causes, that is, the principles;* and that these principles must meet two requirements: first, they must be so clear and evident that the human mind cannot doubt of their truth when it sets itself attentively to consider them; and, secondly, the knowledge of other things must depend on them, in such a way that they can be known independently of these other things, but that these other things cannot be known independently of them; and that we must then seek to deduce from these principles the knowledge of the things that depend on them, in such a way that there is nothing in the whole deductive sequence that is not completely manifest. Only God himself is truly wise; that is to say, only he has a perfect knowledge of all things; but one can say that human beings have more or less wisdom, in proportion to their knowledge of the more important truths. And there is nothing, I think, in all this with which any learned person would not concur.

I would then have turned to the benefits of this philosophy, and would have shown that, since it covers all that the human mind can know, we should regard it as the only thing that differentiates us from the most savage and barbarous peoples; and that the better a nation's philosophers, the more civilized and polite* that nation is; and therefore that nothing benefits a state more than having true philosophers.* Besides, from the point of view of an individual person, it is not only useful to live among people committed to this study, it is incomparably better to engage in it oneself; just as it is better to use one's own eyes to guide oneself, and so enjoy the beauty of colour and light, than to keep them closed and follow the guidance of another person. But even that is better than keeping them closed, when one has no one else to guide one. To live without philosophizing is tantamount to living with one's eyes closed, without making any effort to open them; and the pleasure of seeing all those things that are revealed to us by our eyesight cannot be compared with the satisfaction that comes from knowing everything that is to be discovered with the help of philosophy; and, finally, in order to live according to a standard* and to find our way in this life, we need philosophy even more than we need our eyes in order to walk straight.* The brute beasts, who have only their body to preserve, are continually engaged in supplying it with nourishment; but human beings, whose principal part is their mind, should devote their main efforts to the quest for wisdom, which is the true food of the soul; and I am, moreover, confident that there are many who would not fail in this quest, if they had hope of succeeding and if they realized how capable they were of doing so. There is no soul so devoid of nobility and so captivated by the things of the senses, that it does not on occasion turn aside from them in the search for some higher good, even though it frequently has no idea in what that good consists. The favourites of fortune, who have health, honour, and wealth in abundance, are no more exempt from this desire than anyone else; on the contrary, I am convinced that no one yearns more than they for a higher good, supreme above all those that they possess. Now, this supreme good, from the point of view of natural reason, without the enlightenment of faith,* is nothing other than the knowledge of truth by means of its primary causes, that is to say, wisdom, the study of which is philosophy. And because all these things are entirely true, it would not be difficult to convince people of them, if they were set out in an orderly fashion.

But since we are hindered from believing them by experience, which shows us that those whose profession is philosophy are often less wise and reasonable than others who have never engaged in this study, I would have added here a succinct explanation of the state of our present knowledge and of the degrees of wisdom we have attained. The first degree contains only those notions that are so clear in themselves that they can be acquired without meditation. The second includes whatever we learn through sense-experience. The third, whatever we learn from our dealings with other people. To this we may add a fourth, the reading, not of all books, but especially of those by people capable of giving us good instruction, for this is a kind of conversation with their authors.* And it seems to me that the whole of wisdom, such as it is customarily acquired, is acquired only in these four ways (for I leave divine revelation out of account here, since it does not lead us on by degrees, but raises us all at once to an infallible belief). Now, since the beginning of history there have been great men who have sought to discover a fifth degree in the attainment of wisdom, one incomparably loftier and more certain than the first four; they sought the first causes and the true principles from which it is possible to deduce the reasons for everything we are capable of knowing. It is particularly those who have laboured towards this end that are known as philosophers. And yet to my knowledge none of them up to now have achieved their goal. The first and most important of them whose writings we have are Plato and Aristotle, between whom the only difference is that the former, following in the footsteps of his master Socrates, frankly confessed that he had not yet been able to discover anything certain, and had contented himself with writing down what seemed to him to be probable, imagining for this purpose a number of principles by means of which he tried to explain everything else; whereas Aristotle was less candid, and, although he had been Plato's disciple for twenty years, and his principles were identical to Plato's, he adopted a completely different manner of delivering them, and put them forward as true and certain, although it is highly improbable that he really believed them to be such.* Now these two men were highly intelligent and had a great deal of the wisdom that is acquired by the four means mentioned above, and this gave them great authority, so that those who came after them confined themselves to following their opinions rather than looking for something better. And the main point of controversy between their disciples was whether everything should be doubted, or whether there were some things that were certain. This led to egregious errors on either side. For some of the advocates of doubt extended it even to the actions of life, so that they did not govern their behaviour by common prudence;* and those who upheld the claims of certitude, supposing that it must depend on the senses, put their faith entirely in these; so much so that we are told that Epicurus maintained, in the face of all astronomical reasoning, that the sun is no bigger than it appears.* This is a failing that may be observed in most controversies, in which truth occupies a middle ground between the two opinions being asserted, but each party moves further away from it the harder it tries to contradict the other. But the error of those who inclined overmuch towards doubt was not followed for long, and that of their opponents has been somewhat corrected, inasmuch as it has been acknowledged that the senses deceive us in many things. And yet, it has not, to my knowledge, been entirely eliminated by the proof that certitude is to be found, not in the senses, but in the pure understanding, when it has evident perceptions;* and that, while we have only the knowledge that can be acquired through the first four degrees of wisdom, we should not doubt what appears true, as regards the conduct of life,* but, at the same time, should not regard it as so certain that we cannot change our minds, when compelled to do so by some evident reason. It is because they have failed to acknowledge this truth, or, if any of them have acknowledged it, to act upon it, that, in recent centuries, most would-be philosophers have blindly followed Aristotle, so that they have often distorted the meaning of his writings, crediting him with various opinions that he would never recognize as his own, if he were to come back to this world; and those who have not followed him (among whom there have been many great minds) still had his opinions drummed into them when young (because these are the only opinions that are taught in the Schools), which left them with so many preconceptions that they have been unable to attain the knowledge of the true principles. And although I respect all of them, and do not wish to make myself odious by criticizing them, I can offer a proof of my views that I do not think any of them could deny, namely, that they all have taken as a fundamental principle something their knowledge of which was imperfect. For instance, there are none of them that, to my knowledge, do not suppose that terrestrial bodies have heaviness; but although experience shows us very clearly that the bodies we call heavy fall towards the centre of the earth, we still do not know the nature of this so-called heaviness; that is, we do not know the cause or principle that makes bodies behave in this way, and we have to seek this knowledge elsewhere. The same applies to the void and to atoms, to hot and cold, dry and moist,* to salt, sulphur, mercury, and all the similar things that have been identified as fundamental principles. Now, any conclusion deduced from a principle that is not evident cannot itself be evident, even if the deduction itself is evident;* from which it follows that all the reasoning that philosophers have based on such principles has failed to afford them a certain knowledge of anything, and failed, therefore, to help them a single step further along the road to wisdom. And if they have found any truths, it was only by means of one or more of the four ways described above. And yet I do not want to take away any of the honour to which any of them can lay claim; but I am simply obliged to say, in order to reassure those who have never studied, that just as if, during a journey, you turn your back on your destination, you get further away from it the further and faster you walk, so that, even if you afterwards get yourself back on the right path, you cannot arrive as soon as you would have done if you had not first marched in the wrong direction; likewise, when you start from bad principles, the more you cultivate them and the more carefully you set about drawing various conclusions from them, in the belief that this is the right way to philosophize, the further away you are getting from the knowledge of truth and wisdom. From this we must infer that those who have acquired the least knowledge of everything that has been called philosophy up to now are the most capable of learning the true philosophy.

After having fully explained all these things, I would have wished to indicate the reasons that prove that the true principles, by means of which we may attain that highest degree of wisdom in which the sovereign good of human life consists, are the ones set out in this book. There are two of them and they are quite sufficient. The first is that the principles in question are very clear, and the second that everything else can be deduced from them; for these are the only conditions they need to meet. Now, it is an easy matter to prove that they are very clear. Firstly, by the manner in which I discovered them, that is, by rejecting everything in which I could find the slightest grounds for doubt; for it is certain that those things that, when the effort was made to consider them, were impossible to reject in this way, are the most evident and clear the human mind can know. Thus, when we consider that a person who wishes to doubt everything cannot, however, doubt that he exists, while he is doubting, and that whatever reasons in this way, being unable to doubt itself and yet doubting everything else besides, is not what we call our body, but what we call our soul or our mind,* I took the being, or existence, of this thinking agency* as my first principle, from which I very clearly deduced the following: that there is a God, who is the creator of everything that exists in the world, and who, being the source of all truth, did not endow us with an understanding of such a kind that it can be mistaken in its judgement of things of which it has a very clear and distinct perception. These are the only principles I use as regards immaterial or metaphysical entities. From them I very clearly deduce the principles of bodily or physical entities, namely, that there are bodies extended in length, breadth, and depth, which have various shapes and which move in various ways. These are, in short, the only principles from which I deduce the truth of other things. The second reason that proves these principles clear is that they have been known in all ages, and even accepted by all human beings* as true and indubitable, the only exception being the existence of God, which has been called into question by some, because they have set too much store by sense-perceptions and God can be neither seen nor touched. But although the truths I have enshrined among my principles have been known by everyone in every age, no one until now, to the best of my knowledge, has recognized them as the principles of philosophy, that is to say, as being such that from them we can deduce the knowledge of everything else in the world. This is why it remains for me here to prove that they are such. And it seems to me that there is no better way of doing so than to appeal to experience: I mean, by inviting my readers to read this book. For although I have not covered everything in it (which would be impossible), I think I have explained everything I have had occasion to discuss in such a way that those who read attentively will have good reason to be convinced that, in order to access the highest kinds of knowledge of which the human mind is capable, there is no need to go searching for any other principles besides those I have given here; especially if, having read my writings, they take the trouble to consider how many and how varied are the problems that are there resolved, and if, having also looked through other people's books, they observe how few plausible reasons are put forward there for attempting to resolve them by principles different from mine. And to facilitate my readers' efforts, I could have pointed out that those who have absorbed my principles find it much easier to understand other people's writings, and to evaluate them correctly, than those who have not absorbed them. This is the very opposite of what I said earlier in connection with those who have begun by studying the old philosophy, that the more deeply they have studied it, the less capable, as a rule, they are of assimilating the new one properly.

I would also have added a word of advice about how to read this book. I would suggest reading it all the way through, like a romance,* without greatly straining one's attention, or being held up by any difficulties one encounters, so as simply to get a general idea of the subjects discussed. Afterwards, if one decides that these are worthy of examination, and is curious to know the causes of them, it can be read a second time, so as to follow the sequence of my arguments; but, again, one should not let oneself be put off, if one loses the thread now and again, or if one does not understand all the arguments; simply mark with a pen the places one has found difficult, and read on to the end without a break. Then if one goes back to the book a third time, I venture to say that one will find the solution to most of the difficulties one has noted the previous time; and if any still remain, a final re-reading should put paid to them.

Having examined the characteristics of many categories of intelligence,* I have observed that there are almost none so coarse or so sluggish, that they were incapable of assimilating the correct views, and even of mastering the most lofty sciences, if properly directed. And this can also be proved by reason; for since the principles are so clear, and one should deduce nothing from them save by very evident reasoning, anyone has enough intelligence to understand what follows from them. But, not to mention the hindrance of prejudices,* from which no one is altogether free, although they are most damaging to those who have most deeply studied the bad sciences,* it almost always happens that those of a moderate disposition do not take the trouble to study because they think themselves incapable, whereas the more enthusiastic ones are in too much of a hurry; as a result they often accept principles that are by no means evident, and draw unreliable conclusions from them. This is why I would wish to assure those who lack confidence in their ability that there is nothing in my writings that they will be unable to understand completely if they take the trouble to examine them; and at the same time, however, to warn other readers that even the finest intelligences will need a good deal of time and attention if they are to register everything I have aimed to cover in my works.

Following that, in order to give a clear idea of my goal in publishing this work, I would wish to explain here the proper order one should follow in the search for knowledge. First of all, a person who has got no further than the common and imperfect knowledge that may be acquired by the four means described above should, before anything else, attempt to formulate a moral code sufficient to regulate the actions of his life,* since this is a matter that does not admit of delay, and we should try, above all, to live a good life. After that, he should also study logic: not that of the Schools, for it is, strictly speaking, no more than a dialectic* that teaches one how to pass on to others what one already knows, or even how to find something to say, without any exercise of judgement, about matters of which one knows nothing; it therefore corrupts good sense, rather than increasing it. The logic I mean teaches one to guide one's reason properly in order to discover truths one did not know; and because it takes a good deal of practice, he should spend a long time training himself in it, by applying its rules to straightforward and simple problems, such as those of mathematics. Then when he has got somewhat used to discovering the truth in problems of this kind, he should start applying himself in earnest to philosophy properly so called. The first part of it is metaphysics, which contains the principles of knowledge, including the explanation of the principal attributes of God, and of the immateriality of our souls, and of all the clear and simple notions we find in ourselves. The second part is physics, in which, having found the true principles of material things, we examine in general the composition of the universe as a whole, then, in particular the nature of this earth and of all the bodies most commonly found in proximity to it, such as air, water, fire, magnets, and other minerals. Following which we need also to examine the nature of plants, of animals, and above all of man, so as to be able subsequently to discover the other sciences that are useful to him. Thus, the whole of philosophy is like a tree, the roots of which are metaphysics and the trunk physics, while the branches that grow from the trunk are all the other sciences, which may be reduced to three principal ones, namely, medicine, mechanics, and ethics (by which I mean the highest and most perfect ethics*), which, since it presupposes a comprehensive knowledge of the other sciences, is the ultimate degree of wisdom.

Now, just as it is not from the roots or the trunks of trees that we gather their fruits, but only from the tips of their branches, so the principal benefit of philosophy likewise depends on the parts of it that can only be learned last. But although I know these hardly at all, yet my lifelong zeal to be of service to the public led me, ten or twelve years ago,* to publish a few essays as samples of the things I thought I had learned. The first part of these essays was a *Discourse on the Method of Correctly Conducting One's Reason and Seeking Truth in the Sciences*, where I set out in summary form the main rules of logic and of an incomplete morality, which one may follow on an interim basis, for as long as one does not know a better one. The other parts were three treatises: one on *Dioptrics*, one on *Meteorology*, and finally one on *Geometry*. In the *Dioptrics*, my aim was to show that we could make great progress in philosophy, sufficient to enable us to discover arts that are useful for life, my example being the invention of the telescope, which I explained in the treatise, and which is one of the most difficult ever achieved. In the *Meteorology*, my aim was to bring out the difference between the philosophy I am developing and that of the Schools, where the same subject is commonly discussed. Finally, in the *Geometry*, I sought to demonstrate that I had discovered many things that nobody knew before, and thus to provide good cause to think that many more are waiting to be discovered, intending thus to encourage all human beings to take up the search for truth. Since then, foreseeing how difficult many people would find it to understand the foundations of metaphysics, I attempted to explain the principal points in a book of *Meditations*, which is not very long, but which has been expanded by the objections sent to me* by many very learned people and my own replies to them—by means of which the content of the book has been greatly clarified. Then, finally, when it seemed to me that these previous treatises had adequately prepared the minds of readers to receive the *Principles of Philosophy*, I published these as well, dividing the book into four parts. The first deals with the principles of knowledge, in other words, first philosophy or metaphysics; which is why, in order to understand it properly, it is a good idea to read beforehand my *Meditations* on this subject. The three other parts deal with all the most general elements of physics, namely, the explanation of the primary laws or principles of nature, and the composition of the heavens, the fixed stars, the planets, comets, and generally the whole of the universe; then, in particular, the nature of this earth, and of air, water, fire, and magnets, which are the bodies most commonly to be found in its proximity, and of all the qualities to be observed in these bodies, such as light, heat, heaviness, and so forth. By means of all this I believe I have gone some way to explaining the whole of philosophy in an orderly fashion, without having omitted anything that should have gone before the last subjects I deal with. But to fulfil my plan completely, I would afterwards need to explain in similar fashion the nature of the more specific bodies to be found on earth, namely, minerals, plants, animals, and, above all, human beings; and then, finally, give a precise account of medicine, ethics, and mechanics. I would have to do all this if I am to give my fellow creatures a comprehensive body of philosophy; and I do not feel myself so old, I do not so lack confidence in my powers, I do not find myself so far from the knowledge of what remains to be dealt with, that I would not venture to attempt to fulfil my plan, provided I had the opportunity to carry out all the experiments needed to support and validate my arguments.* However, seeing as I do that these would require heavy expenditure, impossible for a private person like myself, except with support from the public, and being unable to see any prospect of such support, I think that from now on I should be satisfied to study for my own personal edification, and that posterity will excuse me if from now on I cease to work on its behalf.

However, to show why I think I have already been able to be of service to posterity in certain ways, I will here list the benefits that I am convinced may be derived from my *Principles*. The first is the satisfaction of finding many truths revealed there that were unknown before now; for although often the truth does not appeal to our imagination as strongly as falsehoods or fictions, because it appears simpler and less striking, nonetheless the contentment it gives is far more lasting and more solid. The second benefit is that by studying these *Principles* the reader will gradually become accustomed to judging more accurately in all situations, and will thus become wiser. In this way their effect will be the opposite of that of the common philosophy; which, as is easy to observe in the case of those we call pedants,* leaves people less capable of reasoning than they would be if they had never studied it. The third is that the truths it contains, being very clear and certain, will eliminate all sources of dispute, and will thus dispose people's minds to gentleness and harmony: whereas, by contrast, since the controversies of the Schools imperceptibly render those who are trained in them more stubborn and more prone to quarrel over trifles, they are, perhaps, the prime cause of the heresies and disagreements that nowadays plague the world. The last and most important fruit of these *Principles* is that those who work on them may discover many important truths that I have not explained,* and thus, by gradually moving from one to the next, may acquire over time a perfect knowledge of philosophy and ascend to the highest degree of wisdom. For, as we see with all the arts,* that, though at their origins they are crude and imperfect, yet, because they contain an element of truth the effect of which is shown by experience, they gradually develop towards perfection; so it is, that when one has true principles in philosophy, one cannot fail, if one follows them, to come upon further truths; and there is no better proof of the falsity of Aristotle's principles than the fact that no progress based on them has been made in the many centuries during which they have been followed.

I know that some people are so impatient-minded, and so little given to circumspection in what they do, that even on very solid foundations they can build nothing stable; and because these are the type of people who are generally the most likely to rush into print, they might in a very little time ruin everything I have done, and bring uncertainty and doubt into my manner of philosophizing, from which I have carefully attempted to banish them, if their writings were accepted as if they were mine or as filled with my opinions. I have had experience of this not long since in the case of one of those people* who were most firmly believed to be committed followers of mine, and of whom I had somewhere gone so far as to write that 'I placed so much trust in his mind that I did not think he had any opinion that I would not be very willing to accept as my own.' Last year he published a book entitled *Fundamentals of Physics*, in which, although the material on physics and medicine seems to have come entirely from my own writings, both those I have published and another, as yet unfinished, about the nature of animals which came into his posses- sion, yet because he transcribed it incorrectly and rearranged it, and denied certain metaphysical truths* on which the whole of physics depends, I am compelled to disavow it altogether, and to request my readers here never to credit me with any opinion unless they find it explicitly stated in my writings, and to accept no opinion, whether they encounter it in my own writings or elsewhere, as true unless they very clearly see that it follows from the true principles.

I know very well, moreover, that many centuries may go by until all the truths that can be deduced from these principles have been deduced, because the greater part of those that remain to be discovered depend on some specific observations the opportunity for which will never arrive by chance, only by deliberate experiments carried out by highly intelligent people with great care and at great expense; and because it will seldom be the case that the people with the ability to make good use of them will have the resources to carry them out; and also because the majority of highly intelligent people have formed such a low opinion of philosophy in general, on account of the many flaws they have observed in the one that has held the field until now, that they will be unable to commit themselves to the search for a better one. But if in the end the difference they will find between these principles and everybody else's, and the long sequence of truths that may be deduced from them, enable such people to realize how important it is to continue the search for these truths, and how they can lead us to so high a degree of wisdom, so perfect a way of life, and such happiness, I venture to think that none of them will fail to engage in so beneficial a study, or at least to favour and to wish to help with all their power those who are fruitfully engaged in it. My hope is that our descendants will see the successful outcome of this.

PRINCIPLES OF PHILOSOPHY

PART I

ON THE PRINCIPLES OF HUMAN KNOWLEDGE

1. *The seeker after truth must once in his life doubt everything as far as possible.*
Because we came into the world as children, and passed various judgements* on sensible things before we had the full use of our reason, we are diverted from the knowledge of the truth by many prejudices. From these it seems that we can be released only if, once in our life, we make an effort to doubt everything in which we shall find even the slightest suspicion of uncertainty.

2. *What is doubtful must be treated as false.*
Indeed, it will be useful to treat the things we are doubting as actually false, so that we may all the more clearly discover something very certain and very easy to know.*

3. *In the meantime this doubt is not to be applied to the conduct of life.*
But this doubt in the meantime is to be restricted only to the contemplation of the truth. For as far as the conduct of life is concerned, because very often the opportunity to do what has to be done would disappear before we had time to rid ourselves of our doubts, we are often obliged to accept what is only probable;* indeed, sometimes, even if, of two possibilities, neither appears more probable than the other, we have to opt for one or other of them.*

4. *Why we can doubt sensible things.*
Now, therefore, since we are committed purely to the search for truth, we shall doubt first of all whether any sensible or imaginable things exist. First, because we sometimes observe that the senses are in error, and it is prudent never to put too much trust in those who have deceived us even if only once; secondly, because every day in our dreams we seem to perceive or imagine countless objects that exist nowhere; and, to one who doubts in this way, no signs present themselves by which he may certainly distinguish sleep from waking.

5. *Why we can also doubt mathematics.*

We shall also doubt all those other things we previously regarded as most certain; even mathematical proofs, and even those principles we have up to now regarded as self-evident: first, because we have at one time or another seen many people making mistakes in such matters, and accepting as most certain and self-evident things that to us seemed false; secondly, and most importantly, because we have heard that there is a God who is all-powerful and by whom we were created. For we do not know whether perhaps he has decided to create us such that we are always in error, even about things that appear to us to be most certainly known; because this does not seem any less possible than that we should sometimes be deceived, which we have previously known to occur. And if we imagine that our existence depends not on an all-powerful God, but either on ourselves, or on some other being, then the less powerful we suppose whatever cause there is of our existence, the more plausible it will be that we are so imperfect as to be always deceived.

6. *We have free will, so as to be able to refrain from assenting to what is doubtful, and thus to avoid error.*

But, in the meantime, whatever is the source of our being, and however powerful and deceptive it is, we nonetheless know by experience that we have freedom, so that we can always abstain from believing in whatever is not fully certain and properly investigated; and thus we can take care never to be mistaken.

7. *It is not possible for us to doubt that we exist, while we are doubting; and this is the first thing we discover by philosophizing in an orderly fashion.*

Now, rejecting in this way all those things of which we can somehow doubt, and imagining even that they are all false, we readily suppose indeed that there is no God, no sky, no bodies; and that we ourselves do not have hands and feet, or, in short, a body at all; but we do not for all that suppose that we, who are thinking such things, are nothing; for it is self-contradictory to hold that what thinks, while it is actually thinking, does not exist. And therefore this piece of knowledge, *I am thinking, therefore I am*, is the very first and the most certain that presents itself to anyone philosophizing in an orderly fashion.*

8. *The distinction between the soul and the body, or between the thing that thinks and the bodily thing, is hence recognized.**

And this is the best path that leads us to the recognition of the nature of the mind and its distinction from the body. For when we examine what we are, we who are supposing that everything that is distinct from us is false, we see very clearly that no extension, or shape, or local motion, or any similar property of bodies belongs to our nature, and that only thought does, which is accordingly known prior to and more certainly than any bodily thing; for we have already perceived it, and yet we are still doubting everything else.

9. *What thought is.**

By the term 'thought' I mean everything that takes place in us, while we are aware (*nobis consciis*), in so far as there is awareness (*conscientia*) of it in us. And thus not only understanding, willing, and imagining, but also perceiving by the senses, are the same here as thinking. For if I say, I am seeing, or I am walking, therefore I exist; and I am referring to sight or walking as bodily acts, the conclusion is not an absolutely certain one; because, as often occurs in dreams, I may be thinking I am seeing or walking, even though I do not have my eyes open and am not moving from one place to another, and indeed, even though, perhaps, I have no body at all. But if I mean the actual perception or awareness (*sensu sive conscientia*) of seeing or walking, because the reference is then to the mind, which by itself perceives or thinks that it is seeing or walking, the conclusion is completely certain.

10. *What is extremely simple and self-evident is rendered more obscure by logical definitions; and such things are not to be counted as belonging to the knowledge obtained by study.*

I do not here explain many other terms that I have already used, or will use in what follows, because they seem to me to be sufficiently self-evident. And I have often observed philosophers at fault in this, that they were seeking to explain by logical definitions things that were extremely simple and self-evident;* for in this way they actually made them more obscure. And when I said that the proposition, *I am thinking, therefore I am*, is the very first and the most certain that presents itself to anyone philosophizing in an orderly fashion, I did not therefore deny that we had to know other things beforehand, *what* *thought is, what existence is, what certainty is*; and also, *that it cannot come about that what is thinking does not exist*, and so forth; but because these are extremely simple notions that, by themselves, provide knowledge of no existing thing, I therefore deemed that they should not be counted as knowledge.*

11. *In what way our mind is better known to us than the body.*
But now, to make plain how our mind is known not only prior to, and more certainly than, the body, but also more evidently, we should observe that it is absolutely manifest by the natural light* that nothingness has no modifications (*affections*) or qualities; and therefore wherever we discover some modifications or qualities, there will necessarily be found some thing or substance to which they belong; and the more of them we discover in a single thing or substance, the more clearly we know it. But that we can discover more of them in our mind than in any other thing is plain from this, that nothing at all can cause us to know something other than our mind without at the same time bringing us, much more certainly, to the knowledge of our own mind. For instance, if I judge that the earth exists, from the fact that I am touching it or seeing it, certainly, on the same grounds, I should judge all the more that my mind exists; for it could perhaps be the case that I judge that I am touching the earth, even though no earth exists; but it cannot be that I should judge this, and that at the same time my mind that makes the judgement should be nothing; and so on and so forth.*

12. *Why it does not become known equally to everyone.*
Why those who have philosophized in a disorderly fashion have taken a different view is purely and simply because they have never distinguished the mind from the body with sufficient care. And even if they thought that they were more certain that they themselves existed than that anything else did, they failed, however, to realize that 'they themselves' here should be taken to refer to their minds alone; but, on the contrary, they took it as referring only to their bodies, which they saw with their eyes and felt with their hands, and to which they falsely attributed the power of sensation; and this distracted them from perceiving the nature of the mind.

13. *In what sense the knowledge of other things depends on the knowledge of God.*

Now, when the mind, which knows itself and is still doubting about everything else, looks round in all directions, so as to extend its knowledge further, it first of all finds in itself the ideas of many things. As long as it merely contemplates these, and neither affirms nor denies that there is anything resembling them outside itself, it cannot be deceived. It also finds certain common notions,* and from these constructs various demonstrations;* as long as it directs its attention to these, it is entirely convinced that they are true. Thus, for instance, it has in itself ideas of numbers and shapes, and among the common notions, it has *If you add equals to equals, the sums will be equal,** and suchlike. From these it is easy to demonstrate that the three angles of a triangle are equal to two right angles,* and so forth. And it therefore considers these and similar conclusions to be true, as long as it directs its attention to the premises from which it has deduced them. But because it cannot always be attentive to them, when it afterwards remembers that it does not yet know whether perhaps it has been created with such a nature that it is deceived even in matters that appear very obvious to it, it sees that it is right to be doubtful about such things, and that it can have no certain knowledge, until it has identified the source of its existence.

14. *From the fact that necessary existence is contained in our concept of God, it necessarily follows that God exists.*

When the mind, then, considers that among the various ideas it has in itself there is one—that of a supremely intelligent, supremely powerful, and supremely perfect being—that stands out from all the rest, it recognizes that existence is contained in this idea; not only possible and contingent existence, as in the ideas of all the other things it distinctly perceives, but absolutely necessary and eternal existence. And just as, on the basis of its perception that, for instance, having three angles equal to two right angles is necessarily contained in the idea of a triangle, the mind is perfectly convinced that a triangle has three angles equal to two right angles; so, purely on the basis of its perception that necessary and eternal existence is contained in the idea of a supremely perfect being, it must conclude that a supremely perfect being exists.*

15. *Necessary existence is not contained in the same way in the concepts of other things, only contingent existence.*

It will believe this all the more firmly, if it reflects that the idea of no other thing can be found in it, in which it perceives necessary existence to be contained in the same way. For from this it will understand that this particular idea of the supremely perfect being has not been invented by itself, and that it has nothing chimerical about it,* but represents a true and immutable nature, one that cannot not exist, since necessary existence is contained within it.

16. *It is on account of prejudices that the necessity of God's existence is not clearly recognized by all.*

This, I say, will be readily believed by our mind, if it has first freed itself altogether from prejudices. But because we are accustomed to distinguishing essence from existence* in all other things, and also to arbitrarily inventing various ideas of things that do not exist anywhere, and never have, it can readily occur, when we are not fully focused on the contemplation of the supremely perfect being, that we doubt whether perhaps the idea of it is one of those we have invented arbitrarily or, if not that, one of those to the essence of which existence does not belong.

17. *The greater the objective perfection* of any one of our ideas, the greater its cause must be.*

But when we further consider the ideas we have in ourselves, we see, indeed, that these do not much differ from one another in this respect, that they are all certain modes of our thinking,* but that they differ greatly in that one represents one thing, another another thing; and the more objective perfection they contain in themselves, the more perfect their cause must be. For instance, if someone has in himself the idea of some extremely complicated machine, it is reasonable to ask what is the cause of his having it: has he somewhere or other seen such a machine, constructed by someone else? Or has he so thorough a grasp of mechanics or so much intellectual power that, without ever seeing one anywhere, he thought up the idea of it himself? For the whole of the complexity that is contained in that idea purely objectively, as if in a picture, must be contained in the cause of it, whatever that cause may be, not only objectively or representatively, at least as far as its first and principal cause is concerned, but in actual reality, formally or eminently.*

18. *From this we can again infer that God exists.*
Thus, because we have the idea of God, or the supreme being, in ourselves, we can justifiably investigate the cause of our having it; and we shall find in it so much immensity that we are fully certain as a result that it cannot have been implanted in us except by a thing in which there is in reality a full set of all perfections, that is, an actually existent God. For it is completely manifest by the natural light, not only that nothing can come of nothing, and that what is more perfect cannot be produced by what is less perfect, acting as its total and efficient cause;* but also that there can be within us no idea or image of any thing, without there also being some archetype* that exists somewhere or other, whether in our own minds or outside us, and that contains in reality all the perfections of that thing. And because we in no way discover within ourselves these supreme perfections of which we possess the idea, from this alone we rightly conclude that they exist (or, certainly, existed at some time in the past) in something distinct from us, namely, in God; from which it follows very plainly, that they still exist.*

19. *Even though we cannot understand the nature of God, his perfections are still more clearly known to us than any other thing.*
And this is sufficiently certain and plain to those who are accustomed to contemplating the idea of God and his supreme perfections. For although we do not understand these, because it is indeed of the nature of the infinite not to be comprehensible to finite beings like ourselves, nonetheless we can understand them more clearly and distinctly than any corporeal thing, because they fill our thoughts more, and are more simple, nor are they obscured by any limitations.*

20. *We do not exist of ourselves, but were made by God, and therefore he exists.*
But because not everyone recognizes this, and because, whereas those who have the idea of some complicated machine usually know from where they acquired it, we, however, do not likewise remember the idea of God having come to us from God at some particular time, inasmuch as we have always had it, the question still arises,

where our own existence, as beings having an idea of the supreme perfections of God, comes from. For certainly it is entirely manifest by the natural light that a thing that knows something more perfect than itself does not exist of itself: for it would have given itself all the perfections of which it has an idea in itself; nor, again, can it derive its existence from any other being that does not have all these perfections in itself, that is, that is not God.

21. *The continuation of our own existence suffices to demonstrate the existence of God.*

And nothing can obscure the clarity of this proof, as long as we direct our attention to the nature of time or the duration of things;* which is such that its parts do not depend on one another, nor ever exist simultaneously; and therefore from the fact that we now exist, it does not follow that we shall exist at the moment of time immediately following, unless some cause, which must be the same as produced us in the first place, continually reproduces us, so to speak, that is, preserves us. For we can easily see that we have no power in ourselves by which we could preserve ourselves in existence; and that the being that possesses such great power as to preserve us, who are distinct from it, must all the more certainly preserve itself, or rather does not need to be preserved by any being; and in short it is God.

22. *From our manner of discovering the existence of God, we discover at the same time all those of his attributes that are knowable by the natural power of our intelligence.*

Now there is a great advantage to this manner of proving the existence of God, namely, by the idea of him:* because at the same time we recognize what he is, in so far as the weakness of our nature is capable of this. For, indeed, when we turn our attention to this idea which is innate within us, we see that he is eternal, omniscient, omnipotent, the source of all goodness and truth, the creator of all things, and in short that he possesses in himself everything in which we can clearly discern some kind of perfection that is infinite, in other words limited by no imperfection.

23. *God is not corporeal, nor does he have sensations like ourselves, nor does he will the malice of sin.*

For certainly there are many things in which even if we recognize some degree of perfection, we nonetheless detect an element of imperfection or limitation; and these are therefore incompatible with God. Thus, because the nature of a body includes divisibility along with extension in space,* and it is an imperfection to be divisible, it is certain that God is not a body. And although it is in ourselves a kind of perfection to perceive by the senses, yet because in all sensation there is a passive element, and to be passive is to depend on something else, we cannot suppose that God has sensations, but only that he understands and wills—not, moreover, like us, by operations that are in some way distinct, but in such a way that, through one single, always selfsame, and utterly simple action, he simultaneously understands, wills, and produces all things. All *things*, I mean: for he does not will the malice of sin, because this is not a thing.*

24. *From the knowledge of God we can progress to the knowledge of creatures, bearing in mind that he is infinite, and we are finite.*
But now, because God alone is the true cause of all that exists or can exist, it is patently clear that we shall be following the best philosophical path, if we attempt to deduce from the knowledge of God himself the explanation of the things he has created, so as to acquire the most perfect kind of knowledge, that of effects by their causes. In order to undertake this task with sufficient safety and with no risk of going astray, we must make use of this precaution: always to bear in mind to the best of our ability both that God, the author of all things, is infinite, and that we are altogether finite.

25. *We must believe all that is revealed by God,* even when it exceeds our mental capacities.*
Thus, supposing God reveals to us something about himself or about something else that exceeds the natural powers of our understanding, such as, for instance, the mysteries of the Incarnation and the Trinity, we shall not refuse to believe them, even though we do not clearly understand them. Nor shall we be in any way surprised that there are many things, both in the immensity of his nature and also in the things he has created, that exceed our mental capacities.

26. *We should never dispute about the infinite; we should merely regard those things in which we observe no limits, such as the extent of the*

universe, the divisibility of the parts of matter, the number of the stars,
and so on, as indefinite.

In this way we shall never be troubled by arguments about the infinite. For certainly, being finite as we are, it would be absurd of us to make definite statements about the infinite, and thus to attempt, so to speak, to enclose and comprehend it. Therefore, we shall not trouble to answer those who ask whether, supposing a line to be infinite, the half of it would also be infinite, or whether an infinite number is even or odd, and so on and so forth; because no one, it seems, ought to think about these things, except those who think their own minds to be infinite. For our part, however, we shall not assert that those things in which, from some point of view or other, we can find no limit are infinite; we shall, rather, consider them as indefinite. Thus, because, however great an extension we can imagine, we always understand that it could be still greater, we shall say that the magnitude of possible things is indefinite. And because, however many parts a given body can be divided into, we understand that each individual part is still divisible, we shall think that quantity is indefinitely divisible. And because, however great a number of stars we imagine, we believe that yet more could be created by God, we shall suppose that the number of stars is indefinite; and so on and so forth.

27. *The difference between infinite and indefinite.*

And we shall call these things indefinite rather than infinite;* first, so as to reserve the name 'infinite' for God alone, because, in him alone and in every respect, not only do we recognize no limits, but we also positively understand that there are none; secondly, because we do not positively understand in the same way that some other things are devoid of limits in some respect; we only accept, in a negative manner, that their limits, if they have any, cannot be discovered by us.

28. *We should examine not the final causes of created things, only the efficient ones.**

Hence, therefore, we shall never look for explanations of natural things derived from the end God or nature had in view when producing them; for we should not claim so much for ourselves as to think we are party to his counsels. But considering him as the efficient cause of all things, we shall observe what the natural light he has implanted in us shows us we ought to conclude from those of his attributes of which he has wished us to have some knowledge, as regards those of his effects that appear to our senses; yet we should be mindful, as has been stated above [I. 25], that this natural light is to be trusted only so far as it contradicts nothing revealed by God himself.

29. *God is not the cause of errors.*

The first of God's attributes that we should bear in mind here is that he is supremely truthful, and the giver of all enlightenment; so that it is plainly self-contradictory that he should deceive us, or that he should strictly and positively be the cause of the errors to which we know ourselves by experience to be subject. For although, perhaps, to be able to deceive seems to be, among us human beings, a sort of proof of intelligence, certainly the will to deceive never originates in anything other than malice or fear and weakness, and therefore it can never be found in God.

30. *And from this it follows that everything we clearly perceive is true, and the doubts listed above are removed.*

And from this it follows that the natural light, or the faculty of knowing given us by God, can never grasp any object that is not true, in so far as it is grasped by it, that is, in so far as it is clearly and distinctly perceived. For he would justifiably be termed a deceiver if the faculty he had given us were distorted, and apprehended what is false as being true. This puts paid to the extreme doubt that was based on the idea that we did not know whether perhaps our nature was such that we should be deceived even in things that appear to us to be perfectly evident. And, indeed, all the other reasons for doubting listed above are also easily removed with the help of the same principle. For mathematical truths should no longer be suspect to us, because they are supremely clear. And if we bear in mind what is clear and distinct in sensation, in the waking state, and in dreams, and distinguish it from what is confused and obscure, we shall easily recognize what in each case should be regarded as true. Nor is there any need to discuss these matters here at any more length, since they have been already dealt with in various ways in the *Meditations on First Philosophy*, and a fuller explanation of them depends on the knowledge of what follows.

31. *Our errors are only negations if considered in relation to God, privations in relation to ourselves.**

But because, even though God is no deceiver, it nonetheless often happens that we are mistaken, then if we are to investigate the origin and cause of our errors, and learn to avoid them in advance, we must realize that they depend less on the understanding than on the will; nor are they things to the production of which the real concourse of God is required;* but when they are considered in relation to him, they are only negations, and in relation to ourselves, privations.

32. *There are only two modes of thinking in us, namely, the perception of the intellect and the operation of the will.*

Now all the modes of thinking that we experience in ourselves can be reduced to two general kinds, one of which is perception, or the operation of the understanding, while the other is volition, or the operation of the will. For sensation, imagination, and pure understanding are only different modes of perception; just as to desire, to reject, to affirm, to deny, to doubt, are different modes of willing.

33. *We make mistakes only when we pass judgement on a matter we have insufficiently perceived.**

Now, when we perceive something, provided only that we do not definitely affirm or deny anything of it, it is plain that we are not making a mistake; and nor, also, are we doing so when we affirm or deny only what we clearly and distinctly perceive must be affirmed or denied;* but only when (as sometimes happens), even though we do not perceive something correctly, we nonetheless pass judgement on it.

34. *Not only the intellect but also the will is required in the act of judgement.*

And the intellect is certainly required for an act of judgement, because we can pass no judgement on what we do not perceive in any way; but the will is also required, in order to assent to the thing that has been perceived in some way. But a full and comprehensive perception of the thing is not essential to the making of some kind of judgment; for we can assent to many things that we know only very obscurely and confusedly.

35. *The will ranges further than the intellect, and this is the cause of our errors.*

Moreover, the perception of the intellect extends only to the few things that are presented to it, and it is always thoroughly finite. But the will may be said, in a sense, to be infinite, because we never observe anything that can be the object of some other will, even the immense will that is in God, to which our own does not also extend;* so much so, that we readily extend the will beyond those things we clearly perceive; and when we do this, it is hardly surprising that we occasionally fall into error.

36. *God cannot be held responsible for our errors.*

In no way, however, can God be imagined to be the author of our errors, on the grounds that he has not given us an omniscient intellect. For it is of the nature of a created intellect that it is finite; and of the nature of a finite intellect that its range is limited.

37. *The supreme perfection of a human being is to act freely, or at will; and to be worthy of praise or blame as a result.*

But that the will's range is extremely broad is also in accordance with its nature; and there is one supreme perfection in man, that he acts at will, that is, freely, and thus, in a distinctive manner, he becomes the author of his actions, and deserves praise in respect of these. For we do not praise automata for precisely displaying all the movements for which they have been designed, because they display them of necessity; but we do praise their designer, who has made them so elaborate, because he made them not necessarily but freely. By the same token, because, when we embrace the truth, we do so voluntarily, we certainly deserve more credit for embracing it than we would if we could not help embracing it.

38. *Our errors result from a flaw in our behaviour, not in our nature; and though the faults of subordinates can often be attributed to other masters, they can never be blamed on God.*

But our falling into error is a flaw in our behaviour, or in the use of our freedom, not in our nature, inasmuch as our nature is one and the same when we judge wrongly as when we judge rightly. And although God could have given us such perspicacity of intellect that we were never mistaken, we cannot possibly demand this of him as of right.

And, though among us human beings we say that if someone has the power of preventing some evil and does not do so, he is the cause of it, we cannot similarly think that God is the cause of our errors just because he could bring it about that we are never mistaken. For the power that some human beings have over others was established for this purpose, that they should use it to draw their fellow humans away from evil; but the power that God has over all creatures is absolute and free in the highest degree; therefore, we certainly owe him our deepest gratitude, for the good things he has bestowed on us; but we are not at all entitled to complain because he has not bestowed everything upon us that we recognize he could have done.

39. *The freedom of the will is self-evident.*

But that there is freedom in our will, and that there are many things to which we can assent or not assent, as we choose, is so manifest that it must be listed among the primary and most common notions that are innate within us. And this was particularly manifest to us a little while ago, when we were striving to doubt everything, and got to the point of imagining that some all-powerful author of our being was trying to deceive us in all possible ways; nonetheless, we experienced ourselves as having the freedom to be able to abstain from believing in everything that was not entirely clear and certain. And nothing can be more self-evident and more clearly perceived than the things which at that time appeared to us as beyond doubt.

40. *It is certain that all things have been preordained by God.*

But because we now acknowledge God, and perceive him as being possessed of such immense power that we should think it wrong to suppose that anything could be done by us that was not ordained by him beforehand, we can easily become enmeshed in great difficulties, if we attempt to reconcile this divine preordination with the freedom of our will, and to grasp them both simultaneously.

41. *How the freedom of our will and divine preordination can be reconciled.*

But we shall be able to extricate ourselves from these, if we bear in mind that our mind is finite; whereas the power of God, through which he has not only known from all eternity all that exists or can exist, but has also willed and preordained all things, is infinite; and that therefore we can grasp it sufficiently to perceive clearly and distinctly that it exists in God, but do not comprehend it sufficiently to see how it can leave free human actions undetermined; but that we are so aware of the freedom and indifference* that exists in us that there is nothing we comprehend more clearly and perfectly. For it would be absurd if, just because we do not comprehend a thing that we know must be of its nature incomprehensible to us, we doubted another thing, which we do comprehend from inside and experience in ourselves.*

42. *How we make mistakes even though we do not want to make mistakes.*
But now, since we know that all our errors derive from our will, it may seem strange that we should ever make mistakes, since there is no one who wants to be mistaken. But there is a great difference between wanting to make a mistake and wanting to assent to something that happens to involve error. And although there is in fact no one who expressly wishes to make a mistake, there is scarcely anyone who does not often willingly assent to things in which, unbeknownst to him, an error is contained. Indeed, the very desire to attain the truth often causes those who do not rightly know how it is to be attained to pass judgement on things they do not perceive, and thus to fall into error.

43. *We are never mistaken when we assent to what we perceive with sufficient clarity and distinctness.*
Yet it is certain that we shall never accept anything false as true, provided that we give our assent only to what we clearly and distinctly perceive. I say it is certain, because, since God is no deceiver, the faculty of perception he has given us can have no tendency to falsehood. Nor, likewise, can the faculty of assent, when it encompasses only what is clearly perceived. And even if no proof could be provided for this, there is a natural instinct implanted in our souls, in virtue of which, whenever we clearly perceive something, we spontaneously assent to it, and cannot doubt in any way that it is true.

44. *We always judge badly when we give our assent to what is not clearly perceived, even if by chance we stumble upon the truth; and the cause of this is that we suppose that we formerly had a sufficient perception of the matter.*
It is also certain that, when we assent to some reason we do not perceive, we either make a mistake or stumble purely by chance upon the

truth, and hence do not know that we are not mistaken. But, indeed, it rarely happens that we give our assent to what we realize is not perceived by us, because the natural light dictates to us that we should never pass judgement except about what we have knowledge of. On the other hand, we very frequently go astray for this reason, that we think that many things were once perceived by us, and to these, lodged in our memory, we give our assent as if we had properly perceived them when in fact we have never perceived them at all.

45. *What clear and distinct perception is.*
Yet there are a great many people who actually never in their lives perceive anything sufficiently accurately to be able to pass judgement on it with certainty. For in fact, for a perception to be the basis of a certain and indubitable judgement, it must be not only clear, but also distinct. By a 'clear' perception I mean one that is present and manifest to the mind attending to it: thus, we say that we see something clearly when it is present to the perceiving eye and affects it sufficiently strongly and manifestly. But by a 'distinct' perception I mean one that, as well as being clear, is so separated and cut off from all others that it contains absolutely nothing that is not clear.*

46. *The example of pain makes clear how a perception can be clear, even though not distinct; but it cannot be distinct, unless it is clear.*
For instance, while someone is feeling a severe pain, there is a very clear perception of pain in him; but it is not always a distinct one; for people commonly confuse it with an obscure judgement they make about its nature, because they think that in the afflicted part there is something similar to the perception of pain, which is all that they clearly perceive.* And thus a perception can be clear, and yet not distinct; but it can never be distinct, unless it is clear.

47. *In order to correct the prejudices of childhood, we must consider simple notions and what is distinct in each of them.*
And, indeed, in childhood our mind was so immersed in the body that, although it perceived many things clearly, it never perceived any distinctly; and since, nonetheless, it passed judgement on many things, we thus imbibed many prejudices, which many people subsequently never discard. But in order that we may liberate ourselves from them, I will here summarize all the simple notions from

which our thoughts are constructed; and in each of them I will distinguish what is clear from what is obscure, or liable to give rise to error.

48. *Whatever falls under our perception is regarded either as a thing (or a modification of a thing*) or an eternal truth; plus a list of things.*
We consider whatever falls under our perception either as a thing, or a certain modification of a thing; or as an eternal truth, having no existence outside our thought.* As regards what we consider as things,* the most general notions are *substance, duration, order,* and *number,* and any other ones of this kind, which are applicable to all kinds of things.* However, I acknowledge no more than two fundamental categories of thing; first, that of intellectual or mental things, that is, those that pertain to the mind or thinking substance; secondly, that of material things, or, in other words, those that pertain to extended substance, that is, to a body.* Perception, volition, and all the modes of perceiving or willing are predicated of thinking substance; while size, or extension in length, breadth, and depth, shape, motion, position, divisibility of parts, and so forth, are predicated of extended substance. But we experience certain other things in ourselves that should be ascribed neither to the mind alone nor to the body alone, and that, as will be shown in the proper place, derive from the close and intimate union of our mind with the body; namely, the appetites of hunger and thirst, and so forth; and also the emotions, or passions* of the soul that do not consist of thought alone, such as being aroused to anger, joy, sadness, love, and so forth; and finally, all our sensations, such as pain, pleasure* (*titillatio*), light and colours, sounds, smells, tastes, heat, hardness, and the other tactile qualities.

49. *The eternal truths cannot be listed in this way, but do not need to be.*
And we consider all these as things, or qualities or modes of things. But when we recognize that it cannot be that anything should come from nothing, then this proposition, *Of nothing, nothing comes*, is considered not as some existing thing, nor even as the mode of a thing, but as a certain eternal truth, that has its seat in our minds, and is called a common notion, or axiom. Examples of this are: *It is impossible for the same thing to be and not to be at the same time*; *What has happened, cannot not have happened*; *One who is thinking cannot not exist while he is thinking*; and innumerable others.* It would certainly be hard to list these all in their entirety, but it would also be hard not to

know them, when we are thinking about them and are not blinded by any prejudice.

50. *Even though these truths are clearly perceived, they are not all perceived by everyone, on account of prejudices.*

And indeed, with regard to these common notions, there is no doubt that they can be clearly and distinctly perceived, for otherwise it would be wrong to call them 'common notions'; and in fact some of them are not equally deserving of the name as far as some people are concerned, because they are not equally perceived by everyone. This is not, to my mind, because one man's faculty of knowledge is more extensive than another's;* but because, perhaps, these common notions clash with the preconceived opinions of certain people, who therefore cannot grasp them easily; even though many other people, who are free of these prejudices, perceive them with the greatest clarity.

51. *What substance is; and that the term does not apply univocally to God and to creatures.*

As for what we consider as things or modes of things, it is well worth while examining these separately.* By 'substance' we can only mean a thing that exists in such a way that it needs no other thing in order to exist.* And, indeed, one substance only can be understood as needing no other thing at all, namely, God. But we perceive that all other things can exist only by means of the divine concourse.* And therefore the name 'substance' does not apply to God and to them univocally, as they commonly put it in the Schools:* that is, no meaning of this term can be distinctly understood that is common to both God and creatures.*

52. *That the term 'substance' applies univocally to mind and body, and how it can be known.*

However, corporeal substance and the created mind, or thinking substance, can be brought together under this common concept: that they are things that need only God's concourse in order to exist. Yet substance cannot be primarily identified purely in virtue of its being an existent thing, because this, as such, does not by itself affect us;* but we can easily recognize it from some attribute it has, in virtue of the common notion that where there is nothing, there are no attributes, and no properties or qualities. For we conclude, from our perception that some attribute is present, that some existing thing, or substance, to which that attribute can be credited, is necessarily present also.

53. *Each substance has one principal attribute, thought in the case of mind, extension in that of body.*

And, indeed, substance can be known through any of its attributes; but there is, however, one principal property of each substance,* which constitutes the nature and essence of that substance, and to which all other attributes are subordinated. Thus, extension in length, breadth, and depth constitutes the nature of corporeal substance; and thought constitutes the nature of thinking substance. For everything else that can be ascribed to a body presupposes extension, and is only a certain mode of an extended thing;* and, likewise, everything we discover in the mind is only one of the various modes of thinking. Thus, for instance, we cannot conceive of shape except in an extended thing, or motion except in an extended space; nor can we conceive of imagination, or sensation, or will except in a thinking thing. But, on the contrary, we can conceive of extension without shape or motion, and thought without imagination or sense-perception, and so on; as will become evident to anyone who considers the matter carefully.

54. *How we can have clear and distinct notions of thinking and corporeal substance, and also of God.*

And thus we can easily obtain two clear and distinct notions or ideas, one, of created thinking substance, the other, of corporeal substance, if, that is, we carefully distinguish all the attributes of thought from the attributes of extension. Likewise, we can have a clear and distinct idea of an uncreated and independent thinking substance, in other words, God; provided we do not suppose that it adequately discloses everything that is in God, and do not foist on it further properties imagined by ourselves, but concentrate only on the properties that are really contained in it, and which we clearly perceive to belong to the nature of the supremely perfect being. And certainly no one can deny that such an idea of God exists within us,* except one who thinks that there is no knowledge of God whatever in human minds.

55. *How duration, order, and number are also distinctly understood.*

We can also form a very distinct conception of *duration*, *order*, and *number* if we do not foist any concept of substance on them, but consider the duration of each thing as only a mode, in the light of which we conceive that thing, in so far as it continues to exist. And likewise, we shall not suppose that order and number are anything distinct from things that are ordered or counted, but that they are only modes, in the light of which we consider those things.

56. *The meaning of 'modes', 'qualities', 'attributes'.*
And what we mean by 'modes' here is altogether the same as is elsewhere conveyed by 'attributes' or 'qualities'. But when we consider a substance as being affected or altered by these, we call them 'modes'; when the name we give it reflects this alteration,* we call them 'qualities'; and, finally, when, more generally, we consider only that these things are inherent in the substance, we call them 'attributes'. And thus we cannot, strictly speaking, say that there are modes or qualities in God, only attributes, for we understand that there is no variation in him. And likewise, in created things those of their properties that never admit of variation,* like existence and duration, in a thing that exists or endures, should be called, not modes or qualities, but attributes.

57. *Some attributes exist in things, others in thought. The nature of duration and time.*
Some of these, however, exist in the things themselves of which they are called attributes or modes; but others exist only in our thought. Thus, when we distinguish time from duration in the most general sense, and say that it is the measure of movement,* it is only a mode of thought; for we certainly do not conceive one kind of duration in movement and another in things that are not moved; as is plain from this, that, if two bodies are moved for an hour, one swiftly, the other slowly, we do not count a greater quantity of time in the former than in the latter, although much more motion has taken place. But in order to measure the duration of all things, we measure it against the duration of the greatest and most regular movements, which give rise to the years and the days; and we call this duration 'time'. Hence this adds nothing, beyond a mode of thought, to duration in its most general sense.

58. *Number and all universals are only modes of thought.*
Likewise, too, when we consider number not in any particular created

things but only in the abstract or generically, it is merely a mode of thought. The same applies to all other so-called 'universals'.*

59. *How universals are formed; and of the five best-known ones: genus, species, differentia, property, accident.*

Universals are formed purely from this, that we use one and the same idea in thinking about all individuals that resemble one another; we likewise apply one and the same term to all the things represented by this idea. This term is a 'universal'. Thus, when we see two stones, and direct our attention not to their nature, but purely to the fact that there are two of them, we form the idea of that number we call 'two'. And when subsequently we see two birds or two trees, and consider, not their nature, but only the fact of there being two of them, we summon up the same idea as before, which is, in consequence, a universal; likewise, we call this number by the same universal name 'two'. In the same way, when we consider a shape formed by three lines, we form a certain idea of it that we call the idea of a triangle;* and we use the same idea afterwards as a universal in order to represent to our mind all other shapes comprising three lines. And when we observe that among triangles there are some that have one right angle, and others that do not, we form the universal idea of a right-angled triangle, which, considered in relation to the former more general idea, is called a 'species'. And this right-angledness is the universal 'differentia',* by which all right-angled triangles are distinguished from the rest. And because in these triangles the square of the base is equal to the squares of the other two sides, this is a 'property' that belongs exclusively to these triangles. And finally, if we suppose that some triangles of this kind are moving, while others remain at rest, movement will be a universal 'accident' of these triangles.* And in this way we arrive at the five generally recognized universals: genus, species, differentia, property, accident.

60. *On distinctions, and first of all, real distinctions.*

But number in things* arises from the distinction between them. Distinction takes three forms: 'real', 'modal', and 'mental'.* A *real* distinction, strictly speaking, exists only between two or more substances; and we perceive them to be really distinct from one another on this account alone, that we can clearly and distinctly conceive one without the other. For, recognizing that there is a God, we are certain that he can produce whatever we distinctly conceive; so much so that, for example, the fact that we currently have an idea of extended or corporeal substance, even though we do not know for certain if any such substance exists in reality, is nonetheless sufficient for us to be certain that it can exist; and that, if it does exist, whatever part of it we separate out in our thought* is really distinct from the other parts of the same substance. By the same token, from the fact that everyone understands himself to be a thinking thing, and can think away every other substance from himself, it is certain that everyone, considered from this point of view, is really distinguished from every other thinking substance and from all bodily substances. And even if we suppose that God has so closely conjoined some bodily substance with some such thinking substance that they could not be more closely united, and thus that he has fused these two substances into a single entity,* they nonetheless remain really distinct; because, however closely he has united them, he cannot divest himself of the power he previously had to separate them, or to preserve one without the other; and two things that can either be separated, or preserved separately, by God, are really distinct.

61. *On modal distinctions.*

The *modal distinction* takes two forms, namely, first, the distinction between a mode in the strict sense and the substance of which it is a mode, and, secondly, the distinction between two modes of the same substance. We apprehend the first kind when we can definitely perceive a substance clearly without the mode we say is distinct from it, but cannot, on the other hand, conceive the mode without the substance. Thus, there is a modal distinction between shape and motion, on the one hand, and the bodily substance in which they inhere, on the other; likewise, between assertion and remembering, on the one hand, and the mind, on the other. We apprehend the second, on the other hand, when we can definitely recognize one mode without the other, and vice versa, yet neither of them without the substance in which they inhere. So, for instance, if a stone is moving and square, I can certainly conceive its square shape independently of its motion, and conversely its motion independently of its square shape: but I can conceive neither the motion nor the shape independently of the substance of the stone. However, the distinction in virtue of which a mode of one substance differs from another substance (as the motion of one body differs from another body, or from a mind) or from a mode of another substance (as motion differs from duration*) ought to be classified as real rather than modal;* because these modes are not clearly conceived independently of the really distinct substances of which they are modes.

62. *On mental distinctions.*
Finally, there is a mental distinction between a substance and some one of its attributes without which it cannot itself be conceived, or between two such attributes of a single substance. We apprehend it when we cannot form a clear and distinct idea of that substance, if we separate that attribute from it; or when we cannot clearly perceive the idea of one attribute of this kind, if we separate it from another. For instance, because, if a given substance ceases to endure, it ceases to exist, the distinction between the substance and its duration is purely mental; likewise, there is a purely mental distinction between all the modes of thought which we consider as being in objects and the objects themselves, as there is between all these modes in the same object.* I recall that I once, in the Replies to the First Objections to the *Meditations*,* ran this distinction together with the modal kind; but on that occasion there was no need for a rigorous distinction between the two, since it was sufficient for my purpose to distinguish them both from real distinctions.

63. *How thought and extension may be distinctly known, as constituting the nature of mind and body.*
Thought and extension may be considered as constituting the natures of intelligent substance, on the one hand, and corporeal substance, on the other. In that case, they should be conceived only as the thinking substance and the extended substance themselves, that is, as mind and body; by which means they will be most clearly and distinctly understood. Indeed, we have a better understanding of extended substance or thinking substance than of substance by itself, irrespective of its thinking or being extended. For it is far from easy to abstract the notion of substance from the notions of thought or extension, which in fact can be distinguished from it only mentally; and a concept does not become more distinct by our including fewer things in it, but only in our carefully distinguishing what we include in it from everything else.

64. *And how they may also be known as modes of substance.**

Thought and extension can also be regarded as modes of substance, in so far, that is, as one and the same mind can have many distinct thoughts; and one and the same body, while retaining the same quantity, can be extended in many diverse ways; that is, at one moment it can be extended further lengthwise, and diminished in breadth or depth, and immediately after, on the contrary, its breadth can be increased and its length diminished. Moreover, they are both distinguished modally from substance, than which they can be understood no less clearly and distinctly, provided that they are considered not as substances, or certain things separate from others, but only as modes of things. For by this means, because we are considering them as in the substances of which they are modes, we distinguish them from the substances themselves, and recognize what they are in reality. Whereas, on the contrary, if we tried to consider them independently of the substances in which they inhere, we would *ipso facto* be considering them as subsistent things, and thus confusing the ideas of mode and substance.

65. *The proper way to know their modes as well.*

For the same reason, we shall best understand the different modes of thinking (such as understanding, imagining, remembering, willing, and so forth) and also the different modes of extension or pertaining to extension (such as shapes, and the position of their parts, and their motions), if we consider them purely as modes of the things in which they exist; and as far as motion is concerned, we shall best understand it if we consider purely movement in space and do not investigate the force by which it is produced (a matter I shall, however, explain in the proper place*).

66. *How sensation, emotion, and appetite may be clearly known, even though we often pass false judgements about them.*

There remain to be considered sensation, emotion, and appetite. These too can certainly be clearly perceived, if we take great care not to pass any judgement on them that goes further than what is exactly contained in our perception, and what we are intimately aware of. But it is very difficult to stick to this rule, at least where sensation is concerned; because every one of us has judged, from childhood on, that what he perceived by his senses was always some thing existing outside

his mind, and entirely similar to his sensations, that is, to the perceptions he had of them. So that when, for example, we saw colour, we
thought we were seeing a thing situated outside us* and entirely similar to the idea of colour* that we were then experiencing in ourselves;
and on account of the custom of judging in this way, we seemed to be
seeing this so clearly and distinctly that we regarded it as certain and
indubitable.*

67. *Even in judgements about pain we are often mistaken.*
The same is manifestly true of all our other sensations, even of pleasure (*titillatio*) and pain. For even if we do not suppose that these
exist outside ourselves, we do not usually consider them as being in our
mind alone, or in our perception, but as being in the hand or foot, or
some other part of our body.* And, indeed, when, for example, we feel
a pain apparently in our foot, it is not in the slightest more certain
that this is something outside our mind existing in our foot, than that,
when we see light apparently in the sun, this light exists outside ourselves in the sun; but both these beliefs are prejudices springing
from our childhood, as will clearly appear below.

68. *How in these sensations we should distinguish that which is clearly
known from that in which we may be mistaken.*
However, in order to distinguish what is clear from what is obscure,
we must take great care to fix in our minds that pain and colour and
everything else of this kind are clearly and distinctly perceived when
they are regarded purely as sensations or thoughts. When, however,
they are judged to be things existing outside our minds, it becomes
entirely impossible to understand what things they are; indeed, when
someone says that he sees colour in some body, or feels pain in some
limb, this is exactly the same as if he were saying that he sees or feels
something there, but does not in the slightest know what it is; in other
words, he does not know what he is seeing and feeling. For even if
he convinces himself, through inattention, that he has some knowledge of it, on the grounds that he supposes that there is something*
similar to that sensation of colour or pain he is experiencing in himself, if, however, he asks himself what it is that this sensation of colour or pain, apparently existing in the coloured body or the afflicted
part, actually represents,* he will well and truly realize that he does
not know.

69. *Size, shape, and so forth, are known in a completely different way from colours, pains, etc.*

This is especially true if he considers that in relation to the body he has seen, there is a very great difference between, on the one hand, his knowledge of its size, or shape, or motion (I mean local motion: for, by dreaming up various additional kinds of motion* distinct from motion in space, philosophers have only made it more difficult for themselves to understand the nature of motion), or position, or duration, or number, or any similar property, such as it has already been said are clearly perceived in bodies,* and, on the other hand, his knowledge of what it is in the same body that comes across as colour, or pain, or smell, or taste, or any other of those qualities I have said must be linked to our sensations. For even though, when we see some body, we are no more certain that it exists, in so far as it appears as having shape, than in so far as it appears coloured, we recognize far more clearly in it what it is to have shape than what it is to be coloured.

70. *We can form two judgements about sensible objects, by one of which we forestall error, whereas by the other we fall into it.*

It therefore appears that in practice it comes to the same thing when we say that we perceive colours in objects as if we said that we perceive something in objects, the nature of which we do not know, but by which a certain sensation is produced in us that is very vivid and clear, and that is called the sensation of colours.* But from the point of view of the judgements involved there is a very great difference. For as long as we judge only that there is something in objects (that is, in the things, whatever exactly they are, from which sensation comes to us), the nature of which we do not know, we are so far from being mistaken that in fact we are thereby protected from error; because when we realize there is something we do not know, we are all the less prone to pass rash judgements about it. But when we think we perceive colours in objects, even if in fact we do not know what it is that we are then referring to as 'colour', and cannot conceive any similarity between the colour we suppose to exist in the objects, and the colour we experience in our sensation, yet because we do not realize this, and there are many other factors, like size, shape, number, and so forth, in respect of which we clearly grasp that there is no difference between the way they are perceived or understood by us and the way they are or at least can be in reality, we easily fall into the error of judging that what we call 'colour' in objects is something entirely similar to the colour we perceive by our senses, and so supposing that we have a clear perception of something we do not perceive at all.

71. *The prime cause of our errors derives from the prejudices of childhood.* And hence we can recognize the first and most important cause of all error. The fact is that, in our earliest years, our mind was so tightly bound to the body, that it was free to attend only to the thoughts through which it perceived whatever was affecting the body. At that stage it did not yet refer these thoughts to anything situated outside itself, but only felt pain whenever something occurred that was harmful to the body, and pleasure whenever something beneficial occurred. And whenever the body was affected, but with no great beneficial or harmful effects, the mind had certain different sensations, which varied with the parts affected and the ways in which they were affected: namely, what we call sensations of taste, smell, sound, heat, cold, light, colour, and so forth, which represent nothing existing outside the mind.* And at the same time it perceived size, shape, motion, and so forth, which presented themselves to it not as sensations, but as certain things, or modes of things, existing (or at least capable of existing) outside our thought, even if it did not yet realize the difference between these.* And finally, when the mechanism of the body, which is so constructed by nature that it can move in various ways by its own power, turning itself around at random in one direction or another,* by pure chance pursued something beneficial or avoided something harmful, the mind attached to it began to notice that what it was thus pursuing or avoiding existed outside it; and to these things it ascribed not only different sizes, shapes, motions, and so forth, which it perceived as things or modes of things, but also tastes, smells, and so forth, the sensations of which it became aware were being produced in it by the things themselves. And since it related everything to the good of the body in which it was immersed, the more or less it was affected by any object, the more or less of a thing it took that object to be. Hence it came about that it thought that there was much more substance, or corporeality, in stones or metals than in water or air, because it felt more hardness and heaviness in the former than in the latter. In fact, as regards the air, as long as the mind was aware of no wind or cold or heat in it, it regarded it absolutely as non-existent.

And because no more light came to it from the stars than from the tiny flame of a lamp, it therefore could not imagine any stars greater in size than that flame. And because it did not observe the earth turning in a circle, or remark that its surface was curved so as to form a globe, it was all the more readily disposed to think both that it was immobile and that its surface was flat.* From earliest infancy, our mind was imbued with a thousand other prejudices of this sort, which then in later childhood we did not remember we had adopted without sufficient examination, and which we therefore accepted as completely true and evident, as if they had been discovered by the senses or implanted in us by nature.*

72. *Another cause of errors is that we cannot forget prejudices.*
And although, when we reach maturity, and the mind is no longer wholly subservient to the body, and does not relate everything to the body's point of view, but also seeks to discover the truth of things considered in themselves, it realizes that many of the judgements it formerly reached in this way are false; yet, for all that, it does not easily dislodge them from its memory, and as long as they are embedded there, they can continue to cause many errors. For example, since from our earliest infancy we imagined that the stars were tiny, then even though we now have astronomical proofs clearly demonstrating that they are immense, yet our preconceived opinion is still so deep-rooted, that it is extremely difficult for us to imagine them otherwise than we did before.*

73. *The third cause is that we find it tiring to concentrate on those things that are not present to the senses; and therefore we have become accustomed to judge of these, not on the basis of current perceptions, but from preconceived opinions.*
Besides, our mind cannot concentrate on anything without some difficulty and fatigue; and the difficulty is by far the greatest in concentrating on things that are not present to the senses, or even the imagination; whether because this is the mind's nature, on account of its being so closely joined to the body; or because in our earliest years, when the mind was dealing only with sensations and imaginations, it acquired the habit of thinking more, and more readily, about these than about other things. Hence, in any case, it comes about that many people have no conception of any substance that is not imaginable,

and bodily, and also perceptible to the senses. For they do not realize, either, that we can imagine only those things that consist in extension, motion, and shape, even though there are many other things that are intelligible besides these. Nor do they think anything can exist that is not a body; or, indeed, anything that is not a body perceptible to the senses. And because in reality we perceive no thing as it really is by our senses alone, as will clearly be shown below,* it so comes about that all through their lives most people perceive nothing, except confusedly.*

74. *The fourth cause is that we attach our concepts to words that do not properly correspond to things.*

And finally, in order to make use of speech, we attach all our concepts to words by which we express them, and when we entrust them to our memory, it is always together with the words. And since we remember words more easily than things, and scarcely ever have a concept of any thing so distinct that we can separate it from any concept of words, the thoughts of almost all human beings deal with words more than with things; so much so that they very often give their assent to terms they do not understand, because they think that they once understood them, or that they heard them from someone else who did properly understand them.* All these things cannot be thoroughly discussed at this point, because the nature of the human body has not yet been explained; nor has it yet been proved that any bodies exist;* but what has been said here appears to be sufficiently intelligible to help us to distinguish clear and distinct concepts from obscure and confused ones.

75. *A summary of all the rules to be observed in philosophizing correctly.*

Therefore, if we wish to practise serious philosophy, and to track down the truth of all knowable things, we must, first, set aside all our prejudices; in other words, refrain very carefully from putting our trust in any of the opinions we once accepted, unless, after a fresh investigation, we have first discovered them to be true. Secondly, we must reflect in a methodical fashion upon the notions we have in ourselves, and judge all those and only those to be true that, by means of this reflection, we clearly and distinctly know. If we do this, we shall first of all realize that we exist, in respect of our nature as thinking things; along with this, we shall realize also that God exists, and that we depend on him; furthermore, that the truth of all other things can be discovered by considering his attributes, since he himself is the cause of them; and finally, that there is within us, besides the notions of God and our own mind, the knowledge of many eternally true propositions (such as 'nothing can come from nothing'); likewise, the knowledge of a certain corporeal nature, which is extended, divisible, mobile, and so forth; and of various sensations that affect us, such as pain, colours, tastes, and so on, although we do not yet know the reason why they thus affect us.* Moreover, by comparing all this with our earlier and more confused thoughts, we shall acquire the habit of forming clear and distinct concepts of all knowable things. And it seems to me that these few precepts contain the key principles of human knowledge.

76. *Divine authority is to be given precedence over our perception; but, that apart, it is not fitting for a philosopher to assent to anything he has not perceived.*

But besides all these, we must thoroughly fix one paramount rule in our memory: that whatever God has revealed to us is to be believed as supremely certain. And even if perhaps the light of reason, at its brightest and most evident, may seem to suggest otherwise to us, we should nonetheless put our faith in divine authority, rather than in our own judgement. But in all matters of which divine faith has nothing to teach us, it is most unfitting for a philosopher to assume anything to be true that he has never perceived to be true; and to place more faith in his senses, that is, the unreflective judgements of his childhood,* than in his adult reason.

OTHER LETTERS

Reverend Father,

I know that it is very difficult to enter into another person's thoughts, and experience has taught me how difficult my own appear to many people; this is why I am highly obliged to you for the trouble you have taken to examine them; and I can only have the highest respect for you, seeing as I do that you have so assimilated them that they are now more yours than mine. And the difficulties you have chosen to put to me reside more in the subject matter and in my shortcomings as regards expression than in any shortcoming in your own intelligence; for your letter includes the solution of the most important ones. But I shall, all the same, give my views on all of them.

I readily admit that in the case of physical and moral causes which are particular and limited we often find by experience that those that produce a given effect are often incapable of producing several others that appear to us to be easier to produce. For instance, a human being, who can produce another human being, cannot produce an ant; and a king whose orders are obeyed by a whole people is sometimes unable to impose his will on a horse. But in the case of a universal and indeterminate cause it seems to me that it is a common notion* that *quod potest plus, potest etiam minus,** just as it is that *totum est maius sua parte.** And, indeed, this notion, properly understood, extends also to all particular causes, whether physical or moral: for it would be a greater thing for a human being to be able to produce both human beings and ants than to be able to produce only human beings; and a king would be more powerful who could command even horses than one who could command only his subjects; as the poets say* that the music of Orpheus could have an effect even on animals, so as to convey the fullest possible idea of its power.

It is not particularly important whether my second demonstration,* based on our own existence, is considered as different from the first, or merely as a fuller explanation of the first. But, just as my being created is an effect produced by God, so his implanting his idea in me is another of his effects; and there are none of his effects from which his existence cannot be demonstrated. Nonetheless, it seems to me that all these demonstrations from effect to cause come down to one and the same; and, indeed, that they are incomplete if the effects are not evident to us (this is why I chose to focus on my own existence rather than that of the heavens and the earth, of which I am not so certain*), and if we do not combine them with our idea of God. For since my soul is finite, I cannot know that the order of causes is not infinite, except in so far as I have within myself this idea of a first cause; and even if the idea of a first cause that preserves me in existence is accepted, I cannot say that this is God, unless I truly have the idea of God.* I hinted as much, but very briefly, in my Reply to the First Objections,* so as not to show disrespect for the views of others, since it is commonly admitted that *non datur progressus in infinitum;** but I myself do not accept this; on the contrary, I believe that *datur revera talis progressus in divisione partium materiae,** as will appear in my treatise on philosophy,* which has just finished printing.

As far as I know I have never definitely taken the view that God always does what he knows to be most perfect; and it seems to me that a finite mind cannot judge of this point. But I have tried to throw light on the difficulty put to me concerning the cause of errors,* by supposing that God created a most perfect world; because if we suppose the contrary, the difficulty disappears altogether.

I am very much obliged to you for pointing out the passages in St Augustine that might serve as authority for my views; some other friends of mine* had already done much the same; and I am highly satisfied that my thoughts should agree with those of so holy and distinguished a person. For I am by no means one of those people who want their opinions to appear new; on the contrary, I adapt my opinions to those of others, as far as truth allows me to do so.

I regard the difference between the soul and its ideas as exactly the same as that between a piece of wax and the various shapes it can take. And, just as the capacity of the wax to receive various shapes is not, strictly speaking, an action but a passion; so it appears to me that the soul's receiving this or that idea is also a passion;* and that its ideas are produced in it, partly by the objects that affect the senses, partly by impressions in the brain, and partly, also, by preceding dispositions in the soul and by the motions of its will; just as the wax receives its shapes, partly from the other bodies that exert pressure on it, partly from shapes or other qualities already in it, such as its being more or less heavy or soft, and partly also from its motion, when, having been agitated, it has within it the force to continue in motion.

As for our difficulty in learning the sciences, and in clearly representing to ourselves the ideas naturally known to us, this comes from the false prejudices of our childhood, and from the other causes of our errors, as I have tried to explain pretty fully in the book currently in press.*

As regards memory, I believe that the memory of material things depends on the traces that remain in the brain, after some image has been imprinted on it; and that that of intellectual things depends on certain other traces that remain in the mind (*pensée*) itself. But the latter are quite different in kind from the former, and I could not explain them by any example based on corporeal things that would not be very different from them; whereas the traces in the brain enable it to move the soul in the same way as it had moved it formerly, thus causing it to remember something; just as the creases in a piece of paper or linen cause it to be more easily folded thereafter in the same way as it was folded previously than if it had never been folded in 115 that way.

The moral error that occurs when we reasonably believe something that is false because a worthy man has told us it is the case involves no privation, when we assert it only so as to regulate the conduct of our life, in some matter where we are morally incapable of knowing better; and it is thus, strictly speaking, not an error.* But it would be one if we stated it to be true as a matter of physics, because here the witness of a worthy man is insufficient.

As far as free will is concerned, I have not seen what Father Pétau* has written on the subject; but to judge by the way in which you explain your opinion, it seems to me that mine is not very different from yours. For, first of all, I would point out to you that I did not say that man is indifferent only when he is lacking in knowledge; what I said is that he is all the more indifferent* the fewer reasons he is aware of for choosing one alternative rather than the other; and this, it seems to me, no one can deny. And I am in agreement with you, when you say that one can suspend one's judgement; but I tried to explain the reason why one can suspend it. For it is, it seems to me, certain that *ex magna luce in intellectu sequitur magna propensio in* 116 *voluntate*;* so that, when we see very clearly that something is beneficial for us, it is very difficult, and even, as I think, impossible, while we continue to think this, to check our desire for it. But, because the nature of the soul is such that it can be attentive to one and the same thing only for a moment, as soon as our attention is diverted from the reasons that tell us that the thing is beneficial for us, and we sim-ply remember that it appeared desirable to us, then we can come up with some other reason for doubting its beneficial quality, and thus suspend our judgement, or even form the opposite one. So, since you do not regard freedom as consisting precisely in indifference, but in a real and positive power of self-determination, the difference between our opinions is purely verbal; for I admit that this power exists in the will. But because I do not think that, when it is accom-panied by indifference, which you acknowledge to be an imperfection, it is different from what it is when not so accompanied, and because the understanding consists purely in enlightenment, as it does in the case of the blessed who are confirmed in grace, I apply the word 'free' to whatever is voluntary, whereas you wish to confine it to the power of self-determination when it is accompanied by indifference. But as far as terminology is concerned, I desire nothing so much as to follow common usage and examples.

117   As for irrational animals, it is plain that they are not free, because they do not have this positive power of self-determination; but not to be forced or compelled is, in them, a pure negation.

My only reason for not speaking of our freedom to pursue good or evil is that I wished, as far as possible, to avoid the controversies of theology, and to remain within the boundaries of natural philosophy. But I concede to you that wherever there is the possibility of sin, there is indifference;* and I do not think that, in order to act wrongly, we need to see clearly that what we are doing is wrong; it is sufficient that we see it confusedly, or merely remember that we formerly judged it to be wrong, without at all seeing that it was so; that is, without being attentive to the reasons that proved it to be so. For if we clearly saw that it was wrong, it would be impossible for us to sin, as long as we continued to see this; this is why they say that *omnis peccans est ignorans.** And our action is still meritorious,* even when, seeing very clearly what we ought to do, we infallibly do it, without any indiffer-ence, as was the case with Jesus Christ in this life. For since man is capable of not always being perfectly attentive to what he ought to do, it is a good action to be so attentive, and thus to ensure that our will follows the light of our understanding so closely that it is not in the least indifferent. Moreover, I did not write that grace entirely
118 suppresses indifference, only that it inclines us more in one direction

than in the other, and thus that it diminishes indifference without diminishing freedom; from which, it seems to me, it follows that freedom does not consist in indifference.

As for the difficulty of conceiving how God could have been free and indifferent when it came to making it false that the three angles of a triangle are equal to two right angles,* or, in general, that contradictories cannot simultaneously be true, this can readily be removed if we consider that the power of God can have no limits; and if we also consider that our mind is finite, and was created with such a nature that it can conceive as possible things that God wished to be possible in reality, but not with such a nature that it can also conceive as possible what God could have made possible but what, all the same, he chose to make impossible. For the first consideration reveals to us that God cannot have been determined to make it true that contradictories cannot simultaneously be true, and that, in consequence, he could have done the opposite; and the other convinces us that, even though that is true, we should not try to understand it, because our nature is not capable of doing so. And even if God wished it to be true that some truths are necessary, this does not mean that he necessarily wished them to be so; for it is one thing to will them to be necessary, and quite another necessarily to will them so, or to be necessitated to will them so. I readily admit that some contradictions 119 are so obvious that we cannot represent them to our minds without judging them to be entirely impossible; as in the example you put forward, 'that God could have brought it about that creatures were not dependent on him'. But we have no need to think of these in order to recognize the immensity of his power, nor should we conceive any precedence or priority of his understanding over his will or vice versa; for the idea we have of God teaches us that in him there is only a single act, utterly simple and pure; as is very well expressed in these words of St Augustine: *Quia vides ea, sunt, etc.** because in God *videre* and *velle** are one and the same thing.

I distinguish lines from surfaces, and points from lines, as one mode from another; but I distinguish a body from the surfaces, lines, and points that modify it as a substance from its modes. And there is no doubt that some mode that formerly belonged to the bread remains in the Holy Sacrament,* since its external shape, which is a mode, remains in it. As for the extension of Jesus Christ in the Holy Sacrament, I have not given an explanation of it, because I was under

no obligation to do so, and because I refrain, as far as possible, from questions of theology, and because, indeed, the Council of Trent declares that he exists in it, *ea existendi ratione quam verbis exprimere vix possumus*.* I inserted these words deliberately at the end of my Replies to the Fourth Objections,* so as to excuse myself from
120 explaining the matter. But I venture to say that if people were a little more accustomed than they are to my way of philosophizing, they could be brought to understand a way of explaining this mystery,* that would stop the mouths of the enemies of our religion, and that they would be unable to contradict.

There is a great difference between *abstraction* and *exclusion*. If I were to say that my idea of my soul does not represent it as depending on the body and as identified with it, this would be only an abstraction, from which I could only form a negative argument, which would be far from conclusive. But I say that this idea represents the soul to me as a substance that can exist, even if all the properties of the body are excluded from it; and from this I form a positive argument, and conclude that it can exist without the body. And this exclusion of extension is very clearly seen, as regards the nature of the soul, from the fact that we cannot conceive a half of a thinking thing, as you very justly observed.

I would not wish to put you to the trouble of sending me what you were so good as to write about my *Meditations*, since I hope soon to go to France, where I will, if I may, have the honour of seeing you. And in the meantime I beg of you to believe me, etc.

[AT 4]   2. *To Mesland, Egmond-Binnen, 9 February 1645**

173 As regards the freedom of the will, I am in full agreement with what the Reverend Father* has written here. And in order to explain my opinion more fully, I would wish to point out that 'indifference' seems to me to refer, strictly speaking, to the state of the will when it is not impelled in one direction rather than another by a perception of the true or the good; and this was the sense in which I was using it when I wrote that the freedom by which we determine ourselves to objects to which we are indifferent is the lowest grade of freedom. But perhaps other people use the term to denote a positive faculty of determining oneself to either one of two contraries, that

is of pursuing or avoiding, affirming or denying. That such a positive faculty exists in the will, I did not deny. Indeed, I hold that it exists in the will not only with respect to those actions where there are no evident reasons impelling us in one direction rather than in the other, but also with respect to all our other actions; so much so that when a very evident reason moves us in one direction, even if, morally speaking, we can scarcely move in the opposite direction, we can do so in absolute terms. For it is always possible for us to refrain from pursuing a good clearly known to be such, or from assenting to a manifest truth, provided only that we think that it is good to demonstrate the freedom of our will in this way.

It should be noted that freedom can be considered in the acts of the will either before they are performed, or while they are being performed.

And, indeed, when considered in respect of acts before they are performed, freedom involves indifference in the second sense, but not in the first. And although, when we set our own judgement against the commands of other people, we say that we are freer to perform those acts in respect of which we have received no command from others, and in which we are entitled to follow our own judgement, than those that are forbidden us, yet when we consider some of our judgements, or else some of our thoughts, in relation to other judgements or thoughts of ours, we cannot likewise say that we are freer to do those things that appear neither good nor bad to us, or in which we recognize many aspects of good, yet at the same time some negative aspects, than those in which we recognize much more good than bad. For the greater freedom consists either in a greater facility of self-determination, or in a greater exercise of this positive power we have of doing what is worse, even though we see what is better.* And although, if we pursue the course of action that has more good aspects in its favour, we are determining ourselves more easily, yet, if we do the opposite, we are making fuller use of the positive power in question; and thus we can always act more freely in relation to those acts in which we perceive much more good than evil than in relation to those we call *adiaphora*,* or indifferent. And in this sense we perform those acts we are commanded to perform by others, and which we would not otherwise perform of our own accord, less freely than those that are not commanded; because the judgement that they are difficult to perform is opposed to the judgement that it is good to do what we are commanded to do. The more equally we are impelled by those two judgements, the greater the degree of indifference, in the first sense, in which we find ourselves.*

In relation to acts of the will, at the time in which they are being performed, freedom involves indifference, neither in the first, nor in the second sense; because what is being done cannot remain undone, since it is being done. Freedom here consists purely in the ease of per-
175 formance; and thus in this case 'free', 'spontaneous', and 'voluntary' are all one and the same. In this sense I wrote that the more reasons impel me to something, the more freely I am moved to it; because it is certain that in that case our will is moving itself with greater facility and energy.

3. *To the Marquess of Newcastle,* Egmond-Binnen,*
[AT 4]   *23 November 1646*

569   My Lord,
The favours conferred on me by the letters Your Excellency* has been pleased to send me, and the marks they contain of a mind that lends more distinction to your illustrious birth than it receives from it, oblige me to hold them in the highest esteem; but it seems, moreover, that fortune wishes to show that it regards them as among the greatest goods I could possess, since it has delayed them on their way, and not allowed me to receive them, until it has exhausted its efforts to prevent me from doing so.* Thus, I had the honour to receive one last year* which had taken four months to travel here from Paris; and the one I have just received is dated 5 January; but because M. de B.* assures me that you had already been informed of their delay, I need not excuse myself for not replying sooner. And since the matters it pleased you to write to me about are purely concerned with the sciences, which are not at the mercy of changes of time or fortune, I hope that the answer I am now able to give will be no less agreeable to you than if you had received it ten months ago.

I subscribe altogether to Your Excellency's views about alchemists,* and believe that all they do is to utter words remote from common
570 usage, to give the impression that they know what they know nothing about. I believe also that what they say about the resurrection of flowers by their salt is a mere groundless fantasy, and that their extracts

have other properties than those of the plants from which they are taken. This is very clearly proved by experience, inasmuch as wine, vinegar, and brandy, three different products that can be extracted from the same grapes, have such different tastes and properties. Finally, in my view their salt, sulphur, and mercury differ no more from one another than the four elements of the philosophers, hardly more than water differs from ice, foam, and snow; for I think that all bodies are composed of the same matter, and that the sole cause of the variety among them is that the particles of this matter that form some bodies are different in shape or arrangement from those that form others. I hope that Your Excellency will soon be able to see a full explanation of this in my *Principles of Philosophy*, which are about to be published in French.*

I have no particular knowledge about the formation of stones, except that I distinguish them from metals in that the particles that compose metals are notably larger than those of which stones are composed; and I distinguish them from bones, from hard woods, and other parts of animals or vegetables, in that, unlike these, they do not grow by means of some kind of sap that flows through tiny channels into all the parts of their bodies, but only by the addition of further particles which become attached to their exterior, or intro- 571 duce themselves inside their pores. Thus, I am not astonished to find that there are springs where pebbles are produced; for I think that the water of those springs carries with it little particles of the rocks it flows among, and these particles are so shaped that they attach them- selves easily to one another when they come into contact, and when the water, less fast-flowing and agitated than it was in the veins of the rocks, leaves them behind. And almost the same is true of those stones that are produced in the human body.* Nor am I surprised at the way in which bricks are made: for I think that their hard- ness results from the following process: the action of the fire causes the particles of water to escape from among their other particles (I imagine the water particles to be long and slippery, like little eels, and to flow into the pores of other bodies without becoming attached to them; they are the sole cause of the wetness or moistness of these bodies, as I have stated in the *Meteorology**); but the fire also expels all the other particles that are not very hard and firm, as a result of which the remaining particles become more closely attached to one another, so that brick is harder than clay, even though it has larger pores, which other particles of water or air can subsequently enter, thus making it heavier.

As for the nature of quicksilver,* I have not yet carried out all the
572 experiments required for an accurate knowledge of it; but I think that I can nevertheless state that what renders it so fluid is that the particles of which it is composed are so smooth and slippery that they cannot at all become attached to one another, and that, being bigger than water particles, they almost never allow the subtle matter I term the 'second element' to pass through them, only the very subtle matter I term the 'first element'.* This seems to me sufficient in order to account for all its properties known to me up to now; for it is the absence of second-element particles that prevents it from being transparent and renders it very cold; and it is the activity of the first element, combined with the disproportion between the quicksilver particles and those of the air or other bodies, that causes tiny drops of it on a table to appear more globular than those of water; this same disproportion is the reason why it does not cling to our hands as water does, which is why some have thought that it is not wet like water; but it does cling to lead and gold, for which reason we can say that in relation to them it is wet.

I am very sorry to be unable to read M. d'Igby's book,* since I do not understand English; I have had parts of it interpreted to me; and because I am entirely disposed to obey reason, and I know he has an excellent mind, I dare to hope that, if I had the honour of conversing
573 with him, my opinions would coincide entirely with his.

As regards the understanding or thought ascribed by Montaigne* and some others to animals, I cannot share their opinion. It is not that I hold to the common saying that human beings have absolute power over all other animals, for I admit that some of them are stronger than we are, and I believe that there may be some who have a natural cunning capable of deceiving the shrewdest human beings. But I consider that they match or surpass us only as regards those of our actions that are not directed by our mind (*pensée*); for it often happens that we walk or eat without at all thinking about what we are doing; and when we resist what is harmful to us and parry blows directed at us, we do so without the use of our reason, so much so that even if we explicitly willed not to stretch out our hands in front of our head when we are falling, we would be unable to stop ourselves doing so. I think also that we would eat as the animals do, without ever having learned to do so, if we had no thoughts; and it is said that sleepwalkers sometimes swim across rivers in which they would drown if they were awake. As for the movements of our passions, although in our case they are accompanied by thoughts, because we have the faculty of thinking, still it is very evident that they do not depend on thought, because they often occur in spite of us, and that therefore they can exist in 574 animals, and can even be more violent in them than in us, without our being entitled to infer from that that animals too have thoughts.

Finally, there are none of our external actions that can convince an observer that our body is not just a self-moving machine, but that there is also within it a soul that has thoughts, apart from speech, or other signs made in response to situations, without any relationship to passion. I say 'speech or other signs' because the dumb use signs in the same way as we use the voice; and that these signs are 'in response to situations' so as to exclude the speech of parrots, without excluding that of the mad, which is still related to situations even if it is not in accordance with reason; and I add that these words or signs must be 'without any relationship to passion', so as to exclude not only cries of joy or grief, and the like, but also whatever can be deliberately taught to animals; for if you teach a magpie to say 'good day' to its mistress whenever it sees her appear, this can only be through making the utterance of these words an expression of one of its passions; thus, if one has accustomed it to receiving some treat whenever it has said the words, then saying them will be an expression of its hope to eat; and thus all the actions that dogs, horses, and monkeys can be trained to perform are only expressions of their fear, hope, or joy, so that they can perform them without any thinking. Now, it seems to me very noteworthy that speech, thus defined, pertains to human beings alone. For although Montaigne and Charron* have said that there is more difference between one human being and another than between a human being and an animal,* no animal has ever yet been found so perfect that it has used some sign or other to communicate with other animals about something unconnected with its passions; whereas there is no human being so imperfect that he cannot do so; so much so that even deaf-mutes invent particular signs by which they convey their thoughts. This seems to me a very powerful proof that the reason why animals do not speak, as we do, is that they have no thoughts, and not that they are lacking the necessary organs. And it will not do to say that they converse with each other, but that we cannot understand them; for just as dogs and some other animals can express their passions to us, they would also express their thoughts to us, if they had any.

I know very well that animals do many things better than us, but this does not surprise me; but that fact itself serves to prove that they are acting by nature, and by mechanisms, like a clock, which tells the time much more accurately than our judgement can manage.* And no doubt when swallows arrive in the spring, they are acting in this respect like clocks. Everything that bees do is of the same nature; so is the order we can observe in the flight of cranes, and in the fighting of apes, if, indeed, there is any order they are following; and finally, the 576 instinct to bury their dead is no stranger than that of dogs and cats who scrabble at the earth to bury their excrement, even though they almost never bury it completely; which shows that they do so by instinct and without reflection. We can only say that although animals do not perform any action that convinces us that they can think, nonetheless, because the organs of their bodies are not very different from ours, one might conjecture that there is some thought* attached to these organs, as we find by experience in ourselves, although in their case it is much less developed. To this I have no reply to make, except that, if they thought in the same way as we do, they would have an immortal soul as we do; which is not plausible, because there is no reason why we should believe it of some animals, without believing it of all, and that there are many too imperfect for it to be possible to believe in their case, such as oysters, sponges, and so forth. But I fear I may be wearying you by these arguments, and my whole desire is to assure you that I am, &c.

[AT 5]   4. *To Pierre Chanut, The Hague, 6 June 1647**

50   Sir,
As I was passing through The Hague on my way to France, I learned from M. Brasset* that he had sent letters of yours to Egmond;* and although my journey is quite urgent, my intention was to wait for them there; but they were delivered to my house three hours after I left, and were immediately sent back after me. I read them with avidity. I found manifest proofs in them of your friendship and your abilities. I was apprehensive, when I read the first pages,

in which you reported that M. du Rier* had mentioned one of my letters to the queen, who had asked to see it. But afterwards I was reassured, when I reached the place where you write that she listened to its being read with some satisfaction, and I do not know which is the stronger, my admiration at her so easily understanding things that 51 the most learned people judge very obscure, or my joy that she was not displeased by what she heard. But my admiration was redoubled when I perceived the force and weightiness of the objections raised by Her Majesty as regards the extent I have attributed to the universe. And I could have wished that your letter had found me in my usual residence, because there I would have been able to collect my thoughts better than in the bedroom of an inn, and perhaps I should have been able to tackle a question so difficult and so judiciously raised with somewhat more success. Yet I will not put this forward as an excuse; and provided that I may suppose that I am writing to you alone, so that my imagination will not be too much clouded by veneration and respect, I shall attempt to set down here my views on this question in full.

First of all, I recall that Cardinal Cusa* and several other doctors* have supposed the universe to be infinite, without ever incurring censure from the Church on this point; on the contrary, it is thought to be glorifying God to convey the idea of the vastness of his works. And my opinion is less difficult to accept than theirs: for I do not say that the universe is *infinite*, only that it is *indefinite*.* The distinction is not an insignificant one: for in order to say that something is infinite, we must have a reason that demonstrates it to be such, which can only apply in the case of God; but in order to say it is indefinite, it is sufficient that we have no reason that will serve to prove that it has limits. Thus, it seems to me that we cannot prove, or even conceive, any limits to the matter of which the universe is composed. For 52 when I examine the nature of that matter, I find that it consists purely in having extension in length, breadth, and depth, so that whatever has these three dimensions is a part of this matter; and there can be no space that is entirely empty,* that is to say, that contains no matter, because we cannot conceive such a space without conceiving it as having these three dimensions, and, therefore, as having matter. Now, when we suppose the universe to be finite, we imagine there to be, beyond its boundaries, some spaces, with their three dimensions; these, then, are not purely imaginary, as the philosophers term them, but contain matter; but matter can be nowhere except in the universe, and this therefore shows that the universe is extended beyond the limits it has been alleged to have. We therefore have no reason that proves the world to have limits, indeed we cannot even conceive it as having them; hence I call it 'indefinite'. But nonetheless I cannot deny that it does perhaps have some limits known to God, though incomprehensible to me; and that is why I do not positively say that it is 'infinite'.

When its extent is considered in this way, if one compares it with its duration,* it seems to me that this gives us no more than a reason to suppose that there is no time imaginable, prior to the creation of the world, in which God could not have created it, if he had chosen to; and that there are no grounds from thence inferring that he actu-
53 ally created it prior to an indefinite time, since the real or actual exist-ence the world has had for five or six thousand years* has no necessary connection with the possible or imaginary existence it may have had beforehand, in the way that the actual existence of the spaces conceived as existing around a globe (that is to say, of the universe considered as *finite*) is connected with the actual existence of the same globe.* Moreover, if from the indefinite extent of the world we could infer that its duration is eternal as regards the past, that could be inferred all the more from the eternal duration it must have in the future. For our faith teaches that, although the earth and the heavens will pass away,* that is to say, change their appearance, yet the universe, that is to say, the matter of which they are composed, will never pass away; this appears from the promise of our faith that our bodies will enjoy eternal life after their resurrection,* which means that the universe they will exist in must also be eternal. But from this infinite duration of the universe as regards the future, we cannot in fact infer that it has existed up to now from all eternity, since all the moments of its duration are independent of one another.*

As for the prerogatives attributed to man by religion,* which seem difficult to believe in if the universe is supposed indefinite in extent, some explanation is called for. For although we may say that all created things were made for us, inasmuch as we can derive some benefit from them, there is, however, no reason I know of why we are obliged to believe that human kind is the goal of creation. But it
54 is said that *omnia propter ipsum (Deum) facta sunt*;* that God alone is the final cause,* as well as the efficient cause of the universe; and

as far as creatures are concerned, in so far as they are reciprocally of benefit to one another, each of them can credit itself with the privilege that all those from which it benefits were created for its sake. It is true that the six days of creation are described in Genesis in such a way that it appears that humankind is the principal subject; but we may say that the story of Genesis was written for the sake of humankind, and so the Holy Spirit especially emphasized within it what is of concern to humankind, and nothing else is mentioned there except in relation to humankind. And since preachers are concerned to inspire us to love God, their custom is to draw our attention to the various benefits we derive from other creatures, and they say that God made these creatures for our sake, and they do not invite us to consider the other purposes for which we may also say that he made them, since this is no part of their subject matter; and as a result we are strongly inclined to believe that he made them only for our sake. But preachers go further than this, and they say that each individual human being is in debt to Jesus Christ for every drop of blood he shed on the cross, just as if he had died for that person alone. Which is perfectly true; but, just as, nonetheless, he redeemed with that same blood a very great number of other human beings, so I do not see that the mystery of the Incarnation and all the other special benefits God has conferred on man mean that he cannot have con- 55 ferred an infinity of other very great benefits on an infinity of other creatures. And also I do not thence infer that there are intelligent creatures in the stars or elsewhere; by the same token I see no reason to prove that there cannot be; but I always leave questions of this sort undecided, rather than making affirmative or negative statements. It seems to me that the only remaining difficulty is this: that, having believed for a long time that man has great privileges over other creatures, we seem to lose them all once we change our views on this point. But I make a distinction between those of our goods that can be diminished by others' possession of similar goods, and those that remain unaffected by this. Thus, a man who has only a thousand pistoles* to his name would be very rich, if there were no one else in the world who had as much; and he would be very poor if everyone else had much more. And in the same way the glory conferred by the possession of any praiseworthy quality is all the greater, the fewer people possess it; this is why we are prone to envy the glory and wealth of other people. But virtue, knowledge, health, and all other goods in general, considered in themselves without relation to glory, are not in the slightest diminished by being found in many other people; this is why we have no grounds for vexation that there are many other people who possess them too. Now, the goods that may exist in all the intelligent creatures in an indefinite universe are of 56 this latter kind: they do not diminish those that we possess. On the contrary, when we love God, and through him will ourselves united* with all the things he has created, the more we conceive them to be great, noble, and perfect, the more also we esteem ourselves, as being parts of a more perfect whole; and the more reason we have to praise God, on account of the immensity of his works. When the Holy Scriptures speak in various places of the innumerable multitude of angels,* they entirely confirm this opinion; for we judge the least of the angels to be incomparably more perfect than human beings. And this is confirmed likewise by the astronomers, when they measure the size of the stars and find them to be very much larger than the earth; for if the indefinite extent of the universe leads to the inference that it must have inhabitants besides those of earth, the same inference can be drawn from the extent attributed to it by all astronomers; for there are none of them who do not judge that, compared to the heavens as a whole, the earth is smaller than a grain of sand compared to a mountain.

I move now to your question about the causes that often incite us to love one person rather than another, before we know their personal qualities; and I observe two of these, one in the mind, the other in the body. But, as for the cause in the mind, it presupposes so many things concerning the nature of our souls, that I would not dare undertake to display them in a letter. I will speak only of the bodily. It consists 57 in the disposition of the parts of our brain, whether this disposition has been produced in it by the objects of our senses, or by some other cause. For the objects that affect our senses move certain parts of our brain by means of the nerves, and so produce certain creases,* so to speak, which are smoothed out when the object ceases to act; but the part in which they were produced remains subsequently disposed to be creased again in the same way by another object that resembles the preceding one in some respect, even if not in all respects. For instance, when I was a child I loved a girl of my own age, who had a slight squint; as a result of which, the impression produced in my brain by sight, when I gazed at her wandering eyes, fused with the other impression being formed in that organ so as to arouse in me the passion of love, in such a way that, for a long time afterwards, when I saw women with a squint, I was more inclined to love them than others, for the single reason that they had this blemish: and yet I did not know that this was the reason. On the other hand, since I thought about this, and recognized that it was indeed a blemish, I have no longer been affected by it. Thus, when we are inclined to love someone, without knowing why, we may suppose that the cause is that something in them resembles something in another person we loved at an earlier time, even if we do not know what it is. And although it is more commonly a perfection than a blemish that kindles love in us in this way, nonetheless, because it can sometimes be a blemish, as in the example I have just mentioned, a wise man should not let himself give in entirely to this passion, before he has 58 considered the intrinsic qualities of the person for whom we feel this emotion.* But because we cannot love equally everyone whose qualities we observe to be equal, I think we are obliged only to value them equally; and that, since the principal good in this life is to have friendship for some people, we are entitled to prefer those to whom we are attached by our own secret inclinations, provided that we also observe them to possess personal qualities. Moreover, when these secret inclinations have their cause in the mind, and not the body, I believe that we should always go along with them; and their principal distinguishing mark is that those that originate in the mind are reciprocal, which is often not the case with the other kind. But the proofs I have of your affection convince me so strongly that my inclination for you is reciprocated, that I would have to be completely ungrateful, and to break all the rules I think should be observed in friendship, not to be, most fervently, &c.

5. *For Antoine Arnauld,* Paris, 29 July 1648* [AT 5]

Since a number of objections were delivered to me lately* as if coming 219 from a man living in this city, I replied very briefly, because I thought that if I had left anything out, this could easily be remedied in a personal conversation. But since, as I now understand, he is out of town, and he has written to me again in the most courteous terms, I am very willing to answer him; but, because he conceals his name, lest I make some mistake in my superscription, I shall eschew any introductory formula.*

1. He seems to me to have said very truly that the mind, as long as it is united to the body, cannot withdraw itself from the senses,* when it is violently assaulted by both external and internal objects. I add, furthermore, that it cannot withdraw itself from them, when it is attached to a brain that is too moist and soft, such as we find in children, or that is out of order, as with those who suffer from lethargy, apoplexy, or madness, or even with ourselves when we are deeply asleep; for whenever we have a dream we can subsequently remember, we are sleeping only lightly.

2. In order to remember something, it is not sufficient that the thing has previously come to the observation of our mind, and has left some traces in the brain, which will occasion the thing's reappearance in our thoughts; it is also necessary that when it appears for a second time, we should recognize that this is occurring because the thing was formerly perceived by us; thus, certain lines of poetry will often come to a poet's mind which he does not remember having ever read in someone else's works, but which would not have appeared to him as they are if he had not read them somewhere else.

From which it is clear that memory requires not just any traces that have been left in the brain by previous thoughts, but only those that are such that the mind recognizes that they have not always been in us, but that at some time they came to us anew. In order for the mind to be able to recognize this, I think that when the thoughts were first imprinted, it must have been making use of the pure intellect, I mean, so as to realize that the thing that was then coming under its observation was new, or had never been observed by it before; for there can have been no bodily trace of this newness. Thus, therefore, if I somewhere wrote that the thoughts of babies leave no traces in their brains,* I meant no traces of the kind sufficient for memory to operate, that is, of the kind that, while they are being imprinted, we realize they are new by an act of the pure intellect; in the same way as we say that there are no human footprints on a piece of ground on which we cannot recognize any impression of a human foot, even though in point of fact there may be many unevennesses in the ground, resulting from the passage of human feet, and which therefore can in another sense be said to be human footprints. Finally, just as we make a distinction between direct and reflected vision, because the former derives from the first impact of the rays, and the latter from the second impact, so I call the first and most simple thoughts of babies (when they feel pain because some wind is distending their intestines, or pleasure because the blood that is nourishing them is sweet) 'direct', rather than 'reflected', thoughts; but when an adult perceives something by his senses, and simultaneously perceives that he has never had the same sensation before, I call this second perception a 'reflection', and I refer it to the intellect alone, although the sensation is so closely conjoined with it, that they take place at the same time, and seem to be impossible to distinguish.

3. I attempted to remove the ambiguity of the word 'thought' in articles 63 and 64 of Part I of the *Principles of Philosophy*. Just as the extension that constitutes the nature of the body differs greatly from the various shapes or modes of extension it assumes; so thought, or the thinking nature, in which I believe the essence of the human mind consists, is very different from this or that act of thinking, and the mind itself may be the cause of its performing these or those acts of thinking, but not of its being a thinking thing, just as a flame's spreading itself in this or that direction depends on itself as an efficient cause, but the flame itself is not the cause of its being an extended thing.* Therefore, by 'thought' I do not mean some universal entity, comprehending all the modes of thinking, but a particular nature that accommodates all those modes, just as extension is a nature that accommodates all shapes.

4. It is one thing to be aware* of our thoughts, at the time we are thinking them, and another to remember them subsequently; thus, we think nothing in our dreams without at that moment being aware of our thought, although, for the most part, we immediately forget it. Yet it is true that we are not aware of the manner in which our mind sends the animal spirits into these nerves or those; for this manner depends not on the mind alone, but on the union of the mind with the body; we are only aware of the whole action by which the mind moves the nerves, in so far as this action is in the mind, in which indeed there is nothing other than an inclination of the will towards this or that movement; and following this inclination of the will, there is a flow of spirits into the nerves, along with all the other processes requisite to the movement in question; and this takes place in virtue of the proper configuration of the body, of which the mind may know nothing, and also in virtue of the union of the mind with the body, of which, certainly, the mind is aware; otherwise it would not incline its will in order to move the limbs.

But that the mind, which is incorporeal, can move the body is manifest to us not by any process of reasoning or any comparison derived from other things, but by very certain and evident everyday experience; for this is one of the things known by themselves* that we only make more obscure when we try to explain them by reference to other things. Yet I will make use here of a certain comparison.* Most philosophers who think that the heaviness of a stone is a real quality, distinct from the stone itself, think that they understand sufficiently how this quality can move a stone towards the centre of the earth, because they think they have a manifest experience of this occurring. I, on the other hand, who am convinced that there is no such quality in the nature of things, and therefore no real idea of it in the human intellect, believe that they are using the idea they possess of incorporeal substance, in order to provide themselves with an idea of this heaviness; in this way it is not more difficult for us to understand how the mind moves the body, than for them to understand how this kind of heaviness carries the stone downward. And it makes no difference that they say that this heaviness is not a substance; for in fact they conceive it on the model of a substance, since they think it is real and can in virtue of a certain power (that is, God's power) exist without the stone. Nor does it make any difference that they think it a corporeal quality; for if we take 'corporeal' to mean belonging to a body, even though it is itself of another nature, the mind too can be said to be corporeal, since it is fitted to be united to a body; but if we take 'corporeal' to mean partaking of the nature of body, then this heaviness is no more corporeal than the human mind.

5. I conceive the successive duration of things that are moved, or indeed of the motion itself, no differently from that of things that are not moved: for the 'before' and 'after' of any duration whatever becomes known to me through the before and after of the successive duration I encounter in my thoughts, with which other things coexist.

6. The difficulty in grasping the impossibility of a vacuum seems to me to arise, firstly, from the fact that we do not sufficiently reflect that nothing can have no properties; for otherwise, if we realized that in the space we call a vacuum there is genuine extension and hence all the properties that are required to constitute the nature of body, we would not say that it is a proper vacuum, that is, a pure nothingness; and, secondly, from our resorting to the divine power, which we know to be infinite, so that we ascribe an effect to him that we have failed

to notice involves a basic self-contradiction in the concept, that is, it cannot be conceived by us. To me, however, it does not seem that we should ever say, in connection with any thing, that God cannot 224 bring it about, since the whole essence (*ratio*) of truth and goodness depends on his omnipotence;* and, indeed, I would not even venture to say that God could not bring it about that a mountain could exist without a valley or that one plus two should not equal three; I only say that he has implanted a mind in me such that it cannot conceive a mountain without a valley or the sum of one and two not being three, and so forth, and that such things appear to my understanding to involve a self-contradiction. I think that the same should be said of the idea of a space that is entirely empty, or of a nothingness that has extension, or a universe that is limited in space; because whatever boundaries to the universe can be imagined, I understand there to be extension beyond them; nor can a jar be conceived to be so empty that there is no extension (and therefore no body) within its cavity; for wherever there is extension, there is necessarily body.

THE PASSIONS OF THE SOUL

Reply to the First Letter*

Sir,

Among the insults and reproaches I find in the long letter you have taken the trouble to write me, I observe so many things to my advantage that if you were to have it printed, as you declare you intend, I would be afraid that people would imagine that our relations are closer than in fact they are, and that I have asked you to include in your letter a number of things that it would be unseemly for me to reveal to the public myself. This is why I shall not take the trouble to answer it point by point: I will simply give you two reasons for which, it seems to me, you should not publish it. The first is that it seems unlikely to me that what I take to be your intention in writing it will succeed. The second is that my attitude is by no means as you imagine: I feel no indignation or disgust of a kind to quell the desire to do whatever is in my power to benefit the public, to which I regard myself as greatly obliged, since the writings I have already published have been favourably received by many people; moreover, I would not let you read what I had written on the passions, purely so as not to be obliged to show it to other people who would not have benefited from reading it. For, since I wrote it only for a princess whose intelligence is so far above the common run that she grasps with ease what our scholars find most difficult, I did not linger over explanations of anything except what I thought was new. And in case you doubt my words, I promise you to revise this treatise on the passions and to add whatever I shall judge to be necessary to make it more intelligible, and then I shall send it to you to do with it as you will. For I am, &c.

Egmond, 4 December 1648

Reply to the Second Letter*

Sir,

I am entirely innocent of the artifice you wish to believe I resorted to, in order to prevent the publication of the long letter you wrote to me last year. I had no need of it. For, apart from the fact that I do not believe the letter capable of producing the effect you claim it could,* I am not so given to idleness that the fear of the labour I would have to undertake in carrying out various experimental investigations, supposing I had received from the public the necessary support, would get the better of my desire to gain knowledge for myself and to produce a written record that would be useful to other people. But I cannot so easily excuse myself of the charge of negligence you bring against me. For I admit that I have taken longer to revise the little treatise I am sending to you than I had formerly taken to compose it; and yet I have made very few additions to it, and have not altered the style,* which is so straightforward and concise that it will convince readers that my intention was to write of the passions not as an orator or even a moral philosopher would, but simply as a natural philosopher.* Thus, I predict that this treatise will have no better fortune than my other writings; and although its title will perhaps attract a greater number of readers, it will satisfy only those who take the trouble to study it with care. Such as it is, I deliver it into your hands, &c.

THE PASSIONS OF THE SOUL

PART ONE

OF THE PASSIONS IN GENERAL; AND, BY EXTENSION, OF HUMAN NATURE AS A WHOLE

ART. 1.* *That what is a passion in relation to a subject is always action in some other respect.*

There is nothing in which the shortcomings of the sciences we have inherited from the ancients more clearly appear than in their writings on the passions. For although the knowledge of this subject has always been keenly pursued, and it does not appear to be an especially difficult one, inasmuch as everyone experiences the passions in himself, and need not borrow observations from anywhere else in order to discover their nature, nonetheless the ancients' teaching on the subject is so slender, and for the most part so little believable, that I can have no hope of attaining truth except by departing from the paths they have followed.* This is why I shall be obliged to write here as if I were dealing with a matter no one had ever treated before. And, to begin with, I note that whatever newly comes about or happens is generally termed by philosophers both a passion, in relation to the subject to which it happens,* and an action, in relation to the agent that makes it happen; so that, although the agent and the patient are often quite different, the action and the passion are nonetheless one and the same thing, which has two different names because it can be considered in relation to two different subjects.*

ART. 2. *That in order to know the passions of the soul we must distinguish the functions of the soul from those of the body.*

I note further that we can observe no subject that acts more immediately on our soul than the body to which it is joined; and that therefore what is a passion in the soul is commonly an action on the part of the body; and so there is no better path to lead us to the knowledge of our passions than to examine the difference between the soul and the body, so as to know to which of the two we should ascribe the various functions that are to be found in us.

ART. 3. *What rule we should observe for this purpose.*
There will be no great difficulty in this if we take note that everything that we experience as taking place in ourselves, and that we see can also take place in completely inanimate bodies, should be attributed only to our body; and, on the contrary, that everything that takes place in us of which we understand that it can in no way pertain to a body, should be attributed to our soul.

ART. 4. *That the heat and motion of the limbs proceed from the body, and that thoughts proceed from the soul.*
Thus, because we cannot understand the body as thinking in any way, we are right to believe that all the various thoughts that take place in us belong to the soul. And because we do not doubt that there are inanimate bodies that can move in as many different ways as our own, or even more, and which have as much heat as ours, or more (as experience shows with a flame, which alone has much more heat and movement than any of our limbs), we must think that all the heat and all the movements that are found in us, inasmuch as they do not depend on thought, belong only to the body.

ART. 5. *That it is a mistake to suppose that the soul gives movement and heat to the body.*
By this means we shall avoid an extremely serious mistake into which many have fallen;* and which, indeed, I think is the main reason why up to now we have had no good explanation of the passions and the other attributes of the soul. The mistake is this: observing that all dead bodies are deprived of heat and then of movement, people imagined that the absence of the soul was the cause of the absence of movement and heat. Hence they believed, without reason, that our natural heat and all the movements of our bodies depend on the soul; whereas they should have thought, on the contrary, that the soul takes leave of the body at death, purely because the heat has given out, and the organs the function of which is to move the body have become corrupted.

ART. 6. *The difference between a living and a dead body.*
And therefore in order to avoid this error, let us bear in mind that death never occurs from a failing in the soul, but only because one of the main parts of the body becomes corrupted; and let us judge that

the difference between the body of a living man and that of a dead one is the same as that between a watch, or some other automaton (I mean, some other machine that moves itself), when it is wound up and when it has in itself the physical principle of the movements for which it was designed, along with everything else that is required for it to act, and the same watch or other machine when it is broken and the principle of its movement ceases to act.

ART. 7. *A brief explanation of the parts of the body, and of some of its functions.*

To make all this more intelligible, I will briefly explain here how the mechanism of our body is put together. As everybody knows, there is within us a heart, a brain, a stomach, muscles, nerves, arteries, veins, and so forth. Everyone also knows that the food we eat descends into the stomach and the intestines, whence the juices from it flow into the liver and all the veins, where they mix with the blood already there so as to increase its quantity. Those with a smattering of medical knowledge also know about the structure of the heart, and how all the blood in the veins can readily flow from the vena cava into the right-hand side of the heart, from where it flows into the lungs through the vessel known as the arterial vein,* returning from the lungs into the left-hand side of the heart through the vessel known as the veiny artery; from here it finally flows into the main artery, the branches of which are extended throughout the body. Further, those who have not been completely blinded by the authority of the ancients, and who have opened their eyes sufficiently to examine Harvey's opinion* concerning the circulation of the blood, are well aware that all the veins and arteries of the body are like streams along which the blood flows continuously and very swiftly. Its course is from the right-hand cavity of the heart via the arterial vein, the branches of which are dispersed all over the lungs and are joined to the branches of the veiny artery, through which it flows from the lung into the left-hand side of the heart; from there it flows into the main artery, the branches of which, dispersed throughout the rest of the body, are joined to the branches of the vena cava, which bring the same blood back again to the right-hand cavity of the heart. Thus, these two cavities, the right and the left, are like two sluices through each of which the whole of the blood passes every time it circulates round the body. Moreover, it is known that all the movements of the limbs depend on the muscles, and that each of these is paired with an opposite muscle, in such a way that when one of the pair is contracted, it draws towards itself the part of the body to which it is attached, which process simultaneously causes its opposite number to extend; whereas when the latter is contracted, it causes the former to extend, and draws towards itself the part of the body to which they are both attached. Finally, it is known that all these movements of the muscles depend on the nerves, as do all the senses. The nerves are like little filaments or pipes all coming from the brain; and, like the brain, they contain a highly subtle air or wind known as the animal spirits.

ART. 8. *The principle of all these functions.*
But exactly how these animal spirits and these nerves contribute to motion and sensation, is not commonly known. Nor is the bodily principle that causes them to act. For this reason, although I have already said something about this in other writings, I will nonetheless explain it here in a few words. As long as we are alive, there is a continual heat in our hearts, a kind of fire* kept going by the blood from the veins, and this fire is the bodily principle of the movements of all our limbs.

✗ ART. 9. *How the movement of the heart comes about.*
The first effect of this fire is to dilate the blood by which the cavities of the heart are filled; this causes the blood, which now needs to occupy a larger space, to rush from the right-hand cavity into the arterial vein, and from the left-hand cavity into the main artery; then, as this dilation ceases, new blood immediately makes its way from the vena cava into the right-hand cavity of the heart, and from the veiny artery into the left-hand cavity. For there are little flaps at the entry of these four vessels, so arranged that the blood can only enter the heart via the vena cava and the veiny artery, and leave it via the arterial vein and the main artery. The new blood entering the heart is immediately rarefied in the same way as the blood that was there before. And it is in this alone that the pulsation or beating of the heart and the arteries consists; so that the pulsation is repeated whenever new blood enters the heart. It is this also, and this alone, that imparts movement to the blood, and causes it to flow continuously and swiftly along all the arteries and veins. By this means it conveys the heat it has acquired

in the heart to all the other parts of the body, to which it also serves
as nourishment.

ART. 10. *How the animal spirits are produced in the brain.*
But the crucial point here is that all the swiftest and most subtle
parts of the blood that have been rarefied in the heart by its heat are
constantly flooding into the cavities of the brain. And the reason they
flow there rather than anywhere else is that all the blood which has left
the heart via the main artery heads straight for the brain; but since
it cannot all enter there, because the openings are very narrow, only
the most agitated and subtle parts of the blood make their way into
the brain, while the rest is dispersed throughout the rest of the body.
Now, these very subtle parts of the blood form the animal spirits.
And for this to happen they do not need to undergo any further
change in the brain, except being separated from the other denser
parts of the blood. For what I call 'spirits' here are only bodies, and
their only properties are that they are very small and fast-moving, like
the parts of the flame that comes from a torch. As a result they are
never stationary, but while some are flowing into the cavities of the
brain, others are simultaneously flowing out through the pores of the
substance of that organ. Through the pores they are conveyed into
the nerves, and thence into the muscles, by means of which process
they move the body in all the various ways it can be moved.

ART. 11. *How the movements of the muscles are produced.*
For the sole cause of all muscular movements is that some muscles
are contracted while their opposites are extended, as has already been
noted; and the sole reason why one muscle of a pair contracts rather
than its opposite is that one has received a greater quantity of spirits
from the brain than the other (the slightest difference in quantity will
produce this effect). Not that the spirits flowing immediately from
the brain are sufficient of themselves to move the muscles: but they
cause the spirits already in the two muscles to flow, very swiftly, away
from one and into the other. As a result the one from which they have
flowed away becomes longer and slacker; whereas the one into which
they have flowed is rapidly inflated by them, so that it contracts and
pulls along with it the limb to which it is attached. This is easy to
grasp, as long as one bears in mind that the quantity of animal spirits

that flow continuously from the brain towards each muscle is very small, but that there is always a quantity of other spirits contained in a given muscle, and moving about very quickly: sometimes, when they find no passages open for them to flow out of, they simply whirl about in the same place; sometimes they flow into the opposite muscle. Moreover, there are little openings in each muscle through which the spirits can flow from one of the pair into the other, and these are so arranged that, when the spirits from the brain flow into one muscle more vigorously (by however small an extent) than they flow into the other, they open up all the apertures through which the spirits from the second muscle can flow into the first; at the same time they block up all the apertures by which spirits can flow from the first muscle into the second; as a result of all this, all the spirits previously contained in both muscles swiftly collect together in just one of them, which they therefore inflate and contract, while the opposite muscle extends and slackens.

ART. 12. *How external objects act upon the sense-organs.*
We have now only to show the causes that explain why the spirits do not always flow from the brain into the muscles in the same way, and why sometimes they flow in greater quantity into some than into others. For, not counting the action of the soul, which is certainly one of the causes within us, as I shall presently explain, there are two other causes that depend purely on the body, and that must be mentioned here. The first of these consists in the diversity of the movements stimulated in the sense-organs by their objects, a subject I have already explained pretty fully in the *Dioptrics*;* but to spare the reader of this work the need to refer to others, I will repeat what I stated there, namely, that there are three aspects of the nerves to be considered: first of all, their marrow, or inner substance, which takes the form of tiny filaments extending from their point of origin in the brain to the ends of the other limbs to which they are attached; then there is the skin that surrounds them, which is continuous with the skin that encases the brain, and forms little pipes within which the little filaments are enclosed; and finally, the animal spirits, which are conveyed by these pipes from the brain to the muscles, and which keep the filaments entirely free and extended in such a way that the slightest thing that moves the part of the body to which the end of one of the filaments is attached, causes in the same way a movement in the

part of the brain in which the filament originates; just as when you tug on one end of a cord, you cause a movement in the other.

ART. 13. *That the impact of external objects can cause the spirits to flow into the muscles in different ways.*

And I have explained in the *Dioptrics** how the objects of sight are conveyed to us in one way only: by the local motion they impart, via the transparent bodies that occupy the space between them and us, first to the tiny filaments of the optic nerves located at the back of our eyes, and, secondly, to the parts of the brain where these nerves originate. The different forms of this motion cause us to see differences in the objects; and the objects are represented to us not directly by the movements taking place in the eye but by those that take place in the brain. By analogy it is easy to grasp how sounds, smells, tastes, heat, pain, hunger, thirst, and in general all the objects both of our external senses and of our internal appetites also stimulate some movement in our nerves, which is transmitted by them to the brain. These various movements in the brain produce different sensations in our soul; but, moreover, they can also, without the soul's being involved, cause the spirits to flow towards certain muscles rather than others, and thus to produce movements in our limbs. I will prove this here simply by one example. Suppose someone quickly moves his hand towards our eyes, as if he meant to hit us: even if we know that he is our friend, that it is just a game, and that he will take good care not to hurt us, we can nonetheless hardly help closing our eyes. Which shows that our eyes have closed without the involvement of the soul, because they did so against our will (volition being the only or at least the principal action of the soul); and that it happened because the mechanism of our body is so constituted that the movement of the hand towards our eyes stimulates another movement in our brain, which conveys the animal spirits into the muscles that cause the eyelids to come down.

ART. 14. *That differences within the spirits can also cause them to flow differently.*

The other cause for the differences in the flow of animal spirits into the muscles is the variations in their agitation and their composition. For when some of their parts are larger and more agitated than the rest, they flow straight and further into the cavities and pores of the brain, being thus conveyed into other muscles than those they would reach if their impetus were less.

✕ ART. 15. *The causes of these variations.*

These variations may result from the different substances of which the spirits are composed, as we see in the case of those who have drunk a great deal of wine. The vapours of the wine swiftly merge with the blood, and ascend from the heart into the brain, where they are converted into spirits which, being stronger and more abundant than those usually found there, are capable of moving the body in various strange ways. Variations within the spirits can also result from the various dispositions of the heart, the liver, the stomach, the spleen, and all the other parts that contribute to their production. Here we must pay particular attention to certain tiny nerves attached to the base of the heart, which serve both to broaden and to narrow the entries to its cavities, thus causing the blood to dilate to a greater or lesser extent, and thus to produce spirits that are differently disposed. We should also note that, although the blood that flows into the heart comes from all the other parts of the body, it is often conveyed with more force from some parts than from others; this is because the nerves and muscles connected with those parts are impelling or agitating it to a greater extent. In this case, depending on the particular character of the part of the body from which it has flowed more abundantly, the blood will dilate differently in the heart and so produce spirits with different qualities. So, for example, the blood coming from the lower part of the liver, where the bile is to be found, dilates in the heart in a different way from that of the blood that comes from the spleen, which in turn dilates differently from the blood coming from the veins of the arms or legs, and this in turn differently from the juices from food, when, having just emerged from the stomach and the intestines, they swiftly flow through the liver and into the heart.

✕ ART. 16. *How all the limbs can be moved by sense-objects and by the animal spirits without the help of the soul.*

Finally, we should observe that the mechanism of our body is so constituted that all the changes that can take place in the movement of the spirits can cause them to open certain pores in the brain rather than others; and, reciprocally, that when one of these pores is more or less open than usual (however small the difference), owing to the action of the nerves by which the senses operate, this affects the movement of the spirits, and causes them to be conveyed into the muscles that serve to move the body in the way in which it is ordinarily moved by this kind of action. Thus, all the movements we make without the contribution of the will (as often happens when we breathe, walk, or eat, and in general perform all the actions we have in common with brute beasts) depend purely on the configuration of our limbs and on the path along which the spirits, stimulated by the heat of the heart, naturally flow into the brain, the nerves, and the muscles, in the same way as the movement of a watch is produced purely by the power of its mainspring and the arrangement of its wheels.

ART. 17. *The functions of the soul.*

Having thus considered all the functions that pertain to the body alone, it is easy to recognize that there remains nothing in us that we should ascribe to the soul except our thoughts, of which there are two main kinds: the actions of the soul and its passions. By its actions I mean all our volitions, since we experience these as coming directly from our soul, and as apparently depending on it alone. Whereas, on the other hand, the term 'passions' can be applied in general to all the kinds of perception or knowledge to be found within us, because it is often not our soul that makes them what they are, and because they are always produced in us by the things they represent.

ART. 18. *Of the will.*

Moreover, our volitions are of two kinds.* For some are actions of the soul that terminate in the soul itself, as when we will to love God or more generally to apply our thought to some non-material object. Whereas others are actions terminating in our body, as when, purely and simply because we will to go for a stroll, our legs move and we walk.

ART. 19. *Of perception.*

Our perceptions are also of two kinds, some having the soul as their cause, others the body. Those caused by the soul are the perceptions of our acts of will and of all the acts of the imagination or other thoughts that depend on it. For it is certain that we can will nothing without by the same token perceiving that we will it; and although from the point of view of our soul to will something is an action, we can also say that the perception that it so wills is a passion within it. However, because this perception and this act of will are in fact a single thing, it is always labelled by its more noble aspect, and thus is customarily termed not a passion, but an action.

ART. 20. *Of imaginations and other thoughts formed by the soul.*
When our soul sets itself to imagine something that does not exist, for instance, to picture an enchanted palace or a chimera, and also when it sets itself to consider something that is purely intelligible and not imaginable, for instance, to consider its own nature, its perceptions of these things depend mainly on the will that causes it to perceive them. For this reason they are customarily considered as actions rather than passions.

ART. 21. *Of imaginations caused purely by the body.*
Most of the perceptions caused by the body depend on the nerves; but there are others that do not so depend, and that are called imaginations, like those of which I have just spoken; what is different about them, however, is that the will is not engaged in forming them. Therefore, they cannot be classed among the actions of the soul, and they occur purely because, when the spirits are agitated in various ways, and flow into the traces of different impressions formed beforehand in the brain, they randomly take their course through certain pores of the brain rather than others.* Such are the illusions we have in dreams and also the daydreams we frequently have when awake, when our mind wanders carelessly without applying itself of its own accord to anything in particular. Now, although some of these imaginations are passions of the soul, taking the expression in its most specific and restricted sense, and all of them may be called so, taking it in a broader sense,* nonetheless, because they do not have so significant and determinate a cause as the perceptions conveyed to the soul through the agency of the nerves, of which they seem to be only the shadow and the copy, we cannot hope to get a sufficiently distinct idea of them without first considering the varieties of the latter kind.

ART. 22. *Of the difference between the other kinds of perception.*
All the perceptions I have not yet explained come to the soul through the agency of the nerves. Of these there are three kinds: those we

refer* to external objects that act upon our senses; those we refer to our body or some of its parts; and, finally, those we refer to our soul.

ART. 23. *Of the perceptions we refer to external objects.*

Those we refer to things outside us, or in other words to the objects of our senses, are caused (at least when our opinion is not false) by these objects, which stimulate certain movements in the organs of the external senses, and also, through the agency of the nerves, further movements in the brain, which cause the soul to perceive the objects. Thus, when we see the light of a torch and hear the sound of a bell, the sound and the light are two distinct actions that, purely because they stimulate two different movements in some of our nerves and hence in the brain, cause the soul to experience two different sensations, which we so refer to the objects (*sujets*) we suppose to be their cause that we think we see the torch itself and hear the bell itself, rather than simply having the sensation of movements they have caused.

ART. 24. *Of the perceptions we refer to our body.*

The perceptions we refer to our body or to some of its parts are those of hunger, thirst, and our other natural appetites; to these we may join pain, heat, and the other feelings we experience as if in our limbs and not in external objects. Thus, we can feel at the same time, and through the agency of the same nerves, both the cold of our hand and the heat of the flame towards which we move it, or, on the contrary, the warmth of the hand and the cold of the air to which it is exposed. The only difference between the processes that cause us to feel the heat or cold in our hand and those that cause us to feel the heat or cold outside us is that one of these processes occurs in succession to the other, and so we judge that the earlier one is already inside us, whereas the later one is not yet inside us, but in the object that causes it.

ART. 25. *Of the perceptions we refer to our soul.*

The perceptions we refer only to our soul are those of which we feel the effects as taking place in the soul itself, and for which we are usually unaware of any proximate cause to which we can refer them. Such are the feelings of joy, anger, and so forth, which are sometimes excited in us by the objects that act on our nerves, and sometimes also by other causes. Now, although all our perceptions, including both those we refer to objects outside us and those we refer to various feelings in our body, are in truth passions, taking the word in its broadest sense, in relation to our soul, nonetheless in general usage the word 'passion' is used only to denote those perceptions we refer to the soul itself; and it is only these last I have undertaken to explain here in this treatise on the passions of the soul.

ART. 26. *That the imaginations that depend purely on the random movement of the spirits can also be passions just as much as the perceptions that depend on the nerves.*

It remains to point out here that everything that the soul perceives through the agency of the nerves can also be represented to it by the random flow of the spirits, the only difference between these processes being that the impressions conveyed to the brain via the nerves are generally more vivid and distinct than those aroused in the brain by the spirits. This is why I said in article 21 that the latter are, so to speak, only the shadow or the copy of the former. We should also note that in some cases this copy is so faithful a portrait of the thing it represents that we can confuse the two. This applies to the perceptions we refer to external objects, or to those we refer to some parts of our body; but it does not apply where the passions are concerned, inasmuch as these are so close to us, so internal to our souls, that it is impossible for the soul to feel them without their being in reality as it feels them. Thus, often when we are asleep, and even sometimes when awake, we imagine certain things so vividly that we think we see them before us or feel them in our body, without this being the case at all; but even if one is asleep or daydreaming, one cannot feel sad, or moved by some other passion, without the soul's actually having that passion within itself.

ART. 27. *The definition of the passions of the soul.*
Having considered the way in which the passions of the soul differ from all its other thoughts, it seems to me that they can be defined in general as perceptions, or sensations, or emotions of the soul that we refer particularly to the soul itself, and that are caused, sustained, and fortified by some movement of the spirits.

ART. 28. *Explanation of the first part of the above definition.*
They can be called perceptions in the general sense of the word, when it is used to denote all thoughts that are not actions of the soul

(or volitions); but not in the sense in which it is sometimes used, to denote evident knowledge.* For experience shows that those who are most agitated by their passions are not those who know them the best; and that the passions belong to the category of perceptions rendered confused and obscure by the close alliance between the soul and the body. They can also be called sensations, since they are received in the soul in the same way as the objects of the external senses, and are not known by it in any other way. Still better, though, is the expression 'emotions of the soul', not simply because the term 'emotion' can be attached to any change that happens within it,* that is, to all the various thoughts that come to it, but in particular because, of all the different kinds of thoughts the soul can have, there are none that agitate and disturb it as strongly as these passions.

ART. 29. *Explanation of the rest of the definition.*
I add that the passions are referred particularly to the soul, in order to distinguish them from other sensations that we refer either to external objects, like smells, sounds, and colours, or to our body, like hunger, thirst, and pain. I add further that they are caused, sustained, and fortified by some movement of the spirits, first, in order to distinguish them from our volitions, which can be defined as emotions of the soul that we refer to the soul, but that are caused by it, and, secondly, to indicate their immediate cause, which, again, distinguishes them from other sensations.

ART. 30. *That the soul is united equally to all the parts of the body.*
But to understand all these things more perfectly, we need to know that the soul is in a very real sense joined to the whole of the body, and that it cannot strictly speaking be said to be in one of its parts to the exclusion of the rest, first, because the body is a unity and in a sense indivisible, on account of the disposition of its organs, which are so closely connected with one another that, when one of them is removed, the whole body is rendered defective; and, secondly, because the soul is of a nature that has no relation to extension or to the dimensions or other properties of the matter of which the body is constituted, but relates only to the total combination of the body's organs. This appears from the fact that we cannot form the idea of half a soul, or a third of a soul, or of the space occupied by the soul; nor does the soul become smaller if some part of the body

is removed; but it is completely separated from the body when the combination of the body's organs is dissolved.

ART. 31. *That there is a little gland in the brain in which the soul exercises its functions more particularly than in the other parts of the body.*
We need also to know that, although the soul is joined to the whole of the body, there is nonetheless a certain part of the body in which it exercises its functions more particularly than in all the rest. This is commonly believed to be the brain, or perhaps the heart; the brain, because the sense-organs are connected with it; and the heart, because that is where we seem to feel our passions. But, having examined the matter with care, it seems to me that the part of the body in which the soul immediately exercises its functions is by no means the heart, or the brain as a whole, but only the most inward part of it, which is a certain tiny gland* situated in the middle of the substance of the brain, and suspended over the channel through which the spirits of the anterior cavities communicate with those of the posterior cavity in such a way that the slightest movements that take place within it can do much to change the flow of these spirits; while, conversely, the slightest changes in the flow of the spirits can have a major effect on the movements of the gland.

ART. 32. *How we know that this gland is the main seat of the soul.*
The reason that convinces me that the location in which the soul immediately exercises its functions can only be this gland, and not anywhere else in the body, is the consideration that the other parts of our brain are all in pairs, and that, likewise, we have two eyes, two hands, two ears—in fact all the organs of our external senses are double; but, since at any one time we have only one single thought concerning one single object, there must necessarily be some place where the two images that come to us from our two eyes, or the two other impressions that come to us from a single object via the twin organs of our other senses, can be combined into one before they reach the soul, so that they do not represent two objects instead of one. And we can easily grasp how these images or other impressions come together in this gland through the agency of the spirits that fill the cavities of the brain; but there is no other part of the body where they can thus be combined, except as a result of their being combined in the gland.

ART. 33. *That the seat of the passions is not in the heart.**

As for the opinion of those who think the soul receives its passions in the heart, this has nothing to commend it, for it is based only on the fact that they cause us to feel some alteration in that organ; and it is easy to observe that we seem to feel this alteration in the heart purely through the agency of a little nerve that descends to it from the brain; just as pain is felt in the foot through the agency of the nerves of the foot, and the stars are perceived as if in the sky through the agency of their light and the optic nerves: so that it is no more necessary for the soul to exercise its functions immediately in the heart in order to feel its passions there, than it is for it to be in the sky in order to see the stars.

ART. 34. *How the soul and body act on one another.*

Let us then conceive the soul as having its main seat in the little gland in the middle of the brain, from which it radiates outwards to the rest of the body through the agency of the spirits, the nerves, and even the blood, which, since it reflects the impressions of the spirits, can carry them along the arteries to all our limbs. Bear in mind what has been said above about the mechanism of our body, namely, that the little filaments of our nerves are so distributed over every part of it that, as a result of the different movements produced in them by sensible objects, they open the pores of the brain in different ways, which causes the animal spirits contained in the cavities of the brain to flow into the muscles in different ways, by means of which they can move the limbs in all the different ways in which they are capable of being moved; and also that all the other causes that can move the spirits in different ways are sufficient to convey them into the different muscles. Again, the little gland that is the main seat of the soul is so suspended between the cavities containing the spirits that it can be moved by them in as many different fashions as there are differences in objects perceptible by the senses; but it can also be moved in various ways by the soul, which is of such a nature that it receives as many different impressions (or in other words has as many different perceptions) as there are different movements in the gland. And, on the other hand, the mechanism of the body is so constituted that, when the gland is moved in different ways by the soul or by whatever other cause it may be, it pushes the spirits that surround it towards the pores of the brain, which convey them via the nerves to the muscles, by means of which it causes them to move the limbs.

✗ ART. 35. *An example of the way in which the impressions of objects are brought together in the gland in the middle of the brain.*

Thus, for example, if we see some animal coming towards us, the reflected light of its body depicts two images of it, one in each eye, and these two images form two more, through the agency of the optic nerves, on the inner surface of the brain facing its cavities; then, from there, through the agency of the spirits that fill the cavities, these images so radiate towards the little gland surrounded by the spirits that the movement that forms each point of one of the images tends towards the same point in the gland as the movement that forms the point of the other image, which represents the same part of the animal as the first image. By this means the two images in the brain produce only one image in the gland, which acts immediately on the soul so that it sees the figure of the animal.

ART. 36. *An example of how the passions are aroused in the soul.*

Moreover, if this figure is very strange and very terrifying, that is, if it has a close affinity with things that have previously been harmful to the body, this arouses the passion of fear in the soul, and then the passion of boldness, or else that of terror and horror;* which it is depends on one's particular physical temperament or strength of mind, and on whether one has in the past preserved oneself against the harmful things with which the present impression has an affinity, by standing and fighting, or by flight. For in some people past experience produces a disposition in the brain such that the spirits that carry the reflection of the image thus formed on the gland flow partly into the nerves the function of which is to turn our backs and move the legs in order to flee, and partly into the nerves that expand or contract the orifices of the heart, or else agitate the other parts of the body from which the blood is conveyed to the heart, in such a way that the blood is rarefied in an unusual fashion. As a result, it sends spirits to the brain that are conducive to sustaining and augmenting the passion of terror; suitable, that is, for keeping open, or reopening, the pores of the brain that convey the spirits to the same nerves. For simply by flowing into these pores, the spirits produce a particular movement in the gland, designed by nature* to make the soul feel this passion. And because the pores are connected mainly to the little nerves that serve to contract or to expand the orifices of the heart, it is mainly in the heart that the soul seems to feel it.

ART. 37. *How it appears that the passions are all caused by some movement of the spirits.*

And because the same thing happens in all the other passions, that is, they are chiefly caused by the spirits contained in the cavities of the brain, when their flow is directed towards the nerves that serve to expand or contract the orifices of the heart, or to impel the blood from the other parts of the body towards the heart in a different way, or to sustain the same passion in any other way whatever, it is easy to grasp why the above definition of the passions makes reference to their being caused by some particular movement of the spirits.

ART. 38. *An example of the movements of the body that accompany the passions and do not depend on the soul.*

Moreover, just as the flow of the spirits towards the nerves of the heart suffices to produce the particular movement in the gland that causes terror in the soul, so in the same way the simultaneous movement of spirits towards the nerves that serve to stir the legs to flight produces another movement in the same gland by means of which the soul feels and perceives this flight, which can therefore be produced in the body in this way purely by the disposition of its organs, without any intervention by the soul.

ART. 39. *How one and the same cause can arouse different passions in different people.*

The same impression that the presence of a frightening object makes on the gland, and that causes terror in some people, may arouse courage and boldness in others. This is because our brains are not all disposed in the same way, so that one and the same movement of the gland, which arouses terror in some people, has a different effect on others: the spirits flow into the pores of the brain that convey them partly to the nerves that serve to move the hands in self-defence, and partly to those that stir up the blood and push it towards the heart, in the manner necessary to produce spirits capable of sustaining the self-defence and the will to continue it.

ART. 40. *What the main effect of the passions is.*
For we must note that the principal effect of all the passions in human beings is that they incite and dispose their soul to will the acts for which they are preparing the body: so that the sensation of terror encourages it to wish to flee, and that of boldness to wish to fight, and so on.

ART. 41. *What the power of the mind is in relation to the body.*
But the will is so free of its own nature that it can never be compelled; and, to return to my distinction between two kinds of thought in the soul, its actions, that is to say, its volitions, and its passions, taking the word in its most general sense as covering all kinds of perceptions, the former are absolutely in its power and can be changed by the body only indirectly, whereas, on the other hand, the latter depend utterly on the processes that produce them and can be changed by the soul only indirectly, unless it is itself the cause of them. And the action of the soul consists entirely in this: that, by the mere fact that it wants something, it causes the little gland, to which it is closely joined, to move in whatever manner is necessary to produce the effect connected with this volition.

ART. 42. *How we find in our memory the things we wish to remember.*
Thus, when the mind wishes to remember something, this volition causes the gland to incline in different directions successively, thus driving the spirits to different corners of the brain, until they find the one where the object we wish to remember has left its traces. By 'left its traces', I mean that the pores of the brain through which the spirits have formerly flowed on account of the presence of the object have, as a result, become more liable than the others to be reopened in the same way by spirits flowing in their direction. So that, when the new spirits encounter these pores, they flow into them more easily than into the rest, and hence arouse a particular movement in the gland, which represents the same object to the soul, so that it realizes that this is the thing it wanted to remember.

ART. 43. *How the soul can imagine, be attentive, and move the body.*
Likewise, when we wish to imagine something we have never seen, this volition is sufficient to ensure that the gland moves in the way required to drive the spirits towards the pores of the brain by the opening of which the object can be represented. Again, when

we wish to focus our attention on a single object for some considerable time, this volition keeps the gland inclined in the same direction for as long as necessary. Again, finally, when we wish to walk or to move our body in some other manner, this volition causes the gland to drive the spirits to the muscles that produce the desired effect.

ART. 44. *That each volition is naturally joined to some particular movement of the gland; but that by contrivance or habit one can attach it to others.*

Yet when we produce some movement or other effect in ourselves, it is not always through an act of the will. It depends on the various links established by nature or habit between the gland and particular thoughts. Thus, for example, when we wish to focus our eyes on a very distant object, this volition causes the iris to enlarge; and if we wish to focus them on a very near object, this volition causes it to contract. But if we think only of enlarging the iris, we can will this as hard as we like, and it makes no difference; since nature has joined the movement of the gland that serves to direct the spirits towards the optic nerve in such a way as to enlarge or contract the iris, not with the will to enlarge or contract it, but instead with the will to look at distant or near objects. And when in speaking we think only of the meaning we want to convey, that enables us to move the tongue and the lips far more swiftly and effectively than would the mental effort to move them in all the ways necessary to utter the same words. This is because the habit we have acquired in learning to speak has established a link between the action of the soul, which, through the agency of the gland, can move the tongue and the lips, and the meaning of the words that result from these movements, rather than between the soul and the movements themselves.

ART. 45. *What power the soul has over its passions.*

Again, our passions cannot be directly aroused or banished by the action of our will; but they can be indirectly, by the representation of things that are habitually associated with the passions we want to have, and that are contrary to those we wish to reject. Thus, to arouse boldness in oneself, and banish terror, it is not enough to will to do so: we must instead set ourselves to consider the reasons, objects, or examples that will persuade us that the danger is not all that great; that it is always safer to stand one's ground and fight than to run away; that we can look forward to the glory and joy of victory, whereas if we flee we can expect only regret and shame, and so on and so forth.

ART. 46. *The reason why the soul cannot entirely control its passions.*
There is a particular reason why the soul is unable swiftly to change or put a stop to its passions, on account of which the defin- ition of them I gave above makes reference to their being not only caused, but sustained and fortified, by some particular movement of the spirits. The reason is that they are almost all accompanied by some excitation that affects the heart, and by extension the whole of the blood and the spirits, with the result that, until this excitation has ceased, they remain present to our awareness (*pensée*) in the same way as sensible objects are present to it while they act upon the sense-organs. And just as the soul, by concentrating hard on some other thing, can prevent itself from hearing a faint noise or feeling a mild pain, but cannot likewise prevent itself from hearing thunder or feeling fire burning the hand, so it can easily overcome the lesser passions, but not the most violent and intense, until after the excitation of the blood and the spirits has passed. The most the will can do while the excitation is at its height is not to consent to its effects and to restrain many of the movements to which it disposes the body. For instance, if anger makes us raise our hand to strike, the will can normally restrain it; if terror prompts the legs to run, the will can stop them; and so on.

ART. 47. *The real nature of the conflicts that are usually imagined to take place between the lower and higher parts of the soul.*
It is this contradiction between the simultaneous movements that the body, by means of the spirits, and the soul, by means of the will, are tending to arouse in the gland that really accounts for all the supposed conflicts between the lower, so-called 'sensitive', part of the soul, and the higher rational part,* or between the natural appetites and the will. But there is only one soul in us, and it is not in itself divided into different parts: one and the same soul is sensitive and rational, and all its appetites are acts of will. The mistake of seeing it as playing the part of different, and usually opposing, characters comes purely

and simply from failing to make the proper distinction between the functions of the soul and those of the body. It is to the body alone that we should ascribe whatever can be observed within us that is at odds with our reason. So the only conflict at issue here is this one: since the little gland in the middle of the brain can be impelled in one direction by the soul and in another by the animal spirits, which, as I said above [§10], are bodies pure and simple, it often happens that the two impulsions are opposed, and that the stronger one nullifies the effect of the other. Now, we can distinguish two kinds of movement aroused by the spirits in the gland: the first kind represent to the soul either the objects that affect the senses, or the impressions formed in the brain, and exert no pressure on the will; the second kind, those which cause the passions or the accompanying movements of the body, do exert some pressure on it. Although the first kind can often impede the actions of the soul, or else be impeded by them, nonetheless, because they are not directly contrary to them, no conflict is observed to take place. Such conflict is observed only between movements of the second kind and the contrary acts of will: for instance, between the pressure the spirits exert on the gland in order to produce the desire for something in the soul, and the contrary pressure of the soul, as it wills to keep away from that very thing. The main reason why the conflict makes itself felt is that, as has already been stated [§45], the will does not have the power to arouse passions directly, and so is obliged to use the indirect approach and to set itself to consider various things in succession: now, if it happens that one of these thoughts is sufficiently powerful to change the flow of the spirits for a moment, it may happen that the next one is not, and that they immediately resume their former course, since the prior condition of the nerves, the heart, and the blood has remained unchanged. As a result, the soul feels itself impelled, almost simultaneously, to desire and not to desire one and the same thing; and this is what has prompted the idea that there are two conflicting powers within it. There is, however, another way of conceiving a kind of conflict: a cause that produces a certain passion in the soul will often also produce certain movements in the body to which the soul makes no contribution, and which it halts or tries to halt as soon as it perceives them; this is what we experience when something that produces terror also causes the spirits to flow into the muscles that serve to move the legs in order to flee, and they are halted by the will to be courageous.*

ART. 48. *How we recognize strength or weakness in a soul, and why the weakest people are so.*

Now, it is by the outcome of such conflicts that a person can know the strength or weakness of his or her soul. For those in whom the will is most naturally able to vanquish the passions and halt the accompanying movements of the body have, no doubt, the strongest souls. But there are people who do not give themselves the chance to realize their own strength, because they never set the will to fight with its own weapons, but only with those that some passions supply in order to resist others. What I mean by the will's own weapons is firm and definite judgements concerning the difference between good and evil, according to which it has resolved to conduct the actions of its life. And the weakest souls of all are those whose will does not thus determine itself to follow certain judgements, but allows itself to be continually swept away by the passions of the moment, which, being often mutually contrary, enlist it by turns on their own side, and, setting it to fight against itself, reduce the soul to the most deplorable possible state. Thus, when terror is representing death as the ultimate evil, which can be avoided only by flight, if, on the other hand, ambition represents flight as a disgrace worse than death, the two passions pull and push the will in different directions, so that, obeying now one, now the other, it is constantly opposed to itself;* so condemning the soul to wretched slavery.

ART. 49. *That strength of soul is not sufficient without the knowledge of truth.*

It is true that there are very few men so weak and irresolute that they will only what their passion dictates. Most have some definite judgements, according to which they regulate some of their actions. And, although these judgements are often false, and may even be based on some passions by which the will has formerly let itself be vanquished or led astray, nonetheless, because it continues to be guided by them even in the absence of the passion that originally caused them, we can consider them as weapons of the will, and regard strength or weakness of soul as being determined by one's greater or lesser tendency to be guided by them and to resist the contrary passions of the moment. But, for all that, there is a great difference between resolutions derived from some false opinion and those based purely on the knowledge of truth;

inasmuch as if one is guided by the latter, one is certain never to suffer from regret or repentance,* whereas, if one has been guided by the former, then, when one discovers one's error, these feelings are inevitable.

ART. 50. *That there is no soul so weak that it cannot, being properly guided, acquire absolute power over its passions.*

And it is useful here to realize that, although, as has already been pointed out above [§44], every movement of the gland seems to have been attached by nature at birth to a particular thought, it can still be attached to other thoughts by force of habit. Experience shows this in the case of language: words, spoken or written, produce movements in the gland, which were designed by nature to represent to the soul nothing more than the sound of the words or the shape of the letters; and yet, on account of the habit we have acquired of thinking of what they signify when one hears the sound of them or sees the corresponding letters, they generally cause us to apprehend their meaning rather than the shape of the letters or the sound of the syllables. It is also useful to realize that, although the movements in the gland, and also in the spirits and the brain, that represent certain objects to the soul are naturally attached to those that arouse certain passions within it, they can nonetheless, by force of habit, be detached from these and attached to other quite different ones; and, indeed, that this habit can be acquired by a single action and does not require a long apprenticeship. Thus, supposing one is eating a particular kind of meat with gusto, and suddenly comes across something foul in it, the shock of this experience can so alter the disposition of the brain that from then on one will be unable to bear the sight of that kind of meat, even though one used to enjoy eating it. And the same thing can be observed in animals;* for although they are not endowed with reason, or perhaps with any kind of thought, yet all the movements of the spirits and the gland that arouse the passions in us take place in them as well, serving to sustain and fortify not, as in our case, the passions, but the movements of the nerves and muscles that habitually accompany them. Thus, when a dog sees a partridge, it is naturally impelled to chase after it; and when it hears a gun go off, the sound naturally prompts it to flee; but, nonetheless, pointers can normally be trained to halt when they see a partridge, and to run up to it when they hear the sound of the subsequent shot. Now, to know such things is very useful to anyone as an encouragement to concentrate on regulating his passions. For since, with a little well-directed effort, one can change the movements of the brain in animals devoid of reason, it is clear that this can be done even more successfully in human beings, and that even those who have the weakest souls could acquire a very absolute command of all their passions, if one were to take the trouble to train them and guide them properly.

PART TWO

Of the Number and Order of the Passions, and the Explanation of the Six Fundamental Ones

ART. 51. *The ultimate causes of the passions.*

From what has been said above [§29], it is clear that the immediate cause of the passions of the soul is nothing other than the vibration imparted by the animal spirits to the little gland in the middle of the brain. But that is not sufficient to enable us to distinguish the different passions from one another: we need to investigate their sources, and examine their ultimate causes. Now, although they can sometimes be aroused by the action of the soul, when it decides to think about this or that object, and also purely by bodily temperament or random impressions in the brain, as occurs when we feel sad or joyful for no apparent reason, it appears, nonetheless, from what has been said above, that all the passions can also be aroused by objects moving the senses, and that such objects are their most common and important cause; from which it follows that, in order to discover all the passions, we need only consider all the possible effects of these objects.

ART. 52. *Their function, and how we can list them in order.*

I further observe that the objects that move the senses arouse different passions within us, not in respect of all their diverse qualities, but only in respect of the various ways in which they can harm or benefit us, or generally make a difference to us; and that the function of all the passions consists in this alone: that they dispose the soul to will those things that nature determines are useful to us, and to persist in so willing; just as the same excitation of the spirits that is their usual cause disposes the body to the movements that enable us to act accordingly. Hence, if we are to establish a list of them, we need only examine in order all the various ways in which our senses can be moved by their objects so as to make a difference to us. And I shall here enumerate all the principal passions in the order that corresponds to this.

THE ORDER AND CLASSIFICATION OF THE PASSIONS

ART. 53. *Wonderment.*
When our first encounter with some object takes us by surprise, and
we judge it to be new, or very different from what we have previously
experienced or from what we expected it to be, this causes us to wonder at it and be astonished. And because this can happen before we
have any knowledge of whether the thing is beneficial to us or not, it
seems to me that wonderment is the first passion of all. And it has
no contrary, because, if the object that presents itself has nothing in
itself to surprise us, we are not moved by it in any way and we consider it without any passion.

ART. 54. *Esteem and contempt, nobility of soul or pride, and humility or
baseness of spirit.*
Esteem or contempt are connected with wonderment, depending on
whether it is the greatness or the littleness of the object that we marvel at. And in the same way we can esteem or despise ourselves;
which is the origin of the passions, and in consequence the habits, of
magnanimity or pride, on the one hand, and humility or baseness of
spirit.*

ART. 55. *Veneration and disdain.*
But when we esteem or despise other objects we consider as free
causes, capable of doing good or evil, esteem becomes veneration and
mere contempt becomes disdain.

ART. 56. *Love and hatred.*
All the passions mentioned up to now can be aroused in us without our perceiving in any way if the object that causes them is good or
bad.* But when a thing is represented to us as good from our point of
view, that is, as being beneficial to us, that causes us to feel love for it;
and when it is represented as bad or harmful, that stirs us to hatred.

ART. 57. *Desire.*
This consideration of good and bad is the origin of all the other passions: but to treat them in an orderly fashion, I will distinguish them
with respect to time; and considering that they incline us to look
to the future far more than to the present or the past, I shall begin

with desire. For not only when we desire to acquire some good we do not yet have, or to avoid some evil we judge may befall us, but also when we desire only that some good may continue or some evil stay away from us (and there is nothing else this passion can extend to), it is obvious that it is always related to the future.

Art. 58. *Hope, fear, jealousy, complacency, and despair.*

The mere fact of thinking that a good may be acquired or an evil avoided is sufficient to produce the desire for this to come to pass. But when, over and above this, we consider whether our desire is likely to be satisfied or not, the idea that it is likely arouses hope in us, and the idea that it is unlikely arouses fear, of which one variety is jealousy. When hope is extreme, its nature changes and it is called confidence or complacency, whereas, on the contrary, extreme fear turns into despair.

Art. 59. *Indecision, courage, boldness, emulation, faint-heartedness, and horror.*

And we can hope and fear in this way, even if the outcome we are expecting is altogether outside our control; but when it is represented to us as depending on ourselves, there may be difficulty in selecting a course of action or putting it into effect. From the former comes indecision,* which disposes us to deliberate and to seek advice. The second kind of difficulty is met by courage or boldness, of which emulation is one variety. And the contrary of courage is faint-heartedness, as the contrary of boldness is terror or horror.

Art. 60. *Remorse.*

And if one has resolved on some course of action before indecision has been eliminated, this gives birth to remorse, which is related not, like the preceding passions, to the future, but to the present or past.

Art. 61. *Joy and sadness.*

And the consideration of a present good arouses joy in us, and that of an evil, sadness, when the good or evil is represented to us as belonging to us.

Art. 62. *Derision, envy, pity.*

But when it is represented to us as belonging to other people, we may judge whether they deserve it or not; and when we judge that they deserve it, the only passion this arouses in us is joy, inasmuch as, for us, it is a kind of good to see things turn out as they ought. There is only this difference: joy arising from someone's good is grave, whereas joy arising from someone's evil is accompanied by laughter and derision. But if we judge that they do not deserve it, then their good arouses envy, and the evil they suffer arouses pity, both of which are forms of sadness. And it is to be noted that the same passions that relate to present good or evil can frequently also relate to future good or evil, inasmuch as our opinion that they will come to pass represents them as present.

Art. 63. *Self-satisfaction and repentance.*

We can also consider the good or evil, whether present or past, with reference to its cause. And the good that has been done by ourselves gives us an inner satisfaction that is the sweetest of all the passions, whereas the ill we have done gives rise to repentance, the most bitter.

Art. 64. *Favour and gratitude.*

But the good done by others causes us to feel favour towards them, even when it was not done to us; if it was, then favour is reinforced by gratitude.

Art. 65. *Indignation and anger.*

Likewise, the evil done by others, when it does not affect ourselves, causes us to feel only indignation towards them; when it does affect us, it also stirs up anger.

Art. 66. *Glory and shame.*

Moreover, when the good that we possess, or have possessed, is viewed in relation to the opinion others may have of it, this arouses glory in us; when evil is involved, the result is shame.

Art. 67. *Distaste, regret, and gladness.*

And sometimes the continued presence of a good causes boredom or distaste,* whereas the sadness caused by an evil lessens over time. Finally, a good that is past gives rise to regret, a variety of sadness, whereas an evil that is past gives rise to gladness, a variety of joy.

ART. 68. *Why this classification of the passions is different from the one generally accepted.**

The above is what seems to me the best order in which to list the passions. I know well that I am departing here from the opinion of all those who have written about them before, but there is good reason to do so. For their classification is based on their distinction between two appetites in the sensitive part of the soul, one called 'concupiscible', the other 'irascible'.* And because I recognize no distinction of parts in the soul, as I have said above [§47], this distinction seems to me to boil down to saying that it has two faculties, of desire and anger; but since by the same token it has the faculties of wonderment, love, hope, and fear, and thus the capacity to receive all the other passions within itself, or to perform the actions to which these passions impel it, I cannot see why these authors have wanted to reduce them all to desire or anger. Besides, their classification does not include all the principal passions, as I think mine does. I say only the principal ones, because one could distinguish several more specific ones besides: their number of these, indeed, is indefinite.

ART. 69. *That there are only six fundamental passions.*

But the number of simple and fundamental passions is not very great. For if we go over all those I have just listed, we shall easily see that there are only six of this kind: namely, wonderment, love, hatred, desire, joy, and sadness; and that all the others are either compounds of more than one of them or variants of one of them. So in order to prevent the reader from being confused by the sheer number of the passions, I shall here deal separately with the six fundamental ones; and I shall show thereafter how all the others are derived from them.

ART. 70. *Wonderment: its definition and its cause.*

In wonderment, the soul is suddenly taken by surprise, which causes it to consider attentively the objects that it finds rare and extraordinary. Thus, it is caused first and foremost by the impression formed in the brain which represents the object as rare, and consequently worthy of close consideration; and then by the movement of the spirits, which are disposed by this impression, first, to rush towards the part of the brain where it is located in order to reinforce it and preserve it there, and, secondly, to flow from there into the muscles that serve to keep the sense-organs in the same state as they are now, so as to keep the original impression going (supposing it was formed by them in the first place).

ART. 71. *That in this passion no change takes place in the heart or the blood.*

And this passion has one distinguishing feature: we cannot observe any change accompanying it in the heart or the blood, as we can with the other passions. The reason is this: since it is focused not on good or bad but only on the knowledge of the thing that has given rise to it, it has no relationship with the heart or the blood,* on which all the good of the body depends, but only with the brain, where the sense-organs that furnish such knowledge are located.

ART. 72. *What the power of wonderment consists in.*

And yet the impact of wonderment can be very powerful, because of the surprise involved: that is, the sudden and unexpected occurrence of the impression that alters the movement of the spirits. This surprise is so characteristic of wonderment that, when it is encountered in other passions, in almost all of which it is commonly found, its effect being to reinforce them, this is because they contain an admixture of wonderment. And its impact results from two things: first, the novelty of the experience; and, secondly, the fact that the movement it causes is at its most powerful at the beginning. For this kind of movement certainly has more effect than those that are weak at the beginning and intensify only gradually, so that they can be easily diverted. It is also certain that sense-objects new in our experience affect the brain in parts in which it is unaccustomed to be affected; and since these parts are softer or less firm than those hardened by frequent stimulation, the movements produced there have all the more impact. This will not be so difficult to believe if we reflect that the same reason applies to the soles of our feet, which feel a significant impact when we walk, on account of the weight of the body they are supporting, and yet, since they are accustomed to it, we hardly notice this; whereas if they are tickled, the far milder and more gentle touching is almost unbearable, simply because we are not used to it.

ART. 73. *The nature of astonishment.*

And the surprise in question is so powerful when it comes to sending the spirits in the cavities of the brain towards the place where the impression of the object of our wonderment is located that sometimes it drives them all there, and causes them to be so absorbed in retaining this impression that none of them flow on into the muscles, or even divert their course in the slightest from the first traces in the brain into which they have flowed; the result being that the whole body remains motionless as a statue, and we can perceive nothing of the object but the aspect of it first presented to us, so that we can gain no more detailed knowledge of it. This is what is commonly called being astonished; and astonishment is an excess of wonderment that can only ever be bad.

ART. 74. *The utility of all the passions, and the harm they can do.*
Now it is easy to conclude, from all that has been said above, that the utility of all the passions consists purely in this: that they fortify and preserve thoughts in the soul that are good for it to retain, and which otherwise could be easily effaced. Likewise, the only harm they can do is when they fortify and preserve these thoughts for longer than necessary, or fortify and preserve other thoughts on which one should not linger.

ART. 75. *The particular utility of wonderment.*
And we can say of wonderment that its particular utility is to enable us to learn and retain in our memory things of which we were formerly unaware. For we wonder at only what appears to us rare and extraordinary; and nothing can so appear to us except when we were previously unaware of it, or it differs from what we knew; for it is on account of this difference that we call something extraordinary. Now, even when something previously unknown presents itself for the first time to our understanding or our senses, we do not necessarily retain it in our memory for all that, unless our idea of it is fortified in our brain by some passion, or else by the application of our intellect, when determined by the will to concentrate on and think hard about the object. And the other passions can serve to enable us to notice what appears good or evil, but for those that just appear rare we have only wonderment. And so we see that those without any natural inclination to this passion are ordinarily very ignorant.

ART. 76. *The ways in which it can be harmful, and how one can compensate for a lack of it and correct any excess of it.*
But excessive wonderment, and astonishment at the sight of things

that deserve little or no consideration, occurs far more frequently than its contrary. And this excess can entirely suppress or distort the use of reason. That is why, although it is a good thing to be born with some inclination to this passion, since it disposes us to acquire a knowledge of the sciences, we should subsequently try to rid ourselves of it as much as possible. For it is easy to make up for the lack of it by careful reflection and attention, to which our will can always compel our understanding when we judge that the thing we have encountered is worth the trouble; but to eliminate the tendency to excessive wonderment, there is no other remedy than to acquire a knowledge of many things, and to habituate oneself to thinking about whatever may seem most rare and strange.

ART. 77. *That it is neither the most stupid nor the most intelligent people that are most given to wonderment.*

Moreover, although only those who are dull and stupid have no natural tendency to wonderment, this does not mean that the tendency is greatest in the most intelligent people; it is found most in those with a fair amount of common sense who do not, however, have a very high opinion of their own abilities.

ART. 78. *That an excessive tendency to wonderment may become a habit if we fail to correct it.*

And although this passion seems to diminish with experience, since the more often we encounter rare things at which we wonder, the more used we become to getting over this wonderment, and to thinking that whatever comes our way in future will be commonplace, nonetheless, when it is excessive and it causes one to fix one's attention only on objects as they first appear, without gaining any further knowledge of them, it leaves behind it a habit that disposes the soul to linger in the same way on the surface appearance of whatever objects it comes across in future, those, that is, that appear in the slightest way new. This is how blind curiosity can become a lifelong disease: the curiosity, that is, of people who seek out what is rare only to marvel at it, not to understand it; for they gradually become so prone to wonderment that the most trivial things are no less capable of engaging their attention than those that are most worth investigating.

ART. 79. *The definitions of love and hatred.*

Love is an emotion of the soul caused by the movement of the spirits that incites it to will itself to be united* with objects that appear to be beneficial to it. And hatred is an emotion caused by the spirits that incites the soul to will itself separate from objects that present themselves to it as harmful. I say that these disturbances are caused by the spirits, so as to distinguish love and hatred, as passions and therefore dependent on the body, both from the judgements that also prompt the soul to will itself to be united to things it deems good, and to separate itself from those it deems bad, and from the emotion produced in the soul purely by such judgements.*

ART. 80. *What it means to speak of willing oneself to be united with or separate from.*

Moreover, the word 'will' here means not desire, which is a separate passion, related to the future, but the consent in virtue of which one considers oneself henceforth united, so to speak, with the object of one's love, in such a way that one imagines a whole, of which one thinks of oneself as only one part, the beloved object being another. Whereas, on the contrary, in hatred one considers oneself as a whole entirely separate from the thing for which one feels aversion.

ART. 81. *Of the customary distinction between love of concupiscence and love of benevolence.*

Now, it is usual to distinguish two kinds of love,* one of which is termed love of benevolence, and prompts us to wish well to what we love; the other is termed love of concupiscence, that is, it makes us desire the thing we love. But it seems to me that this distinction applies only to the effects of love, and not its nature: for as soon as one has willed oneself united with some object, whatever its nature, one feels benevolence towards it; that is, one wills it united with those things one thinks are beneficial to it; which is one of the chief effects of love. And if one judges that it would be a good to possess it, or to be associated with it in some way other than by the will, one desires it: which is also one of the most ordinary effects of love.

ART. 82. *How very different passions come together in so far as they partake of the nature of love.*

Nor is there any need to distinguish as many different types of love as there are different possible objects of love; for, though the passions, for example, of an ambitious man for glory, of an avaricious one for money, of a drunkard for wine, of a ruffian for a woman he wants to take by force, of a man of honour for his friend or his mistress,* and of a good father for his children, are very different from one another, nonetheless they are alike in that they all partake of the nature of love. But in the first four cases, the men love only the possession of the object of their passion, and have no love for the object itself, for which they feel only desire mingled with other more specific passions. Whereas the love of a good father for his children is so pure that he desires nothing from them, and does not wish to possess them in any further way, or to be joined to them more closely than he is already; but, considering them as his other selves, he seeks their good as he seeks his own, or even more devotedly, because, considering himself and them as forming a whole of which he is not the better part, he often puts their interests before his own, and would not shrink from losing his life in order to preserve theirs. The affection of men of honour for their friends is of the same nature, though seldom so perfect; and their affection for a mistress is largely of this sort, though with a touch of the other sort as well.

ART. 83. *Of the difference there is between mere affection, friendship, and devotion.*

It seems to me that it is more rational to distinguish between different types of love according to the value one sets on the beloved in comparison with oneself. For when one values the object of one's love less than oneself, one has only mere affection for it; when one values it as much as oneself, that is called friendship; and when one values it more, the passion in question may be called devotion. Thus, one may feel affection towards a flower, a bird, or a horse; but, unless one's mind is extremely disordered, one can feel friendship only for human beings. And human beings are so much the proper object of this passion that there is no person so imperfect that one cannot have a very perfect friendship for them when one thinks that one is loved by them and if one has a truly noble and generous soul, as will be explained below in articles 154 and 156. As for devotion, its chief object is no doubt the sovereign Divinity, to whom we cannot but feel it, when we know him as we should; but one can also feel devotion to one's ruler, one's country, one's city, and even to an individual, when one values him much more highly than oneself. Now, the difference between these three kinds of love appears chiefly in their effects: for inasmuch as in all of them one considers oneself as joined and united with the object of one's love, one is always ready to sacrifice the lesser part of the whole one forms with it, in order to preserve the greater; hence, in mere affection, one always puts oneself first, before what one loves, and, on the contrary, in devotion one so far puts the thing one loves before oneself that one does not fear to die in order to preserve it. Examples of this are not uncommon, when someone exposes himself to certain death to protect his ruler or his city, or even sometimes an individual to whom he has devoted himself.

ART. 84. *That there are not so many varieties of hatred as there are of love.*

However, although hatred is directly contrary to love, we cannot distinguish so many varieties of it, because we are less aware of the difference between the evils from which we have willed ourselves separate than we are of that between the goods to which we are united.

ART. 85. *Of attraction and repulsion.*

And I can find only one significant distinction that applies to both love and hatred. It is this: that the objects of both passions can be represented to the soul either by the external senses, or by the internal ones and by its own reason. For we commonly use the terms 'good' and 'bad' for what our internal senses or our reason cause us to judge suitable or contrary to our nature; but we call 'beautiful' or 'ugly' what is thus represented to us by our external senses, especially that of sight, which alone is more highly valued than all the others. This distinction gives rise to two kinds of love, namely, the kind one has for good things, and the kind one has for beautiful things, which might be termed attraction, so as to avoid confusion with the other kind, and also with desire, to which the name 'love' is often applied; and to two kinds of hatred as well, one of which is directed at what is bad, the other at what is ugly; and this last sort can be called repulsion or aversion, to distinguish it from hatred in general. But the most noteworthy point here is that these passions of attraction and repulsion are usually more violent than the other kinds of love and hatred, because what comes to the soul through the senses makes a more powerful impression on it than what is represented to it by its reason; and yet, nevertheless, there is usually less truth in them; so that, of all the passions, these are the ones that are most deceptive and against which one must most carefully guard oneself.

ART. 86. *The definition of desire.*

The passion of desire is an agitation of the soul caused by the spirits that disposes it to will, with reference to the future, those things it represents to itself as beneficial. Thus, we do not desire only the presence of an absent good, but also the preservation of a present one, and, furthermore, we desire the absence of evil, both the evil we are suffering already and the evil we think may befall us in the future.

ART. 87. *That this is a passion without a contrary.*

I know very well that in the Schools they distinguish the passion that tends towards the pursuit of a good, for which they reserve the name 'desire', from the passion that tends towards the avoidance of evil, which they term 'aversion'.* But, inasmuch as there is no good the privation of which is not an evil, and no evil, considered as a positive thing, of which the privation is not a good; and that in seeking wealth, we are necessarily fleeing from poverty, and in fleeing from diseases we are seeking health, and so on, it seems to me that what we have here is always a single impulsion to seek good, and at the same time to avoid the evil that is contrary to it. I observe only this difference, that the desire we have when we are focused on some good is accompanied by love, and then by hope and joy; whereas the same desire, when our focus is on avoiding the evil contrary to that good, is accompanied by hatred, fear, and sadness; for which reason we judge it contrary to itself.* But if we take the trouble to consider it when it relates equally and at the same time to some good we are pursuing and to the opposite evil we wish to avoid, we can very clearly see that both are results of one and the same passion.

ART. 88. *The different varieties of desire.*

It would be more rational to break desire down into as many different varieties as there are different objects we pursue: since, for example, curiosity, which is nothing other than a desire to know, differs greatly from the desire for glory, which in turn differs from the desire for revenge, and so on. But it is sufficient for our purposes to be clear that there are as many varieties of desire as there are of love or hatred, and that the most important and most powerful are those born of attraction and repulsion.

ART. 89. *The desire born of repulsion.*
Now, although, as has already been pointed out, there is only a single passion of desire tending both towards the pursuit of some good and away from the contrary evil, the desire born of attraction is none-theless very different from the desire born of repulsion.* For the attraction and the repulsion, which are indeed quite contrary, are not a good and an evil constituting the object of these desires, but only two emotions of the soul disposing it to pursue two very different things. That is, repulsion has been established by nature to convey to the soul the idea of sudden and unexpected death, in such a way that, although the source of this repulsion may be only the feel of a little worm on the skin, or the noise, or the shadow, of a fluttering leaf, our initial feeling is of an emotion as violent as if our senses were registering a very real danger of death. This immediately gives rise to an excitation that induces the soul to employ all its powers to avoid so imminent an evil; and this is the kind of desire that is commonly called fleeing or aversion.*

ART. 90. *The desire born of attraction.*
On the contrary, attraction has been particularly established by nature to represent the enjoyment of what attracts us as if it were the greatest of all the goods that pertain to human beings, so that as a result we desire this enjoyment very ardently. It is true that there are different kinds of attraction, and that the desires that result from them are not all equally powerful. For example, the beauty of flowers prompts us only to look at them, while that of fruit prompts us to eat them. But the most powerful attraction comes from the perfections we imagine in a person we think may become another self;* for, along with the difference between the sexes, which nature has established both in human beings and in irrational animals, it has also implanted certain impressions in the brain that cause us, at a certain age and stage, to consider ourselves as lacking in ourselves and as if we were merely the half of a whole of which a person of the opposite sex should be the other half;* so that the acquisition of this other half is confusedly represented by nature as the greatest of all imaginable goods. And though we see many people of the opposite sex, we do

not, all the same, desire several at a time in this way, since nature does not prompt us to imagine that we need more than one other half. But when we observe something in one person that attracts us more than what we observe in others at the same time, this determines the soul to feel for that one person the whole of the naturally inspired inclination to pursue the good that nature represents to it as the greatest we can possibly possess; and this inclination or desire thus born of attraction is more commonly called by the name of love than the passion of love described previously* [§79]. And, indeed, its effects are stranger, and it is the principal subject matter of the writers of romance and the poets.

ART. 91. *The definition of joy.*
Joy is an agreeable emotion of the soul: it is the soul's enjoyment* of a good represented to it as its own by the impressions of the brain. I say that the enjoyment of the good consists in this emotion, because in fact the soul receives no other benefit from whatever goods it possesses; and as long as it feels no joy, one could say that it has no more benefit from its goods than if it did not possess them at all. Furthermore, when I spoke of 'a good represented to it as its own by the impressions of the brain', this was to distinguish this kind of joy, which is a passion, from the purely intellectual joy brought about in the soul by its own action, and which can be defined as an agreeable emotion aroused in itself by itself, which is the form taken by its enjoyment of a good represented to it as its own by the understanding. True, as long as the soul is joined to the body, this intellectual joy can hardly ever fail to be accompanied by the corresponding passion; for as soon as our understanding perceives that we possess some good, even if this good is so different from all that pertains to the body that it cannot be imagined, the imagination nonetheless immediately produces some impression in the brain, which gives rise to the movement of the spirits that arouses the passion of joy.

ART. 92. *The definition of sadness.*
Sadness is a disagreeable feeling of weakness, which is how the soul experiences the disadvantage it receives from some evil or lack represented to it as its own by the impressions of the brain. And there is also an intellectual sadness, distinct from the passion, but which hardly ever fails to accompany it.

ART. 93. *The causes of these two passions.*

Now, when intellectual joy or sadness arouse the corresponding passions in this way, their cause is pretty obvious; and it can be seen from their definitions that joy arises from the opinion that one possesses some good, and sadness from one's opinion that one has some evil or lack. But it often happens that we feel sad or joyful without being able distinctly to observe in this way the good or evil that is causing it, namely, when the good or evil makes its impression on the brain without the involvement of the soul, sometimes because it belongs purely to the body, and sometimes, also, because, although it belongs to the soul, the soul is considering it not as good or evil, but in some other form, the impression of which is connected in the brain with that of good or evil.

ART. 94. *How these passions are aroused by goods and evils that pertain only to the body, and in what titillation* and pain consist.*

So, when one is in perfect health, and the weather is more serene than usual, one feels in oneself a cheerfulness that comes from no activity of the intellect, but purely from the impressions made in the brain by the movement of the spirits; and one feels sad in the same way when the body is indisposed, even if one does not know it is. And likewise the titillation of the senses is followed so closely by joy, and pain so closely by sadness, that most people are unable to distinguish them. And yet they differ so markedly that one can sometimes suffer pains with joy, and find titillation disagreeable. But the reason why titillation normally results in joy is that what we call titillation or an agreeable sensation consists in the production, by the objects of the senses, of some movement in the nerves that would be capable of harming them if they were not sufficiently strong to resist it or if the body were indisposed. This results in an impression in the brain, which, being established by nature as an indication of this strength and this good disposition, represents them to the soul as a good that belongs to it, inasmuch as it is united with the body, and thus arouses within it the passion of joy. It is for virtually the same reason that we naturally take pleasure in feeling ourselves stirred by all kinds of passions, even sadness and hatred, when these passions are caused purely by the strange adventures we see represented on a stage,* or by some other similar causes, which, since they cannot harm us in any way, seem to titillate our soul as they affect it. And the reason why pain ordinarily produces sadness is that the sensation we call pain always comes from some influence so violent as to harm the nerves, in such a way that, since this sensation has been established by nature to signify to the soul both the damage the influence in question is causing the body, and the body's weakness (in that it was not able to resist), it represents both of these facts to the soul as evils that are always unpleasurable unless they result in some good that the soul regards as more important.

ART. 95. *How they can also be produced by goods and evils of which the soul is not aware, even though they belong to it; such as the pleasure of risking one's life or remembering some past evil.*

Thus, the pleasure young people* often find in undertaking difficult things and exposing themselves to great dangers, even when they hope for no benefit or glory as a result, comes from the impression in their brain produced by the thought that what they are undertaking is difficult; and this impression, combined with the impression they could form if they were to think that it is a good to feel oneself courageous enough, lucky enough, skilful enough, or strong enough to dare to run so great a risk, causes them to take pleasure in doing so.*
And the satisfaction of old men when they remember the evils they have suffered comes from their representing to themselves that it is a good to have been able to survive through them all.

ART. 96. *The movements of the blood and the spirits that cause the five preceding passions.*

The five passions I have begun to explain here are so attached to or opposed to one another that it is easier to consider them all together than to treat each one separately, as in the case of wonderment; and, unlike wonderment, their cause is not only in the brain, but also in the heart, the spleen, the liver, and all the other parts of the body, in so far as these play a part in the production of the blood and then of the spirits. For although all the veins convey the blood they contain to the heart, it sometimes happens, nonetheless, that the blood in some is propelled there with more force than that in others; and it also happens that the openings through which it enters the heart, or else those through which it leaves, are broader or narrower at some times than at others.

ART. 97. *The main observations* that enable us to discover these move-ments in the case of love.*

Now, if we consider the various changes that observation reveals in our bodies while our soul is agitated by various passions, I observe, in the case of love, when it is found in isolation, I mean, unaccompanied by an intense joy, or desire, or sadness, that the beating of the pulse is steady and much fuller and stronger than usual, that a pleasant warmth is felt in the chest, and that food is digested very quickly in the stomach, so that this passion is beneficial for the health.

ART. 98. *In hatred.*

I observe, on the contrary, that in the case of hatred the pulse is uneven and less full, and often more rapid; that sensations of cold, interspersed with a kind of harsh and prickly heat, are felt in the chest; that the stomach ceases to perform its functions, and is liable to vomit up and reject the food one has eaten, or at least to corrupt it and convert it into bad humours.

ART. 99. *In joy.*

In joy, it is observed that the pulse is steady and more rapid than usual, but less full and strong than in the case of love; and that a pleasant sensation of heat is felt, not just in the chest, but spreading to all the outer parts of the body, along with the blood, which is observed to flow copiously into these; and yet that sometimes one loses one's appetite, because digestion is less thorough than usual.

ART. 100. *In sadness.*

In sadness, the pulse is weak and slow, and it feels as if the heart is being shackled by cords tied tightly around it, and frozen by icicles which spread their cold all over the body; and yet, all the same, one sometimes continues to have a hearty appetite and to feel that the stomach is properly doing its duty, provided that no hatred is mingled with the sadness.

ART. 101. *In desire.*

Finally, I observe this particularly as regards desire: that it agitates the heart more violently than any of the other passions, and sends more spirits to the brain. These flow from the brain into the muscles and render all the senses more acute and all the parts of the body more mobile.

ART. 102. *The movement of the blood and the spirits in love.*

These observations, and several others which it would take too long to write down here, have given me reason to judge that, when the understanding represents some beloved object to itself, the impression made by this thought in the brain sends the animal spirits, through the nerves of the sixth pair, towards the muscles around the intestines and stomach, in the manner necessary to ensure that the juices from food, which are converted into new blood, flow quickly to the heart without lingering in the liver. This new blood, being impelled towards the heart with more force than the blood in the other parts of the body, enters it in greater quantity, and produces in it a greater degree of heat, since it is denser than the blood that has been rarefied several times over on its journeys back and forth through the heart. As a result, the heart also sends spirits to the brain, the parts of which are larger and more agitated than usual; and these spirits, fortifying the impression produced in the brain by the first thought of the beloved object, compel the soul to linger over this thought. It is in this that the passion of love consists.

ART. 103. *In hatred.*

On the contrary, in hatred, the first thought of the object that arouses repulsion sends the spirits in the brain towards the muscles of the stomach and intestines, in such a way that they prevent the juices from food from mingling with the blood, by closing all the openings through which they normally flow; and the thought also sends the spirits towards the little nerves of the spleen and of the lower part of the liver, where the receptacle of bile* is situated, in such a way that the parts of the blood that are normally directed towards those places flow out of them and back towards the heart, mingling with the blood that is in the branches of the vena cava. This causes the heat of the heart to fluctuate, inasmuch as the blood from the spleen is very little heated and rarefied, whereas that from the lower part of the liver, where there is always bile, becomes heated and dilated very quickly. As a result, the spirits flowing towards the brain have parts very unequal in size and their movement is very irregular; and therefore they fortify the ideas of hatred already imprinted in the brain, and dispose the soul to thoughts full of bitterness and rancour.

ART. 104. *In joy.*
In joy the active nerves are not so much those of the spleen, the liver, the stomach, or the intestines, but those in all the rest of the body, especially the nerve around the orifices of the heart, which opens and closes these orifices, and thus enables the blood conveyed by the other nerves from the veins towards the heart to enter and leave the heart in greater quantities than usual. And because the blood that enters the heart at such times has flowed into and out of it repeatedly, having passed from the arteries into the veins, it dilates very promptly and produces spirits the parts of which are equal in size and subtle. As such, they are well suited to forming and fortifying the impressions of the brain that produce calm and cheerful thoughts in the soul.

ART. 105. *In sadness.*
On the contrary, in sadness, the orifices of the heart are much reduced by the little nerve surrounding them, and the blood in the veins is not at all agitated, so that very little of it flows into the heart; but, meanwhile, the channels through which the juices from food flow from the stomach and the intestines towards the liver remain open; as a result, the appetite remains unaffected, except when hatred, which is often combined with sadness, closes the channels.

ART. 106. *In desire.*
Finally, the passion of desire has this distinctive effect: the will to obtain some good or avoid some evil sends the spirits racing from the brain to all the parts of the body that may contribute to the requisite actions, and especially to the heart and the parts of the body that supply it with most blood, so that, receiving a more abundant supply than usual, it sends a greater quantity of spirits towards the brain, both to sustain and fortify the idea of this act of will and to flow from the brain into all the sense-organs and all the muscles that can be brought into play to obtain the desired result.

ART. 107. *The cause of these movements in love.*
And I deduce the reasons for all this from what has been already stated [§50], that there is so close a union between our soul and our body that when we have once linked some bodily action with some thought, then in the future, whenever one of the two presents itself to us, the other will as well. We see this in the case of those people

who, when ill, have taken some potion they found disgusting, and who cannot thereafter drink or eat anything with a similar taste, without again feeling the same disgust; and, likewise, they cannot think of their loathing for medicine without the same taste coming back to their minds. For it seems to me that the first passions our soul experienced when it was first joined to our body must have originated as follows: sometimes the blood, or other liquid entering the heart, was a nutriment more conducive than usual to maintaining the heat of the heart, which is the principle of life; as a result, the soul willed itself united with this nutriment—loved it, in other words; and at the same time the spirits flowed from the brain to the muscles that could pressure or stimulate the parts from which the nutriment had been sent to the heart, so that they would send more of it; and these parts were the stomach and the intestines, the agitation of which increases the appetite, or else also the liver and the lungs, on which the muscles of the diaphragm can exert pressure. That is why the same movement of the spirits has ever after accompanied the passion of love.

Art. 108. *In hatred.*
Sometimes, on the contrary, some extraneous liquid came towards the heart that was not conducive to maintaining its heat, or that might even extinguish it; as a result, the spirits rising from the heart to the brain aroused the passion of hatred in the soul. And at the same time the spirits also flowed from the brain towards the nerves that could send blood from the spleen and from the little veins of the liver towards the heart, to prevent the harmful liquid from entering it; and also towards the nerves that could send the liquid away towards the intestines and the stomach, or even cause the stomach to vomit it up. Hence the same movements ordinarily accompany the passion of hatred. And one can see with the naked eye that there are numerous veins or channels in the liver sufficiently broad for the juices from food to flow from the portal vein to the vena cava, and thence to the heart, without lingering at all in the liver; but that there is also a host of smaller ones where the juices can linger, and which always contain a reserve supply of blood, as the spleen does also. This blood is denser than the blood in the other parts of the body, and can thus better serve as a nutriment for the fire in the heart when the stomach and the intestines fail to supply it.

ART. 109. *In joy.*

It also sometimes occurred in the very earliest stages of our life that the blood contained in our veins afforded nourishment that was pretty conducive to maintaining the heat of our heart, and was sufficiently abundant for the heart to need no nourishment from elsewhere. This produced the passion of joy in the soul. At the same time, it caused the orifices of the heart to open up more widely than usual and the spirits to flow abundantly from the brain, not only into the nerves the function of which is to open these orifices, but also generally into all the other nerves that convey the blood from the veins to the heart; thus preventing further blood from flowing to the heart from the liver, the spleen, the intestines, and the stomach. That is why these same movements are found in conjunction with joy.

ART. 110. *In sadness.*

Sometimes, on the other hand, it occurred that the body was lacking in nutriments, and this must have produced the soul's first experience of sadness, at least of the kind that is not combined with hatred. It also caused the orifices of the heart to narrow, since they were receiving only a small quantity of blood, a good deal of which, moreover, was coming from the spleen, for this is, so to speak, the ultimate reserve, the function of which is to supply the heart with blood when it is not receiving enough from elsewhere. This is why the movements of the spirits and the nerves that function so as to narrow the orifices of the heart in this way and to convey blood there from the spleen are always found in conjunction with sadness.

ART. 111. *In desire.*

Finally, the soul's first desires, when newly joined to the body, must have all been concerned with receiving whatever was beneficial to it, and rejecting whatever was harmful. And to bring these results about, the spirits immediately began moving all the muscles and all the sense-organs in all the ways in which they can be moved. For this reason, whenever the soul now desires something, the whole body becomes more agile and more disposed to move than it is in its habitual state. And when the body is so disposed from some extraneous cause, that renders the desires of the soul keener and more intense.

ART. 112. *The outward signs of those passions.*

What I have written here makes it easy to grasp the cause of the differences in the pulse-rate and the other properties ascribed above to the different passions, without it being necessary for me to linger further on this topic. But, because I have simply described the observable features that go with each one in its pure state, which reveal to us the movements of the blood and spirits that produce them all, I still need to discuss various outward signs that generally accompany the passions, and which are far more readily observed when they are mingled together, as they generally are, than when they are separate. The main signs in question are the expressions of the eyes and face, changes of colour, trembling, lethargy, fainting, laughing, weeping, groaning, and sighing.

ART. 113. *Of the expressions of the eyes and the face.*

There is no passion that is not disclosed by some particular expression of the eyes; and this is so obvious with some passions that the dullest servants can tell from their master's look if he is angry with them or not. But even though these expressions of the eyes are easily perceived, and their meaning known, it is nonetheless far from easy to describe them, because each one comprises a number of changes in the movement and appearance of the eye; and these are both so specific and so small that they cannot each be perceived separately, although the result of their conjunction is perfectly easy to observe. Almost the same can be said of the expressions of the face that also accompany the passions: for although these are more visible than those of the eyes, it is nonetheless no easy matter to distinguish them, and they differ so little from one another that some people's expressions when weeping are almost the same as other people's when laughing. It is true that some expressions are pretty conspicuous, such as the wrinkles of the brow that accompany anger, and certain movements of the nose and lips that go with indignation and derision; but these seem to be more voluntary than natural. And in general any expression of the face or the eyes can be modified by the soul when, desiring to hide its passion, it vividly imagines a contrary one; so that expressions can be used as much in order to conceal as to express one's passions.

ART. 114. *Of changes of colour.*
It is not so easy to help blushing or growing pale when some passion
disposes us to do so, because, unlike the former changes, these ones
do not depend on the nerves and the muscles: they come more directly from the heart, which may be termed the wellspring of the passions, inasmuch as it prepares the blood and spirits to produce them.
Now, it is certain that the colour of the face derives purely from the
blood, which, as it flows continuously from the heart via the arteries
into all the veins, and from the veins back to the heart, colours the
face more or less, depending on the extent to which it is filling the
little veins found near the surface of the face.

ART. 115. *How joy causes blushing.*
Thus, joy makes the face brighter and rosier, because, by opening the
sluices of the heart, it sends the blood flowing more quickly into all
the veins, as a result of which, becoming hotter and more subtle, it
causes all the parts of the face to expand to a certain extent, giving it
a more cheerful and lively appearance.

ART. 116. *How sadness causes pallor.*
Sadness, on the contrary, narrows the orifices of the heart, causing
the blood to flow more slowly into the veins, so that, becoming colder
and denser, it needs to take up less space; as a result, it tends to concentrate in the broader veins, those nearest the heart,* and to leave
the more remote ones, of which those of the face are the most visible.
As a result, the face appears pale and gaunt, especially when the sadness is intense, or very sudden, as we see in the case of horror, where
the element of surprise increases the constriction of the heart.

ART. 117. *How it is that we often blush when sad.*
But it often happens that, far from growing pale when sad, we actually
go red. This must be explained by other passions' being combined
with the sadness, namely, love or desire, and sometimes hatred as
well. For these passions heat or agitate the blood flowing from the
liver, the intestines, and the other inner organs, and so push it towards
the heart, and from there, via the main artery, into the veins of the
face; the sadness constricting the orifices of the heart on either side
is unable to prevent this, except when it is extreme. But even when it
is only moderately intense, it easily prevents the blood that has thus

flowed into the veins of the face from flowing back to the heart, while at the same time love, desire, or hatred are causing more blood to flow from the internal organs into the face. This is why the blood accumulates around the face and turns it red, redder, even, than in joy, because the colour of the blood appears all the more clearly because it is flowing more slowly, and also because more blood can accumulate in this way in the veins of the face than when the orifices of the heart are more wide open. This appears chiefly in shame, which is a composite passion: the combination of love of self and an urgent desire to avoid present disgrace sends the blood flowing from the internal organs towards the heart, and from there through the arteries towards the face, while, at the same time, a moderately intense sadness prevents that blood from flowing back to the heart. The same normally occurs when one weeps; for, as I shall explain presently, tears are mostly caused by a combination of love and sadness. And in anger also, which often involves the combination of a sudden desire for revenge, on the one hand, and love, hatred, and sadness, on the other.

Art. 118. *Trembling.*
Trembling comes from two different causes. One is that sometimes too small a quantity of spirits is flowing from the brain into the nerves, and the other that sometimes too great a quantity is flowing to allow the little channels in the muscles to be fully closed (as was explained in §11, they have to be closed in order to bring about movements of the limbs). The first cause applies in sadness and in terror, and also when one trembles with cold, for these passions, like cold in the air, can so thicken the blood that it no longer supplies enough spirits to the brain for it to send on to the nerves. The other cause often appears in people who ardently desire something, as well as in those who are seriously angry, not to mention those who are drunk: for both these passions, like wine, sometimes cause the spirits to flow into the brain in such quantities that they cannot be dispatched from there into the muscles in a regular fashion.

Art. 119. *Lethargy.*
Lethargy is a tendency, felt in all the limbs, to go limp and motionless; like trembling, it is due to a shortage of spirits in the nerves, but in a different way. For whereas the cause of trembling is that there is

an insufficient quantity of spirits in the brain to obey the impulsion of the gland when it pushes them towards some muscle or other, the cause of lethargy is that the gland is not determining them to flow towards some muscles rather than others.

ART. 120. *How it is caused by love and by desire.*

And the passion that most typically causes this effect is love, combined with the desire for a thing the acquisition of which is not imagined as currently possible; for the soul is so absorbed by love in the contemplation of the beloved object that it sets all the spirits in the brain to display the image of that object before it, and halts all the movements of the gland that do not contribute to this purpose. And it should be observed, as regards desire, that the property I have ascribed to it, of rendering the body more mobile, applies to it only when we imagine the desired object to be such that we can do something there and then that will help us to acquire it; for if, on the contrary, we imagine that it is impossible for the time being to do anything that may help in this way, all the agitation of desire remains inside the brain, without flowing out at all into the nerves, and, being entirely absorbed in fortifying the idea of the desired object in the brain, it leaves the rest of the body in a state of lethargy.

ART. 121. *That it can also be caused by other passions.*

It is true that hatred, sadness, and even joy, when they are very violent, can also cause a certain lethargy, because they engage the whole mind in the contemplation of their object, especially when combined with the desire for some thing towards the acquisition of which we can do nothing for the time being. But because we tend to dwell far more on things with which we will ourselves united than on those from which we will ourselves separate, and lethargy does not involve an element of surprise but requires a certain length of time in order to take shape, it is found much more in love than in the rest of the passions.

ART. 122. *On fainting.*

Fainting is not far removed from death, for we die when the fire in the heart is completely extinguished, but when it is smothered in such a way that a certain amount of heat remains that can subsequently rekindle it, we only faint. Now, there are many indispositions of the body that can cause one to fall unconscious; but none of the passions

is observed to be capable of producing this effect save extreme joy.*
And the way in which I think it does so is by opening the orifices of
the heart far wider than usual, so that the blood from the veins floods
into it so suddenly and abundantly that it cannot be rarefied by the
heat sufficiently quickly to lift the little flaps that close the entries to
these veins;* as a result it drowns the fire, which, when it enters the
heart at the proper rate, it normally sustains.

ART. 123. *Why sadness does not cause fainting.*
It might seem that sudden extreme sadness must so narrow the orifices of the heart that it could also extinguish the fire; but nonetheless
this is not observed to happen, or, if it occurs, it is very rare; I believe
that this is because there can hardly ever be too little blood in the
heart to maintain the heat when its orifices are nearly closed.

ART. 124. *Of laughter.*
What happens in laughter is that the blood that flows out from the
right-hand cavity of the heart through the arterial vein swells the lungs
suddenly and repeatedly, which forces the air they contain out through
the throat, in the form of an inarticulate and explosive vocal utterance;
and both the lungs, as they are inflated, and the air, as it is expelled, put
pressure on all the muscles of the diaphragm, the chest, and the throat,
which causes movement in the muscles of the face connected with
these. And laughter consists purely in this combination of this movement of the face with the inarticulate and explosive vocal utterance.

ART. 125. *Why it does not accompany the greatest joys.*
Now, although it seems that laughter is one of the chief signs of joy,
it nonetheless occurs only when the joy is moderate, and contains an
element of wonderment or hatred. For we find by experience that,
when we feel extraordinary joy, the cause of that joy never sets us off
laughing; in fact, laughter is less readily produced in that state, even
by some extraneous cause, than when we are sad; and the reason for
this is that, when we are most joyful, the lungs are always so full of
blood that they cannot be further inflated at intervals.

ART. 126. *Its principal causes.*
And I have only identified two causes that suddenly inflate the lungs
in this way. The first is sudden wonderment, which, if combined

with joy, can open the orifices of the heart so swiftly that blood flows copiously into the right-hand side of the heart through the vena cava. There it becomes rarefied, and flows out through the arterial vein, inflating the lungs. The other is the mixture of some liquid that increases the rarefaction of the blood. And I can discover none conductive to bringing this about except the most fluid part of the blood that comes from the spleen. If this is pushed towards the heart by some slight stirring of hatred, reinforced by sudden wonderment, it mingles there with the blood from other parts of the body, which joy has dispatched there in great quantity, and then it can cause the blood to dilate much more than usual. It is very like what we see with many other liquids: when they are bubbling away on the heat, and a little vinegar is added to the pot, they suddenly expand. For the most fluid part of the blood that comes from the spleen is of a similar nature to vinegar. Observation also shows us that, in all the situations that can produce this explosion of laughter from the lungs, there is always some element of hatred, or at least of wonderment.* And those whose spleen is not perfectly healthy are liable not only to be sadder than other people, but also, at intervals, to be more cheerful and more disposed to laugh. This is because the spleen sends two kinds of blood towards the heart, one very thick and dense, and this causes sadness; one very fluid and subtle, which causes joy. And if we have been laughing heartily, we often afterwards feel naturally inclined to sadness, because the most fluid part of the blood of the spleen has run out, and the other denser part now follows it to the heart.

ART. 127. *The cause of indignant laughter.*
As for the laughter that sometimes accompanies indignation, it is normally artificial and affected. But when it is spontaneous, it seems to come from the joy of seeing that one cannot oneself be harmed by the evil at which one is indignant, combined with surprise at the novelty or unexpectedness of the evil in question.* So that joy, hatred, and wonderment all contribute to it. Nonetheless, I am inclined to believe that it can also be produced, in the complete absence of joy, by a pure impulse of aversion. This sends blood from the spleen to the heart, where it is rarefied and sent on to the lungs, which, when it finds them almost empty, it easily inflates. And in general whatever can suddenly inflate the lungs in this way causes the external action of laughter,

except when sadness transforms this into the groans and cries that accompany weeping. In this connection, Vives writes of himself* that, if he had gone a long time without food, the first morsels he put in his mouth would inevitably cause him to laugh: the cause of this might be that his lungs, being empty of blood on account of lack of food, were swiftly inflated by the first juices rising from the stomach to the heart, and that this could be brought about purely by imagining himself eating, even before the juice from the food he was eating had got there.

ART. 128. *Of the origin of tears.*

Just as laughter is never caused by the greatest joys, so tears do not come from sadness in its extreme, but only in its moderate form, when it is accompanied or followed by some feeling of love, or also joy. And, in order to understand how they come about, we should bear in mind that, although vapours are continually being exuded in abundance from every part of our body, there are, however, none from which they come in greater quantity than from the eyes, on account of the size of the optic nerves and the multitude of little arteries through which the vapours reach the eye; and, just as sweat is composed purely of vapours which, arising in other parts of the body, are transformed into water when they reach its surface, so tears are composed of the vapours emitted by the eyes.

ART. 129. *How the vapours are changed into water.*

Now, just as in the *Meteorology*,* in the course of explaining how the vapours of the air are converted into rain, I wrote that this is because they are less agitated or more abundant than usual, so I think that, when the vapours exuded by the body are much less agitated than they generally are, even if they are not so abundant, they are still converted into water, which is what causes the cold sweats that sometimes result from weakness when one is ill. And I think that when they are much more abundant, even though they are not at the same time more agitated, they are also converted into water. Hence the sweat that results from exercise. But in that case the eyes do not sweat, because, during physical exercise, most of the spirits go into the muscles whose function is to move the body, and so less goes through the optic nerve to the eyes. And it is all one and the same matter that takes the form of blood while in the veins or arteries, and spirits while in the brain, nerves, or muscles, and vapours when it is exuded from them and becomes air, and, finally, sweat or tears when it condenses as water on the surface of the body or the eyes.

ART. 130. *How it comes about that the eye weeps when hurt.*
And I can only observe two causes for the conversion of the vapours exuded by the eyes into tears. The first is when the shape of the pores they pass through is changed by any kind of accident: because this will delay the movement of the vapours and alter the disposition of the pores, thus causing them to be converted into water. Thus, a mere wisp of straw getting into the eye can cause tears to flow, because the pain it produces changes the disposition of the pores of the eye, in such a way that some of them become more narrow, which slows the passage of the little particles of the vapours; as a result, the vapours, which used to emerge at an equal distance from one another, thus remaining separate, now run into each other, because the disposition of the pores is disturbed; as a result they merge and in this way are converted into tears.

ART. 131. *How sadness makes us weep.*
The other cause is sadness followed by love or joy, or in general some cause that makes the heart push a great deal of blood through the arteries. Sadness is an essential factor, because it cools the whole of the blood, and so narrows the pores of the eyes. But, because in proportion as it narrows them, it also diminishes the quantity of vapours that can pass through them, it is not a sufficient cause for tears unless the quantity of vapours is simultaneously increased by some other cause. And nothing increases it so much as the blood sent to the heart in the passion of love. This is why we observe that those who are sad do not weep continually, but only at intervals, when thinking anew about the objects to which they are attached.

ART. 132. *Of the groans that accompany tears.*
And sometimes, in these cases, the lungs are also suddenly inflated by the abundance of blood flowing into them, which drives out the air they contained. This is forced out through the throat, producing the groans and cries that generally accompany tears. These cries are usually shriller than those that accompany laughter, although they are produced in very much the same way: the reason for the difference is that the nerves that serve to expand or contract the vocal organs,

so as to make the voice lower or higher, are connected with those
that open the orifices of the heart in moments of joy and contract
them in moments of sadness; they therefore cause the vocal organs to
expand or contract in parallel with these emotions.

ART. 133. *Why children and the old are quick to weep.*
Children and old people are more inclined to weep than those in the
middle, but for different reasons. Old people often weep from affection and joy: for the combination of these two passions sends a great
deal of blood to their heart, and hence a great deal of vapours to their
eyes; but their coldness of temperament so inhibits the agitation of
the vapours that they are easily converted into tears, even without
any prior sadness. But if some old people are also prone to weep from
vexation, this disposition comes less from the temperament of their
body than from that of their mind. For this only happens to people
who are so weak that they allow themselves to be completely overcome by pain, fear, or pity on the most trivial grounds. The same
thing happens with children, who seldom weep from joy, but much
more often from sadness, even when it is unaccompanied by love.
For they always have enough blood to produce a large quantity of
vapours, the movement of which being inhibited by sadness, they are
converted into tears.

ART. 134. *Why some children grow pale instead of weeping.*
And yet there are some who grow pale when vexed instead of weeping. This can be a sign of exceptional judgement and courage, that is,
when its cause is that they are coming to terms with some serious evil
and preparing themselves to resist it stoutly, just as an older person
might. But more commonly it is a sign of ill nature, that is, when its
cause is an inclination to hatred or fear, for these are passions that
diminish the matter of which tears are formed.* And, on the contrary,
we see that those who are very quick to weep are inclined to love and
pity.

ART. 135. *Of sighs.*
The cause of sighs is very different from that of tears, although
both presuppose sadness: for although one is prompted to weep
when the lungs are full of blood, one is prompted to sigh when they
are almost empty, and when some imagined hope or joy opens up

the orifice of the venous artery, previously narrowed by sadness; in this case, the little blood that remains in the lungs is rushed to the left-hand side of the heart along the venous artery, being impelled by the desire to obtain the joy in question, which simultaneously stimulates all the muscles of the diaphragm and chest, thus swiftly pushing air into the lungs from the mouth, so as to fill the place vacated by the blood. And this is what is called sighing.*

ART. 136. *Explanation of the effects of passions peculiar to certain people.* Furthermore, although much could be added here of the various effects or causes of the passions, I shall, for the sake of brevity, content myself with repeating the principle on which everything I have written about them is based: namely, that there is so close a union between our soul and our body that when we have once linked some bodily action with some thought, then in the future, whenever one of the two presents itself to us, the other will as well [§107]; and that the same actions are not always attached to the same thoughts [in everyone]. For this is sufficient to account for any particularity of this kind that we can observe in ourselves or other people and that has not been explained here. For example, it is easy to suppose that the strange aversions of some people, on account of which they cannot endure the smell of roses or the presence of a cat,* and suchlike, result simply from the fact that as babies they were seriously troubled by some such objects, or else their mother's feeling when troubled by such objects during pregnancy communicated itself to them.* For it is certain that there is a connection between all the reactions of the mother and those of the child in her womb, in such a way that what is contrary to the one is harmful also to the other. And the smell of roses may have given the child a severe headache while he was still in the cradle or he may have been terrified by a cat, without anyone's noticing and without himself afterwards remembering anything of what had happened, even though the idea of the aversion he felt at the time towards the roses or the cat remains imprinted on his brain for the rest of his life.

ART. 137. *Of the function of the five passions here explained, in so far as they relate to the body.*
Having provided definitions of love, hatred, desire, joy, and sadness, and dealt with all the bodily movements that cause or accompany

them, it remains only to consider their function. In this connection, we should observe that, as established by nature, they are all related to the body, and the soul has a share in them only in so far as it is joined with the body; so that their natural function is to induce the soul to consent and contribute to those actions that serve either to preserve the body or to render it more perfect in some way. And in this sense sadness and joy are the first two to come into play. For the soul is immediately alerted to things that are harmful to the body only by feeling the sensation of pain, which produces in it, first, the passion of sadness, secondly, hatred for the cause of the sadness, and, thirdly, the desire to be rid of it. And, likewise, the soul is immediately alerted to things beneficial to the body only by a certain kind of titillation that first produces joy, then love for what one thinks is the cause of it, and finally the desire to acquire whatever it is that can enable one to go on feeling this joy or to experience a similar joy in future. And this shows that all five are very useful from the point of view of the body, and even that sadness is in some sense primary and more necessary than joy, just as hatred is when compared to love, because it is more important to reject things that are harmful to the body and may destroy it than to acquire those that add some perfection without which one can still exist.

ART. 138. *Of their drawbacks and the means to correct these.*
But although this function of the passions is as natural as it could be, and all animals without reason conduct their lives purely by corporeal movements similar to those which, in us, typically result from the passions, and to which the passions themselves induce our soul to consent, it is not always good, inasmuch as there are many things harmful to the body that initially cause no sadness, or even give rise to joy, while there are others that are beneficial to it, though initially disagreeable. Moreover, they almost always cause both the goods and the evils they represent to appear much greater and more significant than they are, so that they induce us to pursue the goods and flee the evils with more energy and more effort than is beneficial to us. It is as we see with animals, which are often deceived by bait, and which, to avoid little evils, rush into big ones. This is why we should make use of experience and reason to distinguish good from evil, and to know the true value of each, so as not to confuse one with the other and so as to avoid excessive inclinations of any kind.

Art. 139. *Of the function of these passions in so far as they belong to the soul; and, first, of love.*

All this would be sufficient if there were nothing in us but the body, or if it were the best part of us; but, since it is the lesser part, we should consider the passions chiefly in so far as they belong to the soul. In relation to the soul, love and hatred derive from knowledge and take precedence over joy and sadness,* except when these latter two passions take the place of knowledge, of which they are species. And when this knowledge is true, that is, when the things it inclines us to love are truly good, and those it inclines us to hate are truly evil, love is incomparably better than hatred: there can never be too much of it, and it never fails to bring joy. I say that this love is extremely good because, in joining real goods to us, it perfects us accordingly. I say also that it can never be too great, because all that the most extreme love can do is to join us so perfectly to these goods that the love we have for ourselves in particular cannot make any distinction [between them and ourselves*], which I think can never be a bad thing. And it is necessarily followed by joy, because it represents what we love as a good belonging to us.

Art. 140. *Of hatred.*

Hatred, on the contrary, in however small a quantity, is always harmful; and it is never unaccompanied by sadness. I say that it can never be too small, because there is no action to which we are impelled by the hatred of evil, to which we could not be even better impelled by the love of the good to which that evil is opposed, at least when the good and evil are sufficiently known. For I admit that hatred of the evil that is manifested purely in pain is necessary in relation to the body: but here I am talking only of the hatred based on clearer knowledge, and I am considering it purely with respect to the soul. I say also that it is never unaccompanied by sadness, because, evil being nothing but a privation,* it cannot be conceived save in relation to some real subject in which it exists; and there is nothing real that has not some good in itself, so that the hatred that alienates us from some evil alienates us also *ipso facto* from the good to which it is attached, and the privation of this good, being represented to our soul as something it lacks [§92], is a cause of sadness. For example, the hatred that alienates us from someone's bad character alienates us *ipso facto* from dealings with him, in which we could otherwise find some good of which we are vexed to be deprived. And likewise in all other hatreds we can observe some grounds for sadness.

ART. 141. *Of desire, joy, and sadness.*

As for desire, it is plain that, when it derives from true knowledge, it cannot be evil, as long as it is not excessive and is regulated by the knowledge in question. It is plain also that joy cannot fail to be good, and sadness bad, from the point of view of the soul, since the only harm that evils can do to the soul is the sadness they cause, and the only benefit of the good that belongs to the soul is the joy it causes.* So much so that, if we had no body, I would go so far as to say that we could not give ourselves over too much to love and joy, or strive too hard to avoid hatred and sadness. But the bodily movements that accompany these passions can all, when very violent, be harmful to one's health, whereas in moderation they can be beneficial to it.

ART. 142. *Of joy and love, compared with sadness and hatred.*

Furthermore, since hatred and sadness should be rejected by the soul, even when derived from true knowledge, they must be all the more vigorously rejected when derived from some false opinion. But it is worth asking whether or not love and joy are good when their basis is likewise shaky; and in that case it seems to me that, if we consider them strictly as they are in themselves from the point of view of the soul, it is fair to say that, although joy is less solid and love less beneficial than when they have a better foundation, they are nonetheless preferable to equally ill-founded sadness and hatred. So much so that, in situations where we cannot eliminate the risk of being deceived, it is always better for us to incline to the passions aimed at the good than to those concerned with evil, even though the aim of the latter is to avoid that evil. Indeed, often a false joy is better than a sadness based on a true cause.* But I would not venture to say the same of love in relation to hatred. For justified hatred does no more than keep us away from the subject that contains the evil from which it is good to be separated; whereas unjustified love unites us with objects that can harm us, or at least that do not deserve to be as highly valued by us as they are. Such false valuations debase and degrade us.*

ART. 143. *Of the same passions, in so far as they are attributed to desire.*
And one must be quite clear about this: what I have just said about
these four passions holds good only when they are considered precisely in themselves, and do not induce us to perform any action. For,
inasmuch as they cause us to feel desire, through the agency of which
they govern our behaviour, it is certain that all these passions of which
the cause is false can be harmful, and, on the contrary, that all those
that are justified can be beneficial; indeed, when both are equally
unjustified, joy is generally more harmful than sadness, because
sadness inspires caution and apprehension, and thus disposes us in
some sort to prudence; whereas those who abandon themselves to joy
become thoughtless and rash as a result.

ART. 144. *Of desires the outcome of which is purely in our control.*
But, because these passions cannot induce us to perform any action
except through the agency of the desire they arouse, our efforts must
be directed especially to regulating this desire; and it is in this that the
principal utility of moral philosophy consists. Now, just as I pointed out
above [§141] that desire is always good when it derives from true knowledge, so likewise it must necessarily be bad when based on some
error. And it seems to me that the error we most commonly commit
in relation to our desires is to fail to distinguish sufficiently between
things that are entirely in our control and those that are not.* For, as
to those that are entirely in our control, that is, that depend on our
free will, provided we know they are good, we cannot desire them too
fervently, because to do good things that are in our power is to pursue
virtue, and it is certain that we cannot have too fervent a desire for
virtue. Moreover, what we desire in this way cannot fail to turn out
well, because the outcome is entirely in our control, and thus always
procures us all the satisfaction to which we looked forward. But
the mistake we tend to make in this domain is never to desire too
much, only to desire too little; and for this the sovereign remedy is
to liberate our minds as much as possible from all sorts of other, less
beneficial, desires, and then to strive to know very clearly and to consider most attentively* the goodness of what we should desire.

ART. 145. *Of those that depend only on other causes; and of the nature of
fortune.*
As to things that are not in any way in our control, however good

they may be, we should never desire them passionately, not only because they may not come to pass, and may therefore afflict us all the more, the more we wished for them, but mainly because, by occupying our thoughts, they distract us from setting our affections on other things of which the acquisition is entirely in our control. And there are two general remedies for these futile desires: the first is nobility of soul, of which I shall speak below [§153]; and the second is that we should often reflect on divine providence, and remind ourselves that it is impossible that anything should happen in any other way than has been determined from all eternity by this same providence; which therefore appears as a kind of fatality or immutable necessity, to be pitted against fortune, so as to destroy it, as an illusion the source of which is purely in an error of our understanding. For we can desire only what we deem to be in some sense possible; and we can deem things that are not in our control to be possible only in so far as we suppose that they are in the control of fortune, that is, in so far as we judge that they may happen and that similar things have happened in the past. Now, this opinion is based purely on our ignorance of all the causes that contribute to any given effect; for when something we judged to be in the control of fortune does not come to pass, this indicates that one of the causes essential to its occurrence was absent, and therefore that it was absolutely impossible; and that nothing similar has ever in fact occurred, that is, in the absence of a similar essential cause; in other words, if we had not failed to realize this beforehand, we would never have imagined the thing to be possible, and so would never have desired it.

ART. 146. *Of those that depend both on us and on others.*
We must therefore entirely reject the common opinion that there is a fortune* existing outside us which causes things to happen or not, according to its whim, and know instead that all is governed by divine providence, whose eternal decree is so infallible and unchangeable that, excepting those things that are dependent, in virtue of this same decree, on our own free will, we should think that nothing happens in relation to us that is not necessary and so to speak fated, so that we cannot without error desire it to turn out differently. But because most of our desires extend to things that are neither wholly in our control nor wholly in that of others, we must accurately identify the element in them that is wholly in our control, so as to extend our desire

to that alone. For the rest, although we should consider the outcome as entirely fated and immutable, to prevent our desire from dwelling on it, yet we should nonetheless make a point of considering the reasons that make it more or less likely to occur, so as to regulate our actions accordingly. For example, suppose we have business in some place that can be reached by two different routes, one of which is generally far safer than the other. Although perhaps the decree of Providence is such that, if we take what is considered the safer route, we shall nonetheless be robbed on the way, whereas on the contrary we can travel the other route in perfect safety, we should not, for all that, treat the choice between them as a matter of indifference, or fall back on the immutable fatality of that decree; on the contrary, reason requires us to opt for the route that is generally safer; and our desire will have been fulfilled in this respect if we follow that route, whatever evil may befall us as a result. For the evil was, as far as we were concerned, unavoidable; and so we had no reason to wish to be spared it,* but only to do what was best, as far as our understanding could know it; and this, as I suppose, is what we did. And it is certain that when we practise distinguishing between fate and fortune in this way, we easily accustom ourselves to regulating our desires in such a way that, inasmuch as their fulfilment is entirely within our control, they can always bring us perfect satisfaction.

ART. 147. *Of the internal emotions of the soul.*
I will only add one further consideration here that seems to me to be an extreme useful protection against being harmed in any way by our passions: it is that our well-being, and its opposite, depend chiefly on the internal emotions that are produced in the soul by the soul itself, in respect of which they differ from the passions, which always depend on some movement of the spirits. And although these emotions of the soul are often combined with the passions similar to them, they can often also coexist with different ones, and even be triggered by contrary ones. For example, when a husband weeps over the death of his wife, though perhaps (as is sometimes the case) he would be sorry to see her restored to life again, it may happen that his heart is oppressed by the sadness produced by the funeral rites and the absence of a person he had grown accustomed to conversing with; and it may happen that some remnants of love or pity that present themselves to his imagination draw genuine tears from his eyes,

even though all the time he is feeling a secret joy in the innermost part of his soul, which is acting on him so strongly that the sadness and tears that accompany it cannot at all diminish its intensity. And when we read of strange happenings in a book, or see them enacted on a stage, this sometimes causes us to feel sadness, sometimes joy, or love, or hatred, or, in general, any passion, according to the variety of the objects presented to our imagination. But all the time we are enjoying the pleasure of feeling them aroused in us, and this pleasure is an intellectual joy that can derive from sadness, no less than from any of the other passions.*

ART. 148. *That the exercise of virtue is a sovereign remedy for the passions.* Now, inasmuch as these internal emotions touch us more closely, and thus have much more power over us, than the passions, from which they differ, that affect us concurrently, it is certain that, provided our soul has the wherewithal to be contented in itself, all the troubles that come from elsewhere have no power to harm it, but rather serve to increase its joy, inasmuch as, becoming aware that it cannot be hurt by them, it becomes aware of its own perfection. And in order to have this wherewithal to be content, our soul needs only to pursue virtue wholeheartedly. For whoever has lived in such a manner that his conscience cannot reproach him with ever having failed to do all those things that he has judged best (which is what I mean here by 'pursuing virtue') receives thereby a satisfaction that has so much power to make him happy that the most violent surges of the passions are never strong enough to trouble the tranquillity of his soul.

PART THREE

Of the Particular Passions.

ART. 149. *Of esteem and contempt.*

After having discussed the six principal passions, which are, so to speak, the genera, of which the others form the species, I shall here briefly note down the particular characteristics of all the remaining passions, keeping to the same order as I adopted in classifying them above. The first two are esteem and contempt; for although by these terms we generally mean the opinion we have of the value of something, without any passion, nonetheless, because these opinions often give rise to passions to which no particular name has been assigned, it seems to me that these names may as well be applied to them. Esteem, then, in so far as it is a passion, is an inclination on the part of the soul to represent to itself the worth of the thing esteemed; which inclination is caused by a particular movement of the spirits, directed into the brain in such a way that they fortify the impressions that serve this purpose. Whereas, on the contrary, the passion of contempt is an inclination on the part of the soul to consider the baseness or littleness of what it despises, caused by the movement of the spirits that reinforces the idea of this littleness.

ART. 150. *That these two passions are simply species of wonderment.*

Thus, these two passions are simply species of wonderment: for when we do not wonder at the greatness or littleness of an object, we value it neither more nor less than reason dictates, so that in such a case we esteem or despise it without passion. And although often esteem is aroused in us by love, and contempt by hatred, this is not universally so, and it occurs purely because one is more, or less, inclined to consider the greatness, or littleness, of an object in proportion as one has more, or less, affection for it.

ART. 151. *That one may esteem or despise oneself.*

Now these two passions may be applied in general to all kinds of objects; but they are especially noteworthy when applied to ourselves, that is, when it is our own worth that we esteem or despise. And the movement of the spirits that causes them is so manifest in that case that it changes the bearing, the movements, the gait, and in general all the actions of those who conceive a higher or lower opinion of themselves than usual.

ART. 152. *On what grounds one may esteem oneself.*
And because one of the main parts of wisdom is to know in what way and for what reason a person should esteem or despise himself, I shall try here to give my opinion on the matter. I observe only one thing in us that can give us a good reason to esteem ourselves, namely, the use of our free will, and the mastery we have over our volitions. For we can be justifiably praised or blamed only for those actions that depend on this free will of ours, and it renders us in some sort similar to God by making us masters of ourselves, provided that we do not forfeit, by our own weakness, the rights it confers on us.

ART. 153. *The nature of nobility of soul.*
And thus I think that true nobility of soul, in virtue of which a man esteems himself as highly as he may legitimately do, consist in two things and two only: first, he recognizes that there is nothing that legitimately belongs to him, save this freedom to direct his acts of will, and that there is no reason why he should be praised or blamed except for his good or bad use of it; secondly, he feels in himself a firm and constant resolution to make good use of it, that is, never to lack the willpower to undertake and execute whatever he judges to be best. And this is what it means to follow virtue perfectly.*

ART. 154. *That it prevents one from despising others.*
Those who have this knowledge and awareness of themselves convince themselves readily that all other human beings can have the same knowledge and awareness of themselves: because there is nothing in all this that depends on anybody other than oneself. This is why they never despise anybody; and although they often see other people committing wrongful acts* that betray their weakness, they are, nonetheless, more inclined to excuse than to blame them, and to believe that these acts are due more to lack of knowledge than to lack of good will. And since they do not think themselves much inferior to those who have more wealth and honours, or even more intelligence, more learning, or more beauty than themselves, or who in general surpass them in respect of some other perfections, so, likewise, they do not

think themselves much superior to those whom they themselves surpass, since all these things seem to them of very little importance,
compared to good will, in respect of which alone they esteem themselves, and which they suppose is possessed, or at least could be possessed, by all other human beings.

ART. 155. *In what virtuous humility consists.*

So it is that the most noble of soul are customarily the most humble; and virtuous humility consists purely in this: in the light of our
reflection on the infirmity of our nature, and on the wrongful acts
we may have committed in the past, or which we are capable of committing, which are no less serious than those that may be committed
by other people, we do not rate ourselves higher than anyone else, and
we suppose that, since other people have free will no less than we do,
they can make as good use of it as we.

ART. 156. *The properties of nobility of soul; and how it acts as a remedy for all the disorders of the passions.*

Those who are noble in this way are naturally inclined to do great
things, and yet to undertake nothing of which they do not feel themselves capable. And because they value nothing more highly than
doing good to other human beings, for the sake of which they regard
their own interests as unimportant, they are always perfectly courteous, affable, and helpful towards one and all. Moreover, they are
entirely in control of their passions: especially of desires, jealousy,
and envy, since there is nothing the acquisition of which is not in their
control that they think of sufficient value to warrant being greatly
desired; and of hatred, since they esteem all human beings; and of
terror, because they are fortified by confidence in their own virtue;
and, finally, of anger, since, valuing, as they do, very little whatever
is in the control of others, they never give their enemies the satisfaction of acknowledging that they are put out by such things.

ART. 157. *Of pride.*

All those who form a good opinion of themselves on some other
grounds, whatever it may be, have no true nobility of soul, but only
pride, which is always a serious fault, the seriousness of which is
greater in proportion as the justification for one's self-esteem is less.
Self-esteem is least justified when a person has no specific grounds

for pride; that is to say, when he does not think he has some merit in himself for which he should be valued by others, but, setting no store by merit, imagines that glory is something to which one simply lays claim,* so that those who credit themselves with it most actually possess it most. This vice is so unreasonable and so absurd that I cannot but believe that people would never allow themselves to give way to it, if no one were ever unjustly praised; but flattery is so common everywhere that there is no man, however flawed, who does not often find himself esteemed for things that are not at all praiseworthy, and are even blameworthy; and this gives the most ignorant and most stupid people cause to fall into this kind of pride.

ART. 158. *That its effects are the opposite of those of nobility of soul.*
But, whatever the reason for one's self-esteem, if it is other than the intention one feels in oneself always to make good use of one's free will, which is, as I have said, the source of nobility of soul, it always produces a very blameworthy pride, so different from true nobility of soul that it has entirely opposite effects. For since all other goods, such as intelligence, beauty, wealth, honour, etc., are generally more highly valued the fewer people possess them, and are such, indeed, for the most part that they cannot be shared by many people, it follows that the proud seek to degrade all other human beings, and that, being slaves to their desires, their soul is continually troubled by hatred, envy, jealousy, or anger.

ART. 159. *Of bad humility.*
As for baseness or bad humility, it consists chiefly in feeling that one is weak or lacking in resolution, and that—as if one did not have full use of one's free will—one cannot help doing things that one knows one will subsequently regret; and also in the belief that one cannot be self-sufficient or do without several things one's acquisition of which is in other people's control. It is thus directly opposed to nobility of soul; and it often happens that those whose mind is basest are the most arrogant and haughty of people, just as the most noble of soul are the most modest and humble. But, whereas those with the strongest and noblest minds do not allow prosperity or adversity to affect their mood, those whose minds are weak and abject are governed entirely by fortune, and no less conceited in prosperity than humbled by adversity. Indeed, they are often observed to abase

themselves shamefully before those to whom they look for some
benefit or from whom they fear some harm, and at the same time to
lord it insolently over other people from whom they have nothing to
hope or fear.

ART. 160. *The movement of the spirits in these passions.*

Moreover, it is perfectly clear that pride and baseness are not only
vices, but also passions,* since the agitation they produce in those
who have been suddenly puffed up or brought down by some new
circumstance is plainly visible to the onlooker. But one may wonder
whether nobility of soul and humility, which are virtues, can also be
passions, because their motions are less visible, and because it seems
that virtue is less compatible with passion than is vice. And yet I see
no reason why the same movement of the spirits that serves to fortify a thought the basis of which is bad cannot also fortify it when its
basis is sound; and because both pride and nobility of soul consist only
in the good opinion one has of oneself, and differ only inasmuch as
this opinion is justified in the latter and not in the former, it seems
that they can both be attributed to a single passion, aroused by a composite movement, formed of those that occur in wonderment, joy,
and love (love for oneself no less than love for the thing which is the
source of one's self-esteem); and, likewise, on the contrary, the movement that arouses humility, whether virtuous or bad, is a compound of
those involved in wonderment, sadness, and love for oneself, mingled
with the hatred one has for the faults that cause one to despise oneself. And the only difference I can observe in these two movements
is this. The movement of wonderment has two properties: first, it is
intense at the very beginning, on account of the element of surprise;
secondly, it continues at the same level, that is to say that the spirits
continue to move in the brain at the same rate. Of these two properties, the first is encountered far more in pride and baseness than in
nobility of soul and virtuous humility; whereas the second is more
clearly observed in these latter two than in the two former. And the
reason for this is that vice is typically the result of ignorance,* and
that those who know themselves least well are those most prone to
exalt and to abase themselves more than they should, because any
unfamiliar occurrence takes them by surprise; assimilating it to themselves, they become to themselves a source of wonderment, and feel
self-esteem or self-contempt according as they judge that what is

happening to them is to their advantage or not. But because it often happens that something that has boosted their pride is followed by something else that humiliates them, the movement of their passions is fluctuating. On the other hand, there is nothing in nobility of soul that is not compatible with virtuous humility, and nothing external that can change these passions, as a result of which the movements involved in them are steady, constant, and always very consistent. But surprise is not a major factor in producing them, since those who esteem themselves in this way are sufficiently aware of the causes of their own self-esteem. Nonetheless, one can say that these causes (that is, the power to make use of one's free will, which makes one value oneself, and the infirmities of the subject in which this power resides, which set limits to one's self-esteem) are so fascinating that, whenever one sets them afresh before one's mind, they never fail to give rise to wonderment.

ART. 161. *How nobility of soul can be acquired.*
And we must note that what are commonly called virtues are habits in the soul* that dispose it to certain thoughts: they are distinct from the thoughts themselves, but can produce them, and reciprocally be produced by them. We should also note that these thoughts can be produced by the soul alone, but that they are often fortified by some movement of the spirits, and in that case they are both actions of virtue and passions of the soul. And so, although there is no other virtue to which it seems that good birth contributes as much as to the virtue that causes us to esteem oneself only according to our true value, and it is easy to believe that the souls God places in our bodies are not all equally noble and strong (which is why I have called this virtue 'nobility of soul', in keeping with the usage of our language, rather than 'magnanimity', according to the usage of the Schools, where this virtue is not much in evidence*), it is nonetheless certain that a good upbringing can do much to counter the shortcomings a person is born with, and that, if one regularly sets oneself to consider what free will is, and what great advantages follow from abiding by a firm resolution to make the best use of it, and likewise, on the other side, how futile and pointless are all the cares by which the ambitious are beset, one can arouse in oneself the passion and in due course the virtue of nobility of soul; and since this is, so to speak, the key to all the other virtues,* and a universal remedy for all the disorders of the passions, it seems to me that this consideration is worth emphasizing.

ART. 162. *Of veneration.*

Veneration or respect is an inclination of the soul not only to esteem the object revered, but also to submit to it with a certain fear, in the attempt to gain its favour. It follows that we feel veneration only for free causes we judge capable of doing us good or harm, when we do not know which of the two it will be. For towards those from which we expect only good, we feel love and devotion, rather than mere veneration, and towards those from which we expect only evil, we feel hatred; and if we do not judge that the cause of the good or evil is a free one, we do not submit to it in the attempt to gain its favour. Thus, when pagans venerated woods, springs, or mountains, it was not, strictly speaking, these dead things they were revering, but rather the gods they thought presided over them. And the movement of the spirits that arouses this passion is a compound of the movement that arouses wonderment and of the movement that arouses fear, of which more below.

ART. 163. *Of disdain.*

Likewise, what I call disdain is an inclination on the part of the soul to despise a free cause, by judging that, although of its nature it is capable of doing good or harm, it is nonetheless so far below us that to us it can do neither the one nor the other. And the movement of the spirits that arouses it is a compound of those that arouse wonderment and complacency or boldness.

ART. 164. *Of the use of these two passions.*

And what determines whether we make good or bad use of these two passions is nobility of soul, on the one hand, and weakness of mind or baseness, on the other. For the more noble and generous one's soul, the greater one's inclination to render to everyone their due; and thus one has not only a deep humility in relation to God, but also one pays, without reluctance, all the honour and respect due to human beings, to each in accordance with the rank and authority he holds in the world, and one despises nothing but vices. On the other hand, those whose mind is base and weak are subject to sins of excess, sometimes in so far as they venerate and fear things worthy only of contempt, and sometimes in so far as they insolently disdain those that most deserve reverence. And they often oscillate violently, from extreme impiety to superstition, and back again from superstition to impiety, so that there is no vice or disorder of mind of which they are not capable.

ART. 165. *Of hope and fear.*
Hope is a disposition of the soul to persuade itself that what it desires will come to pass, which is caused by a particular movement of the spirits, namely, by that of mingled joy and desire. And fear is another disposition of the soul, which persuades it that the thing will not come to pass. And it is to be noted that, although these two passions are contrary, one may nonetheless have them both together, that is, when one considers different reasons at the same time, some of which cause one to judge that the fulfilment of one's desires is a straightforward matter, while others make it seem difficult.

ART. 166. *Of complacency and despair.*
And neither of these passions ever accompanies desire without leaving some room for the other. For when hope is so strong that it altogether drives out fear, its nature changes and it becomes complacency or confidence. And when we are certain that what we desire will come to pass, even though we go on wanting it to come to pass, we nonetheless cease to be agitated by the passion of desire which caused us to look forward to the outcome with anxiety. Likewise, when fear is so extreme that it leaves no room at all for hope, it is transformed into despair; and this despair, representing the thing as impossible, extinguishes desire altogether, for desire bears only on possible things.

ART. 167. *Of jealousy.*
Jealousy is a species of fear connected with our desire to retain the possession of some good; and it stems not so much from the force of the reasons that make us judge we may lose it, as from the great value we place on it; as a result of which we examine even the slightest grounds for suspicion, and regard them as reasons of great weight.

ART. 168. *In what cases this can be an honourable passion.*
And because we should always be more concerned to preserve very valuable goods than those of less value, this passion may be justified and honourable in certain situations. Thus, for example, a commander in charge of a very important fortress is right to be jealous on that account,* that is, to be on his guard against all the stratagems

by which it might be taken; and a chaste woman is not blamed for being jealous of her honour, that is, for refraining not only from doing wrong, but also from giving the slightest occasion for malicious gossip.

ART. 169. *In what cases it is blameworthy.*

But we laugh at a miser who is jealous of his treasure, that is to say, who feasts his eyes on it and will never let himself be separated from it for fear it will be stolen; for money is not worth the trouble of guarding it so carefully. And we despise a man who is jealous of his wife, because this is an indication that he does not love her in the right way, and that he has a low opinion either of himself or of her. I say that he does not love her in the right way, because if he felt true love for her, he would have no inclination to distrust her. But it is not strictly speaking her that he loves: he loves only the good that he imagines to consist in exclusive possession of her; and he would not fear to lose this good if he did not judge that he is unworthy of it, or else that his wife is unfaithful. Furthermore, this passion relates only to suspicion and distrust, for it is not being jealous in the strict sense of the word to attempt to avoid some evil when there is good reason to fear it.

ART. 170. *Of indecision.*

Indecision is also a species of fear that, holding the soul, as it were, in suspense between several actions it might carry out, causes it to perform none of them, and thus gives it the time to make a proper choice before opting for one of them. In which respect, it is genuinely of some use.* But when it lasts longer than it should, and causes us to squander on deliberation the time we need in order to act, it is very bad. Now I call it a kind of fear, even though it may happen that, when we have a choice between several things that appear to be virtually equal in goodness, we remain uncertain and undecided, without, however, feeling any fear. For this kind of indecision stems purely from the situation, and not from any agitation of the spirits: hence it is not a passion, unless the uncertainty of the choice is aggravated by the fear of making a mistake. But in some people this fear is so habitual and so powerful that often, even though they have no choice to make between alternatives and see only one line of action to pursue or to avoid, it holds them back and causes them to waste time in looking for other possibilities; in this case, there is an excess of indecision, which stems from an excessive desire to do the right thing, and from a weakness of the understanding, which has no clear and distinct notions, only a host of confused ones. That is why the remedy for this excess is to accustom ourselves to form definite and determinate judgements about whatever things we are confronted with, and to believe that we are always doing our duty when we do what we judge to be best, even though, perhaps, we may be judging quite wrongly.

ART. 171. *Of courage and boldness.*

Courage, when it is a passion and not a habit or natural inclination, is a certain heat or agitation that disposes the soul to throw itself vigorously into the performance of the tasks it has set itself, of whatever nature they may be. And boldness is a species of courage that disposes the soul to the performance of the most dangerous tasks.

ART. 172. *Of emulation.*

And emulation is another species of courage, but in a different way. For we can consider courage as a genus divided into as many species as it has different objects, and also into as many species as it has different causes. Boldness is a species in the first sense, emulation in the second. Emulation itself is nothing other than a heat that disposes the soul to undertake things it hopes it can achieve successfully, because it sees others achieving them. It is thus a species of courage of which the external cause is example. I say the external cause, because it must always have an internal cause as well, namely, a disposition of the body such that the power of desire and hope to send abundance of blood to the heart is greater than that of fear or despair to block it.

ART. 173. *How boldness depends on hope.*

For it is to be observed that, although the object of boldness is difficulty, the usual effects of which are fear or even despair (on account of which it is in the most dangerous and desperate enterprises that boldness and courage are most fully employed), we do need to hope, or even to be certain, that the goal we have in view will be attained, if we are to tackle the difficulties in our path with vigour. But a distinction must be drawn here between the object and the goal.* For we cannot be sure of something and at the same time despair of it. Thus, when the Decii charged into the midst of their enemies,* thus dooming themselves to certain death, the object of their boldness was the difficulty of preserving their life during this action, and this difficulty was a source of despair for them, for they were certain they were going to die; but their goal was to give heart to their soldiers by their example, and to enable them to win the victory they hoped for; or else their goal was to attain glory after the death they knew was inevitable.

ART. 174. *Of faint-heartedness and terror.*

Faint-heartedness is directly opposed to courage,* and it is a lethargy or chillness that prevents the soul from throwing itself into the performance of tasks it would accomplish if it were exempt from this passion. And in terror or horror, which is the contrary of boldness, the soul is not only chilled, but paralysed by agitation, and hence powerless to resist the evils it thinks are imminent.

ART. 175. *Of the function of faint-heartedness.*

Now, although I cannot persuade myself that nature has given human beings any passion that is always bad, and that has no good and praiseworthy use, I find it nonetheless extremely difficult to guess what function these two can fulfil. It seems to me only that faint-heartedness has a certain benefit when it causes one to be exempt from the pains one might be encouraged to take for plausible reasons, but for the fact that other more convincing reasons, in the light of which one judged such pains to be futile, gave rise to this passion. For besides exempting the soul from these pains, it is of some use for the body, inasmuch as, by slowing the movement of the spirits, it prevents one from dissipating one's strength. But it is ordinarily very harmful because it distracts the will from useful actions. And because its cause is simply that one has not enough hope or desire, it can be corrected merely by increasing these passions in oneself.

ART. 176. *Of the function of terror.*

As for terror or horror, I cannot see that it can ever be praiseworthy or useful; indeed, it is not a specific passion, but only an excess of faint-heartedness, astonishment, and fear, and this is always blameworthy, whereas boldness is an excess of courage that is always good, provided that the end in view is a good one. And because the principal cause of terror is surprise, there is no better means of freeing oneself from it than to think things out in advance,* and to prepare oneself for all events the fear of which might give rise to it.

ART. 177. *Of remorse.*

Remorse of conscience is a kind of sadness the cause of which is the misgiving that something one is doing or has done may not be good, and it necessarily presupposes doubt. For if one were entirely certain that what one is doing is bad, one would refrain from doing it, inasmuch as the will is drawn only to things that have some appearance of goodness;* and if one were certain something one had already done was bad, one would repent of it, and not only feel remorse. Now, the function of this passion is to get one to examine if the thing one has doubts about is good or not, and to prevent one from doing it again as long as one is uncertain whether it is good. But because it presupposes evil, it would be best of all if one never had reason to feel it; and it can be forestalled by the same methods as those by which one can liberate oneself from irresolution.

ART. 178. *Of derision.*

Derision or mockery is a species of joy mingled with hatred, which stems from the perception of some trivial evil in a person we think deserves it. We feel hatred for the evil, and joy at seeing it in the person who deserves it. And when this occurs unexpectedly, the sudden wonderment causes us to burst out laughing, in accordance with what was said above about the nature of laughter [§§62, 125]. But the evil must be a trivial one: for if it is great, one cannot believe that the person affected deserves it, unless one is extremely ill-natured or unless one hates him bitterly.

ART. 179. *Why those with the greatest shortcomings are generally those most given to derision.*

And we see that those whose defects are very conspicuous, for instance, the lame, the one-eyed, or the hunchbacked, or those who have received some public slight, are particularly given to derision. For, since they wish to see other people as ill-favoured as themselves,* they are delighted by the evils that befall them, and regard them as deserved.

ART. 180. *Of the function of ridicule.*

As for moderate ridicule,* which helpfully rebukes the vices by making them appear ludicrous, though this does not involve laughing at them oneself or displaying any hatred towards individuals, this is not a passion, but one of the qualities of a well-bred man,* which exhibits the cheerfulness of his temperament and the tranquillity of his soul—both marks of virtue—and often also the cleverness of his wit, inasmuch as he succeeds in imparting a pleasing appearance to the things he is ridiculing.

ART. 181. *Of the place of laughter in ridicule.*
And it is not ill-bred to laugh when one hears ridicule of this kind uttered by another person, which may indeed be such that not to laugh at it would be a sign of gloominess. But when the joke is one's own, it is more becoming to refrain from laughter, so as not to appear to be surprised by the things one says, or to be marvelling at one's skill in coming up with them. This only increases the surprise of the hearers all the more.

ART. 182. *Of envy.*
What is commonly named envy is a vice consisting in a perversity of nature whereby some people are vexed by the good they see befalling others. But I use the word here to denote a passion that is not always vicious. Envy, then, in so far as it is a passion, is a species of sadness mingled with hatred which stems from seeing good befall those one thinks unworthy of it. It can be rational to think this only about the goods of fortune.* For as to those of the soul, or even of the body, in so far as one is born with them, to have received them from God before one was capable of doing any evil* is to be sufficiently worthy of them.

ART. 183. *In what way it can be justified or unjustified.*
But when fortune sends goods to someone of which he is genuinely unworthy, and envy is aroused in us only because, in virtue of our natural love of justice, we are vexed that it has been flouted in the distribution of these goods, this is an indignation that can be excusable, especially when the good that is the object of one's envy is such that, in the hands of its possessor, it may be converted into evil; for instance, if a person has been appointed to some office who may do wrong in the performance of his duties. Indeed, when one desires the same good for oneself, and is prevented from obtaining it because others who are less deserving already possess it, this renders the passion more violent, and it is nonetheless still excusable, as long

as the hatred it contains is focused only on the bad distribution of the good one envies, and not on the people that possess or distribute it. But there are few people so just and generous as to feel no hatred for those who have forestalled them in the acquisition of a good that cannot be shared with many, even when those who have acquired it are just as deserving of it, or more so. And what is ordinarily most envied is glory. For although the glory of others does not prevent us from aspiring to glory, it renders it more difficult and more costly to attain.

ART. 184. *Why the envious are prone to livid complexions.*
Moreover, there is no vice so harmful to human happiness as envy. For, apart from the fact that those tainted by it suffer as a result, they also spoil the pleasure of others to the best of their ability. And their complexion is typically livid, that is to say, pale, with a mixture of yellow and black, rather like a bruise. For which reason *livor* in Latin means 'envy'.* This is entirely in accordance with what was said above about the movements of the blood in sadness and hatred. For hatred causes yellow bile, which comes from the lower part of the liver, and black bile, which comes from the spleen, to be dispersed from the heart along the arteries into all the veins; and sadness cools the blood in the veins and makes it flow more sluggishly than usual, which is sufficient to bring about the livid colour in the face. But because bile, whether yellow or black, can also be sent into the veins by several other causes, and envy can propel it there in sufficient quantity to change a person's complexion only if it is very intense and long-lasting, one should not suppose that everyone with this complexion is inclined to that passion.

ART. 185. *On pity.*
Pity is a kind of sadness mixed with love or good will towards those whom we see suffering some evil we think undeserved. It is thus contrary to envy in respect of its object, and to derision in respect of its attitude to that object.

ART. 186. *Those most subject to feelings of pity.*
Those who feel very weak and very exposed to the adversities of fortune seem to be more inclined to this passion than others, because they imagine other people's troubles as capable of befalling them as

well; and so they are stirred to pity more by the love they bear for themselves than by their love for others.*

ART. 187. *How the most noble of soul are affected by this passion.*

Yet, nonetheless, the most noble and strongest-minded of people, such as fear no evil on their own account and hold themselves above the power of fortune, are not immune to compassion when they behold the weakness of other human beings, and hear their laments. For it is a part of nobility of soul to bear good will to one and all. But the sadness involved in their pity has no bitterness; and like that which is caused by the dreadful deeds we see represented on the stage, it resides more in the outer part and in the senses than in the innermost part of the soul; which has, nonetheless, the satisfaction of thinking that it is doing its duty in feeling compassion for the afflicted. And there is a distinction here to be observed, in that, whereas the common man feels compassion for those who complain because he thinks the evils they are suffering are very severe, the pity felt by the greatest men is for the weakness of those they see complaining. For they think that no mishap that may befall us is so great an evil as the faint-heartedness of those who cannot endure it with constancy; and, although they hate the vices, they have no hatred for those they see are prone to them, only pity.

ART. 188. *What kind of people are unaffected by it.*

But only malign and envious characters that naturally hate all mankind, or else those who are so brutish and so blinded by good fortune or brought down by bad that they think that no harm can come to them any more, are insensible to pity.

ART. 189. *Why this passion arouses tears.*

Moreover, under the influence of this passion, people are prone to shed tears very easily, because love sends much blood to the heart, thus causing a great quantity of vapours to issue from the eyes, while the coldness of sadness restrains the agitation of these vapours, and converts them into tears, as was explained above [§131].

ART. 190. *On self-satisfaction.*

The satisfaction permanently enjoyed by those who constantly pursue virtue is a habit in their soul known as tranquillity and peace of conscience. But the satisfaction experienced afresh when we have just carried out some action we think good is a passion, namely, a species of joy, which I think is the sweetest of all, because its cause depends purely on ourselves. However, when this cause is not justified, that is, when the actions from which we derive much satisfaction are not of great importance, or are even morally wrong, it is ridiculous, and serves only to produce pride and impertinent arrogance. This is particularly to be observed in those who think they are devout, when they are only bigoted and superstitious; that is to say, on the spurious grounds that they go frequently to church, recite a great many prayers, wear their hair short, fast, and give alms, they think they are entirely perfect, and imagine that they are such good friends to God that they can do nothing that could displease him, and that whatever their passion dictates to them is a virtuous zeal, even though it sometimes incites them to commit the greatest crimes that human beings can commit, such as betraying cities, assassinating rulers, and exterminating whole peoples, for the simple reason that they do not follow one's own opinions.*

ART. 191. *Of repentance.*
Repentance is directly contrary to self-satisfaction, and it is a species of sadness that comes from the belief that one has committed some bad action; and it is very bitter, because its cause lies only in oneself. This does not mean that it is not very useful, when it is true that the action we repent is bad and we know this certainly to be so, because it encourages us to do better another time. But it often happens that weak-minded people repent of things that they have done without knowing for certain that they have done wrong; they convince themselves they have because they are afraid they have; and if they had done the opposite, they would repent of that in the same way; which is an imperfection in them that deserves pity. And the remedies for this shortcoming are the same as those that serve to eliminate irresolution.

ART. 192. *Of favour.*
Favour is, strictly speaking, a desire to see good befall someone for whom one has good will; but I use the word here to denote this good will in so far as it is produced in us by some good action on the part of the object of our good will. For we are naturally inclined to love those

who do things we judge to be good, even though no advantage to us may result.* Favour understood in this sense is a species of love, rather than of desire, although it is always accompanied by the desire to see good things happening to the object of one's favour. And it is typically combined with pity, since the setbacks by which we see the unfortunate afflicted cause us to think more about their deserving qualities.

ART. 193. *Of gratitude.*

Gratitude is also a species of love aroused in us by some action on the part of the person for whom we feel it, by which we believe that he has done us some good, or at least intended to. Thus, it contains exactly the same elements as favour, but all the more because it is based on an action that concerns us and that we desire to reciprocate. Hence it is much stronger, especially in souls with the slightest degree of nobility and generosity.

ART. 194. *Of ingratitude.*

As for ingratitude, it is not a passion, for nature has not implanted in us any movement of the spirits that arouses it; it is purely and simply a vice directly contrary to gratitude, inasmuch as gratitude is always virtuous and one of the principal bonds of human society. That is why the vice of ingratitude is the exclusive property of brutish and foolishly arrogant men who imagine that they are entitled to everything, or of the stupid, who fail to think at all about the benefits they receive, or of the feeble and abject, who, feeling their own weakness and neediness, grovel to others for their help, and, once they have received it, hate their benefactors, because, since they do not have the intention of returning the benefit, or they despair of being able to do so, and since they imagine that everyone else is mercenary like themselves, and that no one does any good except in the hope of some reward, they think they have got the better of them.

ART. 195. *Of indignation.*

Indignation is a species of hatred or aversion that we naturally feel towards those who do something bad, of whatever kind. And it is often mingled with envy or pity: but its object is nonetheless quite different. For we are indignant only with people who do good or evil to those who do not deserve it, but we feel envy for those who receive the good, and pity for those who receive the evil. It is true that to possess a good of which one is unworthy is, in a sense, to do evil. This may be the reason why Aristotle and his followers, supposing that envy is always a vice, apply the name of indignation to the kind of envy that is not vicious.*

ART. 196. *Why it is sometimes combined with pity, and sometimes with derision.*

There is a sense in which to do evil is also to receive it; for which reason some combine their indignation with pity, others with derision, depending on whether they bear good or ill will towards those whom they see acting badly. Hence the laughter of Democritus and the tears of Heraclitus* may have arisen from the same cause.

ART. 197. *That it is often accompanied with wonderment, and is not incompatible with joy.*

Indignation is often also accompanied with wonderment. For we are in the habit of supposing that everything will be done in the manner we think it should be, that is, in what we judge to be the right manner. That is why, when this does not occur, we are taken by surprise, and respond with wonderment. Moreover, it is not incompatible with joy, although more typically combined with sadness. For when the evil at which we are indignant cannot harm us and we consider that we would not want to act in the same way, that gives us a certain pleasure; which is perhaps one of the causes of the laughter that sometimes accompanies this passion.*

ART. 198. *Of its function.*

Moreover, indignation is far more often observed in those who wish to appear virtuous than in those who really are so. For although those who love virtue cannot see the vices of others without a certain aversion, they are provoked to passion only by the greatest and most conspicuous ones. It is the mark of a prickly and gloomy person to feel great indignation over trivial matters; it is unjust to feel it over matters for which no one is to blame; and it is illogical and absurd not to confine this passion to the actions of human beings, and instead to extend it to the handiwork of God or nature, as those people do, who, never content with the worldly position they were born to or have attained, dare to find fault with the order of the world or the secrets of providence.

ART. 199. *Of anger.*

Anger is also a species of hatred or aversion, which we feel for those who have done or intended some harm, not to anyone in general, but to us in particular. It thus contains the same elements as indignation, all the more because it is based on an action that concerns us and for which we desire revenge. For this desire almost always accompanies it; and it is directly contrary to gratitude, just as indignation is to favour. But it is incomparably more violent than those other three passions, because the desire to repel what harms us and to avenge ourselves is more powerful than any other. It is a combination of desire and the love we have for ourselves that supplies anger with all the agitation of the blood that courage and boldness can produce; and it is owing to hatred that the blood thus agitated is mostly the bilious type that comes from the spleen and the small veins of the liver. When it enters the heart, its abundance and the nature of the bile with which it is mingled cause it to produce a heat that is fiercer and more intense than can be produced by love or joy.

ART. 200. *Why those who go red with anger are less to be feared than those who go pale.*

And the outward signs of this passion vary according to the temperament of the person affected, and the various other passions that form it or are combined with it. Thus, we see some people go pale or tremble when roused to anger, while others go red or even weep; and the common judgement is that the anger of those who go pale is more to be feared than that of those who go red. The reason for this is that when a person is unwilling or unable to take revenge except by looks and speech, he draws on all his heat and strength immediately he is provoked, and this causes him to go red; sometimes, moreover, the regret and self-pity one feels on account of being unable to take any further revenge causes one to weep. And, on the contrary, those who hold themselves in check and resolve on a greater vengeance are saddened by the thought that they are obliged to do this by the action that has angered them; and sometimes also they fear the evils that may befall them as a result of their decision; hence their initial pallor, chill, and trembling. But when afterwards they come to wreak their vengeance, they become all the hotter for being colder at the beginning; just as we see that fevers that begin with a chill are generally the most violent.

ART. 201. *That there are two kinds of anger, and that the kindest people are the most prone to the first kind.*

This helps us to see that we can distinguish two kinds of anger: one that is quick to arise, and the external signs of which are very conspicuous, but that nevertheless has little result and can easily be assuaged; the other that does not appear at first to the same extent, but that gnaws more at the heart and that has more dangerous effects. People of a very kindly and loving disposition are the most prone to the former. For it does not stem from a deep-rooted hatred, but from a sudden aversion that grips them, because, being inclined as they are to imagine that everything should turn out in what they judge to be the best way, whenever they turn out differently, they are immediately filled with wonderment and vexation, often even when they are not personally affected at all, because, being very affectionate, they feel the same kind of concern for those they love as for themselves. So what to another person would be a matter only for indignation is for them a matter for anger; and because, as a result of their inclination to love, they have much heat and much blood in the heart, the sudden aversion they feel necessarily causes a flow of bile to the heart sufficient to cause an immediate effervescence of this blood. But this disturbance is only short-lived, because the surprise wears off, and as soon as they see that the issue that has angered them should not have upset them so much, they repent of their anger.

ART. 202. *That weak and base souls are most liable to be dominated by the latter kind.*

The other kind of anger, in which hatred and sadness predominate, is not so visible initially, except perhaps to the extent that it causes the face to grow pale. But its strength is gradually increased by the agitation that the ardent desire for revenge produces in the blood, which, being combined with the bile that is driven towards the heart from the lower part of the liver and the spleen, arouses a heat in the heart that is both very fierce and very prickly. And just as it is the most noble souls who feel most gratitude, so it is those who are the proudest, basest, and weakest that allow themselves to be dominated by this second species of anger. For insults appear all the greater the more one's pride increases one's self-esteem, and also the more one values the goods that the insult has taken away; which one values the more, the baser and weaker one's soul, since they depend on other people.

ART. 203. *That nobility of soul serves as a remedy against the excesses of this kind of anger.*

Moreover, although this passion has its function, in that it endows us with the vigour to repel an insult, its excesses are, however, to be avoided more carefully than those of any other, because they disturb the judgement and often cause us to commit bad actions that we later come to repent; sometimes they even prevent us from repelling an insult as effectively as we might do if we were less aroused. But, just as there is nothing that renders such anger excessive more than pride, so I think that nobility of soul is the best remedy that can be found for its excesses. For it causes us to set very little store by all the goods that can be taken away, and on the contrary to set great store by freedom and absolute self-mastery, which we forfeit when we are capable of being offended by someone; and thus we feel only scorn, or at most indignation, in the face of insults at which other people would normally take offence.

ART. 204. *Of glory.*

What I call glory here is a species of joy that is based on the love we have for ourselves, and that comes from the belief or hope that one is being praised by some other people. It is thus different from the inner satisfaction that comes from the belief that one has performed some good action. For we are sometimes praised for things we do not think good, and blamed for those we think better. But both glory and inner satisfaction are species of self-esteem, as well as species of joy. For to see one is esteemed by others is a reason to esteem oneself.

ART. 205. *Of shame.*

Shame, on the contrary, is a species of sadness that is also based on love of oneself, and that comes from the belief or fear that one is being blamed. It is, furthermore, a species of modesty or humility and self-distrust. For when one's self-esteem is so strong that one cannot imagine being despised by anyone, one is scarcely liable to shame.

ART. 206. *Of the function of these two passions.*

Now glory and shame have the same function, in that they both incite us to virtue, one through hope, the other through fear. It is only necessary to inform one's judgement regarding what is truly praiseworthy or blameworthy, so as to avoid being ashamed of acting well and letting one's vices feed one's vanity, as so many people do. But it is not a good thing to strip oneself entirely of these passions, as the ancient Cynics did.* For although the people is a very bad judge,* yet, since we cannot live without it, and it matters to us to be esteemed by it, we should often follow its opinions rather than our own, as far as the external aspect of our actions is concerned.*

ART. 207. *Of shamelessness.*

Shamelessness or effrontery, that is, contempt for shame, and often for glory as well, is not a passion, because there is no particular move-ment of the spirits in us that arouses it; but it is a vice opposed to shame, and also to glory, in so far as both of these are good, just as ingratitude is opposed to gratitude and cruelty to pity. And the main cause of shamelessness is the frequent experience of humiliation. For there is no one who, when young, does not imagine that praise is a good and infamy an evil that make much more difference to one's life than they are found to do by experience, when, having been publicly humiliated a few times, one finds oneself entirely stripped of one's honour and despised by all and sundry. This is why some people become shameless, if they measure good and evil purely by bodily com-forts; for they see that they can enjoy these after such humiliations just as much as before, or even, sometimes, much more so, given that they have been released from all the various constraints imposed by honour and that, if their disgrace is accompanied by the loss of worldly goods, there are always charitable people who will provide them with these.

ART. 208. *Of distaste.*

Distaste is a species of sadness that comes from the same cause as previously produced joy. For we are so constituted that most of the things we enjoy are good for us only for a time, and afterwards become disagreeable. This appears most evidently when it comes to food and drink, which are beneficial only as long as we have an appetite, and harmful when the appetite has gone; and because, at that point, they cease to be agreeable to the taste, this passion is known as distaste.

ART. 209. *Of regret.*

Regret is also a species of sadness, which has a particular bitterness, inasmuch as it is always combined with some despair, and with the memory of the pleasure we experienced in enjoying some good.* For we only ever regret those goods that we have enjoyed, and that are so utterly lost that we have no hope of regaining them at the time and in the state in which they are represented by our yearning.

ART. 210. *Of gladness.*

Finally, what I call 'gladness' is a species of joy that is distinctive in this respect, that its sweetness is enhanced by the memory of the evils we have suffered and of which we feel lightened just as if we had thrown off some heavy burden we had been bearing on our shoulders for a long time. And I observe nothing particularly noteworthy about these three passions; indeed, I dealt with them here only so as to conform to the order of the classification I set out above; but it seems to me that the classification has been useful in showing that I was omitting no passion worthy of particular consideration.*

ART. 211. *A universal remedy for the passions.*

And now we are familiar with all the passions, we have much less reason to fear them than we had before. For we see that they are all good of their nature, and that we are to avoid only their misuse or their excess, for which the remedies I have explained above would be sufficient if everyone took the trouble to apply them. But, because among these remedies I have included premeditation and the effort by which one can correct the shortcomings of one's nature, through repeated practice in separating within oneself the movements of the blood and the spirits from the thoughts to which they are habitually attached, I admit that there are few people who are sufficiently prepared in this way for all possible situations, and that the movements aroused in the blood by the objects of our passions follow so swiftly from mere impressions in the brain and the disposition of our organs, without any contribution from the soul, that there is no human wisdom capable of withstanding them if one is not sufficiently prepared. Thus, many people cannot help laughing when tickled, although they take no pleasure in it. For the impression of joy and surprise that in the past made them laugh when this happened is aroused in their imagination, and this causes their lungs to be suddenly inflated against their will by the blood dispatched there by the heart. And, likewise, many who have a strong natural propensity to emotions of joy, or pity, or fear, or anger, cannot help fainting, or weeping, or trembling, or having all their blood stirred up as if they had a fever, when their imagination is strongly affected by the object of one of those passions. But what one can always do in such situations, and I think I can indicate it here as the most general and easy remedy for all the excesses of passion, is this: when one feels one's blood stirred in this way, one must be alert, and remember that whatever presents itself to the imagination tends to deceive the soul and to cause the reasons in favour of the object of one's passion to appear much more convincing than they are, and those against it to appear much less so. And when the action to which passion is persuading one can be put off for a time, then the thing is to refrain from passing any judgement on the spot, and to distract oneself with other thoughts until time and tranquillity have altogether calmed the disturbance in the blood. And, finally, when the passion is prompting one to actions concerning which we must make an immediate decision, the will must direct itself chiefly to weighing and assenting to the reasons contrary to those represented by the passion, even if they appear weaker. When, for instance, one is unexpectedly attacked by an enemy, the situation does not allow for any time to be spent in deliberation. But what I think that those in the habit of thinking about their actions can always do is to make the effort, whenever they feel themselves seized by fear, to turn their thought away from the consideration of danger, by focusing on the reasons why it is always much safer and more honourable to stand and fight than to flee; and, on the contrary, when anger and the desire for revenge spur them on to charge rashly at their attackers, they will remember that it is folly to throw one's life away when one can save oneself without dishonour, and that, if the odds are heavily against one, it is better to retreat honourably or to ask for quarter* than to expose oneself blindly to certain death.

ART. 212. *That it is the passions alone that make for all that is good or bad in this life.*
Furthermore, the soul may have pleasures of its own. But, as for those it shares with the body, these depend entirely on the passions: so much so that those most capable of being moved by passion are those capable of tasting the most sweetness in this life. It is true that they may also taste the most bitterness, when they do not know how to use the passions and fortune is against them. But the greatest benefit of wisdom is that it teaches us to master the passions so thoroughly and to handle them so skilfully that the evils they cause are perfectly bearable, and can even, all of them, be a source of joy.

APPENDIX

A NOTE ON DESCARTES'S PHYSICS

At various points in the correspondence Descartes is called on to explain this or that aspect of his account of the physical world, as developed in the *Principles*. What follows relates only to points raised in the correspondence included in this volume.[1]

In Part III of the *Principles* Descartes develops a general theory of physical phenomena aimed at explaining the nature of the world as it is now by supposing it has developed out of a primordial chaos, in accordance with laws laid down by God. (He emphasizes that this is a heuristic expedient, so as to avoid clashing with the scriptural account of the creation of the world in its present state.) The basic model is that of a universe in which all bodies are composed of the same basic matter (unlike in Aristotelian physics, where there are distinct fundamental qualities combining to form the four elements); this matter is intrinsically divisible and in fact already divided into parts. These parts are all in motion in two different ways. They are each rotating around their centre, and at the same time they are orbiting in a cluster around one of a massive number of centres, forming what Descartes calls vortices (*tourbillons*). The particles are worn by contact into a spherical shape, and the matter shaved off by this process (the *ramenta*, or scrapings) fills the gaps between the spheres (since Descartes denies the possibility of a vacuum). The scrapings form what Descartes calls the first element; the spherical particles the second. There is also a third element, composed of matter the particles of which, on account of their size and shape, cannot be moved as easily as the first two.[2] The elements, then, are not fundamental constituents: they have been formed by a mechanical process. They can be distinguished further as follows: the first element is luminous, the second transparent, the third opaque. Descartes holds that the sun and the fixed stars are composed of the first element, the

---

[1] For an admirable exposition of the science of the *Principles* and other works, see Stephen Gaukroger, *Descartes' System of Natural Philosophy* (Cambridge, 2002).

[2] It later becomes clear that these have been formed by agglomerations of matter of the first element (see III. 94 (though there is no reference to the third element in L, only in F) and IV. 5–8).

heavens of the second, and the earth, the planets, and the comets of the third (III. 46–52).

Some of the particles of the first element will be larger and slower than the others. Being 'scrapings' of the original particles, they will be irregular in shape and prone to catch onto and get attached to other such particles (there seems to be an echo here of the Epicurean explanation of how atoms cluster together; Lucretius, *De rerum natura* 2. 100–4). These combinations of particles combine further to form what Descartes calls 'striated', or 'grooved', particles. He invites us to think of these as little columns with three grooves, the grooves, moreover, being spirally coiled like the shell of a snail; the direction of the spiral coil on a particular particle is determined by the quarter of the heavens from which the particle is travelling: those coming from the southern celestial pole will have the coil turned in the opposite direction from their counterparts coming from the northern celestial pole (they may be compared to screws of which some have a right-hand, others a left-hand, thread). So shaped, these particles are capable of passing through the gaps left by the spherical particles of the second element (III. 88–91).

These particles are extremely important in Descartes's explanation of why the appearance of the heavens alters: that is, why stars sometimes disappear from view. It is not that the star has ceased to exist: rather, it has been obscured in the same way as the sun is obscured by sunspots. What happens is this. The matter of the first element of which the star is principally composed is moving with great rapidity. The grooved particles, along with any other irregularly shaped particles, resist being whirled along in this fashion, and are therefore expelled from the interior of the star and form a layer of the third element on its surface (III. 94). Descartes compares this accretion of irregular particles to a number of branches being tangled together. But this state of things is unstable. The grooved particles are able to pass through holes, or 'pores', in this layer. In fact, they can pass right through the star, albeit in one direction only, depending on the direction of the coil or thread. They cannot return through the pores by which they entered, because as they passed through it was as if they forced the branches in the same direction, thus creating an impenetrable obstacle to their returning in the opposite direction. They therefore pass through the star altogether and emerge on the other side, where they are driven by the motion around the star of the subtle matter of the second element back to the side of the star by which they originally entered (III. 105–8).

A similar process is described in Part IV, with reference to the earth, which Descartes holds was originally a star (IV. 2). Descartes supposes that the earth contains a number of conduits or passages parallel to its axis along which the grooved particles can pass on their way from one pole of the earth to the other. The grooves of the particles, as we saw, can be compared to the thread of a screw, and, likewise, the conduits are so threaded that they can receive only those particles coming from a particular pole, north or south; having passed through a given conduit in one direction, the particles cannot return along it, because their paths would be impeded by the little hairs, or branches, as Descartes calls them, by which the conduit is lined, and which are so angled that, without impeding the original movement, they would block the return movement. Thus, when a particle has passed right through the earth along one of the conduits, it is compelled to make its way back to its starting point via the air above the surface of the planet (IV. 133, 146).

EXPLANATORY NOTES

CORRESPONDENCE WITH PRINCESS ELISABETH OF BOHEMIA

3 *6/16 May 1643*: the two dates reflect the fact that Elisabeth is still using the traditional Julian calendar, rather than, or as well as, the reformed Gregorian calendar. Since the latter had been introduced by a pope (Gregory XIII), some Protestants were reluctant to use it, though it had been adopted by the province of Holland, in which Elisabeth was residing.

M. Pallotti: known also by the French form of his name, Alphonse de Pollot, an Italian Protestant (1602–68) who had settled in the United Provinces, where he became friendly with Descartes and through whom the philosopher and Elisabeth became acquainted. Elisabeth uses the original Italian form of his name.

M. Regius: the Latin form of the name Henri de Roy (1598–1679). A professor of medicine at the University of Utrecht, he was an early disciple of Descartes's; but he aroused the opposition of Voetius, the rector of the university, who had the university senate condemn Descartes's philosophy in 1642. In 1646 he published *Fundamenta physices* ('Fundamentals of Physics'), but Descartes proclaimed his disagreement with him (see also the letter to Elisabeth of December 1646; letter 40).

how the human soul can act on the spirits of the body: right at the start of the correspondence, Elisabeth raises what has always been regarded as a serious difficulty for Descartes's dualistic philosophy. If mind and body are two radically distinct substances, how can the former act on the latter? 'Spirits' here means 'animal spirits', the most volatile part of the blood; see *The Passions of the Soul*, §10.

4 *Your affectionate friend at your service*: Furetière explains in his *Dictionnaire universel* (1690) that this expression would now be used in writing to an inferior, but that 'as recently as 30 or 40 years ago' a similar expression could be used to a person of high rank. Presumably Elisabeth is using it in the respectful rather than the condescending sense.

Egmond aan den Hoef: a village then in the province of Holland, near the town of Alkmaar. Later Descartes moved to the nearby village of Egmond-Binnen (also known as Egmond de Abdij). On Egmond and his residences in the area, see Steven Nadler, *The Philosopher, the Priest, and the Painter* (Princeton, 2013), 8–9, 87–90.

conveying your commands: on the use of 'your' here, rather than the more strictly correct 'her', see the Note on the Text, Translations, and References.

they reveal themselves to be: Descartes shows himself an accomplished rhetorician here, working on one of the commonplaces of rhetorical thought.

Elisabeth's thoughts are 'ingenious', that is, they indicate a powerful and fertile native intelligence (Latin *ingenium*); but rhetoricians and critics urged that this could sometimes produce superficially striking thoughts or expressions that would not stand up to analysis (judgement; Latin *iudicium*). Elisabeth unusually combines both *ingenium* and *iudicium* in a high degree.

5 *certain primary notions*: on these basic indefinable notions, see *Principles*, I. 10.

by causing its sensations and passions: apart from the general notions, then, there are primary notions pertaining, respectively, to the soul, to bodies, and to the composite of soul and body. In each of these categories there is one absolutely primary notion (thought, extension, and union, respectively) and other notions that depend on it, in the sense that they presuppose it. For there cannot be intellectual perceptions and volitions without thought; or shape and motion without extension; or action of the soul on the body (voluntary movement) and of the body on the soul (sensations and passions) without union. Yet these other notions are still primary in the sense that they are irreducible: we could not deduce them from the absolutely primary notions. That is why Descartes says below that 'each of them can be understood only by itself'.

my Reply to the Sixth Objections: in the passage referred to (AT 7. 440–5, OWC 209–13), Descartes explains how he came to realize that many of his early ideas (and by implication everyone else's) had been based on a confusion of mental and bodily categories, and how he learned to distinguish clearly what belongs to body and what to mind. He summarizes the point briefly in the following paragraph.

6 *we referred to them as 'qualities'*: the 'we' is that of the philosophical and scientific community, still ensnared by faulty Aristotelian conceptions of the soul as the 'form' of the body, and of the real existence of qualities like heaviness and heat.

as I hope to show in my Physics: see *Principles*, IV. 20–7, for Descartes's explanation of heaviness.

the soul moves the body: in standard Aristotelian physics heaviness or gravity is conceived as a real quality in a body moving it towards the centre of the earth, without any contact with other bodies being required. Descartes thinks that this conception is an inaccurate representation of a purely physical process; as he explains in the Sixth Replies, the supposed quality seems to function like a mind in the body that guides it towards its destination (AT 7. 442, OWC 211). But that is exactly what is happening when my mind or soul moves some part of my body. Aristotelian physics, then, can't explain the movement of bodies as such; but it provides a model of movement not dependent on physical contact that could help us to understand how movements of the body are caused by the soul. (It is worth noting, however, that an analogous problem arises concerning the relationship of God to the material universe. Suppose he has so ordained it that all its processes result from the operation of a few laws of physics: nonetheless, being omnipotent, he could certainly intervene to change a body's motion (as, for instance, when he works a miracle). It follows that all bodies, beside the capacity to be moved by other bodies, possess an intrinsic capacity to be moved by an immaterial will; but this capacity seems to conflict with a purely mechanical conception. (From the point of view of a human agent, the capacity could be activated only in the particular human body to which he or she is united.)) Descartes goes on to suggest that our propensity to conflate bodily and mental categories is not purely and simply a self-induced intellectual defect; though its effects are harmful when applied to purely physical or purely mental processes, we need this way of thinking in order to understand the relationships between the physical and the mental. This is an interesting suggestion, which, however, Descartes does not develop as fully as would have been required—as Elisabeth's reply clearly shows.

7 *&c.*: thus abbreviated in the original, and standing in for some conventional formula like 'your humble servant'.

with false praise: she discourages Descartes from using the kind of fulsome praise with which his letter begins, since she has come to associate it with empty flattery, and does not need it as an encouragement to do better.

meditation according to your rules: in the preface to the *Meditations*, Descartes asserts that no one will benefit from the work who is not able and willing to meditate seriously and to withdraw their mind from the senses (AT 7. 9, OWC 8).

the interests of my house: *maison*, used of a royal or princely family.

demonstration of a contrary truth: Descartes will be propounding a mechanical theory of motion, and rejecting the idea that bodies are moved by a kind of inner inclination upwards or downwards (such as 'heaviness').

8 *cannot have any communication with it*: the whole paragraph is extremely acute. Descartes has cited the Aristotelian concept of motion as due to a real quality in bodies as a model for conceiving how the soul can move the body. But, as Elisabeth points out, he rejects the Aristotelian theory as an explanation of the process it purports to describe, and promises to prove this in his forthcoming *Principles of Philosophy*. Would it not be more logical to assume that the theory is a pure fiction, one of the confused ideas Descartes seeks in the *Meditations* to jettison, whereby a physical process is mistakenly credited with an immaterial cause, because the senses do not reveal a material one? In short, how can a bad theory of physical motion be a good theory of interaction? Her reference by contrast to the objective reality of the idea of God (which Descartes argues in the Third Meditation cannot be conceived as a fiction; AT 7. 46, OWC 33) shows how carefully Elisabeth has read the *Meditations* and how fully she has assimilated Descartes's way of thinking; far better than any of the Objectors, save Arnauld.

by the soul's informing the body: *par information*. Suppose, drawing on the language of Aristotle, you say that an immaterial intelligent soul 'informs' the body, and can thus move it. But the body is actually moved by the animal spirits (as Descartes will explain in *The Passions of the Soul*). How is the soul then moving the body, unless you treat the animal spirits as partaking of the nature of soul? But if the soul is defined as intelligent, then the spirits must have intelligence, contrary to Descartes's basic dualistic principle.

a few vapours: Elisabeth is picking up a question she urged in her first letter: if the soul is immaterial, why are its functions interrupted in the state of unconsciousness? 'Vapours' in the usage of the time can refer to exhalations from 'humours' inside the body as well as from external sources; Elisabeth may be referring to the soporific effect of the 'vapours' of wine, or to the vapours supposedly arising from the womb that were invoked to explain fainting in women.

9 *aided by the imagination*: Descartes explains the difference between the intellect or pure understanding and the imagination in the Sixth Meditation (AT 7. 72–3, OWC 51–2). The imagination makes mental pictures of things, and as such is particularly helpful in forming ideas of bodies.

to conceive them as a single thing: for an interesting illustration of this view, compare the analysis of love in *Passions*, §§79–80.

10 *both a body and a mind*: 'mind' here translates Descartes's *pensée*, which usually means the faculty or activity of thinking, but sometimes designates the thinking substance or agent. See Third Replies, 2, AT 7. 174, OWC 109. Moreover 'soul' and 'mind' are, for Descartes, synonymous; see *Meditations*, II, AT 7. 27, OWC 19, and Introduction, p. xix. The context seems to require *pensée* to denote the soul, the thing that thinks, rather than thought in general. Descartes seems to be suggesting that we can conceive the soul united to the body as material and extended, in a specific sense, which excludes, for instance, the claim that the soul and the brain are one and the same thing. It is rather, perhaps, that I, the composite of soul and body, am both my soul and my body; and yet my 'I'-ness or self is located in the soul as distinct from the body since it is the soul that makes the body mine, that transforms it from a physical mechanism into the vehicle of a subjective identity.

11 *the extension of that mind*: my perception of three-dimensional space, distinct from the space itself that exists outside my mind.

one of their ministers: Descartes's *Epistle* to his enemy Voetius, published in May 1643, AT 8/2. 1–194; see Introduction.

to deprive the human race of them: allusion to Voetius. Elisabeth is saying that she would have wanted to intervene on Descartes's behalf in the Voetius affair, so ridding him of the attendant vexations, before bothering him again with questions; but that she felt obliged to take advantage of van Bergen's kind offer to take a letter to Descartes.

11 *van Bergen*: Anthony Studler van Zurck, lord of Bergen (*c*.1608–1666). He
    was a close friend of Descartes's and frequently lent him money.

12 *the rule you lay down in that work*: in the Fourth Meditation, Descartes's
    investigation of the causes of error leads him to conclude that we can avoid
    it if we refrain from passing judgement (making assertions) whenever we
    do not have a clear and distinct perception of the truth (AT 7. 56–60,
    OWC 40–3).

    function of the soul: that is to say, perhaps the soul is not simply a think-
    ing thing, but includes some functions connected with the body (as the
    Aristotelians held, for whom the soul is the source of the body's life: this
    view is rejected by Descartes in the Second Meditation; see Introduction,
    pp. xix–xx).

    the scholastics' self-contradictory view: Elisabeth's syntax is not very clear
    here; it is uncertain what 'it' (*elle*) refers to. That the soul is not located in
    a particular part of the body, but is entire both in the body as a whole and
    in any part of it, is argued by Aquinas (*ST* 1. 76. 8), following Augustine,
    De Trinitate, 6. 6. 8.

    as an excuse for myself: in his previous letter, Descartes had suggested that
    to confuse soul and body comes naturally to non-philosophical people,
    whose experience shows them the interaction of the two. This does not
    apply to Elisabeth, who has thought much about the matter; but all her
    thinking has not been able to lift her above doubt, and enable her to accept
    Descartes's solution unreservedly.

    17 November 1643: the exact date of the letter is supplied in *The Corres-
    pondence of Descartes 1643*, ed. T. Verbeek, E.-J. Bos, and J. M. M. van de
    Ven (Utrecht, 2004).

    the three-circle problem: given three tangent circles, to construct a fourth
    tangent to them. This is sometimes known as Apollonius' problem. The
    figures in the text were inserted by Clerselier, the first editor of Des-
    cartes's correspondence.

16 *the problem is planar*: *le problème est plan*: Shapiro glosses 'planar or of the
    second degree' (*Correspondence*, 77).

17 *if he had followed your instructions*: Descartes had told Pollot not to give
    Elisabeth his letter right away in case she wanted to carry on trying to
    work the problem out for herself (AT 4. 43).

    did me the honour of sending me: Elisabeth's solution is lost.

    finds all things equally easy: Descartes repeats this praise of Elisabeth's
    unique combination of abilities in the dedication to the *Principles of Phil-
    osophy*.

20 *8 July 1644*: this letter is printed out of sequence in AT, since the edi-
    tors originally believed it to date from July 1647. They corrected the error
    later (AT 5. 553; see 5. 660). It is plain that in 1647 Descartes would not
    have needed to give Elisabeth this basic account of the workings of the
    passions.

by willing or thinking of something else: on the indirect nature of the mind's power over the body's reactions, see *Passions*, §45.

21 *harmed by the air*: from antiquity on, many diseases were ascribed to the qualities of the air in a particular place.

in the case of various people: according to Descartes, the Dutch astronomer Hortensius (Maarten van den Hove) predicted on the basis of his horoscope to two young men that he would die in 1639, and that they would not long outlive him. He did indeed die in that year. One of the young men then died and the other fell gravely ill, as Descartes suggests, from sheer fear of the prediction's coming true (to Mersenne, 29 January 1640, AT 3. 15).

the business that has brought me to France: negotiations with his family about the division of property.

The present Mijnheer van Bergen made to me: the *Principles of Philosophy*, which are dedicated to Elisabeth.

you alone have demonstrated that science exists: the syntax is imperfect, and one would require something like 'my debt would be already immense'.

you are obliged to construct a new morality: in the dedicatory letter Descartes adumbrates the ethical viewpoint he will set out at more length in *The Passions of the Soul*, according to which truly virtuous behaviour depends on a clear intellectual perception of what is good.

the lowest level to which you there give your approval: in the dedicatory letter Descartes distinguishes those who lack the full knowledge of what is good but are determined to obtain it from those who already possess a higher level of understanding. Elisabeth puts herself in the first class, though he is implying that she belongs in the second.

22 *your definition of heaviness*: for Descartes, heaviness is not an intrinsic property of bodies or of any kind of body; it is an effect of pressure exerted on the earth by the subtle matter that moves constantly through the heavens; the particles that form liquid substances are less subject to this pressure than solid bodies and are therefore lighter (*Principles*, IV. 20–5). In that case, Elisabeth asks, how can he explain the combination of heaviness and liquidity in quicksilver (mercury), which he mentions in IV. 16 and the origin of which he explains in detail in IV. 58? Could it be that its heaviness, when it is in the earth, is due to downward pressure from the earth's outer crust (body E)? But how would this explain the fact that it is heavy when it reaches the surface of the earth?

the picture on p. 225: the page number is that of the original edition. The picture, which illustrates IV. 59, represents the different layers of matter of which the earth is composed.

the spiral-shaped particles: *ces particules, tournées en coquilles*, literally, 'these particles, twisted like a snail's shell'. Descartes also calls them 'grooved particles' (*particules cannelées*). On these particles, see *Principles*, III. 88–90, and the Appendix.

22 *body M*: the solid layer of the earth around its core; Descartes says that it is formed of particles of the first element, and the comparison with sunspots suggests that he is thinking in particular of grooved particles, as Elisabeth certainly takes him to be (*Principles*, IV. 4).

on pp. 133–4: of the original edition; see *Principles*, III. 89.

a shorter way via body C: having passed through the earth the grooved particles return to their original entry point via the outer air. Elisabeth cannot see why they should not follow a direct route back through body C, the inner crust of the earth. Descartes's reply is not very helpful here, but he could have referred her to *Principles*, IV. 133, 146. See also the Appendix.

23 *Le Crévis*: or Le Crévy, not far from Rennes in Brittany; Descartes had gone there for a family gathering, to settle the question of his inheritance.

how much I esteem and honour you: Descartes is referring to the dedication to the *Principles of Philosophy*.

accusations of attempted innovation: we are so inured to the idea that innovation (intellectual, technological, artistic) is good in itself that it is difficult to realize that in the seventeenth century it was commonly perceived as pernicious in unsettling what ought to be regarded as settled.

more rigid and more compact: and thus more liable to experience the pressure from the subtle matter that produces what we know as heaviness.

24 *as in little magnetic stones*: see *Principles*, IV. 166.

M. de P.: Pollot.

with which Fortune persecutes your house: on Elisabeth's family troubles, see Introduction.

25 *those cruel philosophers*: the Stoics.

the events of a play: Descartes often resorts to this image; he develops it in his very next letter. Elisabeth questions it in letter 27; Descartes replies in 28 and uses the comparison again in 31. For other uses, see *Passions*, §§94, 147, 187. See also Henry Phillips, 'Descartes and the Dramatic Experience', *French Studies*, 39 (1985), 408–22.

27 *Sir Kenelm Digby*: (1603–65). One of the most remarkable men of his age, an English Roman Catholic aristocrat, by turns courtier, diplomat, privateer, scientist, and philosopher. He visited Descartes in the Netherlands in 1641. His philosophical treatises *The Nature of Bodies* and *On the Immortality of Reasonable Souls* were published together in 1644.

two places: in fact the summary of the chapters of *The Nature of Bodies* indicates three places where Digby signals his dissent from Descartes: chapters 13 (on reflection and refraction), 26 (on the movement of the heart), and 32 (on sensation).

28 *determination*: I take this to mean the original combination of force and direction affecting the path of the bullet as distinct from the actual movement

that results from the combination of this with other factors, like its striking a resistant or yielding body.

the Louvain doctor: Vopiscus Fortunatus Plemp, commonly known as Plempius (1601–71), with whom Descartes corresponded in early 1638 apropos of the circulation of the blood (AT 1. 497–9, 521–34; 2. 52–4, 62–9). Plempius published the correspondence, but, according to Descartes, mangled the latter's side of it. In 1643 the Dutch doctor Johan van Beverwijck asked Descartes for his views on the matter (AT 3. 682), and Descartes agreed to send him the original authentic documents of his correspondence with Plempius (AT 4. 6). No doubt this is how Elisabeth came to see it.

Dr Jonson: Samson Jonson or Jonsson, court preacher of Elisabeth's mother, the (deposed) queen of Bohemia.

who goes by the name of Albanus: one of the pseudonyms used by the English Catholic priest and philosopher Thomas White (1593–1676), a friend of Digby's.

30 *who died a few days after my birth*: Descartes was born on 31 March 1596; his mother in fact died over a year later on 13 May 1597.

Monsieur le Chevalier d'Igby: Sir Kenelm Digby (see above); the surname of a French chevalier would be preceded by the nobiliary particle 'de', and many English aristocratic families have originally French names, so Descartes perhaps supposes that the initial letter of Digby's name is that particle.

31 *the curse of my sex*: as an unmarried woman of rank it would be unseemly for Elisabeth to visit a man to whom she was not related.

from your new garden: where Descartes was carrying out his botanical investigations.

the University of Groningen: the university authorities had rejected the accusations of atheism and sedition levelled at Descartes by one of their professors, Martin Schoock, a confederate of Voetius'.

32 *the most violent passions*: Descartes is restating what he said in his last letter. In *Passions*, §212, he states that 'those most capable of being moved by passion are those capable of tasting the most sweetness in this life'.

33 *what is happening in Groningen or Utrecht*: Descartes's disputes with Schoock and Voetius. Descartes is picking up the subjects of the last part of Elisabeth's previous letter, and in particular responding to her regret that she cannot come to see him by announcing that he will come to see her.

seeing Your Highness: on the visit announced in his last letter.

34 *Seneca's On the Happy Life*: *De vita beata*, a Stoic treatise by the Roman philosopher Seneca (*c*.4 BC–AD 65).

35 *in French I would say vivre heureusement*: *heureusement* is the adverb corresponding to the adjective *heureux*, the ordinary French word for 'happy'

(*heureusement* being the adverbial form). But *heureux, heureusement* often refer to good fortune (as when we say 'a happy (i.e. fortunate) chance' in English). Descartes wants to distinguish this from genuine happiness, which is independent of good fortune, and which he therefore labels *béatitude*. This word would not seem unfamiliar to those with a knowledge of Latin, in which *beatus* is a frequent word for 'happy', but to a modern English readership it might sound pedantic, except in particular religious contexts (as in the Beatitudes of the Sermon on the Mount). Hence I have preferred to translate *beatitude* as 'happiness', and though 'happiness' too has etymological links with 'hap', another word, though now rare, for 'chance' or 'fortune', the term must here be understood as denoting a state independent of fortune.

35 *quod beatam vitam efficiat*: 'that makes a life happy'.

these are of two kinds: this distinction between what is within our power and what is not within our power derives from the Stoic philosopher Epictetus (*Enchiridion*, §1), and it is essential to Descartes's ethical thought (cf. *Discourse*, III, AT 6. 25–6, OWC 23–4; *Passions*, §144). Descartes does not go so far as Epictetus in asserting that what is not in our control is in effect valueless: he admits that honour, wealth, and health are genuine goods. In this respect, he is closer to Aristotle. But he differs from Aristotle in denying that they are essential to happiness (see *Ethics* 1. 8. 15–17, 1099ª31–ᵇ9).

in the Discourse on the Method: Part III, AT 6. 23–7, OWC 21–5.

36 *carry out all the acts we have judged best*: cf. the definition of virtue in *Passions*, §153.

this kind of virtue: Descartes is challenging rigorist conceptions of virtue, whether Christian or Stoic, that define it in negative terms, in opposition to pleasure, appetite, and passion. The attempt to subdue these fundamental constituents of human nature can never succeed; whereas Cartesian ethics encourages us not to eliminate them, but to regulate them by reason.

37 *natural happiness*: as distinct from the supernatural beatitude of the vision of God in the afterlife. As the next sentence shows, Descartes is careful, while developing a natural vision of the good life, not to exclude a properly Christian perspective.

the book you recommended to me: Seneca, *On the Happy Life*.

seems not to be teaching me anything new: there is nothing backhanded or grudging about this compliment; nothing could have pleased Descartes better than this confirmation of his basic claim, that his philosophy can be followed by anyone prepared to make the effort, and that it does not deliver new and stunning ideas, but simply enables us to make contact with the innate ideas that have been obscured by the prejudices of experience. However, Elisabeth goes on to turn his claim against himself by asserting her own independent critical thinking.

38 *he felt no pain*: Epicurus suffered from recurrent kidney stones, which

eventually caused his death. On his deathbed, he wrote to a friend that the remembrance of all his philosophical contemplations kept him cheerful, despite the pain he was going through. He did not, therefore, deny he was feeling pain, but only claimed that it did not disturb his philosophical cheerfulness. But Elisabeth's basic point is that this imperturbability is a luxury of the philosophical lifestyle, and would be impossible to maintain in a life (like her own) constantly beset with external challenges.

39 *Nunquam de vita iudicatur, semper creditur*: 'we never show any judgement in the matter of living, but always a blind trust' (Seneca, *On the Happy Life* 1. 4, in *Moral Essays*, ed. and trans. John W. Basore, 3 vols., Loeb Classical Library (Cambridge, Mass., 1928–35), ii. 101). All further translations from Seneca are from this edition, except in cases where Descartes or Elisabeth have substituted their own Latin words for Seneca's, in which case the translation is mine.

Sanabimur, si modo separemur a coetu: 'let us merely separate ourselves from the crowd, and we shall be made whole' (*On the Happy Life* 1. 4).

the supreme good: or 'sovereign good'; in ancient moral philosophy, the ultimate good, the true goal of human life, with reference to which all other goods are to be judged.

rerum naturae assentitur: the original has *rerum naturae adsentior* ('I follow the guidance of nature'; *On the Happy Life* 3. 3). Descartes adjusts the quotation to the syntax of his sentence: 'it [the supreme good] follows the guidance of nature'.

40 *ad illius legem exemplumque formari sapientia est*: 'to mould ourselves according to [Nature's] law and pattern—this is true wisdom' (*On the Happy Life* 3. 3).

beata vita est conveniens naturae suae: 'the happy life, therefore, is a life that is in harmony with its own nature' (*On the Happy Life* 3. 3).

the order established by God: this is in fact more or less the sense in which Seneca is using the term 'nature', though he does not think of God as transcending the world in the manner of the Christian God, but more as a world-soul.

rerum naturae . . . sapientia est: 'to follow the guidance of nature and to mould ourselves according to its law and pattern—this is true wisdom'. Descartes is conflating previous quotations.

nisi sana mens est, &c.: 'unless the mind is sound' (*On the Happy Life* 3. 3; my translation). Descartes has slightly modified Seneca's text here, the point being that unless we have a sound mind, we cannot live according to nature.

secundum naturam vivere: 'to live according to nature' (my translation); not an exact quotation but a paraphrase of the position set out in *On the Happy Life* 3. 3.

living according to true reason: Descartes's interpretation is correct.

40 *beatus est . . . beneficio rationis*: 'the happy man is one who is freed from both fear and desire because of the gift of reason' (*On the Happy Life* 5. 1).

beata vita . . . stabilita: 'the life that is happy has been founded on correct and trustworthy judgement' (*On the Happy Life* 5. 3).

all our actions should aim: the identification of the supreme good with the ultimate aim of our activity and with happiness is in Aristotle, *Ethics* 1. 7. 3–5, $1097^a25{-}^b6$.

41 *that of Zeno*: not Zeno of Elea (*c*.490–*c*.430 BC), famous for propounding the paradox of Achilles and the tortoise, but Zeno of Citium (*c*.334–*c*.262 BC), founder of the Stoic school of philosophy.

the supreme good a given individual can possess: a profound insight into the difference of outlook between Aristotelianism and Stoicism. It is often argued nowadays that Stoicism was in part a response to the breakdown in the Hellenistic period of the old city-states, with their strong community ethos, leading to an increasing isolation of the individual. Descartes's own life is in a sense a response to an analogous social transformation.

all the vices were equal: the Stoics taught that all vices are equal, inasmuch as they are all deformities of soul. See Cicero, *Paradoxa stoicorum* 3. 20–6, in *De oratore, Book III; De fato; Paradoxa stoicorum; De partitione oratoria*, ed. and trans. H. Rackham, Loeb Classical Library (Cambridge, Mass., 1942).

42 *unless they know there is a prize to be won*: Descartes's analogy brackets out the question of skill, which an Aristotelian view of virtue as a set of dispositions acquired by practice would emphasize, and emphasizes the intellectual aspect, the need to know that virtue is the only way to happiness.

to attain a correct judgement: cf. Descartes's previous letter and the definition of virtue at *Passions*, §153.

DES CARTES: Descartes's spelling of his name is inconsistent; in a later letter (24) he signs himself 'De Cartes'.

43 *might among them be considered hypothetical*: Elisabeth means that whereas we might think a particular point of view problematic, and thus go into the arguments for and against it, the ancients would feel entitled to accept it as a working hypothesis, and proceed without taking objections into account.

quam nos virtuti . . . voluptati: 'the rule that we Stoics lay down for virtue, this same rule he lays down for pleasure' (*On the Happy Life* 13. 1).

ego enim nego . . . viuat: 'for I deny that any man can live pleasantly without at the same time living virtuously as well' (*On the Happy Life* 10. 1; my translation). Elisabeth has somewhat departed from the text but without altering the meaning.

consequentia summum bonum: goods that 'attend on the highest good' (without actually constituting it) (*On the Happy Life* 15. 2).

the authority of human reason: Montaigne, for instance, treats the inability of philosophers to agree on the fundamentals of ethics as proof of the feebleness of human reason (*Essays*, II. 12, 'An Apology for Raymond Sebond', 651–2).

Rhenen: the town in the Netherlands where Elisabeth's deposed father was living.

44 *a better state after death than it is currently in*: in the *Meditations* Descartes argues for the real distinction between soul and body. As a substance distinct from the body, the soul need not perish when the body dies. We can thus hope for a better life after death, but philosophy cannot give us more than the hope of this. Only faith can give us the conviction that there is a better life after death.

47 *as if they were remedies*: Descartes's previous letter cited various reasons (her age, royal birth, and occupations) why Elisabeth has not had as much time for study as she would have liked. Even if, she replies, she could accept these 'pretexts' as excuses, they would not make up for (or 'remedy') the fact that she is still (as she thinks) ignorant; in fact, these causes should have prompted her to develop her mind all the more, since she was forced to grow up so quickly by her situation and troubles.

that might have prevented me from thinking of myself: Elisabeth bitterly quotes Descartes's words about the spiritual danger of good fortune, by which indeed she has not been overburdened.

subjection to a governess: rather than a lowly teacher and minder of young children, like Jane Eyre, the term here denotes a lady of high birth responsible for the behaviour of a girl of high birth.

48 *instinctive sense*: *sentiment tacite*. *Sentiment* in seventeenth-century French, as well as meaning 'sensation' or 'feeling' (as in passion), can mean 'opinion' or even something like 'perspective'.

'disorders of the soul': this Stoic conception of the passions as disorders is set out at length in, for example, Cicero, *Tusculan Disputations* 4.

49 *prince of Orange*: Frederick Henry (1584–1647), the effective ruler of the United Provinces.

50 *book III of the Principles of Philosophy*: articles III. 1–3 argue that we have no reason to suppose that the universe has limits, and that we should not search for the purposes God had in mind in creating things; in particular, we should not suppose that all things were created essentially for our sake.

51 *the opinions that appear to us most probable*: on the need to rely on probable judgements in matters of behaviour, where strict demonstration is unavailable, and to act with resolution, in order to avoid subsequent regret and repentance, see *Discourse*, III, AT 6. 24–5, OWC 22–3.

52 *the virtues are habits*: see Aquinas, *ST* 1-2. 55. 1.

53 *lived without the revealed Law*: the pagans of antiquity (suicide being

forbidden in Judaism and Christianity). Some ancient schools of philosophy thought suicide legitimate, but not all (see Plato's *Phaedo* for a condemnation of it).

53 *particular providence*: this normally refers to God's concern, not simply for the general order of the world, but for each event within it (see Matt. 10: 29, the text to which Hamlet is referring when he says, 'there's a special providence in the fall of a sparrow'; v. ii. 150). In her next letter, however, Elisabeth explains that she means it with reference to God's specific plan for the salvation of humanity.

55 *the ordinary capacities of the human mind*: in other words, Elisabeth is not to reproach herself for not making better use of the greater quantity of free time she has had than other people, since we should not try to devote all our free time to study, and would achieve little if we did. It is when we compare ourselves to other people and what they have achieved that we discover whether we have made good use of our time.

56 *only a privation*: that is, an absence of some good that ought to be there, not an actual reality. See *Passions*, §140.

thus, for example, tragedies: 'tragedy' here as elsewhere in this volume usually refers to tragic drama, not to real-life 'tragedies'. Descartes frequently uses this example: see letter 12 and note.

57 *the treatise I formerly drafted on the nature of animals*: see AT 4. 247 and Baillet, *Vie*, ii. 272–3, where reference is made to Regius' coming into possession of draft notes in preparation for a treatise on animals; presumably this is the document seen by Elisabeth.

agitation of the spirits: the animal spirits, the most volatile parts of the blood (see *Passions*, §§7, 10). On the distinction between the passions, due to the animal spirits, and other kinds of perceptions or sensations, see §§22–9.

58 *and that of titillation*: *chatouillement*, literally, tickling, used by Descartes as a general term for pleasurable physical stimulation.

an action of their soul, not a passion: judgement, Descartes explains in the Fourth Meditation, is an act of the will.

conceive the danger: a 'judgement' in seventeenth-century philosophical parlance is a proposition; to 'conceive' is simply to form a distinct idea which may or may not be incorporated into a judgement. Descartes concedes that the emotional reaction may arise not from an explicit judgement ('they'll kill us all') but from a conception or idea ('danger'), giving rise to mental images of slaughter and destruction.

59 *between universal and particular causes*: Aquinas' discussion of providence distinguishes the providence of God as the universal cause from that of human beings as the particular cause (*ST* 1. 22. 2 *ad* 4). Nonetheless, he insists that acts of free human will are subject to divine providence.

there are no rational grounds for this conviction: reason teaches us that the

soul can exist without the body and thus experience pleasures that are pre-
cluded by its current embodied state; but it does not follow that it would
experience them, especially if it had sought death voluntarily.

the false philosophy of Hegesias: Hegesias, a philosopher of the Cyrenaic
school, argued that death was a release from the evils of life: he was banned
from teaching this doctrine by King Ptolemy II of Egypt (reigned 283–246
BC), on the grounds that it had persuaded people to commit suicide. See
Cicero, *Tusculan Disputations* 1. 34.

60 *actions depending on our free will*: to regard God's decrees as subject to
being changed by acts of our free will would be to make him dependent on
us and thus to undermine his sovereignty.

even the Arminians: followers of Arminius (Jakob Hermanszoon, 1560–
1609), a Protestant theologian whose teaching moderated some of the
tenets of hard-line Calvinism, especially the radical denial of human free
will; they held that, in the faithful, human free will, albeit with the indis-
pensable assistance of grace, makes a contribution to their perseverance in
union with Christ. Their teaching was condemned at the Synod of Dort
in 1619. Many, though not all, Roman Catholic theologians would have
agreed with them; Descartes, however, writing to a Protestant, mentions
a Protestant theology.

where morals had not been corrupted: Descartes is not arguing (as Adam
Smith is sometimes taken to have argued) that if each of us focuses only on
his own advantage, society as a whole will benefit, by the operations of
an 'invisible hand'; he is arguing that an enlightened sense of one's true
advantage requires one to concern oneself also with the welfare of other
people. See his next letter.

62 *the doctrine contained in one of your previous letters*: 1 September 1645 (letter 22).

as its existence does: our free will, as a faculty, exists only because God has
created it, that is, willed it to exist. But this, says Elisabeth, does not imply
that each of its acts is also willed by God; otherwise it would not be an
act of free will. Elisabeth's concern for human autonomy is striking, given
her Calvinist upbringing.

by his tutor: Digby's tutor at Gloucester Hall, Oxford, was Thomas Allen,
a noted mathematician and astrologer sympathetic to Catholicism. Catholics hold that not all those who die in a state of grace are yet worthy of
heaven; for such people a further temporary purification (purgatory), typically involving a degree of suffering, is necessary. Digby is giving a philosophical justification for the doctrine. Elisabeth rejects the justification; as
a Protestant, she would reject the doctrine itself.

the providence by which, from all eternity: Elisabeth, as noted above, explains
that she is using the term 'particular providence' to denote God's scheme
for the salvation of humanity. The sense it usually bears is of God's concern for all individual events that occur in our world; if Elisabeth uses it

in a different sense, this may be because she is inclined to think that free human acts do not fall within the scope of providence.

63 *an objection from our theologians*: in her previous letter Elisabeth suggested that the Cartesian thesis of the boundlessness of the universe tended to weaken belief in particular providence; she now says, however, that this is not her own personal view but the one a Protestant theologian might be expected to take.

the final cause: the purpose.

64 *the general run of human beings*: Descartes had suggested that Elisabeth has made far more intellectual progress than her contemporaries; in her last letter she refuses to compare herself with them, and then with other people in general.

there are two kinds of excess: 'excess' in English usually has negative implications ('to drink to excess'); but compare the distinction we make between 'excessively prudent' (his prudence tips into over-caution) and 'exceedingly prudent' (she is never taken by surprise and has everything worked out in advance). For Descartes, we might say, to be excessively given to any passion is bad; to be exceedingly given to it is good if the passion is good, that is, regulated by reason.

66 *the folly of one of my brothers*: on 5 November 1645 her brother Edward had married Anne of Gonzaga, daughter of the duke of Mantua, publicly abjuring his Protestantism and professing the Roman Catholic faith. As Lisa Shapiro points out, Elisabeth herself had rejected a proposed marriage with Władisław IV of Poland, because this would have required her to convert to Roman Catholicism (*Correspondence*, 127 n. 90, and cf. 9–10).

the gazette: newspapers had made an appearance in the United Provinces early in the seventeenth century.

67 *The son of the late Professor Schooten*: the son, Franz van Schooten, was applying to succeed his father as professor of mathematics at the University of Leiden.

recommend him to the Curators: the governors of the university.

68 *as being superfluous*: there was another professor of mathematics at the university (Golius); hence the proposal to suppress the elder Schooten's chair.

I was obliged to follow him right to the door: the young man's nervousness in the face of a princess makes him hurry away, and so perpetrate the social blunder of obliging her to get up and follow him, when he should have waited to be dismissed.

a thing that most people will find good: her brother's conversion to Catholicism. Descartes does not display the sympathy that Elisabeth was patently looking for; he prefers a blunt approach to what he judges to be the core issue: whether Edward's reputation will be damaged by his change of religion. One wonders whether this is why there was such a gap until her reply.

69 *king has forbidden duelling*: a pertinent allusion. Louis XIII of France, or rather his minister Richelieu, forbade duelling in 1626, on pain of death, though noblemen continued the practice for many years. The example seems to be inspired by a passage of Aquinas, *ST* I. 22. 2 *ad* 1.

they will not fail to meet, and to fight: Descartes is here enouncing a kind of psychological determinism (such as we find in Hume), whereas in his previous letter he stated that free will entails unpredictability, at least for human observers. In the rest of the paragraph, he sets out a compatibilist view, maintaining that an action can be seen both as the inevitable result of a person's disposition and circumstances, and as voluntary, in that these determinations do not amount to compulsion.

70 *bonum . . . defectu*: 'good is from a perfect [or "positive"] cause, evil from some defect.' Evil is, in other words, a privation.

71 *far advanced in philosophy*: this shows that for Descartes philosophy, as for the ancients, was an art of living, and not merely an intellectual discipline.

even if they do not realize this themselves: Descartes's interest in implicit or subliminal thought processes (compare *Passions*, §95) shows that he is far from assuming, as is sometimes supposed, that the mind is completely transparent to itself.

like the man in the fable: in Aesop's fable 'The Old Man and Death' an old man worn out gathering sticks calls on Death for relief; Death appears and asks him what he wants, and the old man asks for assistance in getting the bundle of sticks up onto his shoulder.

if they were thought to be of another disposition: the benefits are taken as evidence of good will, and responded to accordingly.

72 *those who seek their advantage in other ways*: this passage shows that in his discussion of self-interest, Descartes is not thinking about the workings of the capitalist market but about a way of life dependent on interpersonal relations. In his praise of frankness and condemnation of dissimulation and artifice, he echoes Montaigne (*Essays*, II. 17, pp. 735–8); both are responding to a Machiavellian discourse widespread in early modern Europe, in which dissimulation is upheld as a necessity for rulers and courtiers.

with the republic of Venice: Elisabeth's youngest brother, Philip, had undertaken to command a Venetian regiment against the Turks.

since your departure: Descartes had been at The Hague on 7 March, and must then have given Elisabeth a manuscript of *The Passions of the Soul*, not published for another three years. To read this was therefore the 'occupation' that he left her with, but which she was unable to pursue.

grow as well, . . . : there is a gap in the manuscript here.

sadness always takes away my appetite: in §100 of the published treatise, Descartes maintains that sadness does not diminish the appetite, unless it is combined with hatred.

73 *producing laughter*: in *Passions*, §124, Descartes explains the mechanism of laughter; in §125, he says that it is caused not by extraordinary joy, but by moderate joy mingled with wonderment or hatred. Wonderment ('admiration') is the passion we feel on encountering something surprising because outside our experience (*Passions*, §52).

seems to affect only the brain: since the object does not at this stage appear either good or evil, from the point of view of the well-being of the body, wonderment has no effect on the heart or the blood, only on the brain, as the organ involved in sensory cognition (*Passions*, §71).

the cause of sighs: sadness and desire; see *Passions*, §135.

it exists naturally in all human beings: cf. Aristotle, *Metaphysics* 1. 1. 1, 980^{a}22.

to send you my draft: early modern correspondents very often wrote a letter twice, a rough draft, which could be kept for their records, and a fair copy, which would be sent to the other person. Cf. Elisabeth's letter of 10 October 1646 (letter 37).

74 *colours and ornaments*: standard metaphors for rhetorical devices.

75 *the temperament of the blood alone*: see *Passions*, §51, where Descartes, however, speaks of 'bodily temperament' rather than specifically of the temperament of the blood.

risus sardonicus: this is still the medical term for the phenomenon Descartes describes, where the appearance of a grin is produced by a spasm of the facial muscles due to tetanus or poison.

76 *a certain lethargy*: *une certaine langueur*; see *Passions*, §170, where Descartes excuses indecisiveness (*irrésolution*) up to a certain point. See also his next letter.

in the presence of Hannibal: the great Carthaginian commander Hannibal once attended a lecture on generalship by the philosopher Phormio. Asked for his opinion, he said that he had seen many mad old men, but none madder; the point being that Phormio was pontificating about a subject of which he had no practical experience (Cicero, *De oratore* 2. 18. 75–6).

77 *M. de Beclin*: according to Baillet (*Vie*, ii. 296–7), Becklin was a member of the princess's household.

Your Highness particularly singled out this passage: whether in conversation or in the lost part of her previous letter (25 April 1646; letter 32), we do not know. The passage in question is *Passions*, §170. The tone of this letter is uncharacteristically anxious: Descartes seems to be afraid that Elisabeth has seized on his indulgent attitude to dilatoriness to justify taking her time over some important negotiations she is involved in, which might be jeopardized as a result.

than when it is not: presumably because delay gives time for the other parties involved in or affected by the negotiation to notice how much you stand to gain, and to worry about the effect on their own interests.

78 *your journey*: Descartes was planning to travel to France, but did not do so until the following year (1647).

the prince my brother: Prince Maurice of the Palatinate (1620–52).

our latest misfortune: a French gentleman, L'Épinay (or d'Espinay), was murdered in The Hague in broad daylight by a gang of Englishmen led by Elisabeth's youngest brother Philip. L'Épinay was suspected of having seduced their sister Louise and made her pregnant (in some accounts he had also tried to seduce their mother). Elisabeth was thought to have stirred up her brothers against him. Her mother therefore sent both her and Philip away: she was to travel to Germany, to stay with the electress dowager of Brandenburg (Elisabeth-Charlotte of the Palatinate), who is the aunt referred to below.

Your presence was necessary: Descartes visited Elisabeth after the murder of L'Épinay. He visited her again in response to the appeal in this letter; that was their last meeting.

more necessary to me at this time than security: Elisabeth was anxious that her post might be intercepted and opened; hence her reluctance to use the ordinary messenger service.

commanded me to give an opinion: Machiavelli's *The Prince*. Elisabeth was clearly determined not to let Descartes off giving his opinions on civil prudence.

79 *better than fortresses*: Descartes is loosely rendering the titles of chapters 19 and 20 of *The Prince*, and the conclusion of the latter chapter.

princes who have acquired a state by just means: Machiavelli distinguishes between hereditary and acquired principalities (*The Prince*, ch. 1). He subdivides the latter into those acquired by someone who is seizing power for the first time, and those annexed by the hereditary ruler of another territory. Descartes notes that this latter distinction ignores the moral difference between legitimate and illegitimate ways of gaining power—a difference with political implications.

the most savage of animals: this last sentence is Descartes's summary of what he thinks Machiavelli's precepts amount to. In chapter 8, Machiavelli advocates inflicting those injuries one judges necessary to inflict all in one go, so as not to have to repeat them; in chapter 18 he argues that one must be prepared to break one's word if it would be disadvantageous to keep it and if the circumstances in which one pledged it no longer apply; he also recommends simulation and dissimulation, and maintaining the appearance of a good man even if one is not.

even one who has newly gained power: Descartes is not thinking of the violent usurper, who seizes power by conspiracy and assassination, but of the ruler who gains power by what would generally be regarded as legitimate means, for instance, a war of conquest, which jurists of the time would normally have regarded as acceptable. It would be very harmful for such a ruler to think that he should behave as the violent usurper is compelled to behave.

80 *when they are thought to be so by the agent*: in Descartes's ethics the core precept is to act resolutely in accordance with what one judges to be best (*Passions*, §§148, 153). In that case, one might conceivably do what is wrong while acting in the honest belief that one is acting rightly; but to go against one's conscience must always be wrong, irrespective of the objective moral quality of the action in question.

both the lion and the fox: Machiavelli uses this image in chapters 18 and 19.

to pretend to be friends: in fact, Machiavelli condemns Agathocles, tyrant of Syracuse, for deceiving his friends (ch. 8). In chapter 18, however, he urges that a prince may need to act contrary to friendship.

the law of nations: the unwritten code deemed in the early modern period to regulate dealings between states.

81 *dare not give battle on the Sabbath*: in the early Middle Ages, the Church sought to establish the 'truce of God', whereby fighting between Christians on Sunday was forbidden, but by Descartes's time this was a dead letter.

82 *both the citizens and the soldiers*: Machiavelli discusses this particular problem of the Roman empire in chapter 19.

when he says in his preface: in the dedicatory letter to Lorenzo the Magnificent.

83 *you took the trouble to examine*: Machiavelli's *The Prince*.

the kind of state that is most difficult to govern: Elisabeth's comment is a subtle one: she sees Machiavelli as carrying out a thought-experiment reducing political decision-making to its simplest form, in which the ruler's survival or destruction depends entirely on his own actions without any support from pre-given factors such as hereditary succession or popular support.

84 *the nephew of Pope Alexander*: Cesare Borgia (1475/6–1507) was in fact the son of the future pope Alexander VI, and acknowledged as such, though the children of prominent clerics were often passed off as nephews and nieces. Machiavelli does indeed express admiration for his cunning and ruthlessness.

the hatred of the people: Cesare enforced his rule over the region of Romagna by savage repression carried out by his henchman Remirro d'Orco, then had Remirro murdered and his body, cut in half, exposed to the people (*The Prince*, ch. 7).

Fathers of the Church: the great early Christian theologians, such as St Augustine of Hippo.

paradoxes: probably not in the usual modern sense of verbally self-contradictory statements but in the older sense of positions contrary to the common opinion.

virtue consists only in conformity to right reason: Elisabeth exaggerates Descartes's originality. It is far from true that earlier writers simply discussed individual virtues without putting forward general definitions of virtue. Nor is Descartes original in defining virtue with reference to reason: reason is an essential aspect of Aristotle's conception and it is highlighted in Cicero's influential definition of virtue as 'a habit of the mind in accordance with nature and reason' (*De inventione* 2. 159). This is not to say that Descartes adds nothing original to the definition of virtue.

85 *the miraculous spring*: at Hornhausen, about 110 miles from Berlin, nowadays in the federal state of Sachsen-Anhalt.

the elector: Elisabeth's cousin Frederick William, elector of Brandenburg from 1640 to 1688, known as the Great Elector for his achievement in restoring and reorganizing his states.

86 *as it has many other people*: a literal rendering would give the opposite meaning: 'a good purge could not harm him, as it has done many other people'; but the rendering adopted here seems to make better sense.

the cipher you sent me: this must have been in a postscript, now lost, to Descartes's last letter. Presumably Elisabeth's correspondence was liable to be opened. Ciphers were commonly used for secret diplomatic and military correspondence, and the methods were often highly sophisticated. Descartes was interested in cryptography, as is suggested by the parallel he draws between breaking a cipher and scientific deduction (*Principles*, IV. 205); the passage is mentioned by David Kahn, *The Codebreakers: The Comprehensive History of Secret Communication from Ancient Times to the Internet* (New York, 1996), 1131. Jean-Robert Armogathe, however, suggests in his note on the passage that the cipher Descartes had proposed was of a fairly straightforward type, monoalphabetic substitution (in which each character in the plain text is replaced always by the same letter in the ciphered message); such a cipher can be broken by observing the frequency of the letters, a flaw Elisabeth points out (*Correspondance*, ii. 1002). What she herself proposes is what is technically called a nomenclator: a combination of cipher and code the use of which was widespread in the early modern period. In the form in question here, individual letters are replaced by numbers; but numbers are also allotted to certain important words. The distinction between numbers standing for letters and those standing for a word would be unobtrusively indicated, say, by punctuation marks. See Kahn, pp. xvii, 107, 117. A lively description of the system is provided by Fletcher Pratt, *Secret and Urgent: The Story of Codes and Ciphers* (London, 1939), esp. ch. 4.

this rough draft: see above, notes to p. 73.

87 *the daemon of Socrates*: in the speech at his trial Socrates refers to a kind of inner voice, a sort of divine (*daimonion*) influence that restrains him from certain actions (Plato, *Apology* 31c–d). This passage was often read in the light of another in which Plato speaks of 'daemons' as creatures intermediate between gods and men (*Symposium* 202e–203e), a concept taken up by many later writers (see C. S. Lewis, *The Discarded Image: An Introduction to Medieval and Renaissance Literature* (Cambridge, 1964), 40–2).

Socrates' inner voice was thus taken to be the utterance of such a creature. According to Baillet, Descartes actually wrote a treatise on the Socratic demon, but it was lost and has never been recovered (*Vie*, ii. 408).

87 *one's inner spirit*: *génie*, a synonym of 'daemon' in the above sense; but the word can also mean an inner inclination or disposition, so Descartes is not committing himself to the thesis of a supernatural influence.

the messenger is due to leave: that is, if you have to write on a matter of business, postpone doing so as long as possible, to cut down on the time available for worry.

the instructor of princes: an ironical reference to Machiavelli.

88 *the waters of Spa*: which Elisabeth had taken, with Descartes's approval, in the previous year (May or June 1645; letter 14).

in order to acquire them: a somewhat puzzling expression. The context does not suggest that Descartes is talking about divine grace. The basic point appears to be that contentment and joy augment the qualities that enable us to acquire contentment and joy in the first place, and so indirectly reinforce themselves.

89 *that ordinarily lead to one's winning*: Elisabeth presumably means that you play better when you are in a good mood because you can think more clearly and make better decisions than when anxious or upset; there is nothing mysterious about this, as Descartes seems to be suggesting.

as in that from which I come: Elisabeth is happy where she is for the moment, but would prefer to be where she came from, back in the Netherlands, because her present situation is precarious (the Thirty Years War was still in progress).

the occult qualities of my imagination: Elisabeth is ironically suggesting that Descartes will attribute her good decisions to a secret power in her imagination, contrary to his philosophical dismissal of such powers (so-called 'occult qualities'). Clearly, the fears he expresses in his last letter that Elisabeth will not take what he is saying entirely seriously have been fulfilled.

90 *getting visibly plumper*: as portraits of mid-seventeenth-century ladies show, thinness was not regarded as desirable.

this is especially true of the Lutherans: Elisabeth was brought up a Calvinist, whereas Lutherans were a majority among German Protestants; but the abbey of which she eventually became abbess was Lutheran.

to adorn his library: the ducal library of Wolfenbüttel was one of the largest and finest in Europe, and is still a highly valued research resource.

91 *Regius' book*: *Fundamenta physices* ('Fundamentals of Physics'). Descartes complains that Regius has both plagiarized and garbled his own ideas (to Mersenne, 5 October 1646, AT 4. 510, and 23 November 1646, AT 4. 566; cf. to Huygens, 5 October 1646, AT 4. 517).

the opinions of the Schools: the traditional views of Aristotle in philosophy and Galen in medicine were still the basis of teaching in the universities.

92 *into the lists*: the jousting area. Descartes must mean that no one has ventured on a full-scale critique of the *Principles*; for not counting the Objections to the *Meditations*, Gassendi had published a *Disquisitio metaphysica* in 1644, in which he attacked Descartes's philosophy at length.

the publication of a new philosophy: the Jesuits, who were heavily involved in secondary education, might be more interested in a new textbook (like the *Principles*) than other religious orders; it would be a sign, also, of their distinctiveness and independence.

fluxions: excessive flows of the humours (such as blood) to some part of the body, to be treated by purges and/or bleeding; in this case Elisabeth is probably thinking of what we would call pneumonia, ascribed to cold or to variations of temperature before the role of viruses or bacteria was known.

the queen mother of Sweden: Maria Eleonora of Brandenburg (1599–1655), widow of King Gustavus Adolphus (d. 1632), sister of the previous elector (George William, d. 1640) and thus sister-in-law of Elisabeth's aunt and hostess the electress dowager; she was also the mother of Descartes's later patron Queen Christina.

94 *the princess your sister*: Henrietta; see previous letter.

that were purged in this way: the body was eliminating ('purging') bad or excessive humours through the abscesses; the fact that they have gone away does not prove that the bad humours have disappeared altogether.

those of apothecaries and those of empirics: apothecaries were regular trained practitioners, working to traditionally approved methods; empirics claimed to offer remedies of their own, often preparations of metals or minerals.

paradoxes: again, in the sense of challenges to accepted opinion.

from my unpublished work: if Regius' book included material from Descartes's unpublished writings, this would still be plagiarism, but at least it would contain something new.

95 *another book on medicine in the press*: Regius' *Fundamenta medica* ('Fundamentals of Medicine') was published in 1647.

her ladyship P. S.: Princess Sophia, Elisabeth's youngest sister (1630–1714). She was later married to the elector of Hanover, and their son became George I of Britain. Descartes's letters to Elisabeth were addressed to Sophia, in order to be sent on to Elisabeth, an alternative security measure to the cipher discussed above (Descartes to Sophia, September 1646, AT 4. 495–6). He refers to her as 'her ladyship' ('Mademoiselle') since to give her her proper title ('Her Highness') would clearly identify her to an unintended reader.

Mijnheer Hogelande: Cornelis van Hogelande (1590–1662), a Catholic nobleman, doctor, and close friend of Descartes, to whom he dedicated his *Cogitationes* ('Reflections, in Which the Existence of God, the Spirituality of the Soul, and its Possible Union with the Body, Are Demonstrated; and, in addition, a Brief Account and Mechanical Explanation of the Workings of the Animal Body Is Proposed').

95 *Lady L.*: 'Mad. [i.e. Madame] L.', i.e. Elizabeth's sister Princess Louise (her title is, again, disguised).

96 *we shall go to Crossen*: a town on the river Oder, now part of Poland and known as Krosno Odrzańskie.

on the borders of Silesia: a region now part of Poland, but at the time integrated into the kingdom of Bohemia.

Regius is not patient enough . . . read or heard: literally the sentence means 'he [Jonson] does not give him [Regius] the patience to understand what he [Jonson] has read or heard'.

unable to change his mind: see Descartes's complaint in letter 42: Regius persisted in his intention of publishing material from Descartes's unpublished writings, though he knew this was against Descartes's wishes.

the one I mentioned in my last letter: Dr Weiss.

97 *the injustices inflicted on me at Utrecht*: Voetius' campaign against Descartes.

regent: professor.

has organized disputations: disputation (methodical debate) was a standard procedure in universities; the teacher would often, as here, prescribe the theses (propositions) to be debated. Descartes complained of this in two letters to the curators of the University of Leiden (4 May 1647 and May 1647, AT 5. 2–12, 23).

98 *including these words*: the words of the thesis are missing in the text, but can be restored from the letter to the curators of 4 May 1647, AT 5. 5–6. The condemned theses have a theological dimension; they seem to register concern that Descartes's recommendation of methodical doubt might be extended to the inner God-given conviction that one is saved, a key tenet of Calvinism. But perhaps this was simply a stick to beat Descartes with.

as is usual in all democratic states: Descartes's expression is *états populaires*. The United Provinces was a republic: the supreme authority was the states-general, comprising representatives of the different provinces, which each had their own representative body. Descartes's contempt for this kind of polity is fairly typical among early modern intellectuals (influenced by Aristotle's attitude to democracy), and what one would expect of a seventeenth-century Frenchman used to monarchy.

99 *His Highness the prince of Orange*: William II (1626–50), who succeeded to the title in March 1647 and was sympathetic to France. Alongside its representative structures, each of the United Provinces had a stadtholder (governor), and this office was usually held by the prince of Orange, who thus to some extent fulfilled the role of head of state.

corollary of Professor Triglandius: the proposition asserting that Descartes blasphemously claims that God is a deceiver.

Professor Stuart: Adam Stuart (1591–1654), professor of philosophy at Leiden.

the calumny of Voetius' pupil: Martin Schoock, professor of philosophy at Groningen, who in 1643 published a vicious attack on Descartes's character and alleged beliefs.

100 *which is privileged everywhere*: that is, in all societies theologians enjoy a certain freedom of speech denied to others, and this applies all the more in a democratic state.

you should not follow their advice in asking for it: Elisabeth agrees that Descartes should not, as advised by his friends, appeal directly to the French ambassador and the stadtholder, but simply demand justice; however, she suggests that, even if he is unsuccessful, his stance will probably prompt them to intervene and put a stop to the attacks.

the Münster negotiations: the negotiations leading up to the Peace of Westphalia in 1648, which put an end to the Thirty Years War. Elisabeth's brother Charles Louis was indeed restored to part of his hereditary territory in the Palatinate (Elisabeth's 'own country').

The electress's dower house: at Crossen, where Elisabeth is writing from.

the flies called cousins in French: a variety of mosquito.

dispatches have prevented me: dispatches (*dépêches*) are messages sent express concerning state matters or other issues of importance; those Elisabeth is referring to perhaps related to the Münster negotiations.

the proofs he gives there of the existence of God: in the first treatise of the *Cogitationes*, Hogelande proves the existence of God by arguing that all matter is constantly undergoing change, and therefore is not eternal; the source of this change or motion is not in matter itself; it must therefore have an external and eternal cause. Moreover, the order, beauty, and purpose of the universe indicates that its cause is a divine mind (*Cogitationes, quibus Dei existentia; item animae spiritalitas, et possibilis cum corpore unio, demonstrantur: nec non, brevis historia oeconomiae corporis animalis, proponitur, atque mechanice explicatur. His accessit tractatus de praedestinatione* (Leiden, 1676), 1–10).

in the principles of our knowledge: Descartes's proofs in the *Meditations* start from the idea of God and from my existence as a being possessed of that idea; they make use of basic axioms such as the principle of causality, but, unlike Hogelande's, make no appeal to the visible world. See the Third and Fifth Meditations, and *Principles*, I. 14–21.

which is immaterial: Hogelande tries to explain the union of soul and body by analogy with the 'subtle matter' that can permeate a liquid contained in some vessel and yet, under the influence of heat, can be separated from it in the form of vapour (*Cogitationes*, 11–23). Elisabeth points out that 'subtle matter' is still matter and so cannot explain the union of the soul, a radically immaterial entity, with a material body.

101 *The doctor whom I have mentioned to you before*: Dr Weiss, to whom Elisabeth had lent Descartes's *Principles*.

even if I were to change country: Descartes is responding to Elisabeth's evidently anxious reaction, expressed in her last letter, to the idea that he might decide to leave the United Provinces.

101 *French resident*: Hector-Pierre Chanut, with whom Descartes had already been in correspondence. A resident is a country's representative in another country, of a lower rank than that of ambassador.

the queen: Christina, queen of Sweden, who reigned from 1633 to 1654 and then abdicated, converting to Roman Catholicism (the Swedish state religion was Lutheran). She had strong intellectual and artistic interests.

102 *from several points of view*: Sweden was then a leading European power; Descartes perhaps supposed that if Christina and Elisabeth became friends, Christina might exert her influence in favour of the restoration of Elisabeth's family to the Palatinate.

can excel other people, etc.: see to Chanut, 1 November 1646 (AT 4. 536). It is not clear what 'etc.' refers to.

have been silenced: the curators wrote to Descartes on 20 May 1647, stating that they had forbidden members of the university to mention Descartes or his teachings in their lectures and disputations, and requesting him to refrain from voicing the condemned opinions (AT 5. 29). This pretence of even-handedness disgusted Descartes, since, as he points out in his reply of 27 May, his complaint was not that his opinions were being criticized, but that he was being accused of holding opinions he did not in fact hold (AT 5. 35–9).

the dedicatory epistle: addressed to Elisabeth. See pp. 121–3.

the Swedish correspondence: the exchange of letters with Chanut mentioned in the previous letter.

103 *my plan in writing that letter had failed*: the letter in question is lost, so we can only guess at the plan: but perhaps Descartes was hoping that Chanut would pick up the mention of his correspondence with Elisabeth on the supreme good and pass it on to the queen, so whetting her curiosity.

a letter to the queen: to Christina, 20 November 1647 (AT 5. 81–6).

up to halfway through the sixth: the letters are those of 21 July 1645 (letter 17), 4 August 1645 (letter 18), 18 August 1645 (letter 20), 1 September 1645 (letter 22), 15 September 1645 (letter 24), 6 October 1645 (letter 26).

104 *the people who sent him*: Descartes is diplomatically vague. As French resident, Chanut would be expected to concentrate on advancing French interests: France and Sweden were at the time on friendly terms. For him to encourage a personal friendship between Christina and a Protestant princess might complicate the political situation unpredictably, at a time when negotiations to end the Thirty Years War were delicately balanced.

to discuss it with Your Highness: Descartes represents himself, as before, as hoping to benefit Elisabeth by his new correspondence with Christina. The implication is that perhaps Christina will be so impressed by what she hears of Elisabeth that she will invite the princess to Sweden. But it is fair to wonder whether Elisabeth was altogether happy at having his letters to her readdressed, as it were, elsewhere.

in a language I am in the habit of using: Elisabeth could read Latin, but, unlike contemporary scholars and ecclesiastics, would not use it in every-day speech and writing.

the objections put to you: the *Meditations* were published with a series of objec-tions from philosophers and theologians, and Descartes's replies to these.

M. Gassendi: Pierre Gassendi (1592–1655), author of the fifth set of objec-tions, some of which (like his comment on the ontological argument; AT 7. 322–3, OWC 177–8) are very far from being irrational. His (empiricist) approach to knowledge differs radically from Descartes's.

the Englishman's: Thomas Hobbes (1588–1679), most famous as the author of *Leviathan*, who supplied the Third Objections, based on an empiricist and materialist point of view no less antithetical to Descartes's.

the Treatise on Learning: Descartes's reply shows that he mentioned this project to her in conversation. The noted Jesuit scholar René Rapin reported that one of Descartes's followers possessed fragments, entitled *De l'érudition*, of an unfinished treatise on logic by Descartes (*Réflexions sur la philosophie ancienne et moderne, et sur l'usage qu'on en doit faire pour la religion* (Paris, 1676), 124). Baillet, who mentions this, notes that no such fragments have ever been found (*Vie*, i. 282).

105 *the one before*: the letter of 5 December (letter 48). The letter of 23 Decem-ber is lost.

the ire of the scholastics: Descartes was no doubt reluctant to stir up fur-ther trouble of the kind he had had with Revius and Voetius: but in any case a treatise on learning, which would be bound to be critical of scholas-tic orthodoxy, would have aroused hostile reactions.

who have transcribed it badly: see AT 4. 566–7.

106 *make this necessary*: Descartes probably intended to visit his relations in Brittany, as he usually did when in France, perhaps partly with a view to settling problems about his inheritance (Desmond M. Clarke, *Descartes* (Cambridge, 2006), 378).

the letter about the supreme good: the letter to Christina of 20 November 1647, AT 5. 81–6.

the person I sent it to: Henri Brasset, the French resident at The Hague, who was to have sent it on to Chanut, his counterpart in Stockholm.

that princess: Queen Christina: 'princess' is used here in the more general sense of 'ruler'.

a pamphlet of slight importance: *Notae in programma* ('Notes against a Pro-gramme'), a critique of Regius' *Programma* of 1647.

Mijnheer Hey(danus): Descartes wrote 'Hey', which AT reads as an abbre-viation of 'Heydanus'. Abraham Heydanus, also known as Heyde, was a Calvinist minister and professor of theology, a friend of Descartes's who publicly professed his support for the Cartesian philosophy. But Baillet (*Vie*, ii. 335) suggests that the person referred to is Christiaan Huygens (1629–95), the famous mathematician and scientist, also a friend of Descartes's.

106 *your letter of 7 May*: the letter, in which Descartes announced his imminent departure from the Netherlands, is now lost.

107 *a settlement in England*: in June 1648 Charles I of England, defeated in the first civil war, was still imprisoned in Carisbrooke Castle in the Isle of Wight. Elisabeth may have been hoping that he would negotiate successfully with Parliament; or perhaps she was aware of his secret deal with some of the Scottish Covenanters, his former enemies, who had pledged to invade England and restore him to the throne if he established Presbyterianism as the state religion for three years. The invasion later that year was repelled by Cromwell.

such a thing in Germany: by contrast the negotiations to end the Thirty Years War in Germany, about which Elisabeth is clearly pessimistic, were eventually successful, though not totally so from her family's point of view.

the journey you proposed some time ago: Elisabeth is being discreetly vague through all the rest of this paragraph, as if, again, worried that her letter may be intercepted and opened. In letters 46 (6 June 1647) and 47 (20 November 1647) Descartes had alluded to his desire for Elisabeth and Christina to become friends, which could only happen if Christina invited Elisabeth to Sweden. Now Elisabeth is alluding to the possibility that she may in fact be going to Sweden. 'Your friend' is Chanut, the French resident in Stockholm; the person to whom he had given Descartes's letters is Queen Christina, whose mother was the queen dowager Maria Eleonora of Brandenburg. Maria Eleonora (mentioned in letter 41) was the sister-in-law of Elisabeth's aunt and hostess, the electress dowager of Brandenburg (Elisabeth-Charlotte of the Palatinate).

another person: Elisabeth herself. She continues to refer to herself in the third person in what follows, so that in the translation 'they' and 'them' are used instead of 'she' and 'her'.

those to whom they have obligations: if her family consented to her travelling to Sweden, this would be because they supposed this could be of some political advantage to them, for reasons discussed above (this is confirmed by letter 51). But Elisabeth is perhaps also thinking that she might be able to be of service to Descartes.

108 *the management of government finances*: Descartes is witnessing the earliest stages of a crisis that was very shortly to degenerate into the civil war known as the Fronde (1648–53). French intervention in the Thirty Years War had greatly increased the burden of taxation. The Parlement was not what we call a parliament (a legislative assembly) but the supreme court for the Paris region (the other sovereign courts mentioned here had specific spheres of activity, mostly financial): however, it regarded itself as

entitled to monitor, and if necessary protest against, the laws and decrees made by the Crown. At this time, the king, Louis XIV, was an infant, and his mother, Anne of Austria ('the queen'), was regent, supported by her unpopular minister Cardinal Mazarin. This accentuated the Parlement's sense of its mission.

to carry on the war: the Thirty Years War was drawing to its end, but the fighting was far from over.

those whom fortune has accustomed to its disfavours: Elisabeth would recognize herself in this category.

109 *the court would have snatched away from you*: Descartes, she means, would have come under pressure from the French court to remain in the country. She is probably remembering his mention in letter 49 of the offer of a royal pension, which would, of course, have been dependent on his residing there, and would probably have been tied to other uncongenial obligations.

another journey that was to take place: Elisabeth's journey to Sweden: see letter 50. From the deliberately vague statements that follow, it appears that her mother and brothers had decided that she could be of use to them in Sweden, and wished her to go there. The resistance seems to come from Elisabeth's hosts in Brandenburg, her aunt the electress dowager, and the elector himself. The plan for the journey involved Elisabeth's travelling with the queen dowager of Sweden, but the delays have made it impossible for her to be ready in time to leave with the queen, and have thus effectively sabotaged the whole journey. (The feminine pronouns by which she refers to herself in the original are necessitated by the fact that *personne* ('person') in French is grammatically feminine, irrespective of the gender of the person referred to.)

for the good of a house: as elsewhere, 'house' is used here in the sense of a royal family.

take pleasure in the right objects: Elisabeth has interestingly modified Descartes's statement in his previous letter, giving it a more ethical twist. He argued that, if those most favoured by fortune do not enjoy more pleasures than other people, this is because the pleasures they enjoy have been staled by custom; for Elisabeth, the explanation is rather that they pursue the wrong pleasures.

110 *in rather an extraordinary fashion*: this tortuous paragraph explains why, finally, Elisabeth's journey to Sweden has been called off, in such a way that she herself cannot be blamed. She has been worried that the queen dowager ('the other person') would have to set out for Sweden before she herself could be ready to travel; but this, she is told by the queen, is not the problem; it is that the queen regnant, Christina ('her daughter'), is now opposed to the visit. (The 'woman who uses' 'your friend' is also Christina; 'your friend', as before, is the French resident Chanut.) The pretext given is difference of religion: and, indeed, Elisabeth is a Calvinist, Christina (still) a Lutheran (she did not convert to Roman Catholicism

until 1654). This seems pretty flimsy to Elisabeth: after all, they were both Protestants, and opposed to the Catholic Holy Roman Emperor. So she suspects that the true reason is that the queen dowager has been pressurized by her sister into withdrawing her support for the visit. The sister in question must be Anna Sophia, whose husband, the duke of Brunswick and Wolfenbüttel, now dead, had supported the Imperial cause ('the party opposed to the house of the person mentioned above') and who was herself still, Elisabeth claims, dependent on Imperial financial assistance.

110 *coming to a crisis*: the treaties of Münster and Osnabrück, which brought the Thirty Years War to an end, were to be signed two months later. A few days before the date of this letter, the Scottish army, on which Charles I's hopes of restoration depended, had been defeated by Cromwell at Preston; but the tone of the rest of the letter suggests that Elisabeth had not heard this dire news.

111 *the three letters*: 50 (30 June 1648), 52 (July 1648), and 53 (23 August 1648).

the person to whom it is attributed: Descartes is reluctant to believe that Christina herself is responsible for the insulting withdrawal of the invitation to Elisabeth.

tossed about by the storm winds: a traditional image ultimately inspired by Lucretius: 'Suave mari magno turbantibus aequora ventis | e terra magnum alterius spectare laborem' ('Pleasant it is, when on the great sea the winds trouble the waters, to gaze from shore upon another's great tribulation'; *De rerum natura* ('On the Nature of the Universe'), 2. 1–2, trans. W. H. D. Rouse, rev. Martin Ferguson Smith, Loeb Classical Library, 2nd edn (Cambridge, Mass., 1982)).

112 *the friend*: Chanut.

to whom he had given my letters: Christina.

thanks to his in-laws: Chanut was married to the sister of Descartes's friend and translator Clerselier.

the business concerning Your Highness: the cancellation of Elisabeth's projected visit to Sweden.

the many pieces of bad news: Descartes had recently lost two good friends, the abbé de Touchelaye and Hardy, brother-in-law of the abbé Picot, translator of the *Principles* into French.

while he was in prison: see Plato, *Phaedo* 60b–61d.

a violent agitation of the animal spirits: on the effect of the animal spirits in stimulating the imagination, see *Passions*, §21.

113 *the tragedies of England*: the execution of King Charles I (Elisabeth's uncle) on 30 January 1649. The use of 'tragedy' to refer to terrible real-life events is attested in the seventeenth century, but Descartes is perhaps hinting at the idea he has advanced in previous letters, that we sometimes need to distance ourselves from misfortune by regarding it as something happening in a play.

universally pitied, praised, and missed: quite apart from the fact that he is writing to the executed king's niece, one would expect Descartes, as a Catholic Frenchman, to sympathize with an Anglican king whose wife, Henrietta Maria, was a French princess and a Roman Catholic, and whose fiercest enemies were radical Protestants. Moreover, he met or corresponded with English supporters of the king, such as Sir Kenelm Digby and the marquess of Newcastle.

from a certain place: Sweden.

to whom I sent the treatise on the passions: Christina of Sweden.

114 *the letters enclosed along with it*: along with *The Passions of the Soul*, Descartes had sent Christina a selection of his letters to Elisabeth (see letter 47).

the terms of the German peace treaty: the Peace of Westphalia restored the Lower Palatinate to Elisabeth's brother Charles Louis, but not the Upper Palatinate, which remained under the control of the elector of Bavaria. Descartes supposes that, with more Swedish pressure, the Palatinate might have been restored in full.

come to an agreement by themselves: Descartes's ostensibly general remarks seem to have this particular application: the 'parties with armed force at their disposal' are the major belligerents, in this case, Sweden and France on the one hand and the Holy Roman Empire and Spain on the other. He implies that they agreed to a partial restitution of the Palatinate as an exercise in the balance of forces, and in particular to prevent the new possessor, the elector of Bavaria, from becoming too powerful. If Charles Louis refuses to accept the partial restitution, then they may as well come to another deal that excludes him altogether. In the end, Charles Louis accepted the settlement.

115 *your servant all my life*: as he would have been if born a subject of her family.

were to come to mind: to Christina's mind.

and return only the following year: Descartes was never to return from Sweden, where the winter weather proved fatal to him. If he had accepted the original invitation, to travel there in the spring, so as to return before the winter, things might have turned out very differently.

116 *my decision about the journey to Sweden*: Elisabeth must have asked this question in a now lost reply to the previous letter.

117 *the pursuit of learning*: *l'étude des lettres*, that is, the study of texts, especially in the ancient languages, considered as sources of knowledge. It would encompass history and rhetoric, at least, as well as poetry and drama. In Christina's case, however, it does not extend to philosophy (which for Descartes would include the natural sciences as well), and one can tell that he is not altogether approving of her scholarly enthusiasms.

Herr Freinsheimius: Johann Freinsheim (1608–60), a German by birth, who, after being professor of politics and eloquence at the University of

Uppsala, became Christina's librarian and historiographer. He and Chanut had been instructed to study Descartes's *Principles* so as to assist Christina with her own reading of the work (Chanut to Descartes, 12 December 1648, AT 5. 252–4).

117 *except at the hours she thinks fit to set aside*: that is, Descartes will not be expected to wait around at the palace until Christina finds it convenient to see him, but will visit her only at appointed times. This is a considerable mark of respect on the queen's part. On the other hand, the appointed hour was 5 a.m., which Descartes, as a lifelong late riser, found very inconvenient.

a roundabout route through Cleves: a duchy in Germany, in the northern Rhineland.

118 *that pedants have fastened upon it*: 'pedants' here is a general term of abuse for scholars, commonly deemed in the early modern period to be low-born and lacking in the social graces; here it relates to the misogynistic views they have imbibed from ancient texts such as those of Aristotle, which their unfamiliarity with ladies' society has given them no opportunity to correct from experience.

their philology: the linguistic and literary scholarship for which Christina has been enthusiastic up to now.

in the company of Herr Kleist: identified in Lisa Shapiro's edition (*Correspondence*, 182 n. 205) as Ewald von Kleist, ambassador of Brandenburg to Denmark and Sweden in 1649.

dated 10/20 November: the letter in question is lost.

PRINCIPLES OF PHILOSOPHY

121 *Most Serene Princess Elisabeth*: this is the preface to the original Latin-language edition. 'Serene' here is a conventional honorific title.

the virtues that stand in the middle: Descartes is here endorsing the Aristotelian idea (*Ethics* 2. 6. 4–20, 1106ᵃ26–1107ᵃ27) that virtue is a mean between two opposite vices (courage stands between cowardice and foolhardiness, and so forth).

who are generous: here in the ordinary modern sense of the word, rather than the specifically Cartesian sense (*Passions*, §153).

122 *the single name of wisdom*: the view that the true virtues form a unity, so that you cannot possess one without possessing all, has been advanced by many philosophers: see, for instance, Aquinas, *ST* 1-2. 65. 1.

whatever he knows to be best: cf. the definition of virtue in *Passions*, §153.

123 *some aged gymnosophist*: gymnosophists were ancient Hindu philosophers, whose asceticism included going naked.

grey-eyed Minerva: Minerva is the Roman name for the goddess the Greeks called Athene. In Homer her name is conventionally accompanied by the epithet *glaukōpis*, which is often understood as 'grey-eyed', though it may mean 'flashing-eyed'.

one of the Muses: the nine goddesses responsible for the liberal arts.

one of the Graces: the three goddesses responsible for conferring divine favours; their name can also be understood as 'charm'. Perhaps Descartes prefers the comparison with the Graces because he wants to suggest that Elisabeth's appeal is quite independent of her intellectual accomplishments.

perpetual injustices of fortune: on the misfortunes of Elisabeth's life, see Introduction.

which may here serve as a Preface: this letter-preface was published with the French translation of the text, which appeared in 1647. It is addressed to Claude Picot, the translator.

academically educated: nourris aux lettres, literally 'bred to letters' (in the general sense of the subjects taught at an early modern school).

124 *the discovery of arts*: in early modern usage the term 'art' covers any productive activity, including what we might usually call crafts.

the principles: Descartes uses this word in two senses, both for a fundamental truth on which other truths depend, and for a fundamental reality on which other realities depend or out of which they are made. He often glides from one sense to the other; and, to complicate things further, 'principles' in this preface sometimes refers to the book *Principles of Philosophy*.

civilized and polite: in early modern Europe, the term frequently refers to the quality of manners and behaviour in a whole society, as distinct from an individual accomplishment.

having true philosophers: a claim that will be taken up by Enlightenment thinkers.

125 *live according to a standard*: régler nos mœurs; more literally, 'regulate our behaviour' or 'our morals'. But this sounds as if the aim of philosophy is to control, or even constrain, our lives, whereas the tradition of moral philosophy on which Descartes is drawing is more concerned with enabling us to find a standard by which to live, instead of succumbing blindly to our impulses or prejudices.

in order to walk straight: the metaphor of the journey towards truth, which is exploited systematically in the rest of the preface, is one of Descartes's favourites: see, for instance, *Discourse*, II, AT 6. 14–17, OWC 14–16; III, AT 6. 24–5, OWC 22.

without the enlightenment of faith: Descartes implicitly acknowledges that the Christian faith discloses the possibility of an even higher good, namely, union with God in the afterlife. Cf. the reference to divine revelation below.

a kind of conversation with their authors: Descartes had said this already in the *Discourse on the Method* (AT 6. 5, OWC 7–8). The idea is in Montaigne, *Essays*, I. 26, p. 175.

126 *he really believed them to be such*: whereas Plato wrote in dialogues, which allow for a degree of openness and inconclusiveness, Aristotle wrote systematic treatises, which give an appearance of settling all the points discussed. But his principles were very far from being identical to Plato's. The idea that the ancient philosophers did not seriously believe their own theories can be found in Montaigne, *Essays*, II. 12, pp. 569–72.

by common prudence: the extreme sceptics of the school of Pyrrho, who is reported to have set so little store by appearances that he would walk straight ahead without ever going out of his way, so that his friends had to save him from being run over or falling over precipices (Diogenes Laertius, *Lives of Eminent Philosophers* 10. 62–8; but Descartes's immediate source may be Montaigne, *Essays*, II. 29, p. 800). Elsewhere Montaigne casts doubt on this account, and maintains that the Pyrrhonists regulated their behaviour by appearances (without professing to know the reality behind them) and by the common practices of their society (II. 12, pp. 560–3).

the sun is no bigger than it appears: Epicurus' views on the size of the sun are in Diogenes Laertius 10. 91 and in Lucretius, *De rerum natura* ('On the Nature of Things') 5. 564–73; but, again, in Montaigne, *Essays*, II. 12, p. 667.

127 *when it has evident perceptions*: Descartes himself has offered this proof in the Second Meditation: even when we have rejected all the evidence of our senses as doubtful, we can still encounter certitude (first of all in the Cogito) through the process of thinking, which therefore does not depend on the senses. (Here as elsewhere Descartes uses 'perceptions' to cover intellectual apprehensions, as distinct from sense-perceptions.)

as regards the conduct of life: Descartes consistently holds that in practical life we do not need, and should not aspire to, the standards of certainty we should aim for when searching for the truth (see, for instance, *Discourse*, III, AT 6. 25, OWC 22–3; *Principles*, I. 3). From a practical point of view, I may as well go along with my spontaneous conviction that fire is hot and stones hard (it will help me to avoid being hurt by them); but if I go down the road of philosophical enquiry I must be prepared to call this into question and accept the reasons that show that 'hot' and 'hard' are qualities not of things in themselves but of our perceptions.

hot and cold, dry and moist: 'atoms and the void' are the fundamental realities in Epicurean philosophy; hot and cold, dry and moist, the fundamental qualities of the Aristotelian universe.

even if the deduction itself is evident: a logical deduction from a premiss that is false or doubtful can yield only a false or doubtful conclusion. Descartes here seems to conflate the two senses of 'principle' (fundamental truth and fundamental reality), which is superficially confusing, but not really so: to identify atoms and the void as the ultimate realities is to formulate the principle 'atoms and the void are the ultimate realities'. This principle is anything but evident.

128 *our soul or our mind*: *notre âme ou notre pensée*. See the following note.

this thinking agency: *pensée* again. *Pensée* here clearly does not denote a specific thought (like the thought of Elvis Presley or the thought that it is raining). Nor can it mean 'thinking': Descartes does not believe that he has proved that thinking exists but that I, a thinking thing, exist (this is very clear from the Second Meditation). *Pensée* here functions as a term equivalent to 'mind'; however, in order to show that it is through the act of thinking that I become aware that I exist and am a thinking thing, I have translated it the second time as 'thinking agency'.

129 *accepted by all human beings*: this seems like a wildly optimistic claim, especially to an adept of Montaigne's 'Apology for Raymond Sebond', which delights in listing differences of views among philosophers and differences of belief between peoples. But Descartes does have a point in that many cultures and thought-systems involve belief that something exists besides the material world (and yet in some relation to it) and that we humans are more than just our bodies.

like a romance: *ainsi qu'un Roman*. This word is generally translated 'novel'; but a novel is nowadays understood to be a tale of events that could have happened in real life; whereas in seventeenth-century French a *roman* is generally a fictional tale of love and chivalry, set in some far-off place and time, and for this 'romance' is the proper English equivalent. Pascal, indeed, reportedly referred to Descartes's philosophy as 'the romance of nature, more or less on a par with *Don Quixote*' (*Pensées*, ed. Louis Lafuma (Paris, 1963), no. 1008). But Descartes's suggestion is a serious one: when we read a romance, we immerse ourselves in the unfamiliar world constructed by the author, and follow the unfolding of events within it, without bothering ourselves about everyday reality; likewise, in reading Descartes's *Principles*, we should concentrate on the unfolding argument, and on the coherent vision he constructs, and not get distracted by worrying about whether it corresponds to what we take to be the real world. When we have finished, we realize (or should realize) that we have actually discovered the real world, and that the 'real world' of the established philosophy is simply systematized prejudice (in the sense discussed below).

130 *the characteristics of many categories of intelligence*: this interest in mental typology was widespread in the early modern period. The Spanish doctor Juan Huarte de San Juan (1529–88) produced an influential work entitled *Examen de ingenios para las ciencias* (1575; translated as *The Examination of Men's Wits*), arguing that physical factors, including the constitution of an individual's brain, predetermine one to succeed or fail in various intellectual disciplines. Descartes is reacting against this current of thought. See also *Discourse*, I, AT 6. 1–2, OWC 5.

the hindrance of prejudices: the word does not have the modern sense of irrational hostility to some category of person but the earlier sense of general preconceptions that turn out to have no rational foundation. The word 'prejudice' is retained here to bring out the pejorative overtones always present in Descartes's use of the term. See *Principles*, I. 1.

130 *the bad sciences*: alchemy, astrology, and magic. See *Discourse*, I, AT 6. 9, OWC 10.

sufficient to regulate the actions of his life: compare *Discourse*, III.

131 *no more than a dialectic*: Aristotle distinguished demonstrative argument, which yields scientific knowledge by deduction from premisses that are certain, from dialectic, where the deduction is from premisses that are generally accepted. Descartes turns this distinction against his followers by implying that their premisses are never certain, because they have failed to grasp the true principles. Their arguments therefore never do more than recycle standard views, and they are only useful within a pedagogic context in which Aristotle's authority is taken for granted. Descartes's logic, on the other hand, would meet Aristotle's requirement of generating scientific knowledge ('scientific' here is a standard expression which carries a broad sense, and does not relate only to what we call science).

the highest and most perfect ethics: as distinct from the provisional moral code adopted earlier.

ten or twelve years ago: ten years before, in fact, in 1637.

132 *the objections sent to me*: the *Meditations* were published with six sets of Objections by various writers (including Thomas Hobbes and the distinguished theologian Antoine Arnauld), along with Descartes's replies to these. A seventh set of Objections and Replies was added in a later edition.

133 *to support and validate my arguments*: the role of experiment in Descartes's natural philosophy is not to provide a basis for theory, but to confirm it, or to enable us to decide between alternative explanations. See *Discourse*, VI, AT 6. 63–5, OWC 52–4.

those we call pedants: in early modern France the term is often applied to academics, deemed to be disputatious, hypercritical, and uncouth (see Michael Moriarty, *Taste and Ideology in Seventeenth-Century France* (Cambridge, 1988)).

many important truths that I have not explained: it is not at first clear whether Descartes means that they will discover things he already knows but has not included in the book (for instance, about plants, animals, and the human body), or that, by applying his principles, they will make discoveries he himself had not foreseen. The next sentence seems to confirm the latter reading.

all the arts: not simply in the narrow modern sense of literature, music, painting, and so forth, but all types of productive activity.

134 *one of those people*: Regius (see above, note to p. 3). The source of the quotation is the *Letter to Voetius*, AT 8/2. 163.

certain metaphysical truths: Regius argues that reason cannot prove that the human mind is a substance capable of existing separately from the body.

PART I

137 *various judgements*: F adds: 'some correct and some incorrect'.

very certain and very easy to know: F is fuller here: 'It will be very useful for us to reject as false everything in which we can imagine the slightest doubt, so that, if we discover some things that, despite this precaution, seem to us manifestly true, we may realize that they are also entirely certain and the easiest things that it is possible to know.'

what is only probable: cf. *Discourse*, III, AT 6. 25, OWC 22–3.

one or other of them: F adds: 'and follow it resolutely, just as if we had judged it entirely certain'.

138 *philosophizing in an orderly fashion*: F's version is fuller: 'for we find it so difficult to conceive (*nous avons tant de répugnance à concevoir*) that that which thinks does not truly exist at the same time as it is thinking, that, despite the most extreme suppositions, we cannot refrain from believing that this conclusion "I am thinking, therefore I am" is true'. The language seems to impart a psychological content absent from the original, where *repugnat* is simply a scholastic expression denoting self-contradiction.

139 *is hence recognized*: F gives a fuller version of this paragraph: 'It seems to me also that this approach is by far the best we can choose in order to know the nature of the soul, and the fact that it is a substance entirely distinct from the body; for when we examine what we are, we who are currently thinking that there is nothing that truly is or exists outside our thought, we manifestly know that, in order to exist, we have no need of extension, shape, position in space, or anything else that can be attributed to the body, and that we exist purely inasmuch as we are thinking; and in consequence the notion we have of our soul or our thought is prior to that we have of the body, and more certain, since we are still doubting that any body exists in the world, yet we know for certain that we are thinking.' As in *Discourse*, IV, AT 6. 32–3, OWC 28–9, Descartes moves here from the Cogito (the discovery of his existence from the fact of his thinking) to the assertion of the real distinction between the soul and the body. Yet in the *Meditations* he is careful not to make this move right away: he cannot trust his perception of the distinction until he has deduced the existence of a perfect God, who will guarantee his clear and distinct perceptions. Compare Meditation II, AT 7. 27, OWC 20, and Meditation VI, AT 7. 78, OWC 55. In response to his critics, he insists that the proof of the real distinction between mind and body does not come until the Sixth Meditation: see Second Replies, AT 7. 129–33, OWC 86–9; Third Replies, II, AT 7. 174–6, OWC 109–11; Fourth Replies, AT 7. 219, OWC 140–1; Fifth Replies, II. 3–4, AT 7. 353–7, OWC 186–8.

139 *What thought is*: again F's version of the paragraph is significantly fuller: 'By the word "thinking" I mean whatever happens within us in such a way that we perceive it immediately by ourselves; this is why not only understanding, willing, imagining, but also perceiving by the senses are the same thing here as thinking. For if I say that I am seeing or walking, and infer from that that I exist, then if I mean to speak of the action performed by my eyes or by my legs, this conclusion is not so infallible that I have no grounds to doubt, because it might be the case that I think I am seeing or walking, even though my eyes are closed and I am still in the same place; for this sometimes happens to me when I am asleep, and the same could perhaps occur if I had no body; whereas if I mean to speak only of the action of my thought or of awareness (*sentiment*), that is, of the knowledge within myself that makes it seem to me that I am seeing or walking, this same conclusion is so absolutely true that I cannot doubt it, because it relates to the soul, which, alone, has the faculty of sensation or indeed of thinking in any other way at all.'

extremely simple and self-evident: against Aristotle, who held that definitions were starting points in the process of knowledge, Descartes casts doubt on their utility: cf. *Meditations*, II, AT 7. 25, OWC 18.

140 *they should not be counted as knowledge*: Descartes is responding here to a further critique from the sceptical Epicurean philosopher Gassendi (author of the Fifth Objections) to which he had earlier replied in a letter to Clerselier, the translator of the *Objections and Replies* (AT 9/1. 205–6). The relevant charges are that Descartes is supposedly getting rid of prejudices but that the Cogito depends on the assumption that 'Whatever thinks, exists', and this is a prejudice; moreover, it cannot be a first item of knowledge, since in order to know we are thinking we must know what thought is. In the letter to Clerselier, Descartes explains that he accepts that we have certain primary notions like 'thought' or 'existence' that we cannot get rid of, but that these are not what he means by prejudices: a prejudice is a judgement or assertion, not a notion. Moreover, we discover our own existence in a specific act of thought, which shows primarily that we exist, through which we come to recognize the general truth that whatever thinks, exists. Here, he makes a variant of the first point: general notions like 'thought' or 'existence', or even general propositions like 'what is thinking must exist', are too unspecific to count as knowledge; the Cogito, on the other hand, is a specific insight into the twin facts of one's thinking and one's existence, and into the relation between them: it can therefore count as knowledge.

the natural light: Descartes frequently uses this term for our intuitive knowledge of certain fundamental truths (cf. e.g. *Meditations*, III, AT 7. 38, OWC 28). See John Cottingham, 'Intuition', in Cottingham, *A Descartes Dictionary* (Oxford, 1993).

and so on and so forth: F adds: 'We can draw the same conclusion from every other thing that comes to our mind, that is, that we, who are thinking them, exist, even if perhaps they are false or have no existence.'

141   *common notions*: basic axioms such as those of geometry.

    demonstrations: rigorously conclusive arguments yielding certainty.

    the sums will be equal: the second of the Common Notions listed in the first book of Euclid's *Elements of Geometry*.

    three angles of a triangle are equal to two right angles: Proposition 32 of the first book of Euclid's *Elements*.

    a supremely perfect being exists: this argument, since Kant, has been known as the 'ontological' argument. An earlier version was put forward by St Anselm.

142   *has nothing chimerical about it*: a chimera is a beast in Greek mythology, a compound of lion, snake, and goat. Descartes means that the idea of God is not a fiction, like that of the chimera; that is, it is not an arbitrary assemblage of properties. The properties of the supremely perfect being hang together unalterably, like those of a geometrical triangle: I can't, for instance, imagine an all-powerful God who is subject to change and decay, or who depends on some other being. The argument depends on whether necessary existence can be regarded as a property, like omnipotence and omniscience: Kant famously argued that it cannot, but he had been anticipated by Gassendi, who maintains that existence is not one property among others, on a par with power or intelligence, but the precondition of all properties (see Fifth Objections, AT 7. 323, and Fifth Replies, AT 7. 382–3, OWC 178, 196).

    distinguishing essence from existence: we can think of the essence or nature of a thing while leaving its existence out of account; it is of the essence of a triangle to have three sides, whether or not there are any triangles in the world. Descartes's point is that the concept of God is an exception to this: a concept of a non-existent supremely perfect being is a non-concept, like that of a round square.

    objective perfection: the objective perfection of an idea is the degree of perfection it represents, or that is contained in it. Thus, if A is more perfect than B, the idea of A has more objective perfection than that of B. To take Descartes's example, the idea of the complex machine contains more objective perfection than that of a very simple machine.

    certain modes of our thinking: my idea of a chimera does not differ from my idea of a lion, in so far as a thought of a chimera is just as much a thought as is that of a goat. The two thoughts differ in respect of the reality of the objects they represent (their 'objective' or 'representative' reality). See *Meditations*, III, AT 7. 37, 40, OWC 27, 29.

143   *formally or eminently*: 'formally' here is synonymous with 'actually', 'in reality'. The implication of the term is, furthermore, that the cause of the idea and the objective reality of the idea are on an ontological level. This would be the case, for instance, if someone's idea of a machine were simply a reproduction of an actual identical machine he had seen: the complexity of the machine in the real world would account, formally, for

its complexity in the person's idea. When the effect is accounted for by a cause on a higher level of being, the cause is said to contain the reality of the effect 'eminently'. This is the case if the cause of the idea of the machine is the person himself who has the idea, who has generated it by his intelligence and engineering skill. See Second Replies, 'Reasons proving the existence of God . . .', Definition IV, AT 7. 161, OWC 103.

143 *total and efficient cause*: the 'efficient' cause of something is the cause that actually brings it into being. It will be seen that Descartes's argument depends on the principle of causality asserted here. For another kind of cause traditionally recognized, see §28.

some archetype: a term typically associated with the Platonic philosophy; but Descartes is not using it in quite the same sense. In Plato, the archetypes, or Forms, are the transcendent realities of which empirical realities are a mere copy. For Descartes here the archetype is the external reality behind our ideas, or to put it more precisely, the reality represented by our ideas which provides an explanation of their content (the fact that my idea of a horse represents a maned quadruped is ultimately to be explained by the existence of maned quadrupeds). Take, by contrast, the idea of a unicorn. It has a certain objective reality, in that it represents something definite, distinct from a horse or a griffin (you could say 'that's not a picture of a unicorn'); and this reality requires explanation, just as much as the objective reality contained in the idea 'horse'. Part of its content does indeed come from the idea of a horse, part from that of some horned creature. But its archetype is really the human mind, which combines and develops its perceptions of sensible objects to form images of objects that do not exist. However, the human mind, says Descartes, is incapable of forming an idea like that of a supremely perfect being, the objective reality of which far exceeds the mind's own level of actual or formal reality.

that they still exist: we have the idea of the supreme perfections now, and we may have had it for some time. At the time when the idea was formed in us, therefore, its cause, the supremely perfect being, must have existed. But since a supremely perfect being that goes out of existence is a self-contradictory concept, it must still exist.

obscured by any limitations: F adds: 'Thus there is no speculation that may better help us to perfect our understanding or that is more important than this one, inasmuch as the consideration of an object without limits to its perfections fills us with satisfaction and certitude.'

144 *the duration of things*: F has 'the duration of our lives'.

namely, by the idea of him: traditional proofs of the existence of God lead us to a first mover, or first cause, or a necessary being, or a designer of the universe; but much subsequent argumentation is necessary to establish that this being possesses all the perfections ascribed to God. An exception here is Aquinas' fourth proof of the existence of God (*ST* 1. 2. 3), which argues from degrees of perfection to the existence of a supremely perfect being, the cause of all perfection. Descartes's argument, which may have been indebted to this, establishes God's existence and his nature simultaneously.

145 *extension in space*: for Descartes, the essence of a body is extension; that is, it occupies three-dimensional space. But he thinks of space as intrinsically divisible, and so of bodies as divisible. But what is divisible can be disintegrated, and this is clearly incompatible with perfection.

because this is not a thing: the act of striking someone unprovoked is as physically real as that of caressing them affectionately, and in so far as it obeys the God-given laws of physical nature, it can be said to be willed by him; but the malice, the evil will to harm, is understood by Descartes (following a basic insight of Augustine's) to be a lack, or 'privation', of the good will the agent ought to have; it is thus not a positive reality, and is not therefore willed by God. Cf. *Passions*, §140 and note.

all that is revealed by God: Descartes, as usual, is careful to assert that his method of seeking for clear and distinct ideas does not preclude belief in the mysteries of orthodox Christianity.

146 *indefinite rather than infinite*: this is not merely a matter of terminological precision. If the physical universe is credited with infinity, one of the divine attributes, it might seem natural to regard it too as part of the divine substance, and the distinction between creator and creature would disappear. The result would be more or less Spinozist pantheism. Whether Descartes clearly saw this possible implication we do not know.

We should examine . . . only the efficient ones: F: 'That we should not examine what end God had in view in the creation of each thing, but only how he willed it to be produced.' The distinction between final and efficient causes is Aristotelian (*Physics* 2. 3, 194^{b}16–195^{b}30). The efficient cause is the productive agency: so a builder is the efficient cause of a house, and a doctor of health. The final cause is the purpose, that for the sake of which something is done: thus, the final cause of the house is shelter, and the final cause of exercise is health. Unlike Aristotelian physics, Cartesian physics acknowledges only the first kind of cause. F indeed adds the polemical statement 'we shall altogether discard the search for final causes from our philosophy'. Final causes, however, may be invoked in ethics: see *Principles*, III. 3, AT 8. 81, where Descartes says we may legitimately think that God made all things for our sake (for a detailed discussion of the issue, see to Chanut, 6 June 1647 ('Other Letters', letter 4), AT 5. 53–5). Divine purpose is also visible in the manner in which the soul and body interact for the preservation of the union between them (*Meditations*, VI, AT 7. 87–8, OWC 62).

148 *privations in relation to ourselves*: in the first place, error is not a positive reality, but the absence of truth. A negation is a pure absence: thus, it is a negation in a human being to be unable to fly by his or her own efforts, which is simply to say that human beings can't fly. A privation is the absence of some attribute or capacity in an entity capable of possessing it: so our errors, in relation to us, are privations of the truth we can

in principle discover. F explains the notion of negation more fully: '[our errors] are, in relation to [God], pure negations; that is, he did not give us everything he could have given us, and we see by the same token that he was under no obligation to do so'.

148 *the real concourse of God is required*: the 'concourse' of God is his preservation of the universe in existence, and in particular his support of human actions. When I write '66 + 92 = 157', he is enabling me to perform the physical and mental acts involved: but he is not producing my mistake, which is an absence or negation rather than a positive entity.

We make mistakes . . . a matter we have insufficiently perceived: F is rather more explicit and precise here: 'When we perceive something, we are not in danger of making a mistake if we pass no judgement about it at all; and even if we do pass judgement, provided that we give our assent only to what we clearly and distinctly know must be understood in the object of our judgement, we cannot be mistaken either; but the usual cause of our mistakes is that we very often do pass judgement, even though we do not have a very exact knowledge of what we are passing judgement about.'

must be affirmed or denied: that is to say, we may be able to affirm a partial truth, clearly and distinctly grasped, with certainty. Thus, in the Second Meditation, the Meditator is able to affirm that, qua thinking thing, he is immaterial; but he makes no assertion about the relationship between his thinking self and the body he seems to have but (for all he knows at this stage) may not in fact have.

149 *to which our own does not also extend*: Descartes's point is that while we experience the limitations of our intellect, so that there are some ideas we cannot form, we can want anything of which we can form an idea, even something intrinsically impossible: we can want to run faster than a race-horse or to go to Jupiter or to go back to a moment in the past.

151 *freedom and indifference*: Descartes uses the latter term in the scholastic sense of the power to choose between alternatives (and not merely to do what we want). See the letters to Mesland and the notes ('Other Letters', letters 1 and 2).

comprehend from inside and experience in ourselves: Descartes's point is that, in feeling we are free, we know what it is to be free. We thus 'comprehend' freedom, whereas we do not comprehend God, as is clear from our inability to understand how his power coexists with our freedom.

152 *nothing that is not clear*: F adds, 'to one considering it in the proper fashion', thus highlighting a fundamental problem in Descartes's philosophy: how can one lay down as a universal criterion an experience of clarity and distinctness, which is, as we would say, necessarily subjective? The objection is vigorously put by Gassendi (*Meditations*, Fifth Objections, III. 1, AT 7. 277–9, OWC 170); for Descartes's answer, see Fifth Replies, III. 1, AT 7. 361–2, OWC 190.

which is all that they clearly perceive: the perception of pain may be very vivid, and it makes no sense to say 'I feel as if I am in pain, but I may not be'. But Descartes's point is that pain-sensations are intrinsically confused as to their location: I feel a pain in my foot; but the pain is not 'in' my foot; rather, there is something affecting my foot (a blister, say, or a stone in my shoe) as a result of which a process takes place in my brain that I experience (in my soul) as pain in my foot. The sensation, therefore, is not distinct, since it runs together several things that are of their nature different. We have, says Descartes, a general inveterate tendency to assume that there is something in the object we perceive that resembles our perception of it; that 'greenness' or 'softness', say, are qualities of grass, as distinct from qualities of our perception of it. See *The World*, ch. 1, AT 11. 405–8.

153 *a modification of a thing*: one might expect Descartes to lay more weight on the distinction between a thing and its modifications. But for the moment the key distinction is between two kinds of basic notion: ideas of things (or their modifications) on the one hand, and propositions on the other. F is perhaps clearer here: 'I distinguish all that falls within the scope of our knowledge into two categories: the first contains everything that exists in some way, the latter, all the truths that have no existence outside our minds (*notre pensée*).'

outside our thought: compare F: 'I divide all that falls under our knowledge into two categories: the first contains everything that exists in some way, and the second everything that has no existence outside our thought.'

what we consider as things: under this term Descartes in this paragraph lumps together acts (perception, volition), properties (extension), sensations, passions, and sensible qualities. None of these would normally qualify as a 'thing' in present-day speech: however, I have stuck to Descartes's own terminology. See the last note but one.

all kinds of things: F adds: 'In addition, we also have more specific notions that serve to distinguish them.'

that is, to a body: to judge by the phraseology of L, the 'things' Descartes is thinking of are modifications. F is actually clearer here: 'the chief distinction I observe among all created things is that some are intellectual, that is, they are intelligent substances, or properties belonging to such substances; while others are corporeal, that is, they are bodies, or properties belonging to a body'.

the emotions, or passions: commotiones, sive animi pathemata: Descartes uses the rare Greek word *pathemata*, presumably as an equivalent to the more common *pathos*, generally rendered in this context as 'passion'. F simply has *passions*. The standard Latin equivalent for *pathos*, such as we find in Cicero, is *perturbatio*: but this means 'disorder', and Descartes may have wished to avoid the pejorative implications of the term.

pain, pleasure: omitted from F.

and innumerable others: F adds: 'these are simply truths, and not things existing outside our minds'.

154 *more extensive than another's*: Descartes attaches very little importance to differences of individual intelligence; see the opening of the *Discourse on the Method*, and, above, the letter-preface to the French edition.

examining these separately: F adds: 'in order to distinguish what is obscure from what is clear in our notion of each'.

it needs no other thing in order to exist: it is interesting to compare Descartes's definition with that of Aristotle: 'Substance in the truest and strictest, the primary sense of that term, is that which is neither asserted of nor can be found in a subject' (*Categories* 5, 2ᵃ11–14, in *The Categories; On Interpretation; Prior Analytics*, ed. and trans. Harold P. Cooke and Hugh Tredennick, Loeb Classical Library (Cambridge, Mass., 1938)). A similar definition is found in the work of Eustache de Saint-Paul (Eustachius a Sancto Paulo), whose textbook of scholastic philosophy Descartes rated as the best (to Mersenne, 11 November 1640, AT 3. 232). Eustache defines substance as 'a subsistent being, or one that exists in itself' (*Ens subsistens seu per se existens*). He explains this as meaning that it does not exist, or inhere, in some other being, whereas an 'accident' requires some other entity in which to exist (*Summa philosophiae quadripartita, de rebus dialecticis, moralibus, physicis, & metaphysicis*, 2 vols. (Paris, 1609), i. 96–7). Thus, for instance, the accident of redness cannot exist except in a substance such as a flower or a coat, whereas the existence of a flower or a coat is not, so to speak, attached to that of anything else. To put it another way, the flower or the coat are not modifications of some other thing; at least so it seems to common sense, though Spinoza was to argue differently. Descartes's definition seems in fact to open up the way to Spinoza: see below.

the divine concourse: see above, notes to p. 148.

univocally, as they commonly put it in the Schools: the 'Schools' are the universities. When Descartes uses scholastic technical terms, he often draws attention to them, as if in a somewhat embarrassed fashion. His point is that if finite entities are substances, they are not so in the same sense as God is. A scholastic would say, then, that the term does not apply to them univocally; just as 'good' is not used univocally of a mother and of a fountain pen. But Descartes's explanation of non-univocity asserts the total absence of a common meaning to the term as used of finite beings and of God. In that case, one can see why someone might infer that the term 'substance' can be applied only to God, and not to finite creatures at all. And in fact this is precisely the step taken by Spinoza.

to both God and creatures: F adds: 'but because among created things there are some of such a nature that they cannot exist without some others, we distinguish these from those that need only the ordinary concourse of God, calling the latter kind substances, and the former qualities or attributes of these substances'.

can be known: the whole paragraph is much fuller in F, and runs as follows: 'And our notion of created substance applies in the same way to all of them, that is, to those that are immaterial and also to those that are material or corporeal; for in order to grasp that they are substances, we need only realize that they can exist without the aid of any created thing. But when we ask whether any of these substances really exists, that is, if it is currently found in the world, the fact of its existing in this way is not sufficient for us to perceive it; for it reveals nothing to us that produces any specific knowledge in our minds; it also requires some attributes that we can observe; and from this point of view any attribute is sufficient, because one of our common notions is that nothingness can have no attributes, or properties, or qualities; this is why when we encounter some such attribute, we must rationally conclude that it is the attribute of some substance, and that this substance exists.'

because this, as such, does not by itself affect us: Descartes is implicitly criticizing the scholastic definition, which does not take account of the fact that we have no access to substance in itself, only through its attributes (which term Descartes is substituting for the scholastic 'accident').

155 *one principal property of each substance*: note that, for all his talk of 'things', Descartes's discussion of substance does not begin with the concept of individual entities, but with the ontological stuff, so to speak, of which individual entities are made; whereas for Aristotle, the individual (man or horse, say) is the primary substance (*Categories* 5, 2^{a}13–14). One can, again, read Descartes's departure from the Aristotelian paradigm as opening the door to Spinozist pantheism.

a certain mode of an extended thing: a 'mode' is a modification of a substance, one of the forms in which it can exist. See §56 below.

such an idea of God exists within us: in the Third Objections to the *Meditations* Hobbes does in fact deny that we have an idea of God (AT 7. 180, OWC 113). As if to refute him, F adds 'without any reason' after 'thinks'.

156 *when the name we give it reflects this alteration*: literally 'when from this variation it can be called such'; F adds: 'I call qualities the diverse manners that cause it to be called so.' (Compare Aristotle's definition of quality as 'that in virtue of which men are called such and such'; *Categories* 8, 8^{b}25.) Descartes is distinguishing modes, which alter a substance without affecting its identity, from qualities, considered as those properties (intrinsically variable) that constitute its identity. For instance, water is water, whether or not it is hot; heat is therefore a potential mode of water. Liquidity, however, is a quality of water, inasmuch as if it ceases to be liquid, by freezing or evaporation, it ceases to be water. It would seem to follow, however, that the same property may be a mode in some cases, a quality in others. For instance, a metal heated to melting point acquires liquidity, but its identity as iron or gold remains unchanged.

properties that never admit of variation: in so far as a thing exists, and continues to exist in time, its existence and duration undergo no variation: it does not have any more or less existence at one point in time (t_1) than at another (t_2) and it is existing in time just as much at the first point as at the second (even if it has existed for longer at the second). To put it another way, if a thing exists, it must also have duration. Compare this with a property like heat, which, in a body capable of being heated, can be greater or lesser at one time than at another, or even absent altogether.

156 *the measure of movement*: or 'number' of movement. Descartes is alluding to the Aristotelian definition in *Physics* 4. 11, 220ᵃ24–6. Descartes's point is that time, unlike duration, is not an intrinsic property of things, but the product of our thought: we construct time, so to speak, by measuring one duration against another. Here he may be seen as opening up a line of thought that is fully developed by Kant.

157 *other so-called 'universals'*: the status of 'universal' terms, such as 'humankind' or 'whiteness', referring not to specific entities, but to categories or general properties, independently of the things in which they are embodied, was a key issue in medieval philosophical debates. F has: 'the same applies to all these other general ideas that they classify in the Schools as "universals"'.

the idea of a triangle: it is clear from the context that 'triangle' is a genus, not a specific entity.

the universal 'differentia': in Aristotelian logic the differentia is the distinctive property that marks out a species within a genus (as, here, right-angledness distinguishes the species of right-angled triangles from other triangles). See *Categories* 3, 1ᵇ16–19.

a universal 'accident' of these triangles: unlike the property, which necessarily belongs to each individual member of a given category, things, the 'accident' may or may not belong to the individual.

number in things: in §§58–9 Descartes discussed number as a concept (or 'mode of thought'), abstracted from particular entities. But it is not simply a concept, for there are distinctions between things in reality. These are discussed here.

'real', 'modal', and 'mental': *realis*, *modalis*, & *rationis*. *Rationis* literally means 'of reason'. The French equivalent is '[*la distinction*] *de raison*' or '[*la distinction*] *qui se fait par la pensée*' ('which is made by the mind').

158 *we separate out in our thought*: as Ferdinand Alquié's note on this passage explains, Descartes's point is that we perceive the general realm of body (extended substance) to be divided into particular bodies (individual substances). The distinction between them, though perceived 'in our thought' (*cogitatione*), is therefore real (*OP* iii. 129 n. 1).

a single entity: Descartes is clearly thinking of the union of thinking and extended substance that forms a human being.

159 *motion differs from duration*: this may appear to be an odd example since a body can have both motion and duration (see §57). But the point is presumably that whereas motion pertains only to extended (corporeal) substance, duration can pertain to any substance, be it extended or thinking.

as real rather than modal: when the distinction is modal, only one substance, to which the mode or modes pertain, is involved; the real distinction involves more than one substance.

in the same object: as the annotation in CSMK points out, this passage is to be read in the light of §§57–8. Because these modes of thought are concepts we apply to objects, rather than modes inhering in the object, the distinction between the mode and the object is mental; if it were real, time, number, and so forth would exist independently of the objects in which we consider them. There is quite a difference between L and F here. F reads as follows: 'and in general all the attributes that cause us to have different thoughts of one and the same thing, for instance bodily extension and its property of being divisible into many parts, differ from the body that is the object of our thought, and from one another, only in that we sometimes think confusedly of the one without thinking of the other'. The distinction between the object in question (a body) and these attributes is purely mental, in that there can be no body without extension; and the same goes for the distinction between the two attributes, in that there can be no divisibility without extension.

in the Replies to the First Objections to the Meditations: AT 7. 120–1, OWC 83–4.

160 *as modes of substance*: by contrast with the previous section, where they were considered as distinct substances.

explain in the proper place: see *Principles*, II. 24–54, especially §§43–4. Descartes makes clear that he is using 'motion' only in a restricted sense, not in the broad sense the term has in Aristotelian philosophy, where it can refer to change of all kinds. See also §69 below.

161 *a thing situated outside us*: the error is not in supposing that the physical object we are perceiving (a house, say) is a thing existing outside our minds, but in supposing that its colour (white) is itself a thing, as distinct from a quality of our perception.

the idea of colour: the term 'idea' in Descartes is not restricted to intellectual concepts. Any specific object of our thinking (here in the broad sense of awareness or consciousness) is an idea (he defines the term elsewhere as follows: 'By the term *idea* I understand the form, of any thought whatever, by the immediate perception of which I am conscious of the same thought itself'; Second Replies, AT 7. 160, OWC 102). In other words, to become aware that one is feeling hot is to have an idea of heat; and to see a white house is to have an idea of the colour white (as well as perceiving the form of the object by which we recognize it as a house). The point he is making here, then, is not that our concept of colour is flawed, though it is; rather, the flaw in the concept comes from the misinterpretation of our experience, whereby we assume that the colour white we are seeing is a property of the object, when it is a property of our perception.

as certain and indubitable: F rather accentuates the polemical side of these claims. The last sentence runs as follows: 'Now we have made this kind of judgement in so many situations, and we thought we were seeing this so

clearly and distinctly, because we were in the habit of making such judgements, that it is no wonder that some people subsequently remain so convinced by this false prejudice that they cannot even bring themselves to
doubt it.'

161 *or some other part of our body*: F again explains the point more fully and more
polemically: 'The same preconception has arisen in all our other sensations,
even those of pleasure (*chatouillement*) and pain. For although we did not
believe that there was anything outside us, in external objects, similar to the
pleasure or pain they caused us to feel, we did not, however, consider these
sensations as ideas existing purely in our soul; but we thought that they
were in our hands, our feet, and the other parts of our body; and yet there
is no reason why we should believe that the pain we feel, for example, in the
foot, is something outside our minds (*pensée*) existing in our foot, or that the
light we think we see in the sun exists in the sun in the same way as it does
in ourselves. And if some people still allow themselves to be convinced by so
false an opinion, this is only because they set so much store by their childhood judgements, that they cannot forget them in order to replace them by
sounder ones, as will appear even more plainly in what follows.'

there is something: F adds: 'in the object'.

actually represents: for Descartes, our sensations are signs or representa-
tions of external objects or bodily states; but there are no grounds for
assuming that the relationship of the sign to what it represents is one of
resemblance, and that assumption leads merely to confusion. Sound is
a vibration in the air; but we don't perceive that vibration, we hear a bird
singing or a bell ringing. In general, there is a similar discrepancy between
the causes of our sensations and the sensations themselves, which are
translations of a physical process. See *The World*, ch. 1, AT 11. 3–6. I know
what 'redness' is as a quality of my perception, but I have no idea of what
'redness' is as a supposed quality of the object.

162 *various additional kinds of motion*: presumably Descartes is referring to the
Aristotelian use of the term 'motion' for various kinds of change besides
movement in space.

are clearly perceived in bodies: see §48 above. This distinction between
qualities known with certainty and those known only in confused fashion
is central to Descartes's philosophy, for it allows for scientific and mathematical knowledge to be developed along mechanical lines, diverging
from the promptings of everyday experience. It is ratified by Locke, who
uses the terms 'primary' and 'secondary' qualities in *An Essay concerning
Human Understanding*, 11. i. 7–10. But it was to be questioned by Berkeley
(*Principles of Human Knowledge*: see e.g. §§9, 73).

the sensation of colours: it is correct, therefore, to say that there is something in an object we perceive as red that differentiates it from one we
perceive as green, as long as we do not interpret this as some intrinsic
'redness' or 'greenness'.

163 *nothing existing outside the mind*: F adds: 'but which vary with the variations

that occur in the movements that connect every part of our body to the place in the brain with which [the soul] is closely joined and united'. The place in the brain in question is the pineal gland: see *Passions*, §31.

the difference between these: that is, the baby's consciousness does not clearly register the difference between qualitative sensations (non-representative) and perceptions representing things or their modes, or, by the same token, the difference between itself and external objects. F suggests that there is a sort of virtual awareness of the distinction: 'It [the soul] also perceived magnitudes, shapes, and movements which it did not take for sensations but for things or properties of certain things that seemed to it to exist, or at least to be capable of existing, outside it, even though it did not yet notice this difference.'

in one direction or another: the baby's random movements bring it into contact with objects that produce pleasant or unpleasant sensations (signs of the objects' beneficial or harmful nature); it thus begins to develop its consciousness of self in relation to the world. F is fuller, emphasizing the process whereby the soul's accurate perception of bodies and their objective properties is overlaid by a mistaken ascription to these bodies of the qualities of the sensations they produce: 'But when, at a slightly later stage of life, our body, turning itself here and there at random on account of the disposition of our organs, encountered useful things or avoided harmful ones, the soul closely united to it came to reflect on the things it was encountering or avoiding, and realized, first of all, that they existed outside it; and it ascribed to them not only magnitudes, shapes, movements, and the other properties that truly belong to bodies, and which it conceived very clearly either as things or as properties depending on things, but also the colours, smells, and all the other ideas of this kind that it perceived along with these perceptions.'

164 *that its surface was flat*: the immobility of the earth was a basic tenet of the Ptolemaic system of astronomy, dominant until the early modern period. Galileo argued that it rotated on its axis (the first point at issue here) as well as around the sun. On the other hand, Ptolemy taught that the earth was a sphere, and this was generally acknowledged throughout the Middle Ages, at least by scholars.

implanted in us by nature: again F emphasizes the process by which pseudo-knowledge comes about: 'And in this way a thousand other prejudices took such a strong root in our minds that even when we were fully capable of making good use of our reason, we accepted them as beliefs; and instead of thinking that we had made these judgements at a time when we were incapable of judging accurately, and that as a result they might well be false rather than true, we accepted them as no less certain than if we had had a distinct knowledge of them via our senses, and we doubted them as little as if they had been common notions.'

otherwise than we did before: F adds: 'So great is the power over us of an opinion we have once accepted!'

165 *as will clearly be shown below*: the senses are discussed in detail in *Principles*, IV. 189–98.

perceive nothing, except confusedly: in F, the last sentence reads as follows: 'And inasmuch as it is not our senses that enable us to discover the nature of anything, whatever it is, only our reason, when it becomes involved, it is no wonder that most people perceive things only very confusedly, since there are very few of them who make the effort to direct their reason properly.'

did properly understand them: F sharpens the criticism, implicitly targeted at the teaching of scholastic philosophy: 'this is why they very often give their assent to terms they do not understand, and do not care whether they understand or not, either because they thought they understood them once, or because they thought that their teachers knew what the words mean, and learned their meaning in the same way.' The student is not quite clear what the terms mean, but believes that the teacher does, and that therefore they must be meaningful. F seems to imply a more complicated thought process: 'I don't really understand what a substantial form is; but the teacher seems to, and he must have learned it in the same way as me, when he was a student, so if I just carry on talking about "substantial forms", maybe one day I'll be like him and know what the words really mean.'

that any bodies exist: the demonstration is offered in *Principles*, II. 1. Our sensations must come from something outside ourselves, since they do not depend on our will. Moreover, we have a clear and distinct conception of matter as a substance existing outside us, and extended in space, the parts of which have shape and motion, and cause us to experience various sensations. Were this an illusion, God, the ultimate cause of all our sensations, would be a deceiver; which is incompatible with his nature (as appears from I. 29 and 36).

166 *the reason why they thus affect us*: in *Principles*, II. 3, Descartes argues that the function of sensations is to indicate what can benefit or harm us, in so far as we are a union of body and soul.

the unreflective judgements of his childhood: the point is not that the senses are in themselves unreliable; on the contrary, we can rely on them from a practical point of view. However, from childhood on, as Descartes has explained, we spontaneously misconstrue our sense-experience, so that we believe that the sensible qualities of objects are really 'in' them, instead of being qualities of our perception.

OTHER LETTERS

169 *Father Denis Mesland*: a French Jesuit (1615–72), first a pupil then a teacher at La Flèche, Descartes's old school; he later became a missionary. The letter (in French) was written at Leiden, through which Descartes was passing on his way to France.

a common notion: a basic axiom, like those of geometry. See *Principles*, I. 13.

quod potest plus, potest etiam minus: 'what can do more can also do less'.

totum est maius sua parte: 'the whole is greater than its part'.

as the poets say: *comme on feint*; literally, 'as it is feigned'; but the verb *fein-dre* is very commonly used of poetic fictions.

my second demonstration: in the *Meditations* Descartes's first proof of the existence of God is that he must exist as the cause of the idea of him I have in my mind; he then argues that my very existence must depend on God (AT 7. 41–51, OWC 29–36).

170 *of which I am not so certain*: not that Descartes currently doubts the exist-ence of the heavens and the earth; but the knowledge of their existence depends on that of a non-deceiving God, whereas of his own existence he has an immediate certainty.

the idea of God: the point being that my own existence requires a first cause, but that I cannot affirm this to be God except in the light of my own idea of God as the supremely perfect being.

my reply to the First Objections: see AT 7. 106–8, OWC 79–80. Descartes is there implicitly criticizing the argumentation of Aquinas.

non datur progressus in infinitum: there can be no progression to infin-ity. Aristotle argues in *Physics* 7. 1, 242ᵃ49–63, that motion cannot be explained by an infinite series of movers and more generally in *Metaphys-ics* 2. 2. 1–4, 994ᵃ1–19, that there cannot be an infinite series of causes.

datur revera talis progressus in divisione partium materiae: 'such a progres-sion can in fact exist in the division of parts of matter'.

my treatise on philosophy: in *Principles*, II. 20, Descartes argues that matter is divisible to infinity.

the cause of errors: Descartes investigates this problem in the Fourth Medi-tation, where he supposes for argument's sake that the universe as a whole is perfect, though it may contain local imperfections (AT 7. 55–6, OWC 40). In keeping with his purely philosophical approach, he does not there consider specifically religious explanations, like the doctrine of Original Sin, considered as damaging our intellectual faculties as well as our moral disposition, and his point may be that in the light of this doctrine the problem would disappear.

some other friends of mine: the letter to Colvius of 14 November 1640 (AT 3. 247–8) specifically identifies *De civitate Dei*, 11. 26, where Augustine argues against scepticism in a manner that seems to anticipate the Cogito. Antoine Arnauld suggests a connection with *De libero arbitrio*, 2. 3 (Fourth Objections, AT 7. 197–8, OWC 126).

is also a passion: in the sense that the soul is passive with regard to the ori-gin of its ideas. On this general notion of passion, see *Passions*, §§1–2, 17.

171 *the book currently in press*: the *Principles*; see I. 50, 71–4.

not an error: error occurs, as Descartes explains in the Fourth Meditation, when we choose to commit ourselves to asserting or denying something of which we do not have a clear and distinct perception. In mathematics, metaphysics, and natural philosophy such perceptions are available, and therefore we should never rely on someone else's authority. In matters of conduct not everyone can work out the truth for her- or himself (see the dedicatory epistle to the *Principles*, AT 8/1. 3; p. 122 above); and besides we have to take account of the laws and customs of the community, and the behaviour and values of those among whom we live (*Discourse*, III, AT 6. 23–4, OWC 21–2). In that case it might be reasonable for an individual to accept the word of a worthy man, as a guide to his or her own conduct.

171 *Father Pétau*: Denis Pétau (1583–1652), also known by the Latin form of his name, Petavius; a distinguished Jesuit theologian. The work referred to is *De libero arbitrio libri tres* (Paris, 1643).

all the more indifferent: in the Fourth Meditation, Descartes's discussion of will and choice uses the term 'indifference' to denote the state in which there is no reason inclining me to one alternative rather than the other. He calls this the lowest degree of freedom; I am freer when I have a strong inclination to one alternative, inspired by a clear perception of goodness and truth (or by divine grace, which he also refers to in this passage of the letter) (AT 7. 58, OWC 41). But in scholastic theology indifference denotes a genuine power to choose between alternatives, which for some theologians (especially those of the Society of Jesus) is regarded as essential to human freedom in this life. Descartes is therefore seeking to show how his account of freedom in the *Meditations* leaves room for this conception of indifference.

ex magna luce . . . magna propensio in voluntate: 'a great illumination of the intellect is followed by a great inclination of the will'. Descartes is quoting himself (with a change from 'was' to 'is'): *Meditations*, IV, AT 7. 59, OWC 42.

172 *there is indifference*: Mesland, no doubt, would have wished to point out that sinners are not necessitated to sin, as Calvinist or Jansenist theologians would claim.

omnis peccans est ignorans: 'every sinner is in ignorance'.

our action is still meritorious: a Roman Catholic theological term for an act that (by God's grace) contributes to the agent's salvation.

173 *equal to two right angles*: a proposition from Euclid (*Elements* 1. 32), regarded as a necessary truth because it follows by accurate deduction from definitions and common notions. In Sixth Replies, §6 (AT 7. 432, OWC 204–5), Descartes argues that this necessity is not in the ultimate nature of things, but has been created by God, who could have opted to create a world in which Euclid's proposition would be false. For a fuller statement of this view, see the letters to Mersenne of 15 April 1630 and 6 May 1630 (AT 1. 145–6, 149–50).

Quia vides ea, sunt, etc.: 'because you see them [the things you have created], they exist' (Augustine, *Confessions*, 13. 38).

videre and velle: 'to see and to will'.

the Holy Sacrament: the consecrated host, transformed (or 'transubstanti-
ated'), according to Roman Catholic doctrine, from bread into the substance of the body and blood of Jesus Christ. According to the influential
explanation given by Aquinas, the 'accidents' of the bread and wine (colour, shape, taste, and so forth) remain, but not the substance (*ST* 3. 75. 5).
Descartes denies the existence of real accidents capable of existing apart
from the substance to which they belong (Sixth Replies, 7, AT 7. 434–5,
OWC 206; see Paul Hoffman, *Essays on Descartes* (Oxford, 2009), 23),
though he concedes that one accident (which, however, he calls a mode),
that of shape, does remain.

174 *verbis exprimere vix possumus*: 'in a form of existence that we can scarcely
express in words'. The Council of Trent, held, but not continuously, from
1545 to 1563, restated and clarified Roman Catholic doctrine against the
Reformers. In particular, it reasserted the doctrine of transubstantiation,
which the Reformers rejected, though their own doctrines of the Eucharist show considerable variation from one another. Descartes is quoting
from the Council's decree on the Eucharist, session 13, 11 October
1651 (*Enchiridion symbolorum: definitionum et declarationum de rebus fidei
et morum*, ed. Heinrich Denzinger, rev. Adolf Schönmetzer, SJ, 35th edn
(Freiburg im Breisgau, 1973), §1636.

my Replies to the Fourth Objections: see AT 7. 252, OWC 162. In the Fourth
Objections, Arnauld had already raised the issue of whether Descartes's
metaphysics is compatible with the doctrine of transubstantiation (AT 7.
217, OWC 139–40).

a way of explaining this mystery: in the technical theological sense of a div-
inely revealed truth above human comprehension.

9 February 1645: this letter, written in Latin, is one of two written to Mesland on this date; the other, in French, is a discussion of the Eucharist
(AT 4. 161–72). The fact that it is separate, and in Latin, may suggest that
it was intended for Mesland to pass on to a colleague.

the Reverend Father: either Mesland himself, or, perhaps more probably,
Pétau, mentioned in the previous letter.

175 *though we see what is better*: an allusion to Ovid's lines *video meliora
proboque*, | *Deteriora sequor* ('I see what is better and approve of it, but I fol-
low what is worse'; *Metamorphoses* 7. 20–1). The lines are often discussed
by early modern philosophers preoccupied with akrasia (weakness of will);
see Susan James, *Passion and Action* (Oxford, 1997), 256–7, 273, 275–6.

adiaphora: Descartes uses this Greek term, and then immediately glosses
it, 'indifferent things'.

176 *in which we find ourselves*: the opposing reasons cancel each other out.
In other words, the essence of indifference in this first sense does not
consist in not caring either way, but in not having preponderant reasons on one side rather than the other.

176 *the Marquess of Newcastle*: William Cavendish (1592–1676), a royalist general in the English civil war, who went into exile when the royalist cause was lost. He was created a duke at the Restoration. His wife, Margaret Cavendish, was an able writer and natural philosopher. The letter is in French.

Your Excellency: Furetière (*Dictionnaire universel*, s.v. *excellence*) writes that this form of address is generally used for ambassadors and other people not entitled to be called 'Your Highness', because they are not of princely rank, but whose rank the speaker wishes to exalt.

to prevent me from doing so: on the same day Descartes wrote to Mersenne that Newcastle's letter had arrived only a week earlier, though it had been sent over ten months before (AT 4. 568). In order to palliate any suspicion of discourtesy, he ascribes the delay in its arrival to the jealousy of Fortune, rather than the inadequacy of the postal services.

to receive one last year: Descartes replies to this earlier letter from Newcastle in his letter of October 1645, which also begins by referring to the delay in its arrival (AT 4. 325).

M. de B: Possibly William Boswell, the king of England's resident at The Hague.

Your Excellency's views about alchemists: Descartes refers contemptuously to alchemy in the *Discourse*, AT 6. 9, OWC 10.

177 *about to be published in French*: the French version of the *Principles* appeared in 1647.

that are produced in the human body: such as gallstones or kidney stones.

as I have stated in the Meteorology: *Meteorology*, I, AT 6. 233.

178 *the nature of quicksilver*: Descartes discusses quicksilver (or mercury) in *Principles*, IV. 16 and 58.

the 'first element': on Descartes's conception of the elements, see the Appendix.

M. d'Igby's book: Sir Kenelm Digby's two treatises *The Nature of Bodies* and *On the Immortality of Reasonable Souls* were published together in 1644. See Elisabeth's letter of 24 May 1645 (letter 13).

ascribed by Montaigne: Michel de Montaigne (1533–92), author of the *Essays*. Descartes uses the old spelling 'Montagne'. The reference is to Montaigne's chapter 'An Apology for Raymond Sebond' (*Essays*, II. 12), where, in order to discredit the idea that human beings are unique, he accumulates evidence of animal intelligence.

179 *Charron*: Pierre Charron (1541–1603), author of the influential treatise *De la sagesse* (On Wisdom), where he borrows heavily from Montaigne.

and an animal: 'there is a greater difference between one man and another than between some men and some beasts' (Montaigne, *Essays*, II. 12, p. 520); cf. Charron, *De la sagesse*, 2nd edn (Paris, 1604), ed. Barbara de Negroni (Paris, 1986), I. 34, pp. 207–19; he copies Montaigne's remark on p. 214.

180 *than our judgement can manage*: Descartes's contemporaries would have been better than most of us at working out the time from natural indicators like the position of the sun or the stars in the sky.

there is some thought: *quelque pensée*, perhaps to be understood as 'some mind', in the light of the following sentence.

6 June 1647: the letter to Chanut ('Other Letters', letter 4) is written in French.

M. Brasset: the French resident at the Hague.

Egmond: Descartes's residence at Egmond-Binnen.

181 *M. du Rier*: the queen's doctor.

Cardinal Cusa: Nicholas of Cusa (1401–64), a German theologian, philosopher, and astronomer.

several other doctors: in the sense of 'learned men of recognized academic standing'.

only that it is indefinite: see *Principles*, I. 26–7.

no space that is entirely empty: in denying the possibility of a vacuum, Descartes is for once in agreement with Aristotle. Pascal conducted experiments to demonstrate its possibility in 1648.

182 *if one compares it with its duration*: Descartes's view that the universe has no limits in space might suggest the complementary view that it has no limits in time, that is, that it has existed from all eternity, as Aristotle taught. But this would clash with the Christian doctrine of creation, hence the following discussion.

five or six thousand years: the usual estimate at the time of the duration of the world since the Creation, based on computations from scripture.

the actual existence of the same globe: the prevailing conception of the universe as finite in space implies that imaginary space actually exists outside it; but if the universe is finite in time (because it was created out of nothing) there is no need to suppose that it was somehow preceded by an actually existing 'imaginary' universe. The doctrine of creation is not therefore refutable by a similar argument to that Descartes adduces against the spatial limitation of the universe.

the earth and the heavens will pass away: cf. Matt. 24: 35: 'Heaven and earth will pass away, but my words will not pass away' (New Revised Standard Version).

after their resurrection: Christian doctrine teaches that the bodies of the dead will be resurrected at the Last Judgement and reunited with their souls.

independent of one another: see *Principles*, I. 21.

the prerogatives attributed to man by religion: Descartes seems to be thinking of Gen. 1: 26–9.

omnia propter ipsum (Deum) facta sunt: the Latin phrase appears to be an imperfect reminiscence of a passage in the Vulgate New Testament: either John 1: 3 (*omnia per ipsum facta sunt*: 'through him all things came into being'); or Col. 1: 16 (*omnia per ipsum et in ipsum creata sunt*: 'all things were created through him and for him'); or perhaps a conflation of the two. But in both passages 'him' is clearly Christ. The translations quoted are from the New Jerusalem Bible.

182 *the final cause*: the cause for the sake of which something is done, the efficient cause being the agent that does it. God is the creator of the universe and he created it for his own sake.

183 *a thousand pistoles*: the pistole was originally a gold coin minted in Spain and in part of Italy. As an accounting unit it was the equivalent of ten *livres* (pounds).

184 *will ourselves united*: '*nous nous joignons de volonte*'. This is Descartes's definition of love: see *Passions*, §§79–80.

the innumerable multitude of angels: see e.g. Matt: 26: 53, Rev. 5: 11.

so produce certain creases: cf. the discussion of memory in the letter to Mesland of 2 May 1644 ('Other Letters', letter 1). A crease occurs when two parts of the surface of an object (a folded handkerchief, for instance) that are normally separate come together, and it renders this conjunction easier in future. In the case of the girl with a squint Descartes observes such a conjunction between the part of the brain that registered a visual stimulus, thus occasioning the sight of the girl and her squint, and the part where the physical process experienced by the soul as love was set in motion by the flow of animal spirits.

185 *we feel this emotion*: Descartes's syntax has become uncharacteristically disordered: it should be 'for whom he [the wise man] feels this emotion'.

Antoine Arnauld: (1612–94): the intellectual leader of the Jansenist movement in French Roman Catholicism. A formidable theologian and controversialist, he had also an acute philosophical mind. He drew up the Fourth Objections to the *Meditations*, which Descartes took very seriously. The letter is in Latin.

were delivered to me lately: Arnauld wrote to Descartes on 3 June 1648 (AT 5. 185–91); from Descartes's reply, which is indeed brief (4 June 1648, AT 5. 192–4), it appears that Arnauld's letter was anonymous. As an active proponent of the Jansenist theology, highly unpopular with the authorities, he must have found it advisable to keep a low profile. Descartes's reply assumes the possibility of a meeting for further discussion. In his follow-up letter of July 1648, Arnauld explains regretfully that this is impossible, since he is absent from Paris. Thus, Descartes's second reply, the letter reproduced here, is fuller. Since, as in the earlier letter, his correspondent has concealed his identity, Descartes refers to him in the third person.

186 *any introductory formula*: not knowing (or not being supposed to know) who his correspondent is, Descartes does not wish to address him in a fashion inappropriate to his social position.

withdraw itself from the senses: an expression Descartes uses fairly frequently to designate the state into which one should put oneself when engaged in intellectual thinking: see *Meditations*, Preface to the Reader, AT 7. 9, OWC 8.

leave no traces in their brains: see Fifth Replies, II. 4, AT 7. 356–7, OWC 188. The issue there is whether, since the soul is defined by Descartes as a thinking substance, it must be always thinking.

187 *its being an extended thing*: I have been helped here by Alquié's translation and interpretation of the passage (*OP* iii. 862 and n.). As he observes, the point is that the modes (the particular thoughts or movements) depend on the substance, but the basic attribute (thought or extension) that constitutes its essence does not depend on it.

to be aware: *esse conscios*.

188 *the things known by themselves*: *rebus per se notis*; that is, directly apprehended without need (or possibility) of proof.

a certain comparison: Descartes analyses the scholastic concept of heaviness (or 'weight') as a real quality in the Sixth Replies (AT 7. 441–2, OWC 210–11), and uses it to explain his conception of body–soul union to Elisabeth in the letters of 21 May and 28 June 1643 (letters 2 and 4).

189 *depends on his omnipotence*: again, Descartes insists that what is good and true is so because God has willed it so, rather than the reverse. Cf. the letter to Mesland of 2 May 1644 ('Other Letters', letter 1).

THE PASSIONS OF THE SOUL

193 *Reply to the First Letter*: instead of a conventional preface, the work is preceded by two letters from an anonymous friend of Descartes's. Baillet identifies the friend as Clerselier (*Vie*, ii. 394); but it has been argued that the abbé Picot, the translator of the *Principles*, is a more probable candidate (AT 11. 294–7). He complains in the first letter that Descartes has not shown him the treatise on the passions he is said to have written, and takes this to be a sign that Descartes (perhaps out of a self-aggrandizing strategy) is no longer interested in publishing his works, and thereby benefiting the public. He notes that at the end of the preface to the French edition of the *Principles*, Descartes had listed lack of funds as the obstacle to his pursuing his investigations to their conclusion. He urges him to fulfil his obligations to the public by pursuing and publishing his investigations, since his method is far superior to that of the prevailing scholastic philosophy, unlike which it yields practical results; he should describe his projects sufficiently clearly and plainly to attract the funds necessary to carry out the requisite experiments. Descartes's reply shows that he is concerned that the friend's letter will appear as a devious stratagem inspired by Descartes so as to launch an appeal for funding without appearing to do so.

Reply to the Second Letter: in the second letter the unknown friend says that he has been waiting so long for the revised treatise on the passions that he is beginning to suspect that the promised revision was just a ruse to stop him publishing the first letter, because the implicit appeal for funding it contains would jeopardize Descartes's excuse for giving up his scientific work, namely, lack of the funds for the necessary experiment.

193 *the effect you claim it could*: that is, arousing interest in Descartes's research on the part of potential funders.

194 *the style*: le discours.

as a natural philosopher: en physicien.

195 *ART. 1*: that is, 'Article 1'.

the paths they have followed: the metaphor of the path or journey is a favourite of Descartes's: see, for instance, *Discourse*, II, AT 6. 14, 15, 16–17, OWC 14, 15, 16, and III, AT 6. 24–5, OWC 22; *Principles*, letter-preface, AT 9/2. 8–9 (above, p. 128); 1. 8; 1. 24.

the subject to which it happens: as the reference below to the body as a subject makes clear, Descartes's use of the term 'subject' is very different from that of philosophers from Kant onwards, who use it to refer only to a conscious entity.

two different subjects: Paul Hoffman has shown that this account of the identity of action and passion is taken over from Aristotle, and is, moreover, central to Descartes's approach to the passions ('Cartesian Passions and Cartesian Dualism', in *Essays on Descartes*).

196 *into which many have fallen*: in the Aristotelian tradition, which Descartes is here rejecting, the soul is the principle of life in all living creatures.

197 *the vessel known as the arterial vein*: I use the obsolete English terms corresponding to Descartes's terminology. We would now say that the blood flows from the heart into the lungs via the pulmonary artery, and returns into the heart via the pulmonary vein, then flowing into the aorta.

Harvey's opinion: William Harvey (1578–1657) explained the circulation of the blood in *De motu cordis* ('On the Motion of the Heart', 1628), dissenting from the authoritative view upheld by Galen (second century AD) according to which the venous and arterial systems were independent (hence Descartes's dismissive reference to the authority of the ancients).

198 *a kind of fire*: as Geneviève Rodis-Lewis explains (*Les Passions de l'âme* (Paris, 1970), 154 n. 1), Descartes conceives this fire as a kind of fermentation (*Discourse*, V, AT 4. 46; *La Description du corps humain* (1667), VIII, AT 11. 228).

200 *in the Dioptrics*: the essay on vision published along with the *Discourse on the Method*. The passage in question is in Part IV (AT 6. 109–10).

201 *in the Dioptrics*: Dioptrics, VI, AT 6. 130.

203 *our volitions are of two kinds*: Descartes is adopting a scholastic distinction between 'elicited' and 'commanded' acts of the will: see Aquinas, *ST* 1-2. 1. 1 ad 2.

204 *through certain pores of the brain rather than others*: the movement of the spirits thus revives impressions left by earlier experiences, which we encounter as mental images, rather than reliving the original sensations.

in a broader sense: they are all passions of the soul in the broad sense in that the soul passively receives them and does not cause them; as for the more specific sense that applies to some of them, the point is presumably that such thoughts are sometimes accompanied by affect, and we suppose that the affect is the reason why we are having them (see §§25–9 below).

205 *those we refer*: 'refer' here translates *rapportons*. This term seems to encompass two aspects of perception. We 'refer' a perception first and foremost to what we suppose to be its cause, say, an external object of vision. But we refer it also to the location where we experience it: that is to say, we are said to refer a visual perception to an external object in that what we seem to see is the object out there in the world, whereas in fact we are perceiving a cerebral image of it (in medicine 'referred pain' is pain perceived at a location other than that where the cause of the pain is operative).

207 *to denote evident knowledge*: as noted above, Descartes often uses the word 'perception' of intellectual acts, which can alone yield evident knowledge; sense-perceptions do not do so, and *a fortiori* nor do the passions. See, for instance, *Principles*, I. 30.

to any change that happens within it: 'emotion' in modern English could not, of course, be used in so broad a sense.

208 *a certain tiny gland*: the pineal gland. See Introduction, p. xxii.

the main seat of the soul: not that the soul is located there (how could it be if it is immaterial, as Descartes claims?), but that, as he explains, it is the part of the body on which it acts directly.

209 *not in the heart*: as Rodis-Lewis, following Étienne Gilson, observes in her note on this passage, the belief that the seat of the passions was the heart was the prevailing orthodoxy, upheld both by Aristotelians and Stoics (*Les Passions de l'âme*, 91 n. 1).

210 *terror and horror*: fear (*crainte*) is the initial unpleasant apprehension of danger (what we would call the fight-or-flight response); in some people this tips over into terror and horror (*peur* and *épouvante*), the feeling that goes with the irresistible urge to flee, whereas others are capable of standing firm, and what they experience is boldness (*hardiesse*).

designed by nature: *institué par la nature*. On the whole, Descartes's physics excludes reference to purpose (final causes), but he admits finality in the constitution of human nature, as a composite of body and soul (see *Meditations*, VI, AT 7. 87–8, OWC 62).

214 *the higher rational part*: the idea of a hierarchy of parts of the soul, of which the higher should govern the lower, but between which conflict can take place, can be found in Plato, *Republic* 439d–441c, and in the Aristotelian–Thomist tradition: see Aristotle, *Ethics* I. 13. 9–19, 1102^{a}25–1103^{a}1–3; Aquinas, *ST* 1. 77. 4, 1. 95. 1–2.

215 *the will to be courageous*: the first explanation of the sense of psychological conflict is thus focused principally on the soul. The spirits arouse some passion in it, and the will sets itself to check that passion by launching a train of thought that will tend to produce an opposite passion. The second explanation brings in the body: the arousal of passion has physical effects, and the will sets itself in opposition to these.

216 *constantly opposed to itself*: the will is thus engaged in two kinds of conflict here. Opposing passions recruit its aid in turn, so that at one moment we want to save ourselves by flight and at the next we want to stand our ground so as to avoid disgrace. The will is thus fighting against ambition one moment, terror the next. But in another sense it is fighting against itself, since, being an essentially active power, it is betraying its own nature by allowing its activity to be subordinated to the dictates of passion.

217 *regret or repentance*: the need to avoid these destructive emotions by taking sound decisions at the time is a constant of Descartes's ethical thinking (see *Discourse*, III, AT 6. 25, OWC 23).

can be observed in animals: for excellent accounts of the complexities of Descartes's conception of animals, see John Cottingham, 'A Brute to the Brutes? Descartes's Treatment of Animals', in Cottingham, *Cartesian Reflections* (Cambridge, 2008), 163–72, and Stephen Gaukroger, *Descartes' System of Natural Philosophy* (Cambridge, 2002), 196–214.

220 *humility or baseness of spirit*: magnanimity and pride are not synonymous, nor are humility and baseness of spirit; they are variants, as Descartes explains below (§§151–9), of self-directed esteem or contempt. Descartes here uses the familiar scholastic term 'magnanimity' (greatness of soul), though he explains below why he prefers the term *générosité* (see §161 and Introduction, pp. xxvi–xxvii).

good or bad: good or bad, that is, for us. Our feelings of esteem or contempt, say, can be purely disinterested. Good and bad here have no specifically moral connotation; the same is true even of the word 'evil', when it refers to something that is bad for someone, as distinct from morally wrong.

221 *From the former comes indecision*: *irrésolution*. In general, Descartes attaches great importance to acting resolutely and avoiding fluctuations of feeling about one's own plans or actions. See *Discourse*, II, AT 6. 24–5, OWC 22–3, and cf. §49 above. I have used 'indecision' here, rather than 'irresolution', to draw a distinction he seems to be implicitly making between taking one's time over decisions and failing to act on a decision once taken. However, the second letter to Elisabeth of May 1646 (letter 34) rather undermines this distinction (see also *Passions*, §170 and note).

222 *boredom or distaste*: for clarification of the notion of distaste, see §208.

223 *the one generally accepted*: see Introduction, p. xxiv.

one called 'concupiscible', the other 'irascible': Aquinas explains that the sensitive appetite of the soul, which applies to objects perceived by the senses, contains two distinct faculties, the concupiscible and the irascible. Through the former the soul is inclined to pursue things beneficial to it (from the point of view of the senses), and to avoid things harmful. Through the latter it is inclined to resist whatever interferes with the operations of the concupiscible. The passions pertain to one or other of these faculties and are classified accordingly (*ST* 1. 81. 2, and cf. *ST* 1-2. 23, 1 and 4).

224 *no relationship with the heart or the blood*: the well-being of the body (the effective functioning of its mechanism) depends on the blood's flowing properly to and from the heart. Passions based on the perception of an object as good or bad for us cause the blood to flow in ways that will help us obtain or avoid the object, and so sustain our well-being (ultimately, by preserving the proper flow of the blood): there is an element of feedback here. But since wonderment does not involve such a perception, it can have no effect on the flow of blood.

227 *to will itself to be united*: as Rodis-Lewis observes (*Les Passions de l'âme*, 121 n. 1), the definition of love as a union of wills was traditional: she instances Aristotle, *Rhetoric* 2. 4. 1–4, 1380[b]34–1381[a]11, and Aquinas, *ST* 1-2. 28. 1.

purely by such judgements: on these intellectual emotions (not, strictly speaking, passions because they have no bodily dimension), see §147 below.

two kinds of love: for the distinction, see Aquinas, *ST* 1-2. 26. 4.

228 *his mistress*: *maîtresse* in seventeenth-century French, like 'mistress' in the English of the period, often means simply a beloved woman, with no necessary implication that the parties are in a sexual relationship.

230 *which they term 'aversion'*: see Aquinas, *ST* 1-2. 23. 4.

we judge it contrary to itself: that is, we imagine what is a variant form of a single passion as a separate contrary passion, as do the scholastic philosophers.

231 *the desire born of repulsion*: Descartes has just argued that there is no need to classify aversion as a separate passion from desire. So why should we distinguish repulsion from attraction? His point is that whereas all desire involves a relationship to both good and evil (towards a specific good, and away from the contrary evil), repulsion and attraction work differently. It is not that in feeling attracted to a beautiful picture, say, we feel revulsion for some ugly picture. They are distinct passions, with quite distinct and specific objects; they have distinct and specific functions as regards the body–soul composite; and, phenomenologically (that is, considered as experiences), they are qualitatively very different.

fleeing or aversion: the scholastic term 'aversion' thus has a place, but to denote not a supposed opposite feeling to desire, but a very specific form of negative desire.

become another self: according to Aristotle, one's child is another self, and a friend is another self (*Ethics* 8. 12. 3, 1161[b]28–9; 9. 4. 5, 1166[a]31–2); Descartes applies this notion to objects of sexual desire.

231 *should be the other half*: as Rodis-Lewis notes (*Les Passions de l'âme*, 130 n. 1), there seems to be a reminiscence here of the myth of the Androgyne in Plato's *Symposium* 189d–193d.

232 *the passion of love described previously*: the relationship between the two passions is not a straightforward one. This kind of desire involves a sensuous attraction, which is not necessarily true of love; it also involves a fantasy of perfect happiness which may well be absent from love. It will be seen that whereas repulsion is bound up with the survival instinct, attraction's ties are with the reproductive instinct, which justifies Descartes's identification of them as separate passions.

the soul's enjoyment: 'enjoyment' (*jouissance*) is used in the sense in which we speak of enjoying good health or enjoying the advantages of a good education; that is to say, possessing something in such a way as to derive benefit from it.

233 *titillation*: *chatouillement*, lit. 'tickling'. Descartes frequently uses the term to denote the opposite of pain; he probably avoids the more obvious term *plaisir* ('pleasure') because this can also denote a purely intellectual experience.

represented on a stage: for other references to the experience of theatre, see §§ 147, 187 below, and the letters to Elisabeth of 18 May 1645 (AT 4. 202–3; letter 12) and 6 October 1645 (AT 4. 309; letter 26).

234 *young people*: *jeunes gens*. Descartes is probably thinking particularly of young noblemen who would typically acquire some experience of war.

to take pleasure in doing so: this is a suggestive but difficult passage. It seems to suggest that a merely possible thought can form an impression in the brain. Probably such thoughts are to be seen as inchoate rather than merely potential: distinct enough to produce the brain-impression, not distinct enough to reach full awareness. The theologian Pierre Nicole (1625–95) was to argue for the importance of such 'imperceptible' thoughts. The kind of thinking here somewhat resembles what in logic is called an enthymeme, a process of syllogistic reasoning where one of the premisses is skipped. The full thought process would be: 'to perform a difficult and dangerous task is a proof of good qualities; I am performing a difficult and dangerous task; I therefore possess good qualities'. Such passages as this show that, despite his equation of thought with awareness, Descartes acknowledges the existence of thought processes that do not reach full awareness. See Geneviève Lewis, *Le Problème de l'inconscient et le cartésianisme* (Paris, 1950), and for a discussion of this passage, Michael Moriarty, *Early Modern French Thought* (Oxford, 2003), 86–7.

235 *The main observations*: *expériences*; the alternative or complementary sense of 'experiments' is not relevant here.

236 *the receptacle of bile*: the gall bladder. In English as in French the synonymous medical terms 'bile' and 'gall' are metaphorically associated with feelings of bitterness and resentment.

241 *those nearest the heart*: cf. the analysis of the physiology of sadness in §105. In both cases, Descartes highlights the narrowing of the orifices of the heart: but in §105 this is said to cause a reduction in the flow of blood through the veins to the heart, whereas here the blood tends to flow back to the veins nearest the heart. Presumably, however, with the narrowing of the orifices, less blood actually enters the heart; and its concentration in the veins close to the heart may explain the sensation of cardiac constriction which Descartes associates with sadness.

244 *save extreme joy*: this may seem a curious thesis: after all, people are observed to faint with shock or terror. In seventeenth-century literature, fainting from emotional stress of various kinds is not uncommon, both in male and in female characters. In Corneille's tragicomedy *Le Cid* (1637) the heroine, Chimène, is pressing the king of Castile to put her lover Rodrigue to death for killing her father in a duel. To test her feelings for Rodrigue, the king reports that he has since been killed in battle. Chimène faints, and this is taken as proof of grief, and therefore love for Rodrigue. When she regains consciousness, she protests that one can faint with joy, because excessive pleasure causes lethargy and overwhelms the senses. But no one accepts this explanation (*Le Cid*, IV. v). Camus too lists fainting among the effects of joy, though he also refers to it in connection with other passions such as love and desire, especially in their spiritual form (Jean-Pierre Camus, *Traitté des passions de l'ame* (1614), ed. Max Vernet and Élodie Vignon (Paris, 2014), 409; cf. 186–7, 354).

the entries to these veins: see §9. Descartes seems to be using 'veins' here rather loosely, since, in his description of the normal process of circulation, blood flows into the heart from both the vena cava and the venous artery, and leaves it via the arterial vein and the main artery. In any case, the flow of blood into and out of the heart is normally regulated by a system of flaps or valves, which are opened when the blood is dilated by heating. In this case, there is not time for this process to take place, so the valves remain closed, and the blood cannot escape. As a result the fire of the heart is swamped by the temporary plethora of blood, resulting in unconsciousness.

245 *or at least of wonderment*: compare Hobbes's account: '*Sudden Glory*, is the passion which maketh those *Grimaces* called LAUGHTER; and is caused either by some sudden act of their own that pleaseth them; or by the apprehension of some deformed thing in another, by comparison whereof they suddenly applaud themselves' (*Leviathan*, I. 6).

the evil in question: this is a shrewd comment on the aesthetics of laughter, explaining how, for instance, the sight of horrifying and unexpected villainy in a film can sometimes be strangely amusing. Quentin Tarantino, for instance, is a master of this effect.

246 *writes of himself*: Juan Luis Vives (1493–1540), in *De anima et vita* ('On the Soul and Life'), book III (1538), 'De risu' ('Of Laughter'). On Descartes's reading of Vives, see *Les Passions de l'âme*, ed. Rodis-Lewis, 24–8.

246 *in the Meteorology*: another of the essays published along with the *Discourse on the Method* in 1637 (the other two being the *Dioptrics* and the *Geometry*). The passage in question is in Part V (AT 6. 284).

248 *the matter of which tears are formed*: tears are produced when an unusually large quantity of vapours is sent to the optic nerve; and this requires an unusually copious flow of blood to the heart, such as love and joy tend to produce. Hatred also causes an increase in the flow of blood towards the heart, by diverting blood away from the spleen and liver, but some of this blood is dense and therefore resistant to being heated and rarefied (cf. §103): thus, it is less easily converted ultimately into vapours. On fear, see below.

249 *what is called sighing*: see the letter to Elisabeth, May 1646, AT 4. 410–11 (letter 33).

the presence of a cat: as Geneviève Rodis-Lewis points out in her note on this passage, Descartes is referring to examples from fairly recent history: Henri III of France had an aversion to cats, and Marie de' Medici (wife of Henri IV) and the chevalier de Guise would faint at the sight of a rose (*Les Passions de l'âme*, 162 n. 1).

communicated itself to them: the idea that the experiences of the mother in pregnancy could be passed on to the child was widely accepted.

251 *take precedence over joy and sadness*: from the point of view of preserving the body, sadness and joy are, as we saw, the primary passions, because they are reactions to pain or pleasure, which are the signals of prospective harm or benefit to the body (§137). But from the point of view of the soul, love and hatred are higher passions, in that they involve an idea of something with which we wish to be united or from which we wish to be separated; they have, in other words, a cognitive dimension, and participate more of our intellectual nature. However, Descartes seems to concede that joy and sadness may also reflect a quasi-intellectual apprehension of something.

[*between them and ourselves*]: the words in square brackets seem necessary to bring out the intended meaning. Suppose we were dealing with a false good (say, permanent intoxication). Any degree of love for this would be harmful, because it would attach a false good to ourselves, the possession of which would actually ruin our lives. If the good were real, but only limited (say, worldly success), an excess of love for it would be harmful: our self-love (in so far as it is enlightened) would see our own good as distinct from, and potentially opposed to, the partial good. But if the good is a true one (say, moral virtue), self-love can see no distinction between the pursuit of it and its own concern, the pursuit of what is good for us. So, even from the point of view of self-love, such love can never be excessive. Or one might understand Descartes's point another way. If I love virtue extremely, I will *ipso facto* have assimilated it into myself: so my self-love cannot distinguish me qua individual from me qua virtuous person. To love myself and to love virtue become one and the same.

evil being nothing but a privation: that is, evil does not exist in itself, it consists purely in the absence of some good that ought to be there. Descartes upholds the same view in the Fourth Meditation and in *Principles*, I. 23: it can be found before him in Augustine (*Enchiridion*, 3. 11) and Aquinas (*ST* 1. 48. 1) (for an explanation of the doctrine, see Brian Davies, *The Thought of Thomas Aquinas* (Oxford, 1992), 84–97). From this point of view, reality and goodness are deemed to be metaphysically 'convertible': that which is most real is also most good and vice versa. Hence, as Descartes goes on to say, everything real has something good in it (Satan's will is thoroughly evil, but his willpower would be admirable were the will itself directed to better objects).

252 *the joy it causes*: cf. §91. As regards sadness, Descartes's point is that an objective evil like poverty or ill health does not in itself harm the soul; it does so only when it results in sadness.

a sadness based on a true cause: but cf. to Elisabeth, 6 October 1645 (letter 26), where Descartes argues that it is preferable to know the truth than to be happy in a false belief. However, in the letter he is considering the matter in a fuller ethical perspective, whereas here his point of view is more restricted, to the passions in themselves, as distinct from their impact on our behaviour.

Such false valuations debase and degrade us: cf. to Chanut, 1 February 1647, AT 4. 616.

253 *and those that are not*: this distinction derives from the Stoic philosopher Epictetus, *Enchiridion*, §1. Descartes had made it earlier in the *Discourse*, III, AT 6. 25–6, OWC 23–4.

to know very clearly and to consider most attentively: this is a two-stage process, comprising both the intellectual quest for clear knowledge and the mental discipline of focusing systematically and sustainedly on that knowledge, so as to reverse the conditioning influence of custom, which has induced us to value other satisfactions. There is a strong affinity with the *Meditations* here: see, in particular, the endings of the First and the Third.

254 *there is a fortune*: here Descartes plainly denies the existence of fortune; but his attitude to the concept is more complex than this suggests. See Emma Gilby, 'The Language of Fortune in Descartes', in John D. Lyons and Kathleen Wine (eds.), *Chance, Literature, and Culture in Early Modern France* (Farnham, 2009).

255 *so we had no reason to wish to be spared it*: this might seem an odd thing to say, because the robbed traveller may have many reasons to wish he had escaped the misfortune. Descartes's point is this: if he was robbed, this is because Providence had decreed he was to be robbed. In other words, his being robbed was inevitable, and his not being robbed impossible. But we cannot desire impossible things. The key thing is that if he chose his route according to his best available information, he has no reason to blame himself for his misfortune, and can spare himself the pain of self-reproach. Ferdinand Alquié, however, observes that we cannot rationally

seek success without desiring it, and thus without suffering if things turn out wrong (see his note on the passage in *OP* iii. 1062 n. 1).

256 *no less than from any of the other passions*: Descartes, as noted above, is interested in the experience of theatre (cf. §94). The key distinction, in these examples, is between the passions, which are linked to physical sensations that cause movements of the spirits, and the simultaneous and contrary intellectual emotions (the widower's realization that he is free, or the spectator's awareness that the heroine for whom he fears will not ultimately come to any harm). On these internal emotions, see James, *Passion and Action*, 196–200.

258 *to follow virtue perfectly*: cf. to Elisabeth, 4 August 1645, AT 4. 265–6 (letter 18), 18 August 1645, AT 4. 277 (letter 20).

wrongful acts: *fautes*; this can mean both 'sins' and 'mistakes'. Descartes seems to be playing on both senses: weak people commit what are objectively sins, but subjectively mistakes: they did not aim, as such, to do wrong.

260 *something one simply lays claim to*: literally, 'glory is nothing but a usurpation'.

'Glory' here has the sense of 'honour', 'reputation', 'admiration'. Such people have no idea of true values, and hence no conception of a legitimate claim on other people's esteem; they think that, the more arrogantly they behave, the more admiration they will receive from others. In other words, they are like usurpers, who ignore the legitimate claims of the lawful ruler and seize the throne simply because they can. Other people, however, as the next sentence points out, collude in this imposture by flattery.

261 *not only vices, but also passions*: terms like 'pride', 'baseness', 'humility', 'nobility of soul', and so forth have a double significance. First, they denote moral virtues and defects: these are traditionally regarded as qualities of the soul. Secondly, they denote passions, movements in the body (in particular, the animal spirits) that are registered in the soul. Descartes is therefore concerned both to make the distinction and to explain the potential relationship between the moral quality in the soul and the psychophysical process.

the result of ignorance: the Augustinian theologians of the time, especially those known as Jansenists, explained wrongdoing by the fundamentally disorderly and corrupt appetites of fallen human kind. Descartes, however, could claim that he is speaking purely philosophically: but his stress on the power of free will to achieve virtue would have been challenged by the Augustinians.

262 *habits in the soul*: the definition of virtue as a habit is standard among the scholastics (see Aquinas, *ST* 1-2. 55. 1); its ultimate source is Aristotle (*Ethics* 2. 6. 12, 1106^{b}24–5). However, the idea that it disposes us primarily to thoughts, rather than actions, seems distinctive to Descartes.

where this virtue is not much in evidence: on the translation of *générosité*, see

Introduction. It is not unusual for early modern French writers, especially noblemen, to refer slightingly to the Schools.

the key to all the other virtues: moral nobility thus takes over the role of prudence in Aristotelian thought, charity in that of Augustine (Aquinas combining the two points of view).

264 *jealous on that account*: 'jealous' may seem an odd word to use here, but the *OED* lists one sense of 'jealousy' as 'solicitude or anxiety for the preservation or well-being of something; vigilance in guarding a possession from loss or damage', which is exactly what Descartes is talking about.

265 *it is genuinely of some use*: in the two letters to Elisabeth of May 1646 (letters 33 and 34), Descartes admits that his excusing *je ne sçay quelle langueur* ('a certain lethargy') is palliating a fault of his own, clearly the behaviour pattern in question here. Indeed, in the second letter he identifies this lethargy as an inability to act in accordance with the determinations of our judgement.

266 *the object and the goal*: the object of boldness is difficulty or danger, in the sense that its specific function is to enable us to face down difficulties or dangers, instead of fleeing from them. As with all the passions, its underlying function is to preserve our life, and if that were all we were concerned about, then the impossibility of doing so in a given situation would tend to produce despair; however, we may choose to act boldly for a higher goal, thus overriding the original function of the passion and directing it to a different end (Roman victory instead of personal survival).

the Decii charged into the midst of their enemies: Publius Decius Mus was a Roman consul in 340 BC. According to Livy (*History of Rome* 8. 9–10), he solemnly devoted himself to the gods, calling on them to give the Romans victory. Rushing into the midst of his enemies, he was killed and the Romans triumphed. His son and grandson, also consuls, emulated his heroism. Descartes eliminates the supernatural element in Livy's account.

267 *Faint-heartedness is directly opposed to courage*: 'cowardice' would be the normal translation of Descartes's word *lâcheté*, especially when it is contrasted with courage. But courage for Descartes (see §171) does not in general consist in facing down danger, which is the specific province of boldness: it is more a matter of energy (a sense still available in modern French, as when someone is called a *travailleur courageux*, a vigorous worker). Moreover, in the literal sense, *lâcheté* in seventeenth-century French means physical slackness or feebleness, and Descartes's analysis shows that he regards *lâcheté* more as a lack of vital energy than as what we normally mean by cowardice, namely, excessive fear in the presence of danger. Such a lack of energy we might term 'faint-heartedness', as in the proverb 'faint heart never won fair lady'.

to think things out in advance: a Stoic precept; see e.g. Seneca, *Epistles* 76. 34–5.

268 *things that have some appearance of goodness*: a Thomist doctrine (*ST* 1-2. 8. 1); the will cannot desire evil as such. For Descartes's 'intellectualist' view that we do what is wrong because we do not realize it is wrong, see also §160.

as ill-favoured as themselves: no one would defend Descartes's attitude to disability, though it is conventional for his time. 'Ill-favoured' is a literal translation of *disgraciés*: as Furetière explains, the word *disgracié* is used for what we would call a disabled person (and his examples are the same as Descartes's), as if he or she were regarded as deprived of the favour of heaven or nature. Hence what might appear as the curious assimilation of the disabled to those publicly denied or deprived of the favour of the great.

moderate ridicule: the art of ridicule (*raillerie*) was defended by an influential near-contemporary of Descartes's, Jean-Louis Guez de Balzac (1597–1654), as an essential ingredient of good conversation. Later in the century, Pascal (*Provincial Letters*, 1656–7, letter XI) and Molière (*Tartuffe* (1669), preface) were to assert the value of mockery in restraining and correcting error or vice.

269 *a well-bred man*: honnête homme. This expression became particularly fashionable after the publication of Nicolas Faret's *L'Honnête Homme, ou, L'Art de plaire à la cour* ('The Well-Bred Man, or, The Art of Pleasing at Court') in 1630. It denotes a man (generally assumed to be a nobleman) who excels in the agreeable social qualities.

the goods of fortune: this is a standard expression denoting primarily wealth, and secondarily honours, rank, and so forth. Descartes's attitude to envy is complex. A propensity to it ranks as a vice, which he condemns unequivocally (§184). As a passion, a one-off response to a situation, he sees it as excusable, to the extent that the other person's good fortune may be bad for everyone else (my rival may prove to be a very bad minister) or even simply for ourselves (he will probably be a very good minister, but his appointment means I may never get the chance to be one). Moreover, the passion of envy can spring from a natural love of justice: to that extent, it is justified, as the title of the article suggests. On the other hand, in §§145–6, he has refuted the notion of fortune. If everything is the result of Providence, surely we should not envy those whom for whatever reason God has seen fit to endow with worldly goods, even if they seem unworthy. The overall conclusion must be that it is excusable to feel an immediate pang of envy at someone else's good fortune, but that we must think ourselves out of reacting habitually in that way, if the passion is not to become a vice.

before one was capable of doing any evil: or, by the same token, of doing good. That is, these qualities are gifts of God unrelated to our merits, and as such must have been well bestowed.

270 *livor in Latin means 'envy'*: the word does indeed denote both 'a bluish or leaden colour, a black and blue spot' and 'envy, spite' (*Chambers Murray Latin–English Dictionary*).

271 *their love for others*: the self-interested nature of pity is proclaimed by Hobbes ('*Griefe*, for the Calamity of another, is PITTY; and ariseth from the imagination that the like calamity may befall himselfe'; *Leviathan*, I. 6) and later La Rochefoucauld ('Pity is often a feeling of our own ills, prompted by the ills of other people. It is a clever way of anticipating the misfortunes that could possibly befall us: we help other people so that they will be obliged to help us when comparable circumstances arise; and the services we render them are, strictly speaking, good deeds that we do for ourselves in advance'; *Maxims*, §264, in François de La Rochefoucauld, *Collected Maxims and Other Reflections*, ed. and trans. E. H. and A. M. Blackmore and Francine Giguère (Oxford, 2007)). But, unlike them, Descartes's analysis finds room for a more noble kind of pity, as the next article makes clear.

272 *one's own opinions*: it is very rare for Descartes to adopt this tone of moral indignation, or to pronounce on religious issues in this way. The devout behaviour he describes is not characteristic of any particular sect. His intervention may be explained by vexation at the campaign conducted against him by the Calvinist minister Voetius. But the reference to regicide probably refers to the murder of two successive French kings by Catholic fanatics, Henri III, killed by a Dominican lay brother, Jacques Clément, in 1589, and Henri IV, whose murderer, Ravaillac, was alleged to have been inspired by Jesuit writings justifying tyrannicide. No doubt the St Bartholomew's Day massacre and the atrocities of the Thirty Years War were also in Descartes's mind. In any case, the last sentence, transcending specific polemics, offers a powerful condemnation of the wicked deeds performed in the name of religion. But unlike Enlightenment foes of religion, Descartes is careful to emphasize that this kind of behaviour is the effect of self-delusion, and not an inevitable outgrowth of religion as such.

273 *even though no advantage to us may result*: Descartes, therefore, rejects any attempt to ground moral judgements in egoistic motivations. These hold sway only in the judgements of base people (see §194).

274 *the kind of envy that is not vicious*: see Aristotle, *Ethics* 2. 7. 15, 1108^{a}35–^{b}6.

the laughter of Democritus and the tears of Heraclitus: Democritus was provoked to laughter by the follies that moved Heraclitus to tears. This traditional contrast (Juvenal, Seneca, Lucian, Diogenes Laertius, all cite it) is also mentioned by Vives (Rodis-Lewis, *Les Passions de l'âme*, 206 n. 1); Montaigne also discusses the two philosophers (*Essays*, I. 50, 'Of Democritus and Heraclitus').

that sometimes accompanies this passion: see §127 and note.

278 *as the ancient Cynics did*: whereas the modern use of the word 'cynical' implies contempt for moral values, the ancient Cynics had high moral standards, committing themselves to living in accordance with nature; but as a result they rejected purely social and conventional values such as honour and decency.

278 *the people is a very bad judge*: 'people' here does not, as so often, mean the so-called lower orders as distinct from the privileged, since Descartes would have no particular respect for the judgement of the privileged as such; it means the mass of the community, as distinct from the wise few.

as far as the external aspect of our actions is concerned: Descartes, probably influenced here by Montaigne and the Stoics, makes a sharp distinction between our thoughts, which are entirely in our own control, and outward behaviour, which must be regulated by social canons.

the pleasure we experienced in enjoying some good: regret (*regret*) in this sense is the yearning for some lost and irrecoverable good. Descartes uses it in this sense in §67. In §§45 and 49, however, he uses it with the sense (more current in modern English) of wishing one had acted differently.

279 *no passion worthy of particular consideration*: the fourth rule of Descartes's method is 'to undertake such complete enumerations and such general surveys that I would be sure to have left nothing out' (*Discourse*, II, AT 6. 19, OWC 17). In §68 he claims to have covered all the main passions, unlike earlier writers.

280 *to ask for quarter*: to surrender. The use of this military term (and that of 'retreat') implies that Descartes is thinking of war, rather than personal quarrels, though both situations would be familiar to noblemen of his day.

INDEX

The Oxford World's Classics Website

www.worldsclassics.co.uk

- Browse the full range of Oxford World's Classics online

- Sign up for our monthly e-alert to receive information on new titles

- Read extracts from the Introductions

- Listen to our editors and translators talk about the world's greatest literature with our Oxford World's Classics audio guides

- Join the conversation, follow us on Twitter at OWC_Oxford

- Teachers and lecturers can order inspection copies quickly and simply via our website

www.worldsclassics.co.uk